Lecture Notes in Computer Science   1753

Edited by G. Goos, J. Hartmanis and J. van Leeuwen

Springer
Berlin
Heidelberg
New York
Barcelona
Hong Kong
London
Milan
Paris
Singapore
Tokyo

Enrico Pontelli   Vítor Santos Costa (Eds.)

Practical Aspects of Declarative Languages

Second International Workshop, PADL 2000
Boston, MA, USA, January 17-18, 2000
Proceedings

Springer

Series Editors

Gerhard Goos, Karlsruhe University, Germany
Juris Hartmanis, Cornell University, NY, USA
Jan van Leeuwen, Utrecht University, The Netherlands

Volume Editors

Enrico Pontelli
Department of Computer Science
New Science Hall, Box 30001, MS CS
New Mexico State University
Stewart Street, Las Cruces, NM 88003, USA
E-mail: epontell@cs.nmsu.edu

Vítor Santos Costa
COPPE/Sistemas e Computação
Centro de Tecnologia, Bloco H-319
Universidade Federal do Rio de Janeiro
Cx. Postal 68511, Rio de Janeiro, Brasil, CEP:21945-970
E-mail: vitor@cos.ufrj.br

Cataloging-in-Publication data applied for

Die Deutsche Bibliothek - CIP-Einheitsaufnahme

Practical aspects of declarative languages : second international
workshop ; proceedings / PADL 2000, Boston, MA, USA, January 17- 18,
2000. Enrico Pontelli ; Vítor Santos Costa (ed.). - Berlin ;
Heidelberg ; New York ; Barcelona ; Hong Kong ; London ; Milan ;
Paris ; Singapore ; Tokyo : Springer, 2000
(Lecture notes in computer science ; 1753)
ISBN 3-540-66992-2

CR Subject Classification (1998): D.3, D.1, F.3, D.2, I.2.3

ISSN 0302-9743
ISBN 3-540-66992-2 Springer-Verlag Berlin Heidelberg New York

Typesetting: Camera-ready by author
SPIN: 10719570   06/3142 – 5 4 3 2 1 0   Printed on acid-free paper

Preface

This volume contains the papers presented at the Second Workshop on the Practical Applications of Declarative Languages (PADL'00) held in Boston, MA, USA, January 17–18, 2000. PADL'00 was co-located with the 27th ACM Conference on the Principles of Programming Languages (POPL'00). The event was organized by COMPULOG AMERICAS.

Declarative languages build on a sound theoretical basis to provide attractive frameworks for application development. Indeed, these languages have been successfully applied to vastly different real-world situations, ranging from data base management to active networks to software engineering to decision support systems, to mention a few examples. One major strength of declarative languages lies in the way work on efficient implementation has allowed programmers to take advantage of their strong theoretical foundations. In fact, new developments in theory and implementation often open up new application areas. On the other hand, as declarative languages are applied to novel problems, a number of interesting research issues arise. Well-known issues include designing for scalability, language extensions for application deployment, and programming environments. Thus, applications are both a cause for and benefit from progress in the theory and implementation of declarative systems.

The goal of the International Workshop on Practical Aspects of Declarative Languages (PADL) series is to provide a forum where researchers, practitioners, and implementors of declarative languages may exchange ideas on current and novel application areas and on the requirements for effective deployment of declarative systems. This volume contains the proceedings of the year 2000 workshop, held in Boston, Massachusetts, January 17–18, 2000. Thirty-six papers were submitted in response to the call for papers. These papers were written by authors from fifteen countries from four continents. Each paper was assigned to at least three referees for reviewing. Twenty-one papers were finally selected for presentation at the workshop. Many good papers could not be included due to the limited duration of the workshop. The workshop included invited talks by Peter Lee of Carnegie Mellon University, speaking on "Production-Quality Proof-Carrying Code," and by I.V. Ramakrishnan of SUNY Stony Brook, speaking on "Current Trends in Logic Programming: Prospects and Promises".

The workshop was sponsored and organized by COMPULOG AMERICAS (http://www.cs.nmsu.edu/~complog), a network of research groups dedicated to promoting research in logic programming, by the Association for Logic Programming (http://www.cwi.nl/projects/alp), and by the Department of Computer Science, New Mexico State University (http://www.cs.nmsu.edu/). The workshop was held in cooperation with the ACM Interest Group on Programming Languages. The support of many individuals was crucial to the success of this workshop. Our sincere thanks go to Gopal Gupta for his help in managing and organizing every aspect of the workshop and for sharing his expertise gained from the organization of PADL'99. Thanks are also due to Krzysztof Apt, President of ALP, and David S. Warren, former President of ALP, for their support and encouragement, to Mark Wegman, POPL General Chair, Tomas Reps, POPL Program Chair, Donna Baglio and Maritza Nichols of ACM, for answering various organizational questions, and to the referees for their prompt reviewing of papers. Our thanks to the program committee members for all their help in reviewing and their advice. Finally, our special thanks to all the authors who took interest in PADL'00 and submitted papers.

October 1999   Enrico Pontelli and Vítor Santos Costa

Organization

Program Committee

S. Debray	University of Arizona, USA
B. Demoen	KU Leuven, Belgium
I. Dutra	Federal Univ. of Rio de Janeiro, Brazil
C. Elliott	Microsoft, USA
M. Fahndrich	Microsoft, USA
M. Felleisen	Rice University, USA
G. Filé	University of Padova, Italy
G. Gupta	New Mexico State University, USA
C. Hankin	Imperial College, UK
D. Hislop	U.S. Army Research Office, USA
P. Hudak	Yale University, USA
R. Kieburtz	Oregon Graduate Institute, USA
P. López-Garcia	Univ. Politecnica de Madrid, Spain
L. Naish	University of Melbourne, Australia
E. Pontelli	New Mexico State University, USA (co-chair)
I.V. Ramakrishnan	SUNY Stony Brook, USA
V. Santos Costa	Federal Univ. of Rio de Janeiro, Brazil (co-chair)
F. Silva	University of Porto, Portugal
P. Van Roy	U. Catholique de Louvain, Belgium
M. Wallace	Imperial College, UK
M. Wand	Northeastern University, USA
N-F. Zhou	CUNY Brooklyn College, USA

Organizing Committee

G. Gupta	New Mexico State University, USA
E. Pontelli	New Mexico State University, USA
V. Santos Costa	Federal Univ. of Rio de Janeiro, Brazil

List of Referees

Akira Aiba	Manuel Carro	Agostino Dovier
Dante Baldan	Inês de Castro Dutra	Conal Elliott
Stefano Bistarelli	Saumya Debray	Manuel Fahndrich
Francisco Bueno	Bart Demoen	Matthias Felleisen
Daniel Cabeza	Yves Deville	Gilberto Filé

Kathi Fisler
Mário Florido
Julio Garcia-Martin
Donatien Grolaux
Gopal Gupta
Chris Hankin
David Hislop
Paul Hudak
Dick Kieburtz
Jimmy Lee
Ho-fung Leung
Seng Wai Loke

Luís Lopes
Pedro López-Garcia
Ken McAloon
Luís Moniz Pereira
Tobias Muller
Enrico Pontelli
Alessandro Provetti
German Puebla
C.R. Ramakrishnan
I.V. Ramakrishnan
Francesco Ranzato
Francesca Rossi

Meurig Sage
Vítor Santos Costa
Fernando Silva
Terrance Swift
Ana Paula Tomás
Raul Trejo
Peter Van Roy
Henk Vandecasteele
Mark Wallace
Mitchell Wand
Paul Watson
Neng-Fa Zhou

Table of Contents

First Class Patterns*

Mark Tullsen

Department of Computer Science
Yale University
New Haven CT 06520-8285
mark.tullsen@yale.edu

Abstract. Pattern matching is a great convenience in programming. However, pattern matching has its problems: it conflicts with data abstraction; it is complex (at least in Haskell, which has pattern guards, irrefutable patterns, n+k patterns, as patterns, etc.); it is a source of runtime errors; and lastly, one cannot abstract over patterns as they are not a first class language construct. This paper proposes a simplification of pattern matching that makes patterns first class. The key idea is to treat patterns as functions of type "a→Maybe b"—i.e., "a→(Nothing|Just b)"; thus, patterns and pattern combinators can be written as *functions in the language*.

1 Introduction

A hotly debated issue in the language Haskell [HJW92] has been patterns. What are their semantics? Do we want n+1 patterns? Do we need @-patterns? When do we match lazily and when do we match strictly? Do we need to extend patterns with "pattern guards"? And etc. In this paper I will propose, not another extension, but a simplification to patterns that makes them first class language constructs. I will do so in the context of the language Haskell, although the ideas would apply to any language with higher order functions.

1.1 Patterns Are Too Complex

There is no argument about the elegance of the following simple use of patterns:

```
length []     = 0
length (x:xs) = 1 + length xs
```

Here is another example:

```
zipWith f (a:as) (b:bs) = f a b : zipWith f as bs
zipWith _ _       _     = []
```

---

* This research was supported in part by NSF under Grant Number CCR-9706747.

E. Pontelli, V. Santos Costa (Eds.): PADL 2000, LNCS 1753, pp. 1–15, 2000.

Although the definition of zipWith appears nicely symmetric, we know it is not actually so symmetric: patterns match from left to right and thus zipWith is strict on its first argument but not its second. What if we wanted to modify zipWith to be strict on its second argument? Using a case statement we could write zipWith' as follows:

```
zipWith' f as bs =
  case (bs,as) of                    -- switch the evaluation order
    (b:bs', a:as') -> f a b : zipWith' f as' bs'
    _              -> []
```

Or we could write zipWith' using an irrefutable pattern, ~(a:as), and a guard:

```
zipWith' f ~(a:as) (b:bs) | not(null(a:as)) = f a b : zipWith' f as bs
zipWith' _ _       _                         = []
```

Note that a small semantic change requires a large syntactic change. These last two examples show some of Haskell's pattern matching features. In Haskell, there are numerous pattern matching features added to the simplest form of pattern matching (i.e., that used above to define the length function above):

```
f (x1:x2:xs)     = e        -- 1)  nested pattern matching
f (p1,p2)        = e        -- 2)  tuple patterns
f p _            = e        -- 3)  a wild card symbol
f ('a')          = e        -- 4)  literal patterns
f (xs@(x:xs'))   = e        -- 5)  as patterns
f ~(x:xs)        = e        -- 6)  irrefutable patterns
f (x+2)          = e        -- 7)  n+k patterns
f p | g          = e1       -- 8)  guards
    | otherwise  = e2       -- 9)  an "abbreviation" for True
    where g = e3            -- 10) an extra binding construct
```

Further extensions, such as views [Wad87b, BC93] and pattern guards, have been suggested. Currently ten pages in the Haskell 98 Report[1] are dedicated to pattern matching.

1.2   Patterns Are Not First Class

Pattern matching is not as expressive as one would wish. For example, in Fig. 1 the two functions getC1s and getC2s are virtually identical but we cannot abstract over the commonality to get a more generic function to which we can pass the two constructors, e.g., getmatches C1. Another example where we see the second class nature of patterns is the following

---

[1] Sections 3.1.3, 3.1.7, and 4.4.3.

```
data T = C1 T1 | C2 T2

-- getC1s - Extract all the C1's from a list:
getC1s []          = []
getC1s (C1 d : xs) = d : getC1s xs
getC1s (_ : xs)    = getC1s xs

-- getC2s - Extract all the C2's from a list:
getC2s []          = []
getC2s (C2 d : xs) = d : getC2s xs
getC2s (_ : xs)    = getC2s xs
```

Fig. 1. getC1s and getC2s

```
f x = case x of        g x = case x of
        p1 -> e1               p1 -> e1
        p2 -> e2               p2 -> e2
        p3 -> e3               p3 -> e3
        p4 -> e4
```

in which we would like to abstract out the commonality of f and g. I.e., we would like to write something like the following (where f is defined in terms of g):

```
f x = g x EXTEND p4 -> e4
```

1.3   Other Problems with Patterns

In addition, patterns have various other problems:

1. Patterns are not compatible with abstract data types [Wad87b].
2. The semantics of patterns is less than elegant:
   (a) Patterns impose a left-to-right, top-to-bottom evaluation order. As seen when modifying zipWith above, if we want a different evaluation order, we must either do without patterns or write far less elegant looking code.
   (b) Pattern syntax gives a declarative appearance that does not exist: the defining equation "f p1 p2 = e" is not true in all contexts (unless we ensure patterns are non-overlapping). In Haskell, the order of declarations is insignificant *except* when patterns are used in a sequence of function declarations.
   (c) Patterns engender a multitude of controversies. They beg for extension upon extension: n+k patterns, irrefutable patterns, "as" patterns, guards, and where bindings; currently, a new construct, "pattern guards", is being considered for inclusion in Haskell.

3. Pattern matching does not make it syntactically apparent when a partial function is defined: partial functions arise (a) when patterns are not exhaustive in case expressions, (b) in let bindings "`let (x:xs) = e1 in e2`", and (c) in lambda bindings "λ`(x:xs)->e`". Each of these can be the source of an unintentional run-time pattern match failure. (Though the first could be solved simply by disallowing non-exhaustive patterns.)

4. Pattern matching can seem to not be referentially transparent (at least to the uninitiated); the following two expressions are not equal (the second obviously unintended)

```
case e1 of {1 -> e2 ; ...}
let x = 1 in case e1 of {x -> e2; ...}
```

5. Patterns go against the grain of a higher-order programming style: we only get their convenience when the arguments of a function are made explicit.

1.4   Overview

We have seen many problems with pattern matching. This paper presents an alternative to standard pattern matching. The essence of this alternative is presented in Sect. 2 and Sect. 3 provides some examples; Sect. 4 introduces the "pattern binder" construct (simple syntactic sugar) which makes patterns easier to write; Sects. 5 and 6 present various extensions and Sect. 7 presents several laws for patterns; Sect. 8 compares this approach to other approaches and summarizes.

2   An Alternative to Patterns

The key idea is to use functions of type "`a`$\rightarrow$`Maybe b`" as patterns[2]. A function of this type will be referred to as a pattern-function or sometimes just as a pattern. When a pattern-function is applied, it either fails (returns `Nothing`) or succeeds with some result (returns `Just x`). This section explains the ramifications of using pattern-functions: in Sect. 2.1, I show what we *could* take away from the language, in Sect. 2.2 I show how we can construct patterns using pattern combinators, and in Sect. 2.3 I explain what must be added to the language.

2.1   Simplify the Language

Note that nothing in what follows *requires* that we simplify Haskell as in this section; the point is to explore what we can still do even with such simplicity.

In Haskell, patterns are currently allowed in top-level declarations, lets, lambdas, and case alternatives. We could restrict the language to only allow failure-free

---

[2] In the Haskell Prelude: `data Maybe a = Nothing | Just a`.

patterns in top-level declarations, lets, and lambdas. We could also restrict the form of case expressions.

The syntax of failure-free patterns is as follows (b is for "binding"):

$$b ::= v \qquad \text{variables}$$
$$| \quad (b, ..., b) \quad \text{tuples}$$

The semantics is given by translation. E.g., `f(x,y) = e` is syntactic sugar for `f z = e{fst z/x,snd z/y}`[3]. Also, `case` expressions are restricted such that they are exhaustive over an algebraic type and alternatives cannot contain literals or nested constructors. E.g.,

```
case e of
  x:xs -> e1
  []   -> e2
```

The objective is to eliminate the implicit left-to-right, top-to-bottom evaluation order. A default alternative is allowed (as "`_->e`") when not all the constructors are given. Obviously, we have not lost any of the expressiveness of the language, but we have lost some convenience. Many programs will not miss the lost features, but other programs will be awkward. For example, the function `zipWith3`, defined in the Prelude thus

```
zipWith3 f (a:as) (b:bs) (c:cs) = f a b c : zipWith3 f as bs cs
zipWith3 _ _      _      _      = []
```

becomes awkward to code with these restrictions:

```
zipWith3 f as bs cs =
 case as of
  a:as' -> case bs of
            b:bs' -> case cs of
                      c:cs' -> f a b c : zipWith3 f as' bs' cs'
                      []    -> []
            []    -> []
  []    -> []
```

The functions `zipWith4`, `zipWith5`, `zipWith6` will be even more awkward. Can we define these less awkwardly in the simplified language?

2.2 Use Pattern Combinators

Patterns are just functions, so we need to define functions to construct and manipulate patterns. I use the following type synonym:

---

[3] Due to lifted tuples, this is not always true in Haskell, but I'll ignore this complication.

```
pid x              = Just x
pk x y             = if x == y then Just () else Nothing
pfail _            = Nothing

(p1 .| p2) x       = case p1 x of Just r  -> Just r
                                  Nothing -> p2 x
p1 |. p2           = p2 .| p1
(p1 .* p2) (a,b)   = case p1 a of
                        Just r1 -> case p2 b of
                                      Just r2 -> Just (r1,r2)
                                      Nothing -> Nothing
                        Nothing -> Nothing
(p1 *. p2) (a,b)   = case p2 b of
                        Just r2 -> case p1 a of
                                      Just r1 -> Just (r1,r2)
                                      Nothing -> Nothing
                        Nothing -> Nothing
(p1 .: p2) x       = case p1 x of Just a  -> p2 a
                                  Nothing -> Nothing
(p .-> f) x        = case p x of Just r  -> Just (f r)
                                 Nothing -> Nothing

(p |> f) x         = case p x of Just r  -> r
                                 Nothing -> f x
```

Fig. 2. Pattern Combinators

```
type Pat a b = a → Maybe b
```

Here are the signatures for the pattern combinators:

Pattern Introduction

pid	:: Pat a a	always matches
pk	:: Eq a => a → Pat a ()	"pk x" matches x
pfail	:: Pat a b	never matches

Pattern Combination

(.	),(	.)	:: Pat a b → Pat a b → Pat a b	or match
(.:)	:: Pat a b → Pat b c → Pat a c	then match
(.*),(*.)	:: Pat a c → Pat b d → Pat (a,b) (c,d)	parallel match
(.->)	:: Pat a b → (b→c) → Pat a c	compose match

Pattern Elimination

| (|>) | :: Pat a b → (a→b) → (a→b) | apply pattern |

The definitions are in Fig. 2. The difference between (.|) and (|.) is the order of evaluation, likewise for (.*) and (*.).

2.3   Add One Primitive

For a constructor C we can get the pattern-function corresponding to it using the # primitive

```
C  :: a → b
C# :: b → Maybe a
```

It satisfies the Pattern Law:

```
C# C     = Just ()  -- when C is a nullary constructor
C# (C x) = Just x   -- otherwise
```

In addition the programmer is allowed to define pairs of functions c and $c^\#$, which should satisfy the pattern law (this is unverified). Curried constructors are allowed but the pattern law is more straightforward when constructors are uncurried.

3   Examples

So, what do various functions look like using these pattern combinators? Given the functions list1, list2, and list3, it is useful to have the corresponding pattern-functions list1#, list2#, and list3#[4]:

```
list1 x       = [x]
list2 (x,y)   = [x,y]
list3 (x,y,z) = [x,y,z]

list1# = :# .: (pid .* []#)      .-> \(x,())->x
list2# = :# .: (pid .* list1#)
list3# = :# .: (pid .* list2#)   .-> \(a,(b,c))->(a,b,c)
```

Here is an example where we can structure the code to reflect the types involved very nicely:

```
data Tree a = Leaf a
            | Tree (Tree a, Tree a)

zipTree :: (Tree a,Tree b) → Maybe (Tree (a,b))
zipTree = Leaf# .* Leaf# .-> Leaf
       .| Tree# .* Tree# .:  (zipTree.*zipTree .-> Tree) . zipTuple

zipList :: ([a],[b])  → Maybe [(a,b)]
zipList = []#  .* []#  .-> (\_->[])
       .|  :#  .*  :#  .:  (pid .* zipList .-> uncurry (:)) . zipTuple

zipTuple ((x1,x2),(y1,y2)) = ((x1,y1),(x2,y2))
```

---

[4] The precedences of the pattern operators are from tightest to loosest binding: (.*), (.:), (.->), (.|).

Remember the functions `getC1s` and `getC2s`? We can now write code generic over constructors of different data types[5]:

```
getmatches :: (a → Maybe b) → [a] → [b]
getmatches p = catMaybes . map p

getC1s = getmatches C1#
getC2s = getmatches C2#
```

Here is a "cons" view of a join list:

```
data List a = Nil | Unit a | Join (List a) (List a)

cons x xs          = Join (Unit x) xs

cons# Nil          = Nothing
cons# (Unit a)     = Just (a,Nil)
cons# (Join xs ys) = case cons# xs of
                        Just (x,xs') -> Just (x, Join xs' ys)
                        Nothing      -> cons# ys
```

4   Extension I: Pattern Binders

4.1   The Pattern Binder Construct

At times the higher order approach above seems elegant, but at other times it is clumsy compared to standard pattern matching. The "pattern binder" construct is an attempt to add the minimum of syntactic sugar to make patterns easier to write. Here are some examples:

```
list1#   = {$x:[]}      .-> x
list2#   = {$x:$y:[]}   .-> (x,y)
list3#   = {$x:$y:$z:[]}.-> (x,y,z)

pair x   = {=x:=x:$r} .-> r
```

A pattern binder is "$\{p\} \otimes e$" where e is a Haskell expression, $\otimes$ is a Haskell infix operator, and p is defined as follows:

$$p ::= \$v \qquad \text{variable}$$
$$| \;\; (p, ..., p) \quad \text{tuple pattern}$$
$$| \;\; = e \qquad \text{constant}$$
$$| \;\; \%e\, p \qquad \text{apply any pattern-function}$$
$$| \;\; c\, p \qquad \text{apply } c^{\#} \text{ pattern-function}$$
$$| \;\; c \qquad \text{apply } c^{\#} \text{ pattern-function } (c \text{ nullary})$$

---

[5] The library function `catMaybes` (`:: [Maybe a]->[a]`) extracts the `Just`'s from a list.

Note that c is any constructor or any symbol with a $c^{\#}$ function defined. The pattern binder "$\{p\} \otimes e$" is translated into "$f \otimes (\lambda b \to e)$" as follows (where f is a pattern-function and b is a failure-free pattern):

$$\{p\} \otimes e = f \otimes (\lambda b \to e) \qquad\qquad \text{where } (f, b) = cvt(p)$$

$$\begin{aligned}
cvt(\$v) &= (pid, v) \\
cvt(p_1, p_2, ..., p_n) &= (f_1.* (f_2.* ...f_n)), (b_1, (b_2, ...b_n))) & \text{where } (f_i, b_i) = cvt(p_i) \\
cvt(= e) &= (pk\ e, ()) \\
cvt(\%e\ p) &= (e .: f, b) & \text{where } (f, b) = cvt(p) \\
cvt(c\ p) &= (c^{\#} .: f, b) & \text{where } (f, b) = cvt(p) \\
cvt(c) &= (c^{\#}, ())
\end{aligned}$$

On the one hand, a pattern binder is a subset of standard pattern matching:

1. Only one "case alternative" is allowed.

On the other hand, it extends pattern matching:

1. It allows arbitrary patterns to be applied anywhere inside a pattern using the % construct.
2. It makes matching constants explicit: {=e} gives matching against not just literal constants like 'c' and 1 but any Haskell expression of Eq type. (This construct is not strictly necessary as we could use the % construct to match constants.)
3. It allows us to extend the "de-constructors" by defining $c^{\#}$ functions.
4. It allows arbitrary control structures, with the $\otimes$ pattern-combinator as a parameter.

Although standard pattern matching can also be understood as merely syntactic sugar [Wad87a], this approach is much simpler. The syntax is not as clean as standard pattern matching because everything is explicit. There are a couple ways to make things syntactically nicer (closer to regular patterns):

One, we could allow for dropping the '=' in the {=e} construct: for literals (integer, character, and string constants) this would be unambiguous; if we had a variable, {v}, it could be converted to either "$pk\ v$" or "$v^{\#}$" but these are equivalent when v is a nullary constructor.

Second, we could allow for dropping the '$' in the {$v} construct: Unfortunately, {v} again is ambiguous: if $v^{\#}$ is defined, we do not know whether to use the $cvt(\$v)$ rule or the $cvt(c)$ rule. We could get around this by using the $cvt(c)$ rule whenever $v^{\#}$ is defined. This effectively disallows shadowing of variables. In Haskell, using capitals for constructors is how we distinguish these two. But this is not going to work any more once we start writing "pseudo-constructors" (functions c that have a $c^{\#}$ "de-constructor" defined). So, while we are making hypothetical changes to Haskell, we should drop this restriction. This is a good thing, it enables abstract data types to work better with patterns: it does not matter if a function corresponds to the constructor of an algebraic data type, all that matters is whether a function c has a corresponding $c^{\#}$ function.

4.2 Examples of Pattern Binders

The function `take` from the Haskell Prelude uses a pattern guard "| n>0":

```
take 0 _              = []
take _ []             = []
take n (x:xs) | n>0 = x : take (n-1) xs
take _ _              = error "take"
```

Using pattern binders `take` can be written as follows:

```
take =
    {(=0,            $_)}      .-> []
 .| {($_,            [])}      .-> []
 .| {(%(is (0<)) $n, $x:$xs)} .-> x : take (n-1, xs)
 |> \_                         -> error "take"

 is p x = if p x then Just x else Nothing
```

The function `zipWith3` can be written straightforwardly:

```
zipWith3 f = {($x:$xs,$y:$ys,$z:$zs)}.-> f x y z : zipWith3 f (xs,ys,zs)
             |> \_                     -> []
```

We can create a "view" of the positive integers using the `succ` and `succ#` functions. (In this case the pattern law is being broken unless `succ` and `succ#` are restricted to positive integers.)

```
succ  n = n+1
succ# n = if n > 0 then Just (n-1) else Nothing

factorial =   {succ $n} .-> (succ n * factorial n)
              |> \_       -> 1
```

4.3 Pattern Binders and New Control Structures

Here is an example extracted from an interpreter:

```
doprimitive =
   {Eprim (%getenv $op) : Eint $a1 : Eint $a2 : []} .-> op a1 a2
 |> \_ -> (error "bad primitive")

getenv :: String → Maybe (Int → Int → Int)
getenv x = lookup x [("+",(+)), ("*",(*)), ("-",(-))]
```

Note the type of `getenv`, it is a pattern-function so we can use it inside pattern binders. To add a more informative error message, the code is changed to[6]

```
doprimitive list =
  {$hd:$a1:$a2:[]} 'matchelse list  (error "expect 3 elements")'
  {Eprim $name}    'matchelse hd    (error "head not Eprim")'
  {Eint  $a1'}     'matchelse a1    (error "1st not Eint")'
  {Eint  $a2'}     'matchelse a2    (error "2nd not Eint")'
  {%getenv $op}    'matchelse name  (error (name ++ " invalid prim"))'
  op a1' a2'
  where
  matchelse val dflt pat contin = ((pat.->contin) |> \_-> dflt) val
```

(Note that pattern binders are right associative.) This is a common pattern, but in Haskell one would write nested case expressions marching off to the right of the page. It is nice to put all the exception code off to the right[7]. Here we also see that other functions besides (`.->`) are useful with pattern binders.

4.4   Changing Evaluation Order

Just like patterns, pattern binders have an implicit left-to-right evaluation mechanism for tuples. I.e., `{(p1,p2)}` is translated with (`.*`)—left-to-right evaluation. Pattern binders could be extended to allow for tuples of patterns that would evaluate right-to-left (e.g., `{/(p1,p2)}`). We could also revert to explicit use of the combinators.

5   Extension II: Backtracking

We could extend the pattern combinators to use lists instead of `Maybe`. Success will be `[x]`, failure will be `[]`, and multiple successes will be `[x1,x2,...]`; but it would be even nicer to write the combinators to work with either `Maybe` or lists. We can do this easily because both `Maybe` and lists are monads, specifically, each is an instance of `MonadPlus`:

```
class (Monad m) => MonadPlus m where
    mzero :: m a
    mplus :: m a → m a → m a

instance MonadPlus Maybe where
    mzero                 = Nothing
    Nothing 'mplus' y = y
    x       'mplus' y = x
```

---

[6] In Haskell, `x 'f' y = f x y`. Haskell does not really allow expressions inside the backquotes, though some think it should.

[7] This is similar to Perl's very useful idiom "`($x =~ /pat/) || exception`" where the exception code is off to the right.

```
pid        :: Monad m => b -> m b
pk         :: (Eq a, MonadPlus m) => a -> a -> m ()
pfail      :: MonadPlus m => b -> m c
(.|),(|.) :: MonadPlus m => (a->m c) -> (a->m c) -> (a->m c)
(.:)       :: Monad m     => (b -> m c) -> (c -> m d) -> b -> m d
(.*),(*.) :: Monad m     => (b -> m c) -> (d -> m e) -> (b,d) -> m (c,e)
(.->)      :: Functor m   => (b -> m c) -> (c -> d) -> b -> m d
```

```
pid x            = return x
pk x y           = if x == y then return () else mzero
pfail _          = mzero
(f .| g) x       = f x 'mplus' g x
(|.)             = flip (.|)
(p1 .* p2) (a,b) = do r1 <- p1 a
                      r2 <- p2 b
                      return (r1,r2)
(p1 *. p2) (a,b) = do r2 <- p2 b
                      r1 <- p1 a
                      return (r1,r2)
(p1 .: p2) x     = p1 x >>= p2
f .-> g          = fmap g . f
```

Fig. 3. Monadic Pattern Combinators

```
instance  MonadPlus []  where
    mzero              = []
    mplus              = (++)        -- list append
```

The more general definitions are in Fig. 3. We need a different pattern elimination construct to replace (|>):

```
(||>) :: (a→[b]) → (a→b) → (a→b)
(p ||> d) f x = case p x of {[]->f x; r:_-> r}
```

When we use (|>) we get standard pattern matching because the pattern combinators are instantiated to the Maybe monad, but when we use (||>) we get backtracking because the pattern combinators are instantiated to the list monad. This requires lazy lists for efficiency. The method of using lazy lists for backtracking is explained in Wadler [Wad85] and is also used in combinator parsers [HM96].

6   Extension III: "Value Constructors"

To define the $c^{\#}$ equivalents for various c "pseudo constructors" is often tedious: for example, the list1$^{\#}$, list2$^{\#}$, list3$^{\#}$ from above. If c is an instance of the Eq class, $c^{\#}$ can simply be a shortcut for "pk c", but for *functions* c, the $c^{\#}$

pattern is often trivial (but tedious) to generate. Is there a way to formalize this and automate the construction of the corresponding pattern function for a given function c? One method is Aitken and Reppy's "Abstract Value Constructors" [AR92]. The language can generate $c^{\#}$ for any c that is a value constructor. A value constructor is a function whose definition is of the following form

$$c\, b = v_c$$

where b is a failure-free pattern, all variables are used linearly, and v_c is defined as follows

$$
\begin{aligned}
v_c = \;& x & & (x \text{ a variable}) \\
| \;& (v_c, ..., v_c) & & \\
| \;& C\, v_c & & (C \text{ a constructor}) \\
| \;& k & & (k \text{ a constant}) \\
| \;& c\, v_c & & (c \text{ a value constructor})
\end{aligned}
$$

There are two advantages to using value constructors:

1. It saves the tedium of defining many pattern functions.
2. It gives function/pattern-function pairs that are *guaranteed* to satisfy the pattern law.

7 Pattern Laws

Here are several laws for the monadic pattern combinators. (These are true for any instance of MonadPlus that satisfies the monad laws.)

$$p\; .|\; \texttt{pfail} = p$$

$$p1\; .|\; p2 = p2\; |.\; p1$$

$$(p1\; .\text{->}\; f1)\; .*\; (p2\; .\text{->}\; f2) = (p1\; .*\; p2)\; .\text{->}\; \backslash(x,y)\text{->}(f1\; x, f2\; y)$$

$$(p1\; .\text{->}\; f)\quad .:\; p2\; = p1\; .:\; (p2.f)$$

$$(\texttt{pid}\; .*\; p)\; (x,y) = \texttt{fmap}\; (\backslash y\text{->}(x,y))\; (p\; y)$$

$$(p1\; .:\; p2)\; .\text{->}\; f = (p1\; .:\; (p2\; .\text{->}\; f))$$

If this is true for an instance of MonadPlus (it's true for Maybe and lists)

$$\texttt{m} \gg\!= (\backslash a\text{->}p1\; a\; \texttt{`mplus`}\; p2\; a) = (\texttt{m} \gg\!= p1)\; \texttt{`mplus`}\; (\texttt{m} \gg\!= p2)$$

then (.:) distributes over (.|):

$$p\; .:\; (p1\; .|\; p2)\; = p\; .:\; p1\; .|\; p\; .:\; p2$$

8   Conclusion

8.1   Relation to Other Work

I am not aware of other work that proposes other *alternatives* to the standard pattern matching constructs. However, there is much work related to getting around the infelicities of pattern matching:

The title of Wadler's seminal paper says it all: "Views: A way for pattern matching to cohabit with data abstraction" [Wad87b]. Other work along these lines is [BC93] and [PPN96]. The goal of this line of work is to reconcile pattern matching and abstract data types; the solutions have been to keep pattern matching as is and *add* more to the language. My proposal here could be seen as another way to reconcile the two (if you allow me to reconcile two parties by eliminating one); but the result is that we get the syntactic convenience of patterns even when dealing with abstract data types.

Other work has been aimed at the expressiveness of patterns: Fahndrich and Boyland [FB97] propose a means to add pattern abstractions. My approach is far simpler, although I do not attempt as they do to make patterns statically checkable for exhaustiveness and redundancy. Aitken and Reppy [AR92] have a simple approach to making pattern matching more expressive; I've borrowed their notion of a "value constructor".

Parser combinators are related to this work, though they are only applicable to matching lists. As Hutton and Meijer [HM96] have shown, monads are useful for designing the combinators. Like my patterns, parser combinators could be parameterized over which monad (list or `Maybe`) to use (i.e., whether to do backtracking or not).

Hughes [Hug98] generalizes monads to what he calls arrows. As his arrows are so general, it is not surprising that my combinators can be made into an instance of an arrow, but the interesting thing is that he extensively uses certain combinators which are a generalization of mine: his $***$ is a generalization of my $(.*)$ and his $>>>$ is a generalization of my $(.:)$.

8.2   Summary

So, to summarize what I have proposed: if we add

1. the # primitive for constructing pattern-functions from constructors
2. the pattern binder syntactic construct

then we can use the power of the language to write all the pattern combinators we want, and as a result we could, without much loss

1. restrict patterns in top-level declarations, lets, and lambdas to be failure-free
2. restrict case alternatives to be exhaustive and mutually exclusive over a single algebraic data type

The advantages of this proposal are

1. The extensions needed to the language are trivial.
2. Complicated pattern matching constructs are unnecessary.
3. Pattern matching no longer results in run-time errors.
4. Patterns become first class: we can write our own patterns; we can write our own control structures for sequencing patterns; and we can write programs generic over constructors (e.g., the getC1s and getC2s above).
5. Pattern matching can use backtracking, when needed.
6. Patterns work with abstract data types.

Acknowledgements. Thanks to Valery Trifonov for pointing out the similarities between my pattern combinators and the arrow combinators of John Hughes and thanks to the anonymous referees for many helpful comments.

References

[AR92]   William Aitken and John H. Reppy. Abstract value constructors: Symbolic constants for standard ML. Technical Report CORNELLCS//TR92-1290, Cornell University, Computer Science Department, June 1992.

[BC93]   F. W. Burton and R. D. Cameron. Pattern matching with abstract data types. *Journal of Functional Programming*, 3(2):171–190, 1993.

[FB97]   Manuel Fähndrich and John Boyland. Statically checkable pattern abstractions. In *Proceedings of the 1997 ACM SIGPLAN International Conference on Functional Programming*, pages 75–84, Amsterdam, The Netherlands, 9–11 June 1997.

[HJW92]   P. Hudak, S. P. Jones, and P. Wadler. Report on the programming language Haskell. *SIGPLAN Notices*, 27(5), May 1992.

[HM96]   Graham Hutton and Erik Meijer. Monadic parser combinators. Technical Report NOTTCS-TR-96-4, University of Nottingham, December 1996.

[Hug98]   John Hughes. Generalizing monads to arrows. Submitted for publication, 1998.

[PPN96]   Palao Gostanza Pedro, Ricardo Peña, and Manuel Núñez. A new look at pattern matching in abstract data types. In *Proceedings of the ACM SIG-PLAN International Conference on Functional Programming (ICFP '96)*, volume 31(6) of *ACM SIGPLAN Notices*, pages 110–121. ACM, June 1996.

[Wad85]   P. L. Wadler. How to replace failure by a list of successes. In Jean-Pierre Jouannaud, editor, *Functional Programming Languages and Computer Architecture*, volume 201 of *Lecture Notes in Computer Science*, pages 113–128. Springer Verlag, September 1985.

[Wad87a] Philip Wadler. Efficient compilation of pattern-matching. In S. L. Peyton Jones, editor, *The Implementation of Functional Programming Languages*, chapter 5. Prentice-Hall International, 1987.

[Wad87b] Philip Wadler. Views: A way for pattern-matching to cohabit with data abstraction. In *Conference Record of the Fourteenth Annual ACM Symposium on Principles of Programming Languages*, pages 307–313. ACM, January 1987.

Parallel Functional Reactive Programming

John Peterson, Valery Trifonov, and Andrei Serjantov

Yale University
peterson-john@cs.yale.edu, trifonov-valery@cs.yale.edu
andrei.serjantov@yale.edu

Abstract. In this paper, we demonstrate how Functional Reactive Programming (FRP), a framework for the description of interactive systems, can be extended to encompass parallel systems. FRP is based on Haskell, a purely functional programming language, and incorporates the concepts of time variation and reactivity.

Parallel FRP serves as a declarative system model that may be transformed into a parallel implementation using the standard program transformation techniques of functional programming. The semantics of parallel FRP include non-determinism, enhancing opportunities to introduce parallelism. We demonstrate a variety of program transformations based on parallel FRP and show how a FRP model may be transformed into explicitly parallel code. Parallel FRP is implemented using the Linda programming system to handle the underlying parallelism. As an example of parallel FRP, we show how a specification for a web-based online auctioning system can be transformed into a parallel implementation.

1   Introduction

A common approach to developing parallel programs is to express a sequential specification of the system in a declarative way and to then transform this model into a parallel implementation of it while preserving its semantics. In this work, we develop a framework for expressing models of *interactive systems* such as web servers and databases.

Our work is based on Functional Reactive Programming [PESL98] (FRP), a library of functions and types that extend Haskell [PJ99], a purely functional language, with means for describing interactive systems containing values that vary in time.

At the core of FRP are the notions of *events* and *behaviors*. An event of type Event a denotes a discrete series of occurrences in time, each having a timestamp and a value of type a, while a behavior of type Behavior b may be sampled at any time to yield a value of type b. FRP defines a rich set of functions operating on these datatypes, and is designed to retain the "look and feel" of pure functional Haskell without resorting to constructs such as monads to handle interaction.

To enable the introduction of parallelism into FRP programs, we have extended the basic framework with constructs which enrich the semantics of the models with non-determinism, representing the fact that the order in which two

E. Pontelli, V. Santos Costa (Eds.): PADL 2000, LNCS 1753, pp. 16–31, 2000.
© Springer-Verlag Berlin Heidelberg 2000

computations on separate processors started does not determine the order in which they will finish.

To formalize the process of parallelizing FRP models, we introduce a number of equations which define valid transformations of sequential FRP constructs into parallel ones. Thus, transformations can be performed by means of a well understood meaning preserving process — equational reasoning. This is currently done by hand but possibly could be automated in the future.

2 Basic Concepts

We begin with a simple FRP model of a web server. This system receives requests for web pages (URLs) and reacts by generating events to post the resulting web pages.

```
server          :: Event URL -> Event WebPage
server urls     = urls ==> lookupWebPage
```

This server is a simple *event transformer*. That is, the URL in each incoming event is transformed into a WebPage. Event transformation is a primitive in FRP: the function

```
(==>)           :: Event a -> (a -> b) -> Event b
```

implements this directly. The actual web page generation is performed by the function lookupWebPage, a Haskell function that maps a URL onto a WebPage. We assume (for now) that the web pages are unchanging: thus, lookupWebPage is a pure function that does not perform IO. The semantics of FRP dictate that the resulting events of ==> logically occur at the same time as the stimulus; that is, the clock (event times) associated with the web pages exactly matches the clock in the input event stream. For example, if the incoming event stream is

```
[(1, "f.com/a"), (3, "f.com/b"), (6, "f.com/c")]
```

then the output stream might be

```
[(1, "Page a"), (3, "Page b"), (6, "Page c")]
```

We represent event streams as lists of tuples, each tuple containing an occurrence time and a value. This is not necessarily how events are implemented, but it serves to illustrate the operation of the system. We are simplifying the problem somewhat: requests to a real server would carry for example the IP address and port identifying the client.

This model serves well for a single processor web server, but what about a parallel version of this problem? First, we observe that this system is *stateless*: that is, the generated web pages depend only on the incoming URL, not on previous transactions. We can infer this property directly from the specification: ==> is stateless (by its definition in FRP) and the lookupWebPage function has no interactions with the outside world. Given this property, we can use two processors to serve the requests, dividing the incoming requests among the processors arbitrarily. Rewriting, the new server becomes:

```
server'              :: Event URL -> Event WebPage
server' urls    =   urls1 ==> lookupWebPage .|.
                    urls2 ==> lookupWebPage
  where (urls1, urls2) = splitEvents urls

splitEvents          :: Event a -> (Event a, Event a)
(.|.)                :: Event a -> Event a -> Event a
```

We have added `splitEvents` to the standard FRP primitives like `.|.` (which merges two event streams together) and defined it by the following property:

$$e \quad \equiv \quad \texttt{let (e1,e2) = splitEvents e in e1 .|. e2}$$

This states that each incoming event must be distributed to one or the other of the resulting event streams. Thus `splitEvents` stands for all the different ways of partitioning one event stream into two. We note that the above property does not guarantee referential transparency—two calls to `splitEvents` on the same event stream will produce different results. We are being a little free with the semantics of Haskell here. In reality, there are a family of event splitting functions; for simplicity, though, we are using the same name, `splitEvents`, for every member of this family. Strictly speaking, we should instead give different names to each `splitEvents` in our examples, indicating that they all split event streams in (potentially) different manners. However, as all functions in this family abide by the same property we choose to use the same name for clarity.

To show that `server'` is equivalent to `server`, we need one more FRP equivalence, distributing `==>` over `.|.`:

$$\texttt{(e1 .|. e2) ==> f} \quad \equiv \quad \texttt{(e1 ==> f) .|. (e2 ==> f)}$$

Thus,

```
        server urls
(definition of server)  ≡ urls ==> lookupWebPage
(splitEvents property)  ≡ (let (urls1,urls2)=splitEvents urls in urls1.|.urls2)
                              ==> lookupWebPage
      (let floating)    ≡ let (urls1,urls2) = splitEvents urls in
                           (urls1 .|. urls2) ==> lookupWebPage
       (==> over .|.)   ≡ let (urls1,urls2) = splitEvents urls in
                           (urls1 ==> lookupWebPage).|.(urls2 ==> lookupWebPage)
(definition of server') ≡ server' urls
```

We now have a server that has two calls to `lookupWebPage` rather than one. The next step is to implement this modified server so that these two calls can be placed on different processors. To do this, we step back and go outside of the FRP framework to incorporate explicit message passing into the two resulting processes. We will present this later, after describing the Haskell-Linda system which handles communication across processes. At present, though, we must contemplate a serious semantic issue: non-determinism.

We have already introduced one non-deterministic construct: `splitEvents`. However, in this particular system, the non-determinism of `splitEvents` is not observable: the specific event splitting used cannot be seen by the user. That is, the .|. removes the evidence of non-determinism from the result.

This model, however, still over-constrains a parallel implementation. Why? The problem lies in the clocking of the event streams. The semantics of FRP dictate that the functions applied to an event stream by ==> take no observable time, as previously explained. However, there is no reason to require that these times are preserved. For example, our server could respond to

```
[(1, "f.com/a"), (3, "f.com/b"), (6, "f.com/c")]
```

with a completely different set of timings:

```
[(2, "Page a"), (7, "Page c"), (10, "Page b")]
```

This result is completely acceptable: the fact that "page b" is served before "page c" doesn't matter in this application, assuming we have tagged the event with the requesting IP address and sent it to the right client. If these two pages go to separate processors, there is no reason to delay delivering the result of the second request until the first request is completed. We are not addressing real time issues here: specifying that requests must be served within some fixed time of their arrival is not presently part of our model.

We need to express the fact that our server is not required to maintain the ordering of the output event stream. This is accomplished by placing a pseudo-function in the system model: shuffle is a function that (semantically) allows the timings in an event stream to be re-assigned, possibly re-ordering the sequence of events. This can be thought of as a function that non-deterministically rearranges an event stream:

```
shuffle          :: Event a -> Event a
```

When the model is used sequentially, this function may be ignored altogether. However, when the model is used to generate parallel code, this function produces an event stream whose timing may be altered by parallelization. As with splitEvents, we are using a single name to denote a family of functions. Strictly speaking, each reference to shuffle should have a distinct name. Furthermore, shuffle serves more as an annotation than a function. It is beyond the scope of this paper to precisely define the rules for correctly transforming program containing shuffle and other pseudo-functions but, intuitively, the use of these functions is easily understood. As with splitEvents, we must treat separate uses of shuffle as different functions.

We now change our original system model to the following:

```
server           :: Event URL -> Event WebPage
server urls      = shuffle (urls ==> lookupWebPage)
```

This model states that the results in the output event stream may arrive in a different order to the events in the input stream and therefore permits a more effective parallelization of the system. As with splitEvents, the shuffle function has a number of algebraic properties, to be described later.

3   Implementing Parallelism

3.1   Haskell-Linda

Before looking at the implementation of parallel FRP, we need to examine the low-level constructs that allow parallel programming in Haskell. We have implemented parallel FRP using an existing parallel programming infrastructure: Linda [CGMS94]. We have used Linda (actually Linda/Paradise, a commercial version of Linda) to implement basic parallel programming services, including message passing, message broadcast, object locking, shared objects, and persistence.

The Linda/Paradise system implements a global shared memory called tuple space, storing not just bytes but structured Haskell objects. Three basic access operations, out (write), read, and in (read and remove), are provided instead of the two (write and read) provided by conventional address spaces. These operations are atomic with built-in synchronization. Data transfer between processes or machines is implicit and demand-driven.

In Haskell-Linda, the tuple space is partitioned into a set of *regions*, each containing values of some specific type. All tuple-space operations are performed within the context of a specific region, where the region name is embedded in the operator. Thus, each read, in, or out operation has access to only one part of tuple space. The scope of a reading operation may be further narrowed using a pattern, requiring some set of fields in the object to have known values. Each region may contain an arbitrary number of tuples. Tuple space is shared by all processes: values written by one process may be read by others. Regions for storing higher-order values could also be defined but are not needed in this context.

Haskell-Linda is implemented as a preprocessor that transforms Haskell-Linda code into a pair of programs, one in Haskell and the other in C, connected to Haskell using GreenCard. This was done because C-Linda has no support for dynamically constructed tuple space queries, so a pre-processor has to be used to generate C code at compile time. A distinguished set of declarations, common to all Haskell programs using tuple space, defines the regions and types in tuple space. All tuple space operators are in the Haskell IO monad.

The values in tuple space are not ordered in any way. A read operation may return any value in the designated region matching the associated pattern, regardless of the order in which the values were placed into tuple space. Thus, the basic read operation is non-deterministic when more than one tuple matches the pattern. More complex disciplines can be layered on top of these basic tuple space operations. For example, a reader and writer may preserve the sequence of tuples by adding a counter to the data objects.

All tuple space functions are suffixed by a region name. Thus, the out_R function writes values into region R of tuple space. The function in_R reads and deletes a tuple from R, while read_R does not delete the tuple. Reading functions may optionally select only tuples in which some of the fields match specified values; this is allowed only when the type in the region is defined using named fields. For example, given the tuple space definitions,

```
region R        = TupType
data TupType    = TupType {key :: Int, val :: String}
```

then read_R {key = 1} reads only tuples with a 1 in the key field. There is currently no support for matching recursive datatypes at arbitrary levels of nesting.

Tuple space allows interprocess communication using events. An event producer places event values into tuple space while an event consumer reads and deletes (using in) event values out of tuple space. When multiple producers write events into the same region of tuple space, these events are implicitly combined, as with the .|. operator. When multiple readers take values from the same event, an implicit splitEvents occurs.

3.2   Using Haskell-Linda in FRP

A program written using Functional Reactive Programming is executed by an engine that converts incoming and outgoing events into Haskell-Linda commands. Each FRP process uses a separate engine; a function of type

```
frpEngine :: IO a -> (Event a -> Event b) -> (b -> IO ()) -> IO ()
```

The arguments to the engine are the input event source, the FRP event transformation, and a dispatcher for outgoing events. The event source is an IO action that generates the events stimulating the system. Incoming events are timestamped with their time of arrival; each FRP engine is thus clocked locally rather than globally. When an event moves from one process (engine) to another, the timestamp on the outgoing event is dropped and a new, local time stamp is placed on the event as it enters the new FRP engine. This eliminates the need for global clock synchronization but restricts the way in which a program may be partitioned into parallel tasks.

This engine blocks while waiting for the IO action to deliver a new stimulus. However, multiple FRP engines may be running in separate processes (e.g. using the fork primitive of Concurrent Haskell [PJGF96]) on a processor to keep it busy even when some of its FRP engines have no work to do or are waiting on IO actions.

Returning to the web server example, a program defining a single server process looks like this:

```
region IncomingURL  =  URL
region OutgoingPage =  WebPage

frpProgram          :: Event URL -> Event WebPage
frpProgram urls     =  urls ==> lookupWebPage

main                =  frpEngine
                          in_IncomingURL
                          frpProgram
                          out_OutgoingPage
```

The two-server version of the web server may be executed by running this same program in two different processes that share a common tuple space. The splitEvents and . | . found in the transformed version of the server are implicit in the tuple space operations used by the FRP engines.

To complete the web server, we need to add a process that interfaces between the HTTP server and tuple space. This process simply listens for incoming requests and drops them into the IncomingURL region of tuple space while also listening to the OutgoingPage region and sending web pages to the appropriate IP addresses.

4 Parallel FRP

Parallel FRP augments traditional FRP in three ways:

- it expands the core semantics of FRP with a number of new functions,
- it defines transformation rules that increase the potential for parallelism, and
- it specifies a compilation process that transforms a system specification into a set of FRP processes, running in parallel and communicating via Haskell-Linda.

4.1 Events

The essential property of events in our system is that, using Haskell-Linda, they can be moved from one process to another. For example, consider the following program:

```
pipeline     :: Event Input -> Event Output
stage1       :: Event Input -> Event Middle
stage2       :: Event Middle -> Event Output
pipeline     =  stage2 . stage1
```

We can encapsulate each of the stages as a separate process, and have the result of stage1 passed into stage2 through tuple space. As a side effect, however, the time elapsed in stage1 computations becomes observable — the timing of event occurrences is different in the event streams fed into the two stages since each process uses its own clock to timestamp events based on the actual time of arrival. Thus an expression which reads the timestamp of an event (using e.g. the FRP primitive withTimeE) will have different values in different stages. Additionally, event occurrences can be propagated into the second stage either in the order they are generated by the first stage, or in arbitrary order; the latter approach will in general yield a faster implementation, but changing the order of occurrences may also be observable by the program. Hence there are some restrictions on the programs that can be partitioned into separate processes without losing their meaning.

To get a better grasp of these restrictions, let us first classify event transformers considering their relation with time transforms on events. A *time transform* on events is an endomorphism on Event a which preserves the values associated with event's occurrences, but may alter their times arbitrarily, so they may end up in a different order after going through the time transform. Consider an event transformer f and an event e in the domain of f. Alluding to the obvious (imperative) implementation of events in real time, we call f *stateless* if it commutes with all time transforms — with the intuition that the value of each occurrence of f e depends only on the value of the corresponding (in time) occurrence of e. A *time-independent* event transformer commutes with all monotonically increasing time transforms; in this case the value of an occurrence of f e may depend on values of earlier occurrences of e as well (so f may have some "internal state"). However the event transformers in neither of these classes may observe the timestamps of the input events.

Now we can denote the re-timestamping of the event stream connecting two processes using two marker functions:

```
shuffle, delay  :: Event a -> Event a
pipeline        = stage2 . delay . shuffle . stage1
```

The function shuffle, introduced earlier, represents an unspecified time transform, while delay is an unspecified but monotonically increasing time transform. In effect these functions designate event streams that may be completely reordered (shuffle) or those that may be delayed but remain in the same order (delay). Thus by definition both shuffle and delay commute with stateless event transformers like ==>, while delay also commutes with "stateful" but time-independent operators such as withElemE. Some equivalences involving these functions are:

$$
\begin{array}{rcl}
\texttt{shuffle (e ==> f)} & \equiv & \texttt{(shuffle e) ==> f} \\
\texttt{filterE (shuffle e) p} & \equiv & \texttt{shuffle (filterE e p)} \\
\texttt{delay (withElemE e l)} & \equiv & \texttt{withElemE (delay e) l}
\end{array}
$$

For operators that observe timestamps, such as withTimeE, the placement of shuffle and delay is observable: moving the markers through such an operator changes the meaning of a program. Although we do not give formal proofs of any of these equivalences here, we believe that they could be proved using suitable tools.

Some FRP transformations serve to introduce new opportunities for parallelism. For example, the transformation

$$
\texttt{e ==> (f . g)} \quad \longrightarrow \quad \texttt{e ==> g ==> f}
$$

allows the event transformation to be computed in two stages.

4.2 Behaviors

Unlike events, behaviors are continuously available: they may be observed at any time. In the absence of time transforms in the program, piecewise-constant global behaviors may be implemented directly in tuple space using a single tuple containing the current value of the behavior; our current implementation based on Haskell-Linda has no support for shared non-piecewise-constant behaviors. To illustrate behaviors, we modify the web server example to include a hit count that is passed into the HTML page formatting routine `lookupWebPage`:

```
server            :: Event URL -> Event WebPage
server urls       =  withHits urls1 ==> lookupWebPage .|.
                     withHits urls2 ==> lookupWebPage
 where
  (urls1, urls2) =  splitEvents urls

  withHits        :: Event a -> Event (a, Integer)
  withHits e      =  e 'snapshot' hitCounter

  hitCounter      :: Behavior Integer
  hitCounter      =  stepper 0 hitCounterE

  hitCounterE     :: Event Integer
  hitCounterE     =  urls 'withElemE_' [1..]
```

This program has the same structure as the previous web server except for the addition of `withHits` to the call to `lookupWebPage`. The `withHits` function gets the current value of the hit counter using the FRP primitive

```
snapshot          :: Event a -> Behavior b -> Event (a,b)
```

which samples the behavior at each event occurrence and augments the event value to include the current value of the behavior. The hit counter behavior is generated using the following FRP functions:

```
stepper           :: a -> Event a -> Behavior a
withElemE_        :: Event a -> [b] -> Event b
```

The `hitCounterE` event numbers the incoming URLs while the `hitCounter` behavior makes this value available at all times.

Conversion of hit count to a behavior is not strictly necessary in this small example: we could instead leave it embedded in the event stream. However, using a behavior improves modularity by keeping the event structure separate from the hit count. It also keeps the URL stream from being stateful, allowing easier parallelization.

A behavior such as `hitCounter` can be implemented by maintaining a single tuple in a designated region tuple space, making the current value of the behavior available to all processes. The producer, a **stepper** function, deletes the old tuple and inserts a new one every time the stepped event delivers a new value. Consumers of the behavior perform a **read**, rather than **in**, on this tuple to find the current value of the behavior. The **read** leaves the tuple in tuple space; only the producer removes this tuple. Instead of the point to point communication used to pass events among processes, here we use tuple space to broadcast the current value of the behavior to all processes.

This implementation has a semantic problem similar to the one we encountered earlier when connecting processes using event streams: since the clocks of the various processes are not synchronized, this globalized behavior may be slightly out of date. For example, when a new URL enters the system, the producer may still be updating the hit counter when the web page construction process reads it. Going back to the non-parallel semantics, we again have to introduce some non-determinism. Here, we don't quite know at what time the behavior will be sampled. As with events, we can add a marker function to the program to indicate that it is not necessary to sample the behavior at precisely the current time. The blur function serves this purpose:

```
blur              :: Behavior a -> Behavior a
```

In the above example, adding blur in front of the reference to hitCounter in the withHits function states that it is acceptable to see a value of the hit counter that is close to the current time but perhaps not quite the same. Partitioning a program into independent FRP processes is semantically correct only if all behaviors they share are "blurred."

4.3 Partitioning

Formally, the process of partitioning a specification into a set of parallel programs involves rewriting the program as a set of mutually recursive global definitions. Each definition corresponds to an event or behavior that will be placed in tuple space and is shared by more than one of the processes. The following principles govern this partitioning process:

- Every global event or behavior is associated with a unique region in tuple space.
- Only events that are referenced with either shuffle or delay may be globalized. When the shuffle marker is absent, a hidden counter must be inserted to ensure that tuples are transferred in the correct order. Similarly, a process may only reference global behaviors tagged with blur.
- The semantic marker functions, shuffle, delay, and blur, are removed in translation.
- A .|. or splitEvents used to define a global event is implemented in tuple space.
- Event streams used in more than one process must be sent to multiple regions.
- A process may produce or consume more than one global event stream. However, multiple streams must be combined into a single type stream using a union type such as Either.
- A process that defines (produces) a shared piecewise-constant behavior encodes the associated stepper function in tuple space operations that turn FRP events into IO actions. Exactly one such process must define each shared behavior.

– Exactly one process has to run each "stateful" event transformer task (communicating via event streams without the **shuffle** marker); an arbitrary number of processes may run each stateless event transformer.

The partitioning process is too complex to fully describe here; a small example will make it a little clearer. We split the web server with a hit counter, annotated with marker functions, into three processes: one to keep track of the hit counter and two to serve web pages. We assume that an outside agent places the incoming URLs into two regions, IncomingURL1 and IncomingURL2 (one copy for the page servers and another for the hit counter).

```
-- Tuple space declarations
region IncomingURL1 = URL
region IncomingURL2 = URL
region HitBehavior  = Integer
region OutgoingPage = Webpage


-- This keeps the hit counter up to date
hitCounterProcess   = do out_HitBehavior 0
                         frpEngine
                           in_IncomingURL1
                           (withElem_ [1..] urls)
                           (\h -> do _ <- in_HitBehavior
                                     out_HitBehavior h)


-- Code for both page server processes
pageServer          = frpEngine
                        in_IncomingURL2
                        (\urls -> urls 'snapshot' hitB
                                  ==> lookupWebPage)
                        out_OutgoingPage
    where
      hitB          = makeExternalBehavior read_HitBehavior
```

The function makeExternalBehavior creates a behavior from an IO action. The .|. and splitEvents operations are implicit in the use of tuple space. This code is not restricted to two server processes — an arbitrary number of these server processes may be used since the event transformer in pageServer is stateless.

4.4   Stateful Event Handling

While we have discussed a parallel implementation of the ==> operator, it is much more common to encounter stateful systems: ones in which each transaction modifies the system state for the next transaction. Stateful event processing is typified by the FRP function accumE:

```
accumE            :: a -> Event (a -> a) -> Event a
```

This function takes an initial value and stream of "state update" functions, and produces a stream of values. Thus `accumE v` is a time-independent but not stateless event transformer, and we cannot perform the same sort of parallelization on `accumE` that we could for `==>`, since to compute the value of each event occurrence in general we must wait for the evaluation of the previous occurrence to "update the state." Our approach to parallelizing stateful event streams is to consider a more restricted situation: one in which the state comprises a set of independent substates. For example, the online auction example satisfies this restriction; incoming requests are partitioned by auction, allowing different processes to operate on different auctions in parallel. The structure of the resulting program is quite similar to the construction of the parallel web page server. The only difference is that the splitting of the incoming event stream is dictated by the auction name embedded in each request. For example, if auctions are named by integers, we may choose to use one processor to handle even numbered auctions and another to handle the odd numbered ones. We have investigated two different ways of partitioning the incoming stream of requests:

- Static partitioning: each substate resides on a fixed processor, requests are routed in a statically determined way. Interacting requests are always delivered to the same process.
- Dynamic partitioning: each substate resides in tuple space. To modify a substate, a process locks it. Interacting requests are resolved by blocking processes.

Each of these strategies has advantages and disadvantages. Static partitioning is easily expressed in ordinary FRP terms: filtering and merging, while dynamic partitioning is handled by the FRP drivers. Dynamic partitioning requires a special rule in the partitioner to generate these modified drivers. Dynamic partitioning also presents difficulties for transactions that observe all of the substates at once.

In either case, some domain-specific knowledge must be applied during the transformation process to allow parallel handling of stateful requests.

5   Example: An Online Auction Server

As a demonstration of FRP's suitability for distributed transaction processing, we have built a parallel web-based on-line auction system. This is essentially an event transformer which takes a stream of inputs and turns it into a stream of outputs, both of which are defined below:

```
data Input
  = StartAuction (Maybe Auction) User Item Description Date
  | Bid User Auction Price
  | Query Auction
  | Search Item
```

```
data Output
  = WebPage WebPage
  | MailTo User EmailMessage
```

The whole system consists of a number of independent auctions (each having a unique auction identifier) and a database of all items being auctioned, which can be used to answer queries about auctions involving a particular type of item.

The incoming events of type `Input` get partitioned according to whether they initiate an operation which will update the global state of the system (e.g. starting a new auction), handled by the event transformer `indexStateMachine`, or whether they just relate to the state of a particular auction (e.g. query the price or place a bid), in which case they are passed on to `auctionStateMachine`.

The initial system specification is thus quite simple.

```
auction :: Event Input -> Event Output
auction i = auctionStateMachine auctionReqs .|.
            indexStateMachine indexReqs
  where
    i' = addAuctionNames (delay i)
    auctionReqs = i' 'suchThat' isAuctionReq
    indexReqs = i' 'suchThat' isIndexReq
```

We note, however, that in a real auction the `auctionStateMachine` will be doing most of the work, so we may want either to try to parallelize it, or simply run multiple copies of it concurrently. We take the latter approach, and partition the stream of auction-related events into two. The resulting model is as follows:

```
auction i = auctionStateMachine auctionReqs1 .|.
            auctionStateMachine auctionReqs2 .|.
            indexStateMachine indexReqs
  where
    i' = addAuctionNames (delay i)
    auctionReqs = i' 'suchThat' isAuctionReq
    auctionReqs1 = auctionReqs 'suchThat' evenAuctionNumber
    auctionReqs2 = auctionReqs 'suchThat' oddAuctionNumber
    indexReqs = i' 'suchThat' isIndexReq
```

Another possible partition of this program is to create four processes: one to add the auction names to the input as well direct events to the proper handler (the `suchThat` functions), another to run `indexStateMachine`, and two running `auctionStateMachine`.

6   Related Work

In this work, we are combining the FRP paradigm with a distributed shared memory system (Linda) to produce a new functional environment which facilitates parallel programming. The problem of partitioning applications into their components for execution on different processors is also considered. All of the above have been addressed separately in the following ways:

FRP was originally developed by Conal Elliott for Fran, a language of interactive animations, but has also been used for robotics [PHE99], computer vision [RPHH99], and safety-critical systems [SJ99].

Concurrent functional languages have been implemented in various forms. Concurrent Haskell [PJGF96] extends Haskell with a small set of primitives for explicit concurrency designed around monadic I/O. Concurrent ML [Rep91] formalized synchronous operations as first-class purely functional values called "events." The functional language Eden [BKL98], built on top of Haskell, distinguishes between transformational and reactive systems, and introduces its (slightly more general) versions of splitEvents and .|. as special process abstractions to encapsulate nondeterminism and thus keeps referential transparency within user processes. However, it does not support time-varying behaviors or indeed any notion of time at all.

The Linda architecture has been well studied and widely used with languages like C [CGMS94], extensions of Pascal and object-oriented languages, but has never been integrated with Haskell.

Lastly, the whole idea of efficiently partitioning a problem such as a web server or an online auction into its constituent components to be run in parallel has been addressed mainly by using the concept of skeletons. In the imperative world, languages such as P3L [CDF+97] have been developed which infer a way of partitioning the problem from annotations highlighting regions of code where task parallelism or data parallelism could be exploited. A version of the same system has been implemented for the functional language OCaml [DCLP98].

7 Conclusions

This work is a very preliminary foray into a large design space. We attempt to combine two very different styles of programming: a declarative style of reactive programming and an imperative style of parallel programming, represented here by the Linda tuple space. Our primary contribution is the incorporation of interaction into the semantic framework of the parallel system. While the use of a specific parallel programming technology, Linda, has influenced the way we have built semantic models, these models are ultimately independent of any underlying implementation mechanisms. This initial effort has succeeded in a number of ways:

- This work can be applied to a large variety of problems of practical importance.
- We have developed a reasonable way of incorporating non-determinism into the semantics of FRP in a very controlled fashion. The non-determinism is restricted to behavior and event values without affecting the overall semantics of Haskell.
- Our work combines both operations on discrete messages (events) and unclocked, continuously available values (behaviors).

- We have shown how a declarative, executable specification can be used to synthesize a complex parallel system.

The primary problem with this work is that the transformation strategy is somewhat ad-hoc. There is not yet any systematic way to automate this process or to even test the equivalence between the system model and a generated parallel program. We expect that adding appropriate annotations to the specification would allow further automation.

We have not been able to evaluate the performance of the online auction example in a particularly meaningful way. While we have observed the expected speedup when adding more processors to the system, we have not yet effectively measured the overhead attributed to the use of tuple space.

We have investigated only static partitioning of the model into processes. A more dynamic system would create and destroy processes as needed, allowing a more effective use of resources. This style of programming is easily supported by the underlying Linda system: tuple pattern matching allows, in essence, new global variables to be created and destroyed dynamically. Here, we have approached partitioning in a first-order rather than a higher-order manner. The seems to be no inherent problems in adding dynamic partitioning to our system.

Some features of FRP have not yet been integrated into this framework. For example, time transformation is not supported at present and would be difficult to reconcile with the imperative nature of tuple-space operators. Another shortcoming is the lack of interprocess garbage collection. In the underlying implementation of FRP, events that are no longer needed are removed by the garbage collector. In the parallel system, this would require feedback from the consumer of some particular type of tuple back to the producer, allowing the consumer to signal that its values are no longer needed.

We have not yet addressed real-time performance criteria. For example, we cannot interrupt a computation in progress at the behest of a higher priority task or make any assurances about fairness or response time. Such features would require serious enhancements to the semantics and implementation of FRP.

While the basic transformations to set up pipelines or use multiple processors to service stateless event streams are easily understood, the transformations relating to stateful event or behavior usage are much harder to use and understand. We expect that further practical experience will be necessary to develop a useful and application appropriate set of transformations.

We have not yet formalized the semantic basis for our model. The work of Elliott and Hudak [EH97] provides a semantic basis for a version of FRP in which the notion of event corresponds to an occurrence of an event in our model and the one used in [Ell99], leading to a different treatment of event primitives. A clear semantic definition of FRP would be the first step towards proving formal correctness of our transformations or inferring a valid set of transformations directly from the underlying semantics.

Acknowledgment

We are grateful to Paul Hudak and the anonymous referees for their constructive comments.

References

[BKL98]   S. Breitinger, U. Klusik, and R. Loogen. From (sequential) Haskell to (parallel) Eden: An implementation point of view. In *Proc. Principles of Declarative Programming (PLILP/ALP'98)*, pages 318–334, 1998.

[CDF⁺97]   S. Ciarpaglini, M. Danelutto, L. Folchi, C. Manconi, and S. Pelagatti. ANA-CLETO: a template-based P3L compiler. In *Proc. 7th Parallel Computing Workshop (PCW'97)*, Canberra, Australia, September 1997.

[CGMS94]   N. Carriero, D. Gelernter, T. Mattson, and A. Sherman. The Linda alternative to message passing systems. *Parallel Computing*, 20(4):633–655, 1994.

[DCLP98]   M. Danelutto, R. Di Cosmo, X. Leroy, and S. Pelagatti. Parallel functional programming with skeletons: the OcamlP3L experiment. In *Proc. 1998 ACM SIGPLAN Workshop on ML*, September 1998.

[EH97]   C. Elliott and P. Hudak. Functional reactive animation. In *Proc. ACM SIG-PLAN International Conference on Functional Programming*, pages 163–173, June 1997.

[Ell99]   C. Elliott. An embedded modelling language approach to interactive 3D and multimedia animation. *IEEE Transactions on Software Engineering*, 25(3):291–308, May/June 1999.

[PESL98]   J. Peterson, C. Elliott, and G. Shu Ling. Fran user's manual. http:// research.microsoft.com/~conal/Fran/UsersMan.htm, July 1998.

[PHE99]   J. Peterson, P. Hudak, and C. Elliott. Lambda in motion: Controlling robots with Haskell. In *Proc. 1st International Conference on Practical Aspects of Declarative Languages (PADL'99)*, pages 91–105, January 1999.

[PJ99]   S. Peyton Jones (ed.). Haskell 98: A non-strict, purely functional language. Technical Report RR-1106, Yale University, February 1999.

[PJGF96]   S. Peyton Jones, A. Gordon, and S. Finne. Concurrent Haskell. In *Proc. 23rd ACM SIGPLAN-SIGACT Symposium on Principles of Programming Languages*, January 1996.

[Rep91]   J. Reppy. CML: A higher-order concurrent language. In *Proc. Conference on Programming Language Design and Implementation*, pages 293–305. ACM SIGPLAN, June 1991.

[RPHH99]   A. Reid, J. Peterson, P. Hudak, and G. Hager. Prototyping real-time vision systems: An experiment in DSL design. In *Proc. 21st International Conference on Software Engineering (ICSE'99)*, May 1999.

[SJ99]   M. Sage and C. Johnson. A declarative prototyping environment for the development of multi-user safety-critical systems. In *Proc. International System Safety Conference*, August 1999.

Out-of-Core Functional Programming with Type-Based Primitives*

Tyng-Ruey Chuang and Shin-Cheng Mu

Institute of Information Science, Academia Sinica, Taipei 115, Taiwan
{trc, scmu}@iis.sinica.edu.tw

Abstract. We formulate and experiment with type-based primitives
(such as fold and unfold operations) for out-of-core processing of functional data structures. We follow the view that recursive data types are
fixed points of polynomial type constructors. This view leads to a clear
separation of the semantics and the implementations of recursive data
types. We provide monadic implementations of the type-based primitives
so that the intermediate data structures used for the executions of the
primitives can be placed in out-of-core storage. The parametric module facility of Objective Caml is further used to package the out-of-core
implementations. The resulting out-of-core user code retains the same
program structure of the in-core user code and can be as elegant.

1 Motivation

In programming languages supporting automatic memory management, a program need not explicitly request storage for data during the execution. The
run-time system allocates space for new data, and reclaims space for data that
is not longer used. This helps users write clear and concise programs, and help
users eliminate run-time errors caused by dangling references.

When dealing with very large data structures, however, one may find automatic memory management becomes a performance bottleneck. One may only
want to keep part of the data structure in the core memory (RAM). Other part
of the data structure may better reside in out-of-core memory (i.e., secondary
storage, hard disk). There are several reasons for wanting to do this:

- The data structure is too large to fit into the core memory. It may even
  outgrow the swap space. If entirely put into the heap, it may cause serious
  paging problems.
- The data structure originally resides in a file or in a database. It is shared
  by other applications.
- The data structure is used in a specific way that the memory management
  scheme may not work well. For example, the data structure is repeated
  probed once it is created, but is not referenced for a long period of time

---

* This research is supported, in part, by National Science Council of Taiwan under
contract NSC 89-2213-E-001-005.

E. Pontelli, V. Santos Costa (Eds.): PADL 2000, LNCS 1753, pp. 32–46, 2000.

between two probes. It may be better to write the data structure to out-of-core storage after it is created, and only to read it back at the quest of a probe.

The above situation occurs, for example, when using a functional language to program a PDA (Personal Digital Assistant) that has small core memory size and has no swap space, but equipped with access links to external data sources on the Web.

Our emphasis in this paper is not on providing very efficient library to access the file media or the communication link at run-time. Rather, it is about developing an abstract layer for programming recursive data structures, as well as providing a workable out-of-core implementation underneath the abstract layer. Hence, programming out-of-core data structures can be as elegant as programming in-core data structures (actually the high-level code will look the same).

This paper is organized as follows. In Section 2, we review fundamental concepts in recursive data types. In Sections 3, 4, and 5, we show monadic formulations of the type-based primitives. These primitives are used to perform aggregate operations over recursive data structures, and our formulations make evident the intermediate data structures that are generated and consumed during the operations. Section 6 describes two examples of out-of-core processing of large recursive data structures, as well as their performance results. Sections 7 discusses related work and concludes this paper.

2   Recursive Data Types and Type-Based Primitives

ML-like languages allow one to define recursive data types and recursive functions concisely. Figure 1 shows the definitions, in Objective Caml, of a data type `tree` and several functions based on `tree`. One often calls `tree` a type constructor, or a type function, because it constructs from a type a a new type a `tree`. Functions `fold` and `unfold` are higher-order and polymorphic. We call the two functions *type-based primitives*. They are primitives because functions for computing `tree` values often can be derived or composed from them. They are type-based because their definitions come in a natural way from the definition of the data type `tree`. Note that function `unfold` uses an auxiliary type `option` in its definition. Type `option` is defined as

```
type 'a option = None | Some of 'a
```

As an application, one can define the Fibonacci function as

```
let g x = match x with 0->None | 1->None | n->Some (n-2,n,n-1)
let f (f'n_2, n, f'n_1) = f'n_2 + f'n_1
let fib n = fold (1, f) (unfold g n)
```

which first uses `unfold` to generate the "call tree" needed for evaluating the nth Fibonacci number, then uses `fold` to sum up the result.

```
type 'a tree = Null | Node of 'a tree * 'a * 'a tree

let rec fold (b, f) t = match t with
       Null           -> b
     | Node (x, y, z) -> f (fold (b, f) x, y, fold (b, f) z)

let rec unfold g s = match g s with
       None            -> Null
     | Some (x, y, z) -> Node (unfold g x, y, unfold g z)
```

Fig. 1. Definitions of the data type `tree`, and the `fold` and `unfold` primitives.

Type `tree` as currently defined has two drawbacks. First, the definition dictates the way `tree` values are implemented. The values can only be built from value constructors `Null` and `Node`, and will always reside in the heap space if they are in use. Secondly, the types of `Null` and `Node` are too restrictive.[1] They have types

```
Null : 'a tree
Node : 'a tree * 'a * 'a tree -> 'a tree
```

As a result, the definitions of type-based primitives are less elegant. For example, one needs the auxiliary data type `option` in the definition of `unfold`. The next section describes a more elegant way to define recursive data types.

2.1   Polynomial Data Types and Fixed Points

One can define type `tree` indirectly by expressing it as a fixed point of another type `node`:

```
type ('a, 'b) node = Null | Node of 'b * 'a * 'b
type 'a tree = Rec of ('a, 'a tree) node
```

Type `node` above is not recursive itself. It is called a *polynomial data type* because it can be viewed as the tagged sum of $\mathbf{1}$ and $(b \times a \times b)$, in which value constructors `Null` and `Node` serve as the tags. Type a `tree` is defined to be isomorphic to $(a, a$ `tree`$)$ `node` for type a. This isomorphism is maintained by the following two functions

```
let up n = Rec n
let down (Rec n) = n
```

where up $\circ$ down $= id_{\mathrm{tree}}$ and down $\circ$ up $= id_{\mathrm{node}}$. Note that value constructors `Null` and `Node` now have types

---

[1] Objective Caml does not consider value constructors first-class functions; hence it does not assign types to them. Other ML dialects, e.g. Standard ML of New Jersey, do view value constructors as functions and infer types for them.

```
Null : ('a, 'b) node
Node : 'b * 'a * 'b -> ('a, 'b) node
```

Their types are more flexible than those from the old definitions. As an example, the following definition of `unfold` does not need the auxiliary type `option` anymore.

```
let rec unfold g s = match g s with
    Null            -> up Null
  | Node (x, y, z) -> up (Node (unfold g x, y, unfold g z))
```

Function `unfold` now has type

```
unfold : ('b -> ('a, 'b) node) -> 'b -> 'a tree
```

Many a recursive data type can be defined as the fixed point of a suitable polynomial data type [2,10].

2.2   Generic Definitions with Parametric Modules

A type constructor like `node` not only lifts a pair of types (a, b) to a new data type (a, b) `node`, it also introduces a map function that lifts a pair of functions to a function between the corresponding `node` data types.

```
let map (f, g) t =
    match t with Null -> Null
               | Node (x, y, z) -> Node (g x, f y, g z)
```

Function `map` has type

```
map: ('a -> 'c) * ('b -> 'd) -> ('a, 'b) node -> ('c, 'd) node
```

Type constructor `node` with function `map` form a functor between categories (where objects are types and arrows are typed functions), provided that `map` further satisfies a number of algebraic properties (see, e.g. [3]).

The parametric module facility in Objective Caml [1] can be used to model polynomial type constructors and their fixed points, as shown in Figure 2. The idea is that all base functors we use to construct recursive data types must match the module type BASE. BASE can be thought as as a common interface for all polynomial type expressions with two type variables. A module Node is defined to match this interface. Further, the implementation of the polynomial type expression, and the map function, need not be exposed outside of module Node. A higher-order module Mu takes a module with interface BASE and returns a module with interface MU. Module Mu derives a new type constructor t as the fixed point of Base.t, as well as defines associated functions for t, such as map and hylo. The module name Mu is taken from the greek latter μ which is often used for fixed point binding in the literature.

Function `map` in Mu lifts a function of type $a \rightarrow b$ to a function of type a t $\rightarrow b$ t. Hence, like module Base, module Mu also defines a functor for type

```
let id x = x                (* identity function *)
let ($) f g x = f (g x)     (* infix op. for function composition *)

module type BASE =
sig
  type ('a, 'x) t
  val map : ('a -> 'b) * ('x -> 'y) -> ('a, 'x) t -> ('b, 'y) t
end

module type MU =
sig
  module Base: BASE

  type 'a t
  val up :   ('a, 'a t) Base.t -> 'a t
  val down: 'a t -> ('a, 'a t) Base.t
  val map : ('a -> 'b) -> 'a t -> 'b t
  val hylo: (('a, 'y) Base.t -> 'y) * ('x -> ('a, 'x) Base.t) -> 'x -> 'y
end

module Node =               (* module Node has module type BASE *)
struct
  type ('a, 'x) t = Null | Node of 'x * 'a * 'x
  let map (f, g) t =
      match t with
            Null -> Null
          | Node (x, y, z) -> Node (g x, f y, g z)
end

module Mu (B : BASE) : (MU with module Base = B) =
struct
  module Base  = B

  type 'a t = Rec of ('a, 'a t) Base.t
  let up n = Rec n
  let down (Rec n) = n
  let rec map f t = (up $ Base.map (f, map f) $ down) t
  let rec hylo (f, g) x = (f $ Base.map (id, hylo (f, g)) $ g) x
end

module Tree = Mu (Node)    (* module Tree has module type MU *)
open Node                  (* so one can use Null instead of Node.Null *)
open Tree                  (* so one can use hylo instead of Tree.hylo *)

let g x = match x with 0 -> Null | 1 -> Null | n -> Node (n-2, n, n-1)
let f x = match x with Null -> 1 | Node (m, _, n) -> m + n
let fib n = hylo (f, g) n
```

Fig. 2. Parametric modules and generic definitions of recursive data types.

constructor t. Function `hylo` is a generalization of the fold/unfold primitives. Two special cases of `hylo`, called `cata` and `ana` in the literature, become the fold and unfold primitives:

```
let cata f t = hylo (f,  down) t
let ana  g x = hylo (up, g)    x
```

Functions `map` and `hylo` are known as homomorphism and they satisfy a number of properties [3,10]. In practice, they provide high-level abstractions so that many recursive operations can be derived or composed from them. For example, one can define the Fibonacci function more succinctly using `hylo`, as shown at the last three lines in Figure 2.

Using module facility for fixed point construction has two benefits. First, it provides genericity: As long as a polynomial type constructor can be made into a module that matches `BASE`, it can always be transformed to the corresponding recursive type constructor using `Mu`, without the need to know the actual polynomial type expression. The second benefit is that it encapsulates implementation details. For example, one can provide an out-of-core implementation for module `Mu`. As long as the new implementation still accepts modules of type `BASE` and produces modules of type `MU`, it can be used interchangeable with the original implementation.

2.3 Out-of-Core Data Representations

By providing alternative implementations of the up and down functions in module `Mu`, we can place recursive data structures generated by them in out-of-core storage. Rather than as a pointer in heap, a recursive data structure of type a t can be represented as a position in a binary file. Function `down` reads a node of the structure, which is of type $(a, a$ t) `Base.t`, from the specified position. Function up writes a node of the same type to a fresh location, returning the position. One needs to perform in-core/out-of-core data representation conversions for the nodes. This can be done with the help of Objective Caml's `to_string` and `from_string` functions in the `Marshal` package. Note that the conversions are for individual nodes, not for the recursive structure as a whole, so there is not need to worry about maintaining a stack for recursive traversal. The actual implementation, however, is more delicate as we provide buffered I/O, as well as perform node caching and garbage collection within the buffers. The definitions of `map` and `hylo` functions remain the same: They just use the out-of-core up and down functions, hence process out-out-core recursive data structures. However, `map` and `hylo` may generate intermediate data structures that are still kept in heap. The rest of this paper will show how to move these intermediate data structures to out-of-core storage without affecting user code structure.

Alternatively, we can store that collection of $(a, a$ t) `Base.t` values in a database. Individual $(a, a$ t) `Base.t` values are represented as records in a table, and each is associated with a record ID. The constituting a t fields of these records, moreover, refer to other $(a, a$ t) `Base.t` records using the record IDs.

The table can use the ID as a key, so the ID can be used for fast cross-reference among the records.

3   Monads and Monadic Maps

A monad in functional programming is the encapsulation of a computational process. It encapsulates low-level details of a computational process so they will not clutter high-level program code. For an introduction to monad, see [13]. We adopt the notations used in [2] where a monad is described as a type constructor with two additional functions: unit and %. They are the monadic versions of the identity function and the functional composition operator. We use them to provide additional functionalities for primitives map and hylo. Function unit and operator % satisfy the following two rules: $f \% \, \mathtt{unit} = \mathtt{unit} \, \% \, f = f$, and $f \% (g \% h) = (f \% g) \% h$. They also satisfy additional algebraic properties [2]. For a specific monad, usually there will be more functions (and rules) that serve additional purposes. For example, often there will be a function to extract from a monad the value of the encapsulated computation.

Furthermore, when one programs in monads with a type constructor, one often needs a monadic version of the map function for the type constructor [6]. The following module type BASE'M describes a type constructor t and the associated monadic map function.

```
module type BASE'M =
sig
  module Monad : MONAD
  type 'a t
  val map : ('a -> 'b Monad.t) -> ('a t -> 'b t Monad.t)
end
```

That is, given a function that lifts a value of type a to a monad of type b, the monadic map function lifts a value of type a t to a monad of type b t. To see the difference between this definition and the usual definition of map, compare BASE'M with BASE in Figure 2. Once the monadic map is defined, monadic versions of other type-based primitives can be defined easily [11].

4   Continuation Monads

We use a continuation monad to illustrate monadic definitions of type-based primitives. A continuation monad of type (a, r) t is a computation that when given a continuation k (which has type $a \rightarrow r$) will return the result of applying k to the value (which has type a) in the monad. Figure 3 shows a module type CONT'MONAD for continuation monad, and a module type BASE'M for a type constructor with its monadic map function. Modules ContMonad and Node'M implement the two interfaces, while module Mu'M defines the monadic map and hylo functions. The definitions of the two monadic functions look very similar

```
module type CONT'MONAD =
sig
  type ('a, 'r) t
  val (%) : ('b ->('c, 'r) t) -> ('a ->('b, 'r) t) -> ('a ->('c, 'r) t)
  val unit : 'a -> ('a, 'r) t
  val run  : ('a, 'r) t -> ('a -> 'r) -> 'r
end

module type BASE'M =
sig
  module Monad : CONT'MONAD
  type ('a, 'x) t
  val map : ('a -> ('b, 'r) Monad.t) * ('x -> ('y, 'r) Monad.t) ->
            ('a, 'x) t -> (('b, 'y) t, 'r) Monad.t
end

module ContMonad =   (* module ContMonad has module type CONT'MONAD *)
struct
  type ('a, 'r) t = ('a -> 'r) -> 'r
  let unit a = fun k -> k a
  let (%) f g a = fun k -> g a (fun b -> f b k)
  let run m k = m k
end

module Node'M =       (* module Node'M has module type BASE'M *)
struct
  module Monad = ContMonad
  type ('a, 'x) t = Null | Node of 'x * 'a * 'x
  let map (f, g) t =
      match t with
            Null -> Monad.unit Null
          | Node (x, y, z) -> fun k ->
                g x (fun u -> f y (fun v -> (g z (fun w ->
                k (Node (u, v, w))))))
end

module Mu'M (B : BASE'M) : (MU'M with module Base  = B
       and module Monad = B.Monad) =
struct
  module Base  = B
  module Monad = B.Monad
  open Monad
  type 'a t = Rec of ('a, 'a t) Base.t
  let up n = unit (Rec n)
  let down (Rec n) = unit n
  let rec map f t = (up % Base.map (f, map f) % down) t
  let rec hylo (f, g) x = (f % Base.map (unit, hylo (f, g)) % g) x
end
```

Fig. 3. Continuation monads and monadic type-based primitives.

to their counterparts at module Mu in Figure 2. In the new definitions, function unit is used in place of id, and operator % in place of $. Otherwise the high-level formulations remain the same.

The monadic Fibonacci function, fib'm, furthermore, can be defined using the same reduction and generation function f and g as before (c.f. last few lines in Figure 2). The only difference is that, before they are passed to the monadic hylo function, they are composed with function unit to become monadic as well. The Fibonacci number is extracted from the monad by passing the identity function as the continuation.

```
let g x = match x with 0->Null | 1->Null | n->Node (n-2,n,n-1)
let f x = match x with Null -> 1 | Node (m, _, n) -> m + n
let fib'm n = hylo (unit $ f, unit $ g) n
let fib n = run (fib'm n) id
```

Note that as defined by the monadic map function, the computation inside a monad is order-specific. For a tree node Node (x, y, z), it is in the order of x, y, z, and, finally, the entire tree node. For out-of-core implementations of type-based primitives, one also needs to specify the order of I/O operations for the constituting fields of a recursive data structure. The next section will describe an implementation where a continuation is modeled as a stack, and where an out-of-core implementation of the continuation stacks leads to out-of-core implementations of map and hylo.

5   Stacks as Continuations and Their Out-of-Core Implementations

One can view the intermediate data structure that is being produced and consumed during the computation of a type-based primitive as a continuation. This intermediate data structure records the state of the computation, and can be arranged as a FIFO stack. Usually, this stack is built in the heap without the awareness of the programmer, and is called the run-time stack. However, one can make explicit the run-time stack in the definition of a type-based primitive, and requires the primitive to pass around this stack explicitly in its internal steps. We define a monad to encapsulate this stack in Figure 4.

For flexibility, we enable the programmers to specify, by implementing a module with interface MOVE, the precise order for evaluating a Base.t node. MOVE is declared as following:

```
type ('a, 'b) control = Call of 'a | Return of 'b

module type MOVE =
sig
  module Base : BASE

  type ('a, 'x, 'y) t
```

```
module type CONT = sig
  type 'a t
  val make : ('a * 'a t) option -> 'a t
  val next : 'a t -> ('a * 'a t) option
end

module type MONAD = sig
  module Base : BASE
  type ('a, 'x, 'y) t
  type ('a, 'x, 'y) op = ('x, ('a, 'y) Base.t) control
  val (%) : ((('a, 'x, 'y) op -> ('a, 'x, 'y) t) -> (('a, 'x, 'y) op ->
             ('a, 'x, 'y) t) -> (('a, 'x, 'y) op -> ('a, 'x, 'y) t)
  val call : ('a, 'x) Base.t -> ('a, 'x, 'y) t
  val return : 'y -> ('a, 'x, 'y) t
  val run : ('a, 'x, 'y) t -> 'y
end

module NodeMove : (MOVE with module Base = Node) = struct
  module Base = Node;;   open Node
  type ('a, 'b) marker = Todo of 'a | Done of 'b | Hold
  type ('a, 'x, 'y) t = ('a, ('x, 'y) marker) Base.t
  let expand x = match x with
      Null             -> Return Null
    | Node (u, v, w) -> Call (u, Node (Hold, v, Todo w))
  let reduce y t = match t with
      Node (Hold, v, Todo w) -> Call (w, Node (Done y, v, Hold))
    | Node (Done u, v, Hold) -> Return (Node (u, v, y))
end

module ContMonad (M : MOVE) (C : CONT) :
      (MONAD with module Base = M.Base) = struct
  module Base = M.Base
  type ('a, 'x, 'y) stack = ('a, 'x, 'y) M.t C.t
  type ('a, 'b) sign = Stop of 'a | More of 'b
  type ('a, 'x, 'y) op = ('x, ('a, 'y) Base.t) control
  type ('a, 'x, 'y) t = ('a, 'x, 'y) stack ->
                        ('y, ('a, 'x, 'y) op * ('a, 'x, 'y) stack) sign
  let call x = fun k -> match M.expand x with
      Call (y, z) -> More (Call y, C.make (Some (z, k)))
    | Return y    -> More (Return y, k)
  let return x = fun k -> match C.next k with
      None -> Stop x
    | Some (h, t) -> match M.reduce x h with
                Call (y, z) -> More (Call y, C.make (Some (z, t)))
              | Return y    -> More (Return y, t)
  let (%) f g x = fun k ->
      match g x k with Stop c -> Stop c | More (b, a) -> f b a
  let run m = match m (C.make None) with Stop c -> c
end
```

Fig. 4. Stacks as continuations, in monadic style. Part I.

```
module type MU'M = sig
  module Base  : BASE
  module Monad : MONAD
  type 'a t
  val pair : (('a, 'y) Base.t -> 'y) * ('x -> ('a, 'x) Base.t) ->
                (('x, ('a, 'y) Base.t) control -> ('a, 'x, 'y) Monad.t)
  val hylo : (('x, ('a, 'y) Base.t) control -> ('a, 'x, 'y) Monad.t) ->
                (('x, ('a, 'y) Base.t) control -> ('a, 'x, 'y) Monad.t)
end

module Mu'M (M : MONAD) : (MU'M with module Base = M.Base and
        module Monad = M) = struct
  module Base  = M.Base
  module Monad = M
  type 'a t = Rec of ('a, 'a t) Base.t
  let (%) = Monad.(%)
  let pair (f, g) x =
      match x with Call  a -> Monad.call  (g a)
                 | Return b -> Monad.return (f b)
  let rec hylo h x = (hylo h % h) x
end
```

Fig. 5. Stacks as continuations, in monadic style. Part II.

```
    val expand : ('a, 'x) Base.t ->
                    ('x * ('a, 'x, 'y) t, ('a, 'y) Base.t) control
    val reduce : 'y -> ('a, 'x, 'y) t ->
                    ('x * ('a, 'x, 'y) t, ('a, 'y) Base.t) control
  end
```

A value of type t describes a move for accessing the continuation stack. The type variable 'x in the definition of type constructor ('a, 'x, 'y) t is the same type variable 'x in the type of the generation function g : 'x -> ('a, 'x) Base.t. Similarly, the 'y in ('a, 'x, 'y) t is the same 'y in the type of the reduction function f : ('a, 'y) Base.t -> 'y. This means that a move can access to values whose types are 'x or 'y. Function expand takes as an argument the result of the generation function g, and decides what to do next. It can either produce a pair of values: A value of type 'x to be expanded again, and a next move, of type ('a, 'x, 'y) t, to be pushed to the continuation stack. That is, it produces the Call part of a control value. Or an expand operation can call the reduction function and return a value of type ('a, 'y) Base.t (i.e., the Return part). Similarly, function reduce takes as an argument the result of the reduction function f. It takes a next move from the continuation stack, and decides either to expand or to reduce further. Figures 4 shows a module NodeMove that specifies a left-to-right evaluation order for values of type Node.t.

Module ContMonad in Figure 4 will generate a module with interface MONAD that is used to define the monadic function hylo (shown in Figure 5). Module

ContMonad is parameterized by a module M that specifies the evaluation order for computing Base.t values, and a module C that implements the continuation stack. Hence, ContMonad can produce monads that use customized traversal routines, as well as monads that use out-of-core storage for continuation stacks. Two lifting functions are described in the generated module: Functions call and return. Function call produces a monad for the result of the generation function g, and function return produces a monad for the result of the reduction function f. Note that in module ContMonad, call is defined to use expand to decide the next move. Likewise, return uses reduce to extract a move from the continuation stack.

In Figure 5, we show how the monad generated by ContMonad module is used to build monadic type-based primitives. To save space, we show only the part about function hylo. Note that one needs an auxiliary function pair to group the generation function and reduction function together before passing them to hylo. This also helps make the definition of hylo tail-recursive. Again, the monadic Fibonacci function can be defined to use the original reduction and generation functions.

```
let g x = match x with 0->Null | 1->Null | n->Node (n-2,n,n-1)
let f x = match x with Null -> 1 | Node (m, _, n) -> m + n
let fib'm n = hylo (pair (f, g)) n
let fib n = run (fib'm n)
```

In Figure 4, the continuation in module ContMonad has type stack, which is defined as

```
type ('a, 'x, 'y) stack = ('a, 'x, 'y) M.t C.t
```

where M is a module that implements module type MOVE, and C implements CONT. The make function in CONT will make a continuation (either by adding a move to an existing continuation, or by constructing an empty one). The next function will see if a continuation is empty, and, if not, will extract a move from it. The two functions are the same as the up and down functions for list data type, and can be implemented to use out-of-core storage. Note that the only place in module ContMonad where an empty continuation is created is in function run, and the continuation is never used after run returns its result. This means that the out-of-core storage for the continuation can be reclaimed just before run returns. One can also show that for an out-of-core recursive data structure t created by $t = $ hylo (f, g) x, t will never be shared by others. However, t may be intermixed with dead intermediate data in the out-of-core storage. The following expression performs an out-of-core garbage collection to move t (but none of the dead intermediate data) to a new storage: hylo (New.up, Old.down) t. Here, New is the module with a fresh out-of-core storage, and Old the original module where t is built.

time (in sec.)	all in-core	out-of-core lists with in-core continuation stacks	out-of-core lists with out-of-core continuation stacks
	867	1047	283

Maximum segment sum. List length: 2,000,000. System RAM: 128 MB.

time (in sec.)	all in-core	out-of-core trees with out-of-core continuation stacks
insert 5×10^5 nodes	4460	10036
insert 10^6 nodes	> 18 hours	30161

Building splay trees. Tree sizes: 500,000 and 1,000,000. System RAM: 20 MB.

Table 1. In-core and out-of-core performance results of the two examples.

6   Examples and Performance Results

We show two examples and their performance results, under separate memory setup. The first example is the maximum segment sum problem which uses lists in a sequential matter. The program is executed with a conventional memory system of 128 MB. The second example builds splay trees and performs a lot of random access to tree nodes. The program is executed under just 20 MB of core memory of which the OS is taking away 14 MB. The two examples are executed on a Pentium Pro 200 MHz PC running Linux 2.2.10. The programs are compiled by the Objective Caml native code compiler (version 1.07).

6.1   Maximum Segment Sum

Given a list of integers, the *maximum segment sum* problem is to find out the maximum of the sums of the non-empty contiguous segments of the list. This problem is interesting because there is a linear time algorithm [3] that makes two passes over the lists using function `hylo`. The intermediate lists (i.e., the continuation stacks) generated and consumed by the `hylo` function can be as long as the original input list. When the input list is very long, both the input list and the intermediate list create storage management problem for the heap. Using our method, we can put both the input list and the intermediate list on out-of-core storage. The execution time for a list of 2,000,000 random integers is shown in Table 1. It shows that implementing out-of-core continuation for `hylo` does pay off as it reduces execution time significantly.

6.2   Building Splay Trees

Splay trees are efficient self-adjusting binary trees [12]. A splay operation moves up a node x in the tree by either a single rotation, or a double rotation, depending on the position of x in the tree. In splay tree, after a usual tree operation on node x (e.g., inserting a node x), one then splays on x and changes the structure of the tree. Splay tree operations are interesting to us (besides its optimal time complexity, in an amortized sense) because it is not obvious how type-based primitives can be used to model splay operation. The problem is that although there are two children for each node in the tree, only one child is rotated during a splay operation. However, if type **tree** is used, the two children will have the same type; hence a type-based primitive will work on both children, which is wrong.

It turns out that the way to describe a tree node during a splay operation is to define a auxiliary type constructor **splay'node**:

```
type ('a, 'b, 'x) splay'node = N | S of 'b * 'a * 'b
    | L  of 'x * 'a * 'b        | R of 'b * 'a * 'x
    | LL of ('x * 'a * 'b) * 'a * 'b
    | LR of ('b * 'a * 'x) * 'a * 'b
    | RL of 'b * 'a * ('x * 'a * 'b)
    | RR of 'b * 'a * ('b * 'a * 'x)

let map (f, g, h) t = ... the map function for splay'node ...

type ('a, 'b) splay'tree =
    Rec of ('a, 'b, ('a, 'b) splay'tree) splay'node

let rec hylo (f, g) t = (f $ map (id, id, hylo (f, g)) $ g) x
```

where type variable `'x` marks the subtree to be rotated. That is, besides type variable `'x` that acts as a fixed point holder, two additional type variables are needed.

We write a program to use the above definitions to build a tree by repeated insert-and-splay operations, both for in-core and out-of-core cases. Building trees this way will generate many intermediate tree nodes as well as intermediate trees. Hence, we employ write buffer garbage collection (Section 2.3) and out-of-core garbage collection (Section 5) to reduce storage usage. We also run the program with a very small system memory setup to stress test both the in-core and out-of-core implementations. As shown in Table 1, our out-of-core implementation is not always better than the in-core implementation. However, in cases where an in-core execution will spend most of its time swapping the heap space (as the > 18 hours case shows), our implementation still performs well.

7 Related Work and Conclusion

Monads have long been shown to bring another level of abstraction, and to improve the overall structure of functional programs significantly [13]. Type-based primitives like **map** and **hylo** help structure and transform programs [3,10], and new language extension has been proposed and implemented to develop programs that can be systematically applied to user-defined data types [2,7]. Several researchers have demonstrated how to use monads in combination with type-based primitives to achieve further abstraction [2,6,8,11].

Monadic data types are used to maintain single-threaded access to data structures [4], and to make modular interpreters [5,9]. Type-based approach to compact printing and parsing of functional data structures is shown in [8]. However, it seems that until now no one had addressed the need of out-of-core processing of functional data structures. Although Objective Caml provides library support to marshal data between in-core and out-of-core storage [1], the library is not suitable for exporting and importing data structures of very large size. Neither can it perform incremental marshaling, or place continuation stacks in out-of-core storage. We have shown how to formulate and implement type-based primitives for out-of-core processing of functional data structures. The resulting program structure for out-of-core user code is as elegant as the in-core user code.

References

1. The caml language. Web site at `caml.inria.fr`.
2. Roland Backhouse, Patrick Jansson, Johan Jeuring, and Lambert Meertens. Generic programming: An introduction. In *Advanced Functional Programming*, pages 28–115, 1999. Lecture Notes in Computer Science, Vol. 1608, Springer–Verlag.
3. Richard Bird and Oege de Moor. *Algebra of Programming*. Prentice Hall, 1997.
4. Chih-Ping Chen and Paul Hudak. Rolling your own mutable ADT: A connection between linear types and monads. In *The 24th Symposium on Principles of Programming Languages*, pages 54–66. ACM Press, January 1997.
5. David A. Espinosa. *Semantic Lego*. PhD thesis, Graduate School of Arts and Sciences, Columbia University, 1995.
6. Maarten Fokkinga. Monadic maps and folds for arbitrary datatypes. In *Memoranda Informatica*, pages 94–28. University of Twente, June 1994.
7. Patrick Jansson and Johan Jeuring. Polyp: A polytypic programming language extension. In *The 24th Symposium on Principles of Programming Languages*, pages 470–482. ACM Press, January 1997.
8. Patrick Jansson and Johan Jeuring. Polytypic compact printing and parsing. In *European Symposium on Programming*, pages 324–333, 1999. Lecture Notes in Computer Science, Vol. 1576, Springer–Verlag.
9. Sheng Liang, Paul Hudak, and Mark Jones. Monad transformers and modular interpreters. In *The 22nd Symposium on Principles of Programming Languages*, pages 333–343. ACM Press, 1995.
10. Erik Meijer, Maarten Fokkinga, and Ross Paterson. Functional programming with bananas, lenses, envelopes and bared wire. In *Functional Programming Languages and Computer Architecture*, pages 124–144, August 1991. Lecture Notes in Computer Science, Vol. 523, Springer–Verlag.
11. Erik Meijer and Johan Jeuring. Merging monads and folds for functional programming. In *Advanced Functional Programming*, pages 228–266, May 1995. Lecture Notes in Computer Science, Vol. 925, Springer–Verlag.
12. Robert Endre Tarjan. *Data Structures and Network Algorithms*. Society for Industrial and Applied Mathematics, 1983.
13. Philip Wadler. Monads for functional programming. In *Advanced Functional Programming*, pages 24–52, May 1995. Lecture Notes in Computer Science, Vol. 925, Springer–Verlag.

A Functional Logic Programming Approach to Graphical User Interfaces

Michael Hanus*

Informatik II, RWTH Aachen, D-52056 Aachen, Germany
hanus@informatik.rwth-aachen.de

Abstract. We show how the features of modern integrated functional logic programming languages can be exploited to implement graphical user interfaces (GUIs) in a high-level declarative style. For this purpose, we have developed a GUI library in Curry, a multi-paradigm language amalgamating functional, logic, and concurrent programming principles. The functional features of Curry are exploited to define the graphical structure of an interface and to implement new graphical abstractions, and the logic features of Curry are used to specify the logical dependencies of an interface. Moreover, the concurrent and distributed features of Curry support the easy implementation of GUIs to distributed systems.

1 Introduction

The implementation of graphical user interfaces for application programs is a non-trivial task which is usually supported by specific libraries. Although it is clear that any serious programming language must have a library for implementing GUIs, there are many different approaches to structure those libraries. In this paper we propose a GUI library for integrated functional logic languages (see [6] for a survey) and show how the features of such integrated languages can be exploited to provide a nice structure for the implementation of GUIs.

In this paper, we consider the language Curry [7,11], a modern multi-paradigm declarative language which integrates functional, logic, and concurrent programming paradigms. Curry combines in a seamless way features from functional programming (nested expressions, lazy evaluation, higher-order functions), logic programming (logical variables, partial data structures, built-in search), and concurrent programming (concurrent evaluation of expressions with synchronization on logical variables). Curry also provides additional features in comparison to the pure paradigms (compared to functional programming: search, computing with partial information and constraints; compared to logic programming: more efficient evaluation due to the deterministic and demand-driven evaluation of functions, more flexible search strategies) and supports programming-in-the-large with specific features (types, modules, encapsulated search).

* This research has been partially supported by the German Research Council (DFG) under grant Ha 2457/1-1 and by the DAAD under the PROCOPE programme.

E. Pontelli, V. Santos Costa (Eds.): PADL 2000, LNCS 1753, pp. 47–62, 2000.

```
runWidget "Hello"
      (TkCol [] [TkLabel [TkText "Hello world!"],
             TkButton tkExit [TkText "Stop"]])
```

Fig. 1. A simple "Hello world" GUI

```
TkCol [] [
   TkEntry [TkRef val, TkText "0"],
   TkRow [] [TkButton (tkUpdate incrText val) [TkText "Increment"],
            TkButton (tkSetValue val "0")    [TkText "Reset"],
            TkButton tkExit                  [TkText "Stop"]]]
   where val free
```

Fig. 2. A specification of a counter GUI

In order to avoid reinventing the wheel, our GUI library is based on Tcl/Tk [14]. The main purpose of this contribution is to provide a suitable structure to access the components of Tcl/Tk in a high-level way from Curry programs. We will see that the functional *and* logic features of Curry supports together a good structure to describe GUIs.

In order to get an impression of the proposed structure of GUI implementations, Fig. 1 shows a simple but complete implementation of a "Hello world" GUI based on our library. The GUI is started by the I/O action `runWidget` which takes a string (the title of the main window) and a specification of a GUI as an argument. This specification is basically a description of the hierarchical layout of the various GUI elements. In this simple example, the GUI is a column (`TkCol`) of two elements: a label element (`TkLabel`) containing a text and a button (`TkButton`) which terminates the GUI by the action `tkExit` when the button is pressed.

Beyond the hierarchical layout structure, GUIs have also a logical structure which connects the different elements of a GUI. For instance, different buttons refer to the manipulation of particular entry fields in a GUI. As a simple example, consider the counter GUI shown in Fig. 2. Since clicking the increment button should increase the value of the entry field by one, there is a connection between the action of the "Increment" button and the value shown in the entry field (and similar for the "Reset" button). Many GUI libraries (e.g., [14,19]) solve this problem by forcing the programmer to assign explicit names (strings) to the different GUI elements which are subsequently used as references to them. Since these names are strings, often no consistency checks are done so that runtime errors can occur when a name is referred but does not exist. Moreover, new graphical abstractions which combine several elements are difficult to define since the necessary names can clash with other existing names. To avoid these problems, we use logical variables ("fixed but unknown widget references") to refer to the different GUI elements. If a reference to some GUI element is necessary, we introduce for this purpose a logical variable ("TkRef val" in Fig. 2) which can be used in actions like tkSetValue or tkUpdate to manipulate these elements. Thus, a GUI in our framework is a partially instantiated data structure[1] where multiple occurrences of a logical variable denotes the logical dependencies inside the GUI. In Fig. 2 the entry field showing the current value of the counter is referred by the logical variable val. Clicking the "Increment" button causes the invocation of the event handler "tkUpdate incrText val" that applies the function incrText (which increments the textual representation of a number by one) to the string shown in the entry element referred by val. Similarly, this field is set to the string "0" by pressing the "Reset" button.

2   Basic Elements of Curry

This section provides a brief overview of Curry as necessary to understand our approach to GUI programming. More details about Curry's computation model and a complete description of all language features can be found in [7,11].

From a syntactic point of view, a Curry program is a functional program[2] extended by the possible inclusion of free (logical) variables in conditions and right-hand sides of defining rules. Thus, a Curry program consists of the definition of functions and the data types on which the functions operate. Functions are evaluated in a lazy manner. To provide the full power of logic programming, functions can be called with uninstantiated arguments (logical variables). The behavior of such function calls depends on the evaluation annotations of functions which can be either *flexible* or *rigid*. Calls to rigid functions are suspended if a demanded argument, i.e., an argument whose value is necessary to decide the applicability of a rule, is uninstantiated (*"residuation"*). Calls to flexible functions are evaluated by a possibly non-deterministic instantiation of the demanded arguments to the required values in order to apply a rule (*"narrowing"*).

Example 1. The following Curry program defines the data types of Boolean values and polymorphic lists (first two lines) and functions for computing the concatenation of lists and the last element of a list:

```
data Bool   = True | False
data List a = []    | a : List a

conc :: [a] -> [a] -> [a]
conc eval flex

conc []      ys = ys
```

---

[1] Since the GUI library does not export any constructor for the argument type of TkRef, the type system ensures that no ground values can be inserted as arguments of TkRef.

[2] Curry has a Haskell-like syntax [15], i.e., (type) variables and function names start with lowercase letters and the names of type and data constructors start with an uppercase letter. The application of *f* to *e* is denoted by juxtaposition (*"f e"*).

```
conc (x:xs) ys = x : conc xs ys

last xs | conc ys [x] =:= xs   = x    where x,ys free
```

The data type declarations define `True` and `False` as the Boolean constants and `[]` (empty list) and `:` (non-empty list) as the constructors for polymorphic lists (a is a type variable ranging over all types and the type `List a` is usually written as `[a]` for conformity with Haskell).

The (optional) type declaration ("`::`") of the function `conc` specifies that `conc` takes two lists as input and produces an output list, where all list elements are of the same (unspecified) type.[3] Since `conc` is explicitly defined as flexible[4] (by "`eval flex`"), the equation "`conc ys [x] =:= xs`" can be solved by instantiating the first argument `ys` to the list `xs` without the last argument, i.e., the only solution to this equation satisfies that `x` is the last element of `xs`.

In general, functions are defined by (*conditional*) *rules* of the form "$l \mid c = e$ **where** *vs* **free**" where l has the form $f\,t_1 \ldots t_n$ with f being a function, $t_1, \ldots, t_n$ data terms and each variable occurs only once, the *condition* c is a constraint, e is a well-formed *expression* which may also contain function calls, and *vs* is the list of *free variables* that occur in c and e but not in l (the condition and the **where** parts can be omitted if c and *vs* are empty, respectively). The **where** part can also contain further local function definitions which are only visible in this rule. A conditional rule can be applied if its left-hand side matches the current call and its condition is satisfiable. A *constraint* is any expression of the built-in type `Constraint`. Each Curry system must support at least equational constraints of the form $e_1 =:= e_2$ which are satisfiable if both sides e_1 and e_2 are reducible to unifiable data terms (i.e., terms without defined function symbols). However, specific Curry systems can also support more powerful constraint structures, like arithmetic constraints on real numbers or finite domain constraints for applications in operation research problems, as in the PACS implementation [9]. *Expressions* are of the following form:

$e ::= c$	(constants like numbers or identifiers)
x	(variables x)
$(e_0\ e_1 \ldots e_n)$	(application)
if b then e_1 else e_2	(conditional)
$e_1 =:= e_2$	(equational constraint)
e_1 & e_2	(concurrent conjunction of constraints)
e_1 &> e_2	(sequential conjunction of constraints)
let $x_1, \ldots, x_n$ free in e	(existential quantification)

Curry has also a polymorphic type system which ensures that the expressions e, e_1, e_2 in the last three alternatives are always constraints.

The operational semantics of Curry, as precisely described in [7,11], is a conservative extension of lazy functional programming (if no free variables occur

---

[3] Curry uses curried function types where $\alpha \text{->} \beta$ denotes the type of all functions mapping elements of type α into elements of type β.

[4] As a default, all non-constraint functions are rigid.

in the program or the initial goal) and (concurrent) logic programming. Due to the use of an optimal evaluation strategy [1], Curry can be considered as a generalization of concurrent constraint programming [17] with a lazy (optimal) evaluation strategy. Due to this generalization, Curry supports a clear separation between the sequential (functional) parts of a program, which are evaluated with an efficient and optimal evaluation strategy, and the concurrent parts, based on the concurrent evaluation of constraints, to coordinate concurrent program units.

Monadic I/O: Since the implementation of GUIs in a declarative language requires some knowledge about performing I/O in a declarative manner, we sketch the I/O concept of Curry which is identical to the monadic I/O concept of Haskell [20]. In the monadic approach to I/O, an interactive program computes a sequence of actions which are applied to the outside world. *Actions* have type "IO α" which means that they return a result of type α whenever they are applied to (and change) the outside world. For instance, getChar of type IO Char is an action which reads a character from the standard input whenever it is executed, i.e., applied to a world. Actions can only be sequentially composed. For instance, the action getChar can be composed with the action putChar (which has type Char -> IO () and writes a character to the terminal) by the sequential composition operator >>= (which has type IO α -> (α -> IO β) -> IO β), i.e., "getChar >>= putChar" is a composed action which prints the next character of the input stream on the screen. The second composition operator >> is like >>= but ignores the result of the first action. Furthermore, done is the "empty" action which does nothing (see [20] for more details).

Disjunctive computations: A difficulty in combining logic-oriented languages with I/O is the fact that the meaning of I/O operations becomes unclear when a computation is split into two disjunctive paths. In Curry this problem is solved by encapsulating possible non-deterministic computations between I/O operations (see [10] for details). We do not further discuss this technique here but remark that non-deterministic search is not performed for goals containing global variables but only for goals where all unbound variables are existentially quantified in this goal. Since we will create GUIs via global variables ("ports", see below), non-deterministic steps (i.e., a potential copying of GUIs in a disjunctive computation) are automatically avoided (i.e., suspended) if they include a reference to a GUI. This provides for a conceptually clean integration of GUI programming in a logic language (in contrast to low-level Tcl/Tk libraries like in Sicstus-Prolog).

3   Object-Oriented and Distributed Programming

GUI programming as proposed in this paper is based on the techniques for object-oriented and distributed programming in Curry. Therefore, we sketch these features in this section. More details and examples can be found in [8].

It is well known [18] that concurrent logic programming languages provide a simple way to implement (concurrent) objects. An object can be seen as a constraint or predicate processing a stream of incoming messages. The local state of the object is a parameter which may change in recursive calls when a message is processed. Thus, the general type of an object o is

```
o :: st -> [mt] -> Constraint
```

where st is the type of the local state and mt is the type of the messages which can be sent to the object. For instance, a simple counter object which understands the messages Inc, Get v, and Stop can be implemented in Curry as follows (the predefined type Int denotes the type of all integer values and success denotes the always satisfiable constraint):

```
data CounterMessage = Inc | Get Int | Stop

counter :: Int -> [CounterMessage] -> Constraint
counter eval rigid

counter n (Inc   : ms) = counter (n+1) ms
counter n (Get v : ms) = v=:=n & counter n ms
counter _ (Stop  : ms) = success
```

The type declaration for counter (which can be omitted since types are reconstructed in Curry by a type inference algorithm) specifies that a counter object keeps an integer as local state and understands messages of type CounterMessage. Since counter is declared as a rigid function, an expression "counter n s" can reduce only if s is a bound variable.

The evaluation of the constraint "counter 0 s" creates a new counter object with initial value 0 where messages are sent by constraining the variable s to hold the desired messages. For instance, the constraint

```
let s free in  counter 0 s  &  s=:=[Inc, Inc, Get x, Stop]
```

is successfully evaluated by binding x to the value 2.

In realistic applications, the stream of messages is not instantiated at once but incrementally constrained by various other objects (message senders). In order to allow a dynamic extension of senders and to ensure the sending of messages in constant time, Janson et al. [12] proposed the use of port constraints which have been generalized in Curry to provide a high-level approach to implement distributed systems [8]. In principle, a *port* can be considered as a multiset (of messages) where the individual elements are not directly accessible. There are two primitive constraints on ports, where "Port a" denotes the type of a port to which messages of type a can be sent:

```
openPort :: Port a -> [a] -> Constraint
send     :: a  ->  Port a -> Constraint
```

The evaluation of "openPort p s" where p and s are uninstantiated variables establishes a *port constraint* which is satisfied iff all elements in the port p also occur in the message stream s and vice versa. A message m is sent to the port p by evaluating the constraint "send m p" which constrains (in constant time) p and the corresponding stream s to hold the element m. From a logic programming point of view, p and s are partially instantiated variables that are more and more constrained by solving the constraint "send m p". In contrast to the purely functional part of Curry, the communication is performed in a strict manner to avoid a communication overhead in a distributed system, i.e., the message m is reduced to a data term before sending it.

With the use of ports, we can define a generic constraint new

```
new :: (st -> [mt] -> Constraint) -> st -> Port mt -> Constraint
new obj st p = let s free in  openPort p s &> obj st s
```

to create new objects with initial state st and communication port p. Thus,

```
let cp free in  new counter 0 cp  &  client1 cp  &  client2 cp
```

creates a counter with two different clients. Each client can increment the counter by solving the constraint "send Inc cp". The current state of the counter can be asked by "send (Get x) cp" so that x is unified with the current counter value. Thus, free variables in messages provide an elegant method to return values to the sender without explicitly creating reply channels.

In order to support the programming of distributed systems, where different components run on different machines in the Internet, ports can be declared as *external* so that they are accessible from outside. This feature together with concrete examples for distributed applications using ports can be found in [8].

4   A Functional Logic GUI Library

A main objective of our GUI library is a design which smoothly interacts with the features of the base language Curry. In particular, a careful design is necessary to deal with features like non-determinism and search. We solve this by using ports for GUI communication. Therefore, we introduce a new primitive I/O action

```
openWish :: String -> IO (Port TkMsg) .
```

"openWish t" creates a new GUI window with title t and returns a *communication port* for this GUI. The (abstract) data type TkMsg[5] is the type of possible messages for GUI communication. These are only used in the implementation of the GUI library but not visible to the user of the library. The important design issue is the fact that a GUI communication port is always external and created by such an I/O action. Since the GUI communication port is a global variable, disjunctive computations or search are not performed for subexpressions containing a reference to such a port (compare Sect. 2). This behavior is perfectly intended since it avoids the potential duplication of GUIs in different disjunctive branches of a computation. Nevertheless, the non-deterministic features of the base language can be used inside a GUI if the search computations are encapsulated and do not refer to the global port.

After the creation of a GUI communication port gp, we can run a GUI specification gs (like the one shown in Fig. 2) by the constraint "runWidgetOnPort gs gp". Basically, runWidgetOnPort communicates with

---

[5] Most of the identifiers defined in the GUI library are prefixed by Tk since the library is based on the Tcl/Tk toolkit. Similarly, the name openWish refers to the fact that the windowing shell wish is used for the communication with the Tk toolkit.

the port gp by translating the GUI specification gs into appropriate Tcl commands (see Sect. 7). The I/O action runWidget (see Fig. 1) composes the functionality of openWish and runWidgetOnPort: it creates a new GUI communication port and runs the GUI specification on this port. Note that runWidget executes a GUI as an I/O action whereas runWidgetOnPort executes a GUI as a (concurrent) constraint. Therefore, runWidget is usually applied when one GUI is executed as the main program (Fig. 1), whereas runWidgetOnPort is applied when one GUI should be executed concurrently to other activities (e.g., other concurrent objects or GUIs, see Sect. 5).

Layout structure of a GUI: A GUI specification is a description of the hierarchical layout structure of the GUI together with the actions that should be performed when, for instance, a GUI button is pressed. To be more precise, a GUI specification is a term of the following data type (here we list only the widgets used in the examples of this paper):

```
data TkWidget a = TkButton (Port TkMsg -> a) [TkConfItem a]
                | TkCheckButton              [TkConfItem a]
                | TkEntry                    [TkConfItem a]
                | TkLabel                    [TkConfItem a]
                :
                | TkRow [TkCollectionOption] [TkWidget a]
                | TkCol [TkCollectionOption] [TkWidget a]
```

Thus, a GUI specification is a simple widget (like a button or entry), a row (TkRow) or a column (TkCol) of widgets.[6] The first parameter of TkRow/TkCol specifies additional options for the geometric alignment for widget composition, like centering, left alignment, expanding subwidgets if extra space is available:

```
data TkCollectionOption = TkCenter | TkLeft | ... | TkExpand
```

A button widget (TkButton) is intended to perform an action whenever the user presses this button. Therefore, an event handler is associated to each button widget (first parameter). Other widgets can also contain event handlers but they are optionally associated in the list of configuration items (see below). Since these event handlers are responsible for an event of a specific GUI, *event handlers* have type "Port TkMsg -> a" where a is the result type of the event handler which is either Constraint (for GUIs executed concurrently to other objects) or IO () (for GUIs executed as an I/O action). Consequently, this type variable is also a parameter for the entire GUI structure.

Logical structure of a GUI: Before discussing event handlers in more detail, we must understand the concept to describe the logical structure of GUIs. As mentioned in the introduction, GUIs have a layout structure *and* a logical structure. While the layout structure is simply described by composing simple widgets into widget collections (TkRow and TkCol), the logical structure contains dependencies between different widgets and their event handlers. For instance, pressing

---

[6] The row/column organization of widgets is sufficient for our purposes but one can also extend the library to cover other forms of widget collections (see also Sect. 6).

some button usually results (after some computation) in the update of one or
more other widgets. Although many GUI libraries (e.g., [14,19]) are based on
user-selected strings to identify the different widgets, we propose to use logical
variables to refer to individual widgets which avoids many programming errors
and provides for better abstractions. For this purpose, each primitive widget can
have a number of items to configure the widget, like[7]

```
data TkConfItem a =
        TkRef TkRefType         -- a reference to this widget
      | TkText String           -- an initial text contents
      | TkWidth Int             -- the width of a widget
      | TkBackground String     -- the background color
      | TkCmd (Port tkMsg -> a) -- an associated event handler
      :
```

Most of these configuration items directly correspond to similar options in the
Tk toolkit with the exception of TkRef. Since TkRefType, the type of all widget
references, is abstract, i.e., no constructors of this data type are available to
the user of the GUI library, the only reasonable way to use the TkRef item is
with a free logical variable as shown in Fig. 2. If we run a GUI specification on
a concrete port, this variable will be instantiated to a unique widget reference
which is not visible to the user. The important point is that this variable can also
be used in event handlers for other widgets in the same GUI. For this purpose,
there are the following primitives to construct event handlers for GUIs:

```
tkExit     :: Port TkMsg -> IO ()
tkGetValue :: TkRefType -> Port TkMsg -> IO String
tkSetValue :: TkRefType -> String -> Port TkMsg -> IO ()
tkUpdate   :: (String->String) -> TkRefType -> Port TkMsg -> IO ()
```

tkExit terminates the GUI, tkGetValue gets the (String) value currently stored
in the widget referred by its first argument, tkSetValue sets the value stored
in the referred widget, and tkUpdateValue updates the value according to an
update function. The same set of primitives is also available for GUIs executed
as a concurrent constraint:

```
tkCExit     :: Port TkMsg -> Constraint
tkCGetValue :: TkRefType -> Port TkMsg -> String -> Constraint
...
```

The event handlers attached to some widget are automatically invoked with the
current GUI communication port whenever a GUI specification is executed by
runWidgetOnPort (or runWidget), see also the examples in Fig. 1 and 2. Thus,
a GUI specification is executed by sending commands that create the widget
layout through the communication port followed by a scheduler which invokes
the corresponding event handlers whenever the user performs some action on
the GUI (see Sect. 7 for more details).

---

[7] Note that not all configuration items are meaningful for all widgets. This is checked
   at run time in our library, but in can be also checked at compile time with a more
   sophisticated type system, as proposed in [3].

To change the configuration of widgets dynamically (e.g., changing colors, deactivating or activating buttons and entries), there is also a primitive

```
tkConfig :: TkRefType -> TkConfItem a -> Port TkMsg -> IO ()
```

which adds a configuration item to a particular widget in a GUI.

5   Example: A Calculator

We have already seen in Fig. 1 and 2 two specifications of simple GUIs using our library. However, many interactive applications contain a state which is shown and modified by a GUI. To demonstrate the implementation of these kinds of applications with our GUI concept, we present in the following the implementation of a simple calculator GUI as shown to the right. We model the calculator as an object which accepts the following messages:

```
data CalcMsg = Button Char | Display String
```

The message "Button c" is sent whenever the button c (e.g., '1', '2',...,'+', '*',...) is pressed. The message "Display s" is sent to get the current value of the operand, i.e., the argument s (which is usually an unbound variable) is instantiated with the current operand of the calculator. The calculator's local state is a pair (d,f) with the current operand d and an accumulator function f to be applied to d (this idea is due to [19]). With the techniques sketched in Sect. 3, we can implement calculator objects as follows (the rigid Boolean function == tests the equality of two ground expressions, i.e., $e_1 == e_2$ reduces to True if both e_1 and e_2 are reducible to identical ground data terms; $(e\ op)$ denotes the partial application of the operator op to the left argument e):

```
calcMgr :: (Int,Int->Int) -> [CalcMsg] -> Constraint
calcMgr eval rigid
calcMgr (d,f) (Display s : ms) = s=:=(show d) &> calcMgr (d,f) ms
calcMgr (d,f) (Button b  : ms)
  | isDigit b = calcMgr (10*d + ord b - ord'0', f) ms
  | b=='+'    = calcMgr (0, ((f d) +)) ms
  | b=='-'    = calcMgr (0, ((f d) -)) ms
  | b=='*'    = calcMgr (0, ((f d) *)) ms
  | b=='/'    = calcMgr (0, ((f d) 'div')) ms
  | b=='='    = calcMgr (f d, id) ms
  | b=='C'    = calcMgr (0, id) ms
```

Since the GUI needs a reference to the calculator object, we add it as a parameter cm to the GUI:

```
calc_GUI cm = TkCol [] [TkEntry [TkRef display, TkText "0"],
                        TkRow [] (map cbutton ['1','2','3','+']),
                        TkRow [] (map cbutton ['4','5','6','-']),
                        TkRow [] (map cbutton ['7','8','9','*']),
                        TkRow [] (map cbutton ['C','0','=','/'])]
```

```
where display free
      cbutton c = TkButton (button_pressed c) [TkText [c]]
      button_pressed c gp = let d free in
                            send (Button c) cm &>
                            send (Display d) cm &>
                            tkCSetValue display d gp
```

Here we exploit the higher-order features of the base language: To create the individual buttons, we use a generic function cbutton which is mapped on the particular lists of characters. The event handler button_pressed for each button sends a corresponding Button message to the calculator and shows the new operand of the calculator in the display widget. A new calculator application on a given GUI communication port gp is created by the following function:

```
runCalcOnPort gp
| let cm free in
  new calcMgr (0,id) cm & runWidgetOnPort (calc_GUI cm) gp
= done
```

Now the complete application is started by

```
openWish "Calculator" >>= runCalcOnPort
```

This implementation is modular similarly to the classical model-view-controller paradigm of Smalltalk-80 [13]. The application (represented by calcMgr) is completely independent to the user interface. All the programming techniques of the base language (laziness, higher-order functions, constraints, search etc.) can be used to implement the application. Due to the independence of the user interface and the application, it is also possible to have several GUIs (which represents the applications in different ways) for one application. In our implementation above, this is easily possible by changing the function runCalcOnPort to start one application together with several concurrent GUIs. This feature of our GUI design is also useful for developing GUIs for distributed applications where the GUI shows and manipulates different components of a distributed system. For instance, we have implemented a GUI for sending emails where the email address can be inserted by querying an address server running on some other machine. Due to lack of space, we omit a concrete example for this, but from the previous example it should be obvious how to use the distributed features of Curry (see Sect. 3 and [8]) in GUIs.

6   Application-Oriented Extensions

This section shows how the features of the base language can be exploited to define new application-oriented graphical elements for GUIs. As a simple example (which is often predefined in GUI libraries), consider the implementation of a radio button column as a new GUI element. A radio button column is a column of check buttons where at most one button is "on", i.e., if the user activates a button in this column, all other buttons must be set to "off" (for the sake of simplicity, the values "off" and "on" are represented by the strings "0" and "1"). This can be implemented by the following function, where "radioButtonCol r labs cmd" creates a new radio button column with reference r, labels labs (i.e., the strings shown at each button) and event handler cmd which is called whenever the user presses a button (the auxiliary functions gen_vars n returns a list of n unbound variables, $l!!i$ returns the i-th element of the list l, and remove i l removes the i-th element from the list l):

```
radioButtonCol r labs cmd
  | r =:= gen_vars (length labs)  = TkCol [TkLeft] (gen_rb 0)
  where gen_rb i = if i==(length labs) then []
           else TkCheckButton [TkText (labs!!i), TkRef (r!!i),
                               TkCmd (rbcmd (r!!i) (remove i r) cmd)]
             : gen_rb (i+1)

rbcmd sel oth cmd gp =
  tkGetValue sel gp >>= \sv ->   --get state sv of this checkbutton
  (if sv=="1" then foldr (>>) done (map (\o->tkSetValue o "0" gp) oth)
              else done ) >>
    cmd gp
```

Thus, each button of a radio button column is a check button with an event handler which sets the other buttons (oth) to "off" whenever it is turned on, followed by the execution of the event handler cmd for the radio button. Two operations are important on radio buttons: get the index of the activated button in the column (or -1 if there is no active button) and activate a particular button. These operations can be defined as follows:

```
getRadioValue [] _ = return (-1)
getRadioValue (r:rs) gp = tkGetValue r gp >>= \rval ->
  if rval=="1" then return 0
               else getRadioValue rs gp >>= \rspos ->
                    return (if rspos>=0 then rspos+1 else -1)

setRadioValue [] _ _ = done
setRadioValue (r:rs) i gp =
  tkSetValue r (if i==0 then "1" else "0") gp >>
  setRadioValue rs (i-1) gp
```

Due to the functional dimension of the base language, we can use radio button columns like any other widget in GUI specifications. For instance, a "traffic light GUI" as shown to the right, where the user can click on two traffic lights and the program ensures the pairwise exclusion of both red and green lights, is implemented by the following simple GUI specification:

```
TkRow [] [radioButtonCol l1 ["Red","Yellow","Green"] (ex l1 l2),
          radioButtonCol l2 ["Red","Yellow","Green"] (ex l2 l1)]
  where l1,l2 free
ex l1 l2 gp = getRadioValue l1 gp >>= \sel ->
              if sel>=0 then setRadioValue l2 (2-sel) gp else done
```

The event handler **ex** ensures that, whenever the user selects **Red** (**Yellow**, **Green**) for one traffic light, the other light switches to **Green** (**Yellow**, **Red**).

In a similar way, one can implement other more advanced graphical abstractions. For instance, one can define sets of radio buttons which are not simply mutually exclusive, like in the traffic light example, but must satisfy more complex constraints ("constraint buttons"). Due to the constraint logic programming features of Curry, such abstractions are fairly easy to implement. The usefulness of constraints in the design of user interfaces has been discussed elsewhere [16].

Note the importance of the use of free logical variables for widget references to built new graphical abstractions. If one assigns fixed strings to refer to widgets, as for instance in [14,19], name conflicts can easily occur.

7 Implementation

The entire GUI library is implemented in Curry based on the connection to the Tcl/Tk toolkit [14]. The only extension which has been added to Curry is the connection to a windowing shell **wish** via the I/O action **openWish** (see Sect. 4). The messages sent to this port are of the following type:

```
data TkMsg = TkPut String | TkGet String
```

If the message "TkPut s" is sent to the port, the string **s**, which must be a valid Tcl command, is added to the input stream of the **wish**. On the other hand, the message "TkGet s" unifies the argument variable **s** with the next line of the output stream of the **wish**. These two messages are sufficient to implement **runWidgetOnPort** in Curry. First of all, the GUI specification is translated into a Tcl/Tk script to create the GUI layout which is sent to the **wish** via the message **TkPut**. Additionally, **runWidgetOnPort** creates a call-back list for handling the GUI events. If the user manipulates the GUI (e.g., press a button) so that an event occurs for which an event handler is defined, the **wish** emits a message on its output stream. This message is analyzed by the scheduler in **runWidgetOnPort** which calls the responsible event handler stored in the call-back list. Furthermore, the primitive event handlers like **tkGetValue** and **tkSetValue** are implemented by sending Tcl/Tk scripts that set or extract the corresponding GUI values.

Although all communication between the Curry system and Tcl/Tk is done by strings which have to be interpreted on both sides, this kind of implementation is efficient enough in our practical experiences. This is due to the fact that the communication in interactive applications tends to be slow since the user is usually much slower than the system. Therefore, the connection to Tcl/Tk through a port is sufficient for implementing practical systems. Furthermore, this technique supports an easy reuse of this library in other Curry implementations.

8 Conclusions and Related Work

We have presented a library for implementing GUIs in the functional logic language Curry. We have exploited the functional as well as the logic features of

Curry for the design of the library. The functional features are used to define the layout structure of GUIs and to built new application-oriented graphical abstractions. The logic features (logical variables) are used to specify the logic dependencies inside a GUI. This allows a compact and readable specification of GUIs as expressions of a particular data type rather than a sequence of actions to built the GUI. As far as we know, this is the first approach to design a functional logic GUI library. Nevertheless, we want to relate it to some other approaches for GUI programming in declarative languages.

TkGofer [3] extends Gofer, a lazy functional language similar to Haskell, with a library for GUI programming. Similarly to our approach, the implementation is based on Tcl/Tk. TkGofer uses a monadic approach for GUI programming which forces the user to an imperative style. The different widgets are defined in a flat and sequential order and are later composed to a hierarchical layout structure by **pack** operations, similarly to Tcl/Tk scripts. This has the disadvantage that the layout structure is not defined together with the individual widgets and each widget must be given a name—even if they are used only once like the labels or buttons in Fig. 1 and 2. Furthermore, TkGofer is based on a sequential functional language. Thus, logic programming techniques like constraint solving as well as features for concurrent and distributed programming are not available.

The same holds for Fudgets [2], a GUI concept for lazy functional languages. Fudgets are processes accepting messages (for manipulating the state) and delivering messages (for sending information about an event). Primitive fudgets, like buttons, text inputs etc., are composed to more complex entities by connecting the input and output streams of the different fudgets. This approach makes it necessary to pass the GUI events via streams to the corresponding widgets to be manipulated by these events, which leads to less intuitive GUI specifications than using direct references to the corresponding widgets as in our approach.

Haggis [5] is a further GUI framework for Haskell. It is based on monadic I/O and uses concurrent processes to handle events. Instead of specifying a handler to be invoked when an event occurs, a new process is created that waits for this event. This has the drawback that widgets have two handlers in Haggis (one for the layout and one for the event handling).

Our proposal for GUI programming is not just an adaptation of existing GUI library designs to an integrated functional logic language, but it exploits the features of such an integrated language to support simple and readable GUI specifications. Moreover, the features of the base language like higher-order functions, constraints, and concurrency can be used to build new application-oriented graphical abstractions in a simple way and to support a modular connection of the application program to the user interface. In particular, the distribution features of Curry largely simplify the implementation of user interfaces for distributed systems.

The current definition of Curry has also some limitations which restricts the design of our GUI library. Currently, Curry has a Hindley-Milner like polymorphic type system [4]. It has been shown in [3] that a richer type system including type classes can improve the structure of a GUI library so that more errors can be caught at compile time. Since this is independent on the design issues discussed in this paper, we plan for the future to refine the design of our GUI library with a more sophisticated type system. Another topic for future work is to add the possibility to dynamically change the layout structure of GUIs which is currently not supported.

References

1. S. Antoy, R. Echahed, and M. Hanus. A Needed Narrowing Strategy. In *Proc. 21st ACM Symposium on Principles of Programming Languages*, pp. 268–279, 1994.
2. M. Carlsson and T. Hallgren. Fudgets - A Graphical User Interface in a Lazy Functional Language. In *Conference on Functional Programming and Computer Architecture (FPCA'93)*. ACM Press, 1993.
3. K. Claessen, T. Vullinghs, and E. Meijer. Structuring graphical paradigms in TkGofer. In *Proc. of the International Conference on Functional Programming (ICFP'97)*, pp. 251–262. ACM SIGPLAN Notices Vol. 32, No. 8, 1997.
4. L. Damas and R. Milner. Principal type-schemes for functional programs. In *Proc. 9th Symposium on Principles of Programming Languages*, pp. 207–212, 1982.
5. S. Finne and S. Peyton Jones. Composing Haggis. In *Proc. of the Fifth Eurographics Workshop on Programming Paradigms for Computer Graphics*. Springer, 1995.
6. M. Hanus. The Integration of Functions into Logic Programming: From Theory to Practice. *Journal of Logic Programming*, Vol. 19&20, pp. 583–628, 1994.
7. M. Hanus. A Unified Computation Model for Functional and Logic Programming. In *Proc. 24th ACM Symposium on Principles of Programming Languages*, pp. 80–93, 1997.
8. M. Hanus. Distributed Programming in a Multi-Paradigm Declarative Language. In *Proc. of the International Conference on Principles and Practice of Declarative Programming (PPDP'99)*, pp. 376–395. Springer LNCS 1702, 1999.
9. M. Hanus, S. Antoy, J. Koj, R. Sadre, and F. Steiner. PACS: The Portland Aachen Curry System. Available at http://www-i2.informatik.rwth-aachen.de/~hanus/pacs/, 1999.
10. M. Hanus and F. Steiner. Controlling Search in Declarative Programs. In *Principles of Declarative Programming (Proc. Joint International Symposium PLILP/ALP'98)*, pp. 374–390. Springer LNCS 1490, 1998.
11. M. Hanus (ed.). Curry: An Integrated Functional Logic Language (Vers. 0.5). Available at http://www-i2.informatik.rwth-aachen.de/~hanus/curry, 1999.
12. S. Janson, J. Montelius, and S. Haridi. Ports for Objects in Concurrent Logic Programs. In *Research Directions in Concurrent Object-Oriented Programming*. MIT Press, 1993.
13. G. Krasner and S. Pope. A Cookbook for using the Model-View-Controller User Interface in Smalltalk-80. *Journal of Object-Oriented Programming*, Vol. 1, No. 3, pp. 26–49, 1988.
14. J.K. Ousterhout. *Tcl and the Tk toolkit*. Addison Wesley, 1994.
15. J. Peterson et al. Haskell: A Non-strict, Purely Functional Language (Version 1.4). Technical Report, Yale University, 1997.
16. M. Renschler. Configuration Spreadsheet for Interactive Constraint Problem Solving. In *Proc. of the ComputlogNet Industrial Conference on Advanced Software Applications*, Manchester, 1998.
17. V.A. Saraswat. *Concurrent Constraint Programming*. MIT Press, 1993.

18. E. Shapiro and A. Takeuchi. Object Oriented Programming in Concurrent Prolog. In E. Shapiro, editor, *Concurrent Prolog: Collected Papers*, volume 2, pp. 251–273. MIT Press, 1987.
19. T. Vullinghs, D. Tuijnman, and W. Schulte. Lightweight GUIs for Functional Programming. In *Proc. 7th Int. Symp. on Programming Languages, Implementations, Logics and Programs (PLILP'95)*, pp. 341–356. Springer LNCS 982, 1995.
20. P. Wadler. How to Declare an Imperative. *ACM Computing Surveys*, Vol. 29, No. 3, pp. 240–263, 1997.

Using Static Analysis to Compile Non-sequential Functional Logic Programs*

Julio Mariño and Juan José Moreno-Navarro

Universidad Politécnica de Madrid
Dpto. LSIIS - Facultad de Informática.
Campus de Montegancedo s/n, 28660, Madrid, SPAIN.
jmarino@fi.upm.es

Abstract. The efficient implementation of functional logic languages relies on finding (if it exists) an optimal evaluation order for the arguments of functions. The problems of finding the best evaluation order, and the sequentiality of program rules are both difficult and can benefit from using static analysis techniques. The second problem is of special interest because the parallel evaluation of arguments is out of the question due to the possibility of backtracking and sharing of free logical variables among different arguments. However, the lack of sequentiality is often syntactic rather than semantic. In this paper we show that an adequate use of type information and strictness analysis can help a compiler to (i) derive an efficient evaluation order, and (ii) generate sequential code from most programs. Data structures (new versions of definitional trees) are introduced to take advantage of this kind of information and manage run time tests when the computation cannot be made sequential at compile time.

Keywords: Sequentiality, Abstract Interpretation, Functional Logic Programming.

1 Introduction

The compilation of pattern matching in functional programming and unification in Prolog is one of the strong points of declarative languages as it relieves the programmer of specifying a lot of control. The first implementations of the functional logic language Curry are appearing now but impose a number of restrictions to programs (as overlapping rules) that we try to relax in this paper.

The relationship between *sequential term rewriting systems* [6] and the implementation of lazy functional programming languages is well known – see, for instance [12,11] for an introduction to the subject. The typical example is *parallel or*, defined by the equations in figure 1.a. One would expect any system with lazy evaluation to give the answer true to the calls

---

* This research was partly supported by the Spanish CICYT project TIC96.1012-C02-02.

E. Pontelli, V. Santos Costa (Eds.): PADL 2000, LNCS 1753, pp. 63–80, 2000.

```
> or true (loop e)                > or (loop e) true
```

where (loop e) is any non-terminating expression. But in practice what we get is a hung terminal – at least for one of the calls. The problem is that given a call (or e_1 e_2) there is no information on which argument has to be reduced first and the compiler favors one of them.

In other cases, there is a safe order to try the evaluation of arguments, but actual implementations are unable to perform the sequentiality analysis required to generate sequential code. For instance, certain "lazy" Hope interpreter is bound to the left-to-right order and thus the program in figure 1.b loops with (left (loop 0) 0) but (right 0 (loop 0)) gives the desired 0. This problem is solved in a widely used Haskell interpreter by statically reordering the arguments but some sequential programs, like the one shown in figure 1.c still cause trouble – the call (lr (loop 0) 0 0) works fine, but (lr 2 (loop 0) 1) loops.

Our own compiler (Sloth [13]) for the functional logic language Curry [5] is able to generate sequential code for all these examples by performing sequentiality analysis based on the so called *definitional trees* [1]. For the last example the decision tree in figure 2.a is built. Depending on the value of the third argument to lr, the first or the second argument is evaluated. For a given set of rules there may exist several definitional trees [1]. The class of programs for which a definitional tree exists is that of *inductively sequential programs*[1,2].

For those cases (as parallel or) where no definitional tree exists, *parallel definitional trees* have been proposed [1,3]. These imply simultaneous reduction of arguments and, being Curry a functional logic language, those arguments can contain free variables and even share them. This leads to a risk of reevaluation and speculative work even more serious than in functional systems. It does not mean that the implementation is not possible (see [4]), but the complexity and inefficiency is very high. For more arguments in favor of sequentialization, see [9].

So it seems that parallel evaluation should be avoided as much as possible and that means that a compiler should generate parallel trees only as a last resort or even allow the user to choose a incomplete evaluation, issuing the opportune warnings at compile time. Fortunately, most functional programs are inductively sequential and some of those that are not, can be rewritten into an equivalent sequential one. A typical example is merging two sorted lists of numbers (figure 1.d) If we just look at the left hand side it looks like a parallel-or in disguise, but if we look at the right hand sides we immediately see that both arguments to merge are demanded. A programmer would write, in fact, a modified version where the second rule is rewritten as

```
merge (x:xs) []    = x:xs
```

---

[1] Sloth is actually a translator from Curry into Prolog written itself in Prolog and is able to obtain every possible definitional tree via backtracking. Additional criteria to choose among them exist but are beyond the scope of this paper.

a) or true x   = true   c) lr x 0 0 = 0
    or x   true = true   lr 1 2 0 = 1
    or false false = false   lr 2 y 1 = 2
                                       lr 3 1 1 = 3

b) dec left: num -> num -> num;   dec right: num -> num -> num;
    --- left x 0 <= 0 ;   --- right 0 x <= 0 ;
    --- left 1 1 <= 1 ;   --- right 1 1 <= 1 ;

d) merge []   ys   = ys
    merge xs   []   = xs
    merge (x:xs) (y:ys) | x <= y = x:(merge xs (y:ys))
                         | x >= y = y:(merge (x:xs) ys)

Fig. 1. Sample definitions with different sequentiality problems

instead. This more or less corresponds with the classic notions of *strong* and *weak* sequentiality.[2]

The thesis of this work is that for the vast majority of programs, the information obtained from type inference and strictness analysis can help a compiler to generate sequential definitional trees for programs even when they are not syntactically (strongly) sequential. For the merge rules, the tree in figure 2.b is produced.

Typing information is important here for two reasons. On one hand, if the most general type of a given argument fixes a type constructor, we know all the possible data constructors that can appear at that position of the tree. On the other hand, if the type of a parameter is polymorphic the information is that this parameter is not "touched" by pattern matching during reduction.

Let us show an example where higher order strictness analysis is desirable. Figure 3 shows a higher order generalization of the merge function. The (functional) parameters indicate the task to be done when the selected element comes from the first list, the second, or both, and what to do when one of the lists is empty. This function can be used to define list union, intersection and difference. Although hiMerge is not sequential, it could be reasonable to generate code for its two possible sequential versions – let them be called $hiMerge_1$ and $hiMerge_2$. Then union can be executed calling either $hiMerge_1$ or $hiMerge_2$ directly, difference can call $hiMerge_1$ and only intersection would need to call the parallel evaluation code.

The paper is organized as follows. Section 2 introduces background notions needed in subsequent sections, including the model language used in this paper and its operational semantics. Section 3 presents definitional trees and introduces some notions and properties necessary for the analysis. Section 4 defines a denotational semantics which is then applied in section 5 to yield a strictness

---

[2] We are using the fact that for constructor systems *left-* and strong sequentiality are equivalent[15].

analyzer for our language. Code generation based on the information from the analyzer is discussed in section 6. Section 7 concludes.

2   Preliminaries

In this section we introduce the main concepts needed to understand the operational principles of the subset of Curry considered in this paper. For a complete description of the syntax and operational semantics of Curry the reader is referred to the draft [5].

Syntax. We assume a ranked set $TC = \bigcup_n TC^n$ of type *constructors* and a countably infinite set TV of *type variables*. Any data type is uniquely denoted by an algebraic term $\tau \in \mathcal{T}(TC \cup TV)$ or a function type $(\tau_1 \to \tau_2)$. Next, we assume a set $DC = \bigcup_n DC^n$ of typed *data constructors*, a countably infinite set VS of *variable symbols*, and a set FS of *function symbols* f/n with declared principal type $f : \tau_1 \to \ldots \to \tau_n \to \tau$ where τ is not a function type. The *arity* of a data constructor $c \in DC^n$ is n and is denoted $ar(c)$. In practice, type and data constructors are both defined via **data** declarations of the form **data** $\kappa\ \tau_1 \ldots \tau_k = c_1\ \tau_{11} \ldots \mid \ldots \mid c_n\ \tau_{n1} \ldots$.

Expressions are given by the grammar $e ::= x \mid d \mid (e_1\ e_2)$ where $x \in VS, d \in DC^0$. Expressions must be well typed in the sense of a Milner system. A program is a set of defining rules of the form $f\ e_1 \ldots e_n = e$ for every $f \in FS$. Several restrictions are imposed on the rules in a program in order to ensure confluence of reduction, and the following are used somewhere in the paper: (i) for every rule $(l = r)$, l is a *pattern*, i.e. it has a single function symbol at its top and no variable occurs twice in l; (ii) rules must be well typed; (iii) for every pair of program rules $(l_1 = r_1), (l_2 = r_2)$, if l_1 and l_2 have a unifier σ then $\sigma(r_1) = \sigma(r_2)$. Observe that we are not forbidding overlaps.

When looking at the syntactic shape of the left hand sides of defining rules, a total application $(f\ e_1\ \ldots\ e_n)$ is treated as the algebraic term $f(e_1, \ldots, e_n)$ and then the standard notation for positions and substitutions is used. A position is a string of natural numbers that identifies a path to a subterm in a term. The expression t/p denotes the subterm of t at position p, i.e. $f(e_1, \ldots, e_n)/i.p = e_i/p$

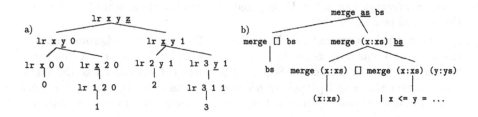

Fig. 2. (sequential) definitional trees

```
hiMerge :: (Int->[Int]->[Int]) -> (Int->[Int]->[Int]) ->
           (Int->[Int]->[Int]) -> ([Int]->[Int]) -> ([Int]->[Int]) ->
                    [Int] -> [Int] -> [Int]

hiMerge f g h a b []     ys    = b ys
hiMerge f g h a b xs     []    = a xs
hiMerge f g h a b (x:xs)(y:ys)|x < y  = f x (hiMerge f g h a b xs (y:ys))
                              |x == y = g x (hiMerge f g h a b xs ys)
                              |x > y  = h y (hiMerge f g h a b (x:xs)ys)

union        = hiMerge (:) (:) (:) id id
intersection = hiMerge (curry snd) (:) (curry snd) (const []) (const [])
difference   = hiMerge (:) (curry snd) (curry snd) id (const [])
```

Fig. 3. Higher-order merge and operations on sets

and $t/\epsilon = t$, with ϵ the empty string. Replacement of t/p by t' is abbreviated $t[p \leftarrow t']$. The topmost symbol of term t is denoted $root(t)$.

Narrowing. The operational mechanism we will deal with is *narrowing*. Narrowing can be viewed as a generalisation of term rewriting where matching is replaced by unification. Informally, to *narrow* an expression e means to apply a substitution that makes it reducible, and then reduce it. More formally: let $l = r$ be a variant of a program rule sharing no variables with e. Then e is *narrowable into* e', *at position* u, *using* $l = r$, via σ_{out}, iff $e/u \notin VS$ and there exists a substitution σ_{in} such that $\sigma_{\text{in}}(l) \equiv \sigma_{\text{out}}(e/u)$ and $e' \equiv \sigma_{\text{out}}(e[u \leftarrow \sigma_{\text{in}}(r)])$, This is written $e \leadsto_{u,l = r,\sigma_{\text{out}}} e'$ or simply $e \leadsto_{\sigma_{\text{out}}} e'$, when the position and rule can be determined from the context. We write $e_0 \leadsto^*_\sigma e_n$ to denote that there is a narrowing sequence $e_0 \leadsto_{\sigma_1} e_1 \leadsto_{\sigma_2} \cdots \leadsto_{\sigma_n} e_n$ with $\sigma = \sigma_n \circ \cdots \circ \sigma_2 \circ \sigma_1$. If $e \leadsto^*_{\sigma_{\text{out}}} e'$ holds and e' is a *value* – an expression without defined function symbols – we speak of a *computation* for the goal e with *result* e' and *answer* σ_{out}, denoted $e \Downarrow \sigma_{\text{out}} \| e'$. Otherwise, if e' is not a value and cannot be further narrowed, we speak of a *failed computation*.

Example 1. The following rules define a predicate to compare two natural numbers

```
0     =< y     = true
(s x) =< 0     = false          TC⁰ = {nat, bool}
(s x) =< (s y) = x =< y         DC⁰ = {true : bool, false : bool, 0 : nat},
                                DC¹ = {s : nat → nat}
                                FS² = {(=<) : nat → nat → bool}
```

For the expression $g = x =< s\ 0$ the following are successful computations:

$$g \Downarrow \{x \mapsto 0\}\|\text{true}, g \Downarrow \{x \mapsto s\ 0\}\|\text{true}, g \Downarrow \{x \mapsto s\ (s\ z)\}\|\text{false}.$$

□

Approximation Framework. In this paper, the "abstraction framework" for abstract interpretation is used. A triple (X, α, Y) where X is a cpo, Y is a complete lattice and where $\alpha : X \to Y$ is strict and continuous, is called an *approximation*. The function α is usually referred to as an *abstraction mapping*. The notation $\alpha(v)$ is usually abbreviated $v^{\natural}$ when α is known. The abstraction mapping can be extended to an *approximation* relation (denoted $\propto$) in the following way: $u \propto v$ if $\alpha(v) \leq u$ or if u, v are functions such that $x \propto y \Rightarrow (u\ x) \propto (v\ y)$. An abstract semantic function is one that approximates the standard one.

3   Needed Narrowing and Definitional Trees

Unrestricted application of the narrowing rule is too nondeterministic and many strategies have been proposed to improve this. The one used in Curry is *needed narrowing*[2], a lazy strategy where the program is translated into a set of definitional trees, one for every function symbol being defined. Definitional trees are given by the grammar

$$DT ::= \text{branch } (\textit{Pattern, Pos } [, DT]^+) \mid \text{rule } \textit{Rule} \mid \text{or } (DT\ [, DT]^+)$$

where *Pattern* stands for patterns made up of data constructors and different variables as in the left hand sides of program rules, *Pos* are positions defined in the standard way and *Rules* are program rules. Trees without "or" nodes are called *(inductively) sequential*, otherwise they are *parallel* definitional trees. Definitional trees are used like the *case*-expressions in [16]:

Definition 1 (Definitional Tree). T *is a* definitional tree *for pattern* π *iff one of the following cases holds:*

1. T *is rule($l = r$) where $l = r$ is a program rule such that l is a variant of π.*
2. T *is branch(π, o, $T_1, \ldots, T_k$) where the T_i are definitional trees for $\pi[o \leftarrow c\ x_1 \ldots x_{ar(c)}]$, being c a data constructor suitable to appear at o and the x_j fresh variables.*
3. T *is or($T_1, \ldots, T_k$) where the T_i are definitional trees for π.* ∎

Example 2. Consider the definition for natural number comparison in example 1. The following tree[3] is a definitional tree for x =< y that covers all the rules in its definition. Its graph is displayed in fig. 4.

```
branch(1, rule(0 =< y = true),
        branch(2, rule((s x) =< 0 = false),
              rule((s x) =< (s y) = x =< y)))
```

□

The set of program rules $R(T) = \{l_i = r_i \mid \text{rule}(l_i = r_i) \text{ is a subtree of } T\}$ is called the set of rules in tree T. A definitional tree T_f, $f \in FS$ for pattern $(f\ x_1 \ldots x_{ar(f)})$ such that $R(T)$ is the set of rules defining f in the program is called a *definitional tree for function symbol f.*

Given expression e built with the symbols in a program and a set of definitional trees for the defined symbols in *FS* a position in e can be chosen to apply

---

[3] We have not printed the π's as they can be inferred from the leaves of the tree.

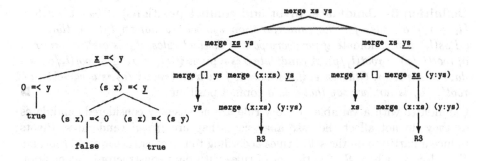

Fig. 4. Definitional trees for (=<) and merge

narrowing. This is done by first looking for an outermost application $f\ e_1 \ldots e_n$ where f is a defined function symbol, and then descending some e_i according to f's definitional tree. This is formally defined as a function λ that takes a definitional tree T and a term t with a function symbol at its root as arguments and that yields a set of triples $(position, rule, substitution)$.

Definition 2 (Strategy). $\lambda(t, T)$ *is the least set that satisfies:*

$$\lambda(t,T) \supseteq \begin{cases} \{(\epsilon, l = r, mgu(t,l))\} & \text{if } T = rule(l = r) \\ \lambda(t, T_i) & \text{if } T = branch(\pi, o, T_1, \ldots, T_k) \wedge \\ & \exists i, \sigma.\sigma(t) = \sigma(pattern(T_i)) \\ \{(o.p, rul, \sigma \circ \tau)\} & \text{if } T = branch(\pi, o, T_1, \ldots, T_k) \wedge \\ & root(t/o) = g \in FS, \tau = mgu(t, \pi), \\ & T_g \text{ is a definitional tree for } g, \\ & \text{and } (p, rul, \sigma) \in \lambda(\tau(t/o), T_g) \end{cases} \blacksquare$$

Only those narrowing steps $t \leadsto_{u,l=r,\sigma} t'$ where $(u, l=r, \sigma) \in \lambda(t, T)$ and T is the definitional tree for the topmost symbol of t, are allowed.

A simple way to understand how a definitional tree works is by giving the incremental construction of the set of its rules that unify with a given pattern π, denoted $\Omega_T(\pi)$:

Proposition 1 (Abstract behaviour of a definitional tree). *Given a definitional tree T for f and a pattern π for f, the set*

$$\Omega_T(\pi) = \{rule \in R(T) | \pi \text{ and rule unify}\}$$

can be computed in the following way:

$$\Omega_T(\pi) = \begin{cases} \{(l = r)\} & T = rule(l = r) \text{ and } l \text{ unifies with } \pi \\ \emptyset & T = rule(l = r) \text{ and } l \text{ does not unify with } \pi \\ \Omega_{T_i}(\pi) & T = branch(\pi', o, T_1, \ldots, T_k) \text{ and } root(\pi/o) = c_i \\ \Omega_{T_1}(\pi) \cup \ldots \cup \Omega_{T_k}(\pi) & T = branch(\pi', o, T_1, \ldots, T_k) \text{ and } root(\pi/o) \in Vars \\ \Omega_{T_1}(\pi) \cup \ldots \cup \Omega_{T_k}(\pi) & T = or(T_1, \ldots, T_k) \end{cases} \blacksquare$$

Our compiler is able to build a sequential tree for a set of rules, if it exists. We provide some concepts needed for the specification of the algorithm.

Definition 3 (Candidate, pivot and conflict positions). *Given a set* $S = \{l_i = r_i\}$ *of rules for the same function symbol, (a nonempty) position* $o \in \cap Pos(l_i)$ *is a* candidate *if for every pair of distinct rules, if p is a strict prefix of o, $root(l_i/p) = root(l_j/p)$. A candidate o is a* pivot *if* $\forall l_i = r_i \in S.root(l_i/o)$ *is a data constructor. Otherwise, if there are i, j such that $root(l_i/o)$ is a variable and $root(l_j/o)$ is not, we say that o is a* conflict *position.* ∎

Candidates with a variable in every rule are not usually considered candidates as they do not affect the case analysis – they are *trivial* candidates. Pivots induce a partition on the set of rules according to the constructor at its root, i.e. $S = \bigcup_i S_{o,c_i}$, where S_{o,c_i} is the set of rules with data constructor c_i at position o. Pivots which induce a partition with a single element are *trivial* pivots and do not affect the case analysis. Our algorithm is based on the following lemma:

Lemma 1. *A sequential definitional tree exists for a given function symbol defined by the set of rules S, iff S has a single rule (or a rule subsumes all), or if there is a (nontrivial) pivot o such that $\forall i. S_{o,c_i}$ has a sequential tree.* ∎

Definition 4 (Algorithm). *The set $\Delta(S, \pi)$ of definitional trees for pattern π and set of rules S – whose left hand sides are instances of π – can be defined as the least set that satifies:*

$$\Delta(S, \pi) \supseteq \begin{cases} \{rule(l = r)\} & if\ S = \{l = r\} \\ \{branch(\pi, o, T_1, \dots, T_k)\} & if\ o\ is\ a\ pivot \wedge \forall i. T_i \in \\ & \quad \Delta(S_{o,c_i}, \pi[o \leftarrow c_i\ x_1 \dots x_{ar(c_i)}]) \\ & \quad being\ the\ x\text{'}s\ fresh\ variables. \end{cases}$$

∎

When no sequential tree exists, it is interesting to have a trace of where did the conflicts occur. The following definition tries to formalize this idea:

Definition 5 (Sequentiality formula). *The* sequentiality formula *of a set of rules S, notation $Seq(S)$, is defined recursively in the following way: If S has a sequential tree, $Seq(S) = \top$. Otherwise, let $C = \{p_i\}$ the set of (nontrivial) candidate positions of S. Then, we define*

$$Seq(S) = \bigvee_i \mathbf{Prefix}(S, p_i) \wedge \Pi_{p_i}(S)$$

To define $\mathbf{Prefix}(S, p)$ *let p' range over the set of strict prefixes of p and let l be a left hand side of a rule in S. Then*

$$\mathbf{Prefix}(S, p) = \bigwedge_{p'} p' = root(l/p')$$

Each $\Pi_{p_i}(S)$ *is given by:*

1. *If p_i is a pivot:* $\Pi_{p_i}(S) = \bigwedge_{c_j} p_i = c_j \wedge \mathbf{Seq}(S_{p_i, c_j})$
2. *If p_i is a conflict:* $\Pi_{p_i}(S) = p_i \wedge \bigwedge_{c_j} p_i = c_j \wedge \mathbf{Seq}(S^*_{p_i, c_j})$
   where $S^*_{p_i, c_j} = S_{p_i, c_j}$ *plus all the conflicting rules with the variable at p_i substituted by $c_j\ x_1 \dots x_{ar(c_j)}$, being the x's fresh variables.* ∎

Example 3. Consider the following definitions:

```
berry x       false true  = 0          deep (g false y    )  = D1
berry true  y     false = 1            deep (g x       false) = D2
berry false true  z      = 2           deep h                 = D3
```

Then $\mathbf{Seq}(\text{berry}) = 1 \vee 2 \vee 3$, i.e. the set of rules does not admit a sequential tree, but once any of the arguments gets to *hnf* – *head normal form*, a constructor on top – the rest of the evaluation would be sequential. This results as the simplification of

$$[1 \wedge ((1 = \mathbf{true} \; \wedge \top) \vee (1 = \mathbf{false} \; \wedge \top))] \vee$$
$$[2 \wedge ((2 = \mathbf{true} \; \wedge \top) \vee (2 = \mathbf{false} \; \wedge \top))] \vee$$
$$[3 \wedge ((3 = \mathbf{true} \; \wedge \top) \vee (3 = \mathbf{false} \; \wedge \top))]$$

The second definition shows non-topmost conflicts. It simplifies to

$$\mathbf{Seq}(\text{deep}) = [1 = \text{g} \wedge (1.1 \vee 1.2)] \vee 1 = \text{h}$$

□

A parallel tree for `merge xs ys` comprising the definition above appears in fig. 4. Parallel trees are not as good at specifying control as sequential ones. On one hand, although a generalization of the aforementioned strategy exists to sets of positions, this is in general too nondeterministic. The fact that as soon as one of the arguments to `merge` is in hnf the parallel reduction of the other argument can be stopped and then jump to purely sequential code – $\mathbf{Seq}(\text{merge}) = 1 \vee 2$ – is not explicit in the tree above. Observe as well that the third rule is covered by both subtrees. On the other hand, consider a expression `merge (f xs ys) (g xs zs)` where `xs` is a (free) logical variable shared among the two arguments to `merge`. It is well known from logic programming that parallel evaluation of goals with shared variables is inherently inefficient.

4 A Denotational Semantics

A simple denotational semantics for our subset of Curry follows. This is a purely functional semantics, that is, it does not capture such aspects as computed answers, but suffices for the purposes of this paper. The approach is similar to that of previous papers on Babel, but has been modified in order to fit into a metalanguage inspired by that in [8]. This makes proving the continuity of the interpretation transformer and the safety of the subsequent approximation a straightforward task. Another difference with other work is that a higher order language is now considered.

We first define some of the semantic domains involved. H is the cpo completion of the Herbrand universe formed with all the (data) constructors in a program. An interpretation for a certain program P maps every function symbol to a value in D. We regard constructors as free, and thus have a standard denotation.

DOMAINS	$D \cong H + [D_\perp \to D_\perp] + \sum_i \{(c\ d_1 \ldots d_i)	c \in DC^i,\ \forall k.d_k \in D\}$
	$Int = FS \to D$
SEMANTIC FUNCTIONS	$\mathbf{F}_P : Int$
	$\mathbf{R} : Rule \to Int \to Int$
	$\mathbf{E} : Exp \to Int \to D$

$\mathbf{R}[\![f\ t_1 \ldots t_n = r]\!]i = \lambda fs.(fs = f) \to \lambda x_1 \ldots x_n.\bigsqcup_{Var(t_j)}(t_1 \doteq x_1 \wedge \cdots \wedge t_n \doteq x_1) \to$
$\mathbf{E}[\![r]\!]i$
$\mathbf{F}_P = lfp(\bigsqcup_{rule \in P}(\mathbf{R}[\![rule]\!]))$

Fig. 5. Denotational semantics

Regarding the semantic functions, $\mathbf{E}$ is just evaluation of expressions according to the semantics of the program, and can be defined as the homomorphic extension of the semantics for function symbols ($\mathbf{F}_P$). It is needed in order to evaluate the right hand sides of rules. $\mathbf{R}$ is the interpretation transformer associated with each rule of the program and represents the amount of information added by every possible application of that rule. The symbol ($\doteq$) denotes domain equality and ($\cdot \to \cdot$) is shorthand for ($\cdot \to \cdot|\perp$). For every equational program P, $\mathbf{F}_P$, $\mathbf{R}$ and $\mathbf{E}$ are continuous.

5   A Simple Strictness Analysis

By "simple" we mean a forward strictness analysis much in the style of [10] (two-point domain), but higher order. The differences are in the presentation and the treatment of pattern matching and higher-order functions.

A strictness analysis can predict undefinedness in functional expressions. Domain-theoretically, this amounts to detect bottoms as the result of semantic (complete) functions. In our system, only D will be treated as dynamic, and its approximation is obtained by approximating its first-order subdomains by 2-point lattices where $\perp$ represents undefined values and $\top$ represents everything, i.e. the supremum of the powerdomain.

Example 4. Consider natural number addition as defined by

```
0       + m = m
(s n) + m = s(n + m)
```

Its semantics is given by

$$\mathbf{F}[\![+]\!] = \lambda x.\lambda y.lfp(\lambda i.(x \doteq 0 \to \mathbf{E}[\![y]\!]i) \sqcup (\bigsqcup_{N,M}(x \doteq (s\ N) \to \mathbf{E}[\![s(N+M)]\!]i)))$$

after some simplification of the formula. The strictness analysis of the addition rules is

$$\begin{aligned}
\mathbf{F}^\sharp[\![+]\!] &= \lambda x.\lambda y.lfp(\lambda i.(x \leftrightarrow \top \wedge \mathbf{E}^\sharp[\![y]\!]i) \vee (\exists n,m.\ x \leftrightarrow \top \wedge \mathbf{E}^\sharp[\![s(N+M)]\!]i)) \\
&= \lambda x.\lambda y.lfp(\lambda i.(x \leftrightarrow \top \wedge y) \vee (\exists n,m.\ x \leftrightarrow \top \wedge \top)) \\
&= \lambda x.\lambda y.(x \wedge y) \vee x \\
&= \lambda x.\lambda y.x
\end{aligned}$$

That is, the analysis says that if the first argument is undefined so is the result.□

ABSTRACT DOMAIN $D^{\sharp} \cong 2 + [D^{\sharp} \to D^{\sharp}]$

APPROXIMATION

$\bot^{\sharp} = \bot$ $(\lambda x.e)^{\sharp} = \lambda x.(e^{\sharp})$

$c^{\sharp} = \top$ if $c \in DC^0$ $(\bigsqcup_{v_1 \ldots v_n} e)^{\sharp} = \exists v_1 \ldots v_n.e^{\sharp}$

$c^{\sharp} = \lambda x_1 \ldots \lambda x_n.\top$ if $c \in DC^n$ $(b \to e)^{\sharp} = b^{\sharp} \wedge e^{\sharp}$

                    $(x \doteq e)^{\sharp} = x \leftrightarrow e^{\sharp}$

Fig. 6. Strictness analysis

For every program P, $\mathbf{F}_P^{\sharp} \propto \mathbf{F}_P$, which is straightforward using properties of the metalanguage.

5.1 Computing the Approximation

Effectively computing the abstract denotation for the function symbols in a program implies the ability of manipulating propositional formulae and deciding on their equality — in order to detect fixed points.

Our implementation is based on BDD's (binary decision diagrams) which are normalized representations of propositional formulae. Thanks to normalisation, coimplication reduces to syntactic equality. This more or less fits our needs, whenever the functions tested for equality are of the form $\lambda x_1.\lambda x_2 \ldots \lambda x_n.P$ where P is a propositional formula. That is, in order to test the equality of $\lambda \tilde{x}_i.P$ and $\lambda \tilde{y}_i.Q$ the lists of parameters $[\tilde{x}_i]$ and $[\tilde{y}_i]$ are renamed out with a unifier θ and then $P\theta$ and $Q\theta$ are tested for logical equivalence.

5.2 Dealing with Function Spaces

When higher order functions like map, foldr, etc, occur in the program the former method no longer applies, as the abstraction of a higher-order function is a higher-order boolean function. A possible way to overcome this is to translate equality between higher order boolean functions to an isomorphic first order problem.

If we have $f : \text{bool} \to T$ then by Shannon's expansion theorem

$$f(x) \leftrightarrow (x \wedge f(\top)) \vee (\neg x \wedge f(\bot))$$

— where $(\vee, \wedge)$ are really higher order disjunction and conjunction if T is a function type. Making $f_{\bot} = f(\bot)$, $f_{\top} = f(\top)$ we obtain an isomorphism

$$(\text{bool} \to T) \leftrightarrow (T \times T)$$

i.e. a function type is translated into a product which in turn can be treated via currying.

Example 5. The higher order function $F : (\text{bool} \to \text{bool}) \to \text{bool} \to \text{bool}$ defined as

$$F = \lambda f.\lambda x.\ f(\top) \wedge x$$

translates to F' : bool $\to$ bool $\to$ bool $\to$ bool with definition

$$F' = \lambda f_\perp.\lambda f_\top.\lambda x.\ f_\top \wedge x$$

□

For types $(H \to T)$ with $H \neq bool$ the combinatory explosion seems excessive to apply this method. Fortunately enough, this kind of "very" higher order functions where some arguments are expected to be functions which expect functions as arguments do not occur very frequently in real programs, so we consider this a limitation of our analyzer.

6   Application to Code Generation

In this section, we show how to apply a strictness analysis to the compilation of equational programs. The method tries to produce sequential code in most cases when the (sequential) definitional tree does not exist. In short, the idea is to look for the causes of the non-sequentiality, and use that information to help the strictness analyzer to find the desired solutions. The easiest solution consists in a source code transformation that splits conflicting rules in strict positions. The new program has less conflicts so it is easier to find a sequential definitional tree for it. The transformed program is denotationally equivalent to the original one.

Conflicts are a necessary condition – but not sufficient – for the lack of sequentiality in a function's definition. The requirement that conflicts have to be candidates makes them less likely to appear in deep positions of a pattern. Due to space limitations we will restrict ourselves to the treatment of "topmost" conflicts. Deeper conflicts can be approached by using a source code transformation, similar to those in [9], that brings the conflicts to the top positions. Of course, the use of a richer strictness analyzer is also possible.

6.1   Program Transformation by Rule Expansion

Let P be a program and let f be a function symbol for which a sequential tree could not be built, and let $f\ \pi_1 \ldots x \ldots \pi_n = r$ be a conflicting rule for f in position i. That implies x is of a constructed type instance $\kappa\ \tau_1 \ldots \tau_k$ defined by

$$\textbf{data}\ \kappa\ \tau_1 \ldots \tau_k = c_1\ \tau_{11} \ldots\ |\ \ldots\ |\ c_n\ \tau_{n1} \ldots$$

Suppose that the analysis says that f is strict in i. We obtain a new program P' by replacing the conflicting rule by the set of rules resulting from applying the substitution $\{x \mapsto c_j\ y_1 \ldots\ y_{aj}\}$ to it, for every constructor c_j in the type declaration, where the y's are fresh variables. The next proposition establishes that programs P and P' are denotationally equivalent.

Proposition 2. *Let P be a program and let P' be the program obtained from the previous transformation for the function f and strict position i. Then $\mathbf{F}_P[\![f]\!] = \mathbf{F}_{P'}[\![f]\!]$* ■

After deleting subsumed rules the resulting rule set can be sequential, otherwise a different position is tried. As the number of conflicting positions is usually small, the expanding rule step does not require a big number of iterations.

Example 6. Take the rules for function merge:

```
merge []        ys      = ys      (1)
merge xs        []      = xs      (2)
merge (x:xs) (y:ys) = (R3)   (3)
```

the left hand sides are essentially a parallel-or, but the strictness analysis gives $merge^{\sharp} = \lambda xs.\lambda ys.xs \wedge ys$. Trying the conflict at position 1 we get $merge^{\sharp} \perp \top = \perp$, so the second rule is rewritten into:

```
merge []        [] = []      (2a)
merge (x:xs) [] = x:xs   (2b)
```

Rule (2a) is subsumed by (1) and the set of rules is sequential with the following definitional tree:

Mixing overlapping and logic variables has some inherent drawbacks – repeated solutions. Moreover, the new program can have a strange behavior. Let *goal*= merge any_list []. Then we have:

$$goal \Downarrow \{any\_list \mapsto []\} \| []$$
$$\Downarrow \{any\_list \mapsto x:xs\} \| x:xs$$

The second outcome is unexpected, instead of the more natural $goal \Downarrow \epsilon \|$ any_list.[4] The reason is that in changing the actual rules of the program, while the (functional) denotation of the program does not change, the operational or *computed-answers* semantics is different.

6.2   Extended Definitional Trees

We can study the non-sequentiality problem as well as this issue of the computed answers in a broader framework. Definitional trees are only able to manage situations when there is not *syntactic* overlapping, but in some cases, overlapping does not imply non-sequentiality as the merge example shows. Definitional trees can be extended to handle such these cases. The key idea is to introduce a new kind of branch node adding a case for variables (*vbranch*). If the evaluated argument is a constructor, there are two possible subtrees to select: the subtree associated with the corresponding constructor as well as the variable branch. If the argument is a free variable, all the subtrees can be selected. More formally, extended definitional trees are defined as follows:

---

[4] The other solution is redundant, of course.

Definition 6 (Extended definitional tree). T *is an* extended definitional tree *for pattern π iff one of the following cases holds:*

1. T *is rule($l = r$) where $l = r$ is a program rule such that l is a variant of π.*
2. T *is branch(π, o, $T_1,\ldots,T_k$) where the T_i are definitional trees for $\pi[o \leftarrow c\ x_1 \ldots x_{ar(c)}]$, being c a data constructor suitable to appear at o and the x_j fresh variables.*
3. T *is vbranch(π, o, $T_1,\ldots,T_k$, T_{k+1}) where*
   - *the T_i ($1 \leq i \leq k$) are as before.*
   - *T_{k+1} is a extended definitional tree for π, provided that it does not branch on position o.*
4. *T is or($T_1,\ldots,T_k$) where the T_i are definitional trees for π.* ■

The same narrowing strategy defined in section 3 can be applied to extended trees. We can see, however, that the definition of $\Omega_T(\pi)$ can be refined after the inclusion of *vbranch* nodes:

$$\Omega_T(\pi) = \begin{cases} \ldots & \\ \Omega_{T_i} \cup \Omega_{T_{k+1}}(\pi) & T = vbranch(\pi', o, T_1, \ldots, T_k, T_{k+1}) \\ & \text{and } root(\pi/o) = c_i \\ \Omega_{T_1}(\pi) \cup \ldots \cup \Omega_{T_k}(\pi) \cup \Omega_{T_{k+1}}(\pi) & T = vbranch(\pi', o, T_1, \ldots, T_k, T_{k+1}) \\ & \text{and } root(\pi/o) \text{ is a variable} \\ \ldots & \end{cases}$$

Definition 7 (Semantically inductive sequential function definitions). *An operation f is semantically inductive sequential iff there exists an extended definitional tree T for f such that*

- *the rules contained in T are all and only the rules defining f, and*
- *vbranch nodes are only used at strict positions of f.* ■

Given a set of semantical inductively sequential rules for f and a strictness analysis information that detects strict positions of f, the following algorithm produces an extended definitional tree without *or*-nodes for it.

Definition 8 (Algorithm for extended trees). *Define $S_{o,\_} \subseteq S$ as the set of rules with a variable at position o. The set $\Delta^*(S, \pi)$ of extended definitional trees for pattern π and set of rules S (subsumed by π) can be defined as the least set that satifies:*

$$\Delta^*(S, \pi) \supseteq \begin{cases} \{rule(l = r)\} & \text{if } S = \{l = r\} \\ \{vbranch(\pi, o, T_1, \ldots, T_k, T_{k+1})\} & \text{if } o \text{ is strict or a pivot,} \\ & \forall i. T_i \in \Delta^*(S_{o,k_i}, \pi[o \leftarrow c_i x_1 \ldots x_{ar(c_i)}]) \\ & \text{and } T_{k+1} \in \Delta^*(S_{o,\_}, \pi), \text{ provided} \\ & \text{that position } o \text{ is not used for} \\ & \text{branching in } T_{k+1}. \\ (\text{branch case as before } \ldots) & \text{if } S_{o,\_} \text{ is empty} \end{cases}$$ ■

The extended tree for the `merge` example follows:

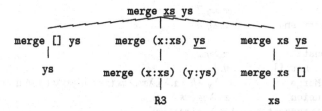

We can now establish the correctness of the algorithm in the following terms:

Proposition 3. *Let f be an inductively sequential function and T a (parallel) definitional tree for it. Let T' be the extended definitional obtained as the result of the previous algorithm. Then for all f-patterns π, we have $\Omega_T(\pi) = \Omega_{T'}(\pi)$* ■

6.3   Run-Time Tests to Handle Parallel Definitions

The previous method does not ensure the construction of a (extended) definitional tree in all the cases. However, if not enough strict conflicts have been found, then the sequentiality formula can be used to select "good" candidates among the other conflicts and a run-time test can then branch to sequential code produced using the previous steps. In order to introduce these run-time tests we modify again the notion of definitional trees to add a kind of or-node to check whether some of the arguments are already constructor-rooted and a (sequential) extended definitional tree can be used. Otherwise a parallel tree is used.

Definition 9 (Or-checked extended definitional tree). *The definition of extended definitional trees is augmented with the following check-or nodes:*

5. *T is check-or $((F_1, T_1), \ldots, (F_k, T_k), T_{k+1})$ where the T_i are sequential extended definitional trees for π, the F_i are sequentiality formulae defined for the set of rules considered and T_{k+1} is an or-rooted definitional tree.* ■

The operational semantics can be easily modified to cope with *check-or* nodes. Roughly speaking, the calling expression is analyzed to check if all the arguments satisfy F_i. In this case, the (sequential) definitional tree T_i is used. Otherwise, the parallel subtree is used.

Or-checked extended definitional trees can be generated from the sequentiality formula. The idea is to select a set of implicants of the sequentiality formula in conjunctive form as the F_i. These implicants will be of the form

$$\bigwedge_j p_j \wedge \bigwedge_k p_k = c_k$$

The associated definitional tree is obtained using the previous algorithm for extended definitional trees assuming that every position p_j is strict, and using only those rules for which the root symbol at position p_k is c_k.

Due to space limitations, we defer the formal definition of this construction to an extended version of this paper. This will also contain the extension of Ω for or-checked extended definitional trees and the correctness theorem.

FUNCTION	STRICTNESS SEMANTICS
id	$\lambda x.x$
(:)	$\lambda x.\lambda y.\top$
curry snd	$\lambda x.\lambda y.y$
[]	$\top$
const	$\lambda x.\lambda y.x$
const []	$\lambda y.\top$
hiMerge	$\lambda f.\lambda g.\lambda h.\lambda a.\lambda b.\lambda xs.\lambda ys.(xs \wedge b\ ys) \vee (ys \wedge a\ xs)$
union	$\lambda xs.\lambda ys.(xs \wedge ys)$
intersection	$\lambda xs.\lambda ys.(xs \vee ys)$
difference	$\lambda xs.\lambda ys.xs$

Fig. 7. Strictness analysis for the hiMerge example

7   Results and Conclusion

Curry, unlike most declarative languages, has included in the current draft the operational behaviour associated with the compilation of patterns as part of the language definition. This is due, in part, to the fact that in the same way as in a functional language with lazy evaluation, sequentiality is more crucial than in an eager one, in a functional logic language there is a greater risk of speculation. The reason is that parallel strategies are harder to implement in the presence of partial information.

The issue of sequentiality in functional logic languages differs from the functional case in two other aspects. On one hand, textual order is no longer significant, as nondeterminism is accepted, so optimizations like those in [7] no longer apply. The other difference is the problem of preserving output substitutions.

We have shown that although complete, present compilation techniques in Curry are inefficient for non strongly sequential programs, and that it is feasible to produce a more efficient unification code using information from a strictness analyzer. This means taking into account the bodies of the rules, not only the left hand sides.

Even in the presence of higher order functions — a key feature of functional logic languages — strictness can be used to improve sequentiality. Figure 7 shows the results of applying the method to the example in figure 3. For the three functions union, difference, intersection, only intersection would need, in the worst case, parallel code or run-time tests.

It has been shown that the formalism of definitional trees must be enhanced to take full advantage of the analysis. The reason is that current definitional trees assume that all indexing information comes from constructor symbols actually present in the program rules and this is used to produce output substitutions. In other words, the definition of sequential definitional trees is too restrictive to take advantage of strictness information not present syntactically in the left hand sides. More specifically, the property that different branches in a *branch* node are indexed by different constructors at a given position should be separated from the actual substitution applied at that node, and that is exactly what extended definitional trees provide.

For the case of parallel definitions, the techniques in 6.3 make possible to move or-nodes to the top of the tree, thus improving on previous algorithms proposed for its construction.

In this paper we have used a purely functional denotational semantics, in part to make it as self contained as possible, and then the problem of output substitutions is solved operationally. A different approach would be to use a denotational semantics that capture output substitutions from the beginning, like a higher order version of that in [17].

Rather than expecting too much from a powerful strictness analyzer we have relied in reasonable approximations to take advantage of the simplest. For instance, the treatment of higher order domains is justified by a measure of the type of the function analyzed, and the applicability of a simple strictness analysis is based on the way sequentiality conflicts tend to appear. Anyway, the main goal of showing the strictness analysis we are considering at the moment is to give the whole picture of our technique, not to present it as state of the art in static analysis.

This commitment to the pragmatics of a programming language distinguishes this paper from other work (e.g. [14]) that approaches the issue of (non strong) sequentiality in the field of TRS's. Questions on the use of a programming language and notions like its semantics (and its abstractions) or higher order are usually sidestepped.

In this paper we have considered narrowing as the only evaluation mechanism. Curry allows goals to be evaluated using both narrowing and *residuation* — essentially suspension of goals with free variables. Recently the treatment of residuation, with evaluation annotations, has been integrated into the formalism of definitional trees, making its extension a less trivial question than shown here.

References

1. Sergio Antoy. Definitional trees. In *Proc. of the 4th Intl. Conf. on Algebraic and Logic Programming*, number 632 in Springer LNCS, pages 143–157, 1992.
2. Sergio Antoy, Rachid Echahed, and Michael Hanus. A needed narrowing strategy. In *Proc. 21st. ACM Symposium on Principles of Programming Languages*, pages 268–279, Portland, 1994.
3. Sergio Antoy, Rachid Echahed, and Michael Hanus. Parallel evaluation strategies for functional logic languages. In *International Conference on Logic Programming*, 1997.
4. Daniela Genius. Sequential implementation of parallel narrowing. In *Proc. JIC-SLP'96 Workshop on Multi-Paradigm Logic Programming*, pages 95–104, 1996.
5. Michael Hanus et al. Curry: an integrated functional logic language. http://www-i2.informatik.rwth-aachen.de/~hanus/curry/report.html.
6. G. Huet and J.J. Lévy. Call by need computations in non-ambiguous linear term rewriting systems. Technical Report Rapport Laboria 359, IRIA, august 1979.
7. Luc Maranget. Compiling lazy pattern matching. In *Proc. of the 1992 conference on Lisp and Functional Programming*. ACM Press, 1992.

8. Kim Marriot, Harald Søndergaard, and Neil Jones. Denotational abstract interpretation of logic programs. *ACM Transactions on Programming Languages and Systems*, 16(3):607–648, may 1994.

9. J.J. Moreno-Navarro, H. Kuchen, R. Loogen, and M. Rodríguez-Artalejo. Lazy narrowing in a graph machine. In H. Kirchner and W. Wechler, editors, *2nd International Conference on Algebraic and Logic Programming, Nancy (France)*, pages 298–317. CRIN (Centre de Recherche en Informatique de Nancy), LNCS, Springer Verlag, October 1990.

10. A. Mycroft. The theory and practice of transforming call-by-need into call-by-value. In *Proc. International Symposium on Programming*, pages 269–281. Springer LNCS 83, 1980.

11. Michael O'Donnell. *Handbook of Logic in Artificial Intelligence and Logic Programming*, chapter Equational Logic Programming. Oxford University Press, 1994.

12. S. L. Peyton-Jones. *The Implementation of Functional Programming Languages*. Prentice-Hall, 1987.

13. José María Rey and Julio Mariño. Implementación de Curry mediante su traducción a Prolog. Master's thesis, Facultad de Informática, Universidad Politécnica de Madrid, 1997. In Spanish.

14. R. C. Sekar and I. V. Ramakrishnan. Programming in equational logic: Beyond strong sequentiality. *Information and Computation*, 1(104):78–109, 1993.

15. S. Thatte. A refinement of strong sequentiality for term rewriting with constructors. *Information and Computation*, 72:46–65, 1987.

16. Philip Wadler. Efficient compilation of pattern matching. In Peyton-Jones, editor, *The Implementation of Functional Programming Languages*, pages 78–103. Prentice-Hall, 1987.

17. F. Zartmann. Denotational abstract interpretation of functional logic programs. In P. Van Hentenryck, editor, *Static Analysis: Proceedings of the Fourth International Symposium*, volume 1302 of *Lecture Notes in Computer Science*, pages 141–156. Springer, 1997.

GNU Prolog: Beyond Compiling Prolog to C

Daniel Diaz[1] and Philippe Codognet[2]

[1] University of Paris 1, CRI, bureau C1407
90 rue de Tolbiac, 75013 Paris, FRANCE
diaz@univ-paris1.fr
[2] University of Paris 6, LIP6, case 169
8 rue du Capitaine Scott, 75015 Paris, FRANCE
Philippe.Codognet@lip6.fr

Abstract. We describe in this paper the compilation scheme of the GNU Prolog system. This system is built on our previous experience of compiling Prolog to C in wamcc. The compilation scheme has been however redesigned to overcome drawbacks of the compilation to C. In particular, GNU-Prolog is based on a low-level mini-assembly platform-independent language that makes it possible to avoid the phase of compiling C code, and thus speeds up drastically compilation time. It also makes it possible to produce small stand alone executable files as the result of the compilation process. Interestingly, GNU Prolog is now compliant to the ISO standard and includes several extensions (constraint solving, OS interface, sockets, global variables, etc). The overall system is efficient and comparable in performances with commercial systems.

1 Introduction

GNU Prolog is a free Prolog compiler supported by the GNU organization (http://www.gnu.org/software/prolog). The development of GNU Prolog started in January 1996 under the name Calypso. Discussions with the GNU organization in late 1998 makes it released as a GNU product in April 1999: GNU Prolog.

GNU Prolog is based on our experience with wamcc. The main novelty of wamcc [4] was to translate Prolog to C but with also the idea of translating a WAM branching into a native code jump in order to reduce the overhead of calling a C function, see [4] for details. wamcc shown that this approach was an attractive alternative to the classical solution consisting in a WAM emulator. Indeed, the performances of this unoptimized system were close to commercial systems based on a highly optimized emulator. Moreover, many ideas of wamcc have inspired the designers of some Prolog systems since its diffusion in 1992. From the user point of view the main advantage of wamcc was its ability to produce stand alone executables while most other Prolog systems need the presence of the emulator at run-time. There is however a serious drawback when compiling Prolog to C, which is the size of the C file generated and the time taken to compile such a big program by standard C compilers (e.g. gcc). Indeed, a Prolog

E. Pontelli, V. Santos Costa (Eds.): PADL 2000, LNCS 1753, pp. 81–92, 2000.
© Springer-Verlag Berlin Heidelberg 2000

program compiles to many WAM instructions (e.g. the 3000 lines of the GNU Prolog compiler give rise to 12000 WAM instructions) and trying to inline each WAM instruction could lead to a very big C file that cannot be handled by the C compiler. In order to cope with big Prolog sources we decided, in wamcc, to translate most WAM instructions to a call to a C function performing the treatment. Obviously the execution is a bit slowed down but the compilation is much faster (and the executable is smaller). However, even with this solution, the C compiler took too much time for big sources, especially in trying to optimize the code produced.

The novelty of the GNU Prolog compilation scheme is to translate a WAM file into a mini-assembly (MA) file. This language has been specifically designed for GNU Prolog. The idea of the MA is then to have a machine-independent intermediate language in which the WAM is translated. The corresponding MA code is mapped to the assembly language of the target machine. In order to simplify the writing (i.e. porting) of such mappers the instruction set of MA must be simple, in the spirit of the LLM3 abstract machine for Lisp [3], as opposed to the complex instruction set of the BAM designed for Aquarius Prolog [8]. Actually, the MA language is based on 11 instructions, mostly to handle the control of Prolog and to call a C function (performing most of the treatment). This new compilation process is between 5-10 times faster than wamcc+gcc. The rest of this paper is devoted to a detailed explanation of this compilation scheme.

Moreover, wamcc had been designed as an experimental platform to provide a sound basis for various extensions (like Constraint Logic Programming). Due to this choice, several functionalities were missing in wamcc (e.g. no floating arithmetic, no stream support,...) and the whole system was not robust enough. The main goal of GNU Prolog was then to provide a free, open, robust, extensible and complete Prolog system. Like wamcc it should be able to produce efficient stand alone executables but overcoming all limitations cited above.

GNU Prolog is a complete system including: floating point numbers, streams, dynamic code, DCG, operating system interface, sockets, a Prolog debugger, a low-level WAM debugger, a line editing facility with completion on atoms, etc. GNU Prolog offers more than 300 Prolog built-in predicates and is compliant to the ISO standard for Prolog [7] (GNU Prolog is today the only free Prolog system really compliant to this standard). There is also a powerful bidirectional interface between Prolog and C, featuring implicit Prolog ↔ C type conversion, transparent I/O argument handling, non-deterministic C code, ISO error support, etc. This is a key point to allow users to write their own extensions. Finally, GNU Prolog includes a very efficient constraint solver over finite domains inspired from clp(FD) [5,6] containing many predefined constraints: arithmetic constraints, boolean constraints, symbolic constraints, reified constraints; there are more than 50 FD built-in constraints/predicates, and several predefined labeling heuristics. Moreover the solver is extensible, and new high-level constraints can be easily defined by the user and defined in terms of simple primitives.

The rest of this paper is organized as follows. Section 2 introduces the MA language while section 3 describes how this language can be mapped to a specific architecture. Section 4 is devoted to the link phase. Performance evaluation is detailed in Section 5, and a short conclusion ends the paper.

2 The Mini-Assembly Language

2.1 Overview

We here describe the mini-assembly (MA) language. The idea of the MA language is to have a machine-independent intermediate language in which the WAM is translated. The design of MA comes from the study of the C code produced by wamcc. Indeed, in the wamcc system, most WAM instructions given rise to a call to a C function performing the treatment (e.g. unification, argument loading, environment and choice-point management). The only exceptions were obviously instructions to manage the control of Prolog and some short instructions that were inlined. The MA language has been designed to avoid the use of the C stage and thus has instructions to handle the Prolog control, to call a C function and to test/use its returned value. The MA file is then mapped to the assembly of the target machine (see section 3) from which an object is produced. Thus, the wamcc sequence: $WAM \rightarrow C (\rightarrow assembly) \rightarrow object$ becomes in GNU Prolog: $WAM \rightarrow MA \rightarrow assembly \rightarrow object$.

In order to simplify the writing of translators of the MA to a given architecture (i.e. the mappers), the MA instruction set must be simple: it only contains 11 instructions.

2.2 The MA Instruction Set

Here is a description of each MA instruction:

pl_jump *pl_label*: branch the execution to the predicate whose corresponding symbol is *pl_label*. This symbol is an identifier whose construction is explained later in section 2.3. This instruction corresponds to the WAM instruction execute.

pl_call *pl_label*: branch the execution to the predicate whose corresponding symbol is *pl_label* after initializing the continuation register CP to the address of the very next instruction. This instruction corresponds to the WAM instruction call.

pl_ret: branch the execution to the address given by the continuation pointer CP. This instruction corresponds to the WAM instruction proceed.

pl_fail: branch the execution to the address given by the last alternative (ALT cell of the last choice point pointed by the WAM B register). This instruction corresponds to the WAM instruction fail.

jump *label*: branch the execution to the symbol *label*. This instruction is used when translating indexing WAM instructions to perform local control transfer (e.g. try, retry or trust). This instruction has been distinguished from pl_jump (even if both can be implemented/translated in a same manner) since, on some machines, local jumps can be optimized.

call_c *fct_name* (*arg* , ...): call the C function *fct_name* passing the arguments *arg*,... Each argument can be an integer, a float (C double), a string, the address of a label, the address or the content of a memory location, the address or the content of a WAM X or Y register. This instruction is used to translate most of the WAM instructions.

fail_ret: perform a Prolog fail (like pl_fail) if the value returned by the previous C function call is 0. This instruction is used after a C function call returning a boolean to indicate its result (e.g. functions performing the unification).

jump_ret: branch the execution to the address returned by the previous C function call. This instruction makes it possible to use C functions to determine where to transfer the control. For instance, the WAM indexing instruction switch_on_term is implemented via a C function accepting several addresses and returning the address of the selected code.

move_ret *target*: copy the value returned by the previous C function call to *target* which can be either a memory location or a WAM X or Y register.

c_ret: C return. This instruction is used at then end of the initialization function (see below) to give back the control to the caller.

move *reg1* , *reg2*: copy the content of the WAM X or Y register *reg1* to the register *reg2*.

It is worth noticing the minimality of the language which is based on a very restricted instruction set. Note however the presence of the move instruction to perform a copy of WAM X or Y registers. We could instead invoke a C function to perform such a move (using call_c). However, those moves between registers are rather frequent and the invocation of a C function would be costly. There is thus a compromise to find between the minimality of the instruction set and the performance. Obviously, it is possible to extend this instruction set (e.g. adding arithmetic instructions) but this will complicate much more the writing of the mappers to assembly. Performance evaluation will show that this instruction set gives good results.

Beside these instructions, the MA language include several declarations which are presented now. The keyword local specifies a local symbol (only visible in the current object) while global allows other object to see that symbol.

pl_code local/global *pl_label*: define a Prolog predicate whose corresponding symbol is *pl_label*. For the moment all predicates are global (i.e. visible by all other Prolog objects). But local will be used when implementing a module system.

c_code local/global/initializer *label*: define a function that can be externally called by a C function. The use of initializer ensures that this function will be executed first, when the Prolog engine is started. Only one function per file can be declared as initializer.

long local/global *ident* = *value*: allocate the space for a **long** variable whose name is *ident* and initializes it with the integer *value*. The initialization is optional (i.e. the = *value* part can be omitted).

long local/global *ident(Size)*: allocate the space for an array of *Size* longs whose name is *ident*.

The $WAM \rightarrow MA$ translation can be performed in linear time w.r.t. the size of the WAM file (the translation is performed on the fly while the WAM file is read).

2.3   Associating an Identifier to a Predicate Name

Since the MA language is later mapped to the assembly of the target machine only classical identifiers can be used (a letter followed by letters, digits or the underscore character). In particular, it is necessary to associate such an identifier (referenced as *pl_label* in section 2.2) to each predicate. Since the syntax of identifiers is more restrictive than the syntax of Prolog atoms (which can include any character using quotes) GNU Prolog uses an hexadecimal representation where each predicate name is translated to a symbol beginning with an X followed by the hexadecimal notation of the code of each character of the name followed by an underscore and the arity. For instance append/3 is coded by the symbol X617070656E64_3 (61 is the hexadecimal representation of the code of a, 70 is associated to p, ...). The linker is then responsible for resolving external references (e.g. call to built-in predicates or to user predicates defined in an other object). The output of the linker is filtered by GNU Prolog to decode eventual hexadecimal notations in case of errors (e.g. undefined predicate, multiple definitions for a predicate).

2.4   An Example

We here present the MA code associated to the simple clause p(T,g(U),V):- q(a,T,V,U). Associated WAM instructions are shown as comment.

```
% gplc -M t.pl
% more t.ma
pl_code global X70_3                    ; define predicate p/3
   call_c   Get_Structure(at(2),1,X(1)) ; get_structure(g/1,1)
   fail_ret
   call_c   Unify_Variable()            ; unify_variable(x(3))
   move_ret X(3)
   move     X(0),X(1)                    ; put_value(x(0),1)
   call_c   Put_Atom(at(3))             ; put_atom(a,0)
   move_ret X(0)
   pl_jump  X71_4                        ; execute(q/4)

long local at(4)                         ; table for 4 atoms
```

```
c_code initializer Object_Initializer  ; object initializer
   call_c   Create_Atom("t.pl")         ; atom #0 is 't.pl'
   move_ret at(0)
   call_c   Create_Atom("a")            ; atom #3 is 'a'
   move_ret at(3)
   call_c   Create_Atom("g")            ; atom #2 is 'g'
   move_ret at(2)
   call_c   Create_Atom("p")            ; atom #1 is 'p'
   move_ret at(1)
   call_c   Create_Pred(at(1),3,at(0),1,1,&X70_3)
   c_ret                                ; define predicate p/3
```

It is easy to see that most WAM instructions give rise to a C function call
(e.g. call_c Get_Structure()). Calls to functions that can fail (unification) are
followed by a fail_ret that performs a Prolog fail if the returned value is 0. Note
the presence of the MA instruction move to perform a copy of WAM registers
(associated to the WAM instruction put_value(x(0),1)).

According to the encoding presented in section 2.3, the symbol X70_3 is
associated to p/3 (and X71_4 to q/4) .

It is worth noting how atoms are managed. All atoms are classically stored
in a hash-table. To cope with separate linking the hash-table must be built
at run-time (while it is possible to compute hash-values at compile-time in
the presence of a single file). For that the function Object_Initializer is
first invoked. It is responsible for updating the atom table with atoms needed
by the object. The hash value of each atom is then stored in a local array
(at($atom\_number$)) and is used by instructions handling atoms (e.g. put_atom)
or functors (e.g. get_structure). The initialization function also updates the
predicate table with predicates defined in the object. Both properties (pub-
lic/private, static/dynamic, user/built-in) and the address of the code of each
predicate are added. The knowledge of the address of the code is only necessary
for meta-call (e.g. to implement call/1) since all other references are resolved by
the linker. The way the initializer function is automatically invoked at run-time
is explained later in section 4.

3   Mapping the Mini-Assembly to a Target Machine

The next stage of the compilation consists in mapping the MA file to the assembly of the target machine. Since MA is based a reduced instruction set, the
writing of such translators is simplified. However, producing machine instructions is not an easy task. The first translator was written with the help of a C
file produced by wamcc. Indeed, compiling this file to assembly with gcc gave us
a first solution for the translation (since the MA instructions corresponds to a
subset of that C code). We have then generalized this by defining a C file (now
independently from wamcc). Each portion of this C code corresponds to a MA
instruction and the study of the assembly code produced by gcc is a good starting point. This gives a first information about register conventions, C calling

conventions,... However, to further optimize the assembly code it is necessary to refer to the technical documentation of the processor together with the ABI (Application Binary Interface) used by the operating system. Our experience is that such a backend for a new architecture can be produced within a week.

Here is the interesting portion of the linux/ix86 assembly code corresponding to the definition of p/3 (the associated MA code is shown as comment):

```
% gplc -S t.pl
% more t.s
fail:
    movl    1028(%ebx),%eax # fail
    jmp     *-4(%eax)


    .globl X70_3            # pl_code  global X70_3
X70_3:
    movl    at+8,%eax       # call_c   Get_Structure(at(2),1,X(1))
    movl    %eax,0(%esp)    #    arg    at(2)
    movl    $1,4(%esp)      #    arg    1 ($1=immediate value)
    movl    4(%ebx),%eax
    movl    %eax,8(%esp)    #    arg    X(1)
    call    Get_Structure
    testl   %eax,%eax       # fail_ret
    je      fail
    call    Unify_Variable  # call_c   Unify_Variable()
    movl    %eax,12(%ebx)   # move_ret X(3)
    movl    0(%ebx),%eax    # move     X(0),X(1)
    movl    %eax,4(%ebx)
    movl    at+12,%eax      # call_c   Put_Atom(at(3))
    movl    %eax,0(%esp)
    call    Put_Atom
    movl    %eax,0(%ebx)    # move_ret X(0)
    jmp     X71_4           # pl_jump  X71_4

.data
    .local at               # long local at(4)
    .comm  at,16,4
```

Here again, a crucial point is that the mapping $MA \rightarrow assembly$ is executed in linear time w.r.t. the size of the MA file (the translation is done on the fly while the MA file is read). Obviously the translation to the assembly of the target machine makes room for several optimizations. For instance the ix86 mapper uses the ebx register as a global register to store the address of the bank of WAM registers (consisting in 256 X registers followed by control registers: H, B, ...). Maintaining this address in ebx makes it possible to load/store (into/from a processor register) any WAM register with only one machine instruction. More generally, it is possible to use machine registers if it is ensured that they are saved and restored by functions using them (the ABI gives this information).

Note the definition of a `fail` label which performs a WAM `fail`. The associated code first loads the value of the B register (pointer to the last choice-point) and then branches to the value of the `ALT` cell of that choice-point (stored at the offset -1(*4 bytes) from B).

Another optimization used in this translation consists in using an original argument passing scheme. Under ix86, arguments are passed into the stack (as usually for CISC processors). The classical way to call a C function is then to use push instructions to initialize arguments, to call the function and, after the return of the function, either to use several pop instructions or to perform a stack pointer adjustment (adding a positive number to it). Many optimizing C compilers try to group these stack adjustments delaying them as long as possible to only perform one addition. GNU Prolog does better by avoiding all adjustements. This is done by reserving at the start of the Prolog engine enough space in the stack [1] and then copying arguments on that space (cf. `movl` ..., offset(`%esp`) instructions with offset a positive integer). This could not be done when compiling to C in `wamcc` (like many other optimizations included in the GNU Prolog mappers).

4   Linking

All objects are linked together at link-time with the GNU Prolog libraries: Prolog built-in predicate library, FD built-in constraint/predicate library and run-time library. This last library contains in particular functions implementing WAM instructions (e.g. `Get_Structure()`,...). Linked objects come from: Prolog sources, user C foreign code or FD constraint definition. This stage resolves external symbols (e.g. a call to a predicate defined in another module).

Since a Prolog source gives rise to a classical object, several objects can be grouped in a library (e.g. using `ar` under Unix). The Prolog and FD built-in libraries are created using this way (the user can also define his own libraries). Defining a library allows the linker to extract from it only the needed objects, i.e. those containing statically referenced functions/data. For this reason, GNU Prolog offers an option to generate small executables by avoiding the inclusion of most unused built-in predicates. To cope with meta-calls in that case, GNU Prolog provides a directive to force the linker to include a given predicate. To further reduce this size of the executables the linker should exclude *all* (instead of *most*) unused predicates. To do this we should define a built-in predicate per Prolog file (similarly to what is done for the C standard library) since the object is the unit of inclusion of the linker (i.e. when a symbol is referenced the whole object where this symbol is found is linked). For the moment built-in predicates are grouped by theme, for instance, a program using `write/1` will give rise to an executable also containing the code of `writeq/1`, `display/1`,... In the future we will define only one predicate per file. In the same spirit we will also define only one C function associated to a WAM instruction per file (e.g. to avoid to link the code of `Put_Structure()` if this instruction is not used).

---

[1] enough to store the maximal number of arguments of library functions.

In section 2.4 we have mentioned the role of the initializer function (called Object_Initializer in our example). It is worth explaining how this function is invoked. Indeed, the Prolog engine must be able to find dynamically at run-time all objects selected by the linker and execute their initializer function. The solution retained in GNU Prolog consists in marking all objects with magic numbers together with the address of the initializer function. At run-time, a pertinent portion of the data segment is scanned to detect each linked object (thanks to the magic numbers) and invoke its initializer.

5 Prolog Performance Evaluation

5.1 Compilation

Table 1 presents the performances of the GNU Prolog compilation scheme on a classical set of benchmarks, times are in seconds and sizes in KBytes. We have also added the GNU Prolog p12wam sub-compiler since it is a more representative example. For each program, one can find: the number of lines of the Prolog source

Program	Lines	object time	size	executable time	size
boyer	362	0.520	44	0.650	154
browse	88	0.200	11	0.420	129
cal	131	0.190	11	0.320	118
chat_parser	905	1.430	113	1.620	221
ham	48	0.120	8	0.240	110
nand	518	0.850	61	1.020	310
nrev	52	0.100	4	0.280	112
poly_10	86	0.160	10	0.360	120
queens (16)	60	0.080	3	0.170	111
queens_n (10)	37	0.070	4	0.270	112
reducer	307	0.420	30	0.570	148
sendmore	52	0.110	7	0.360	114
tak	24	0.060	2	0.200	110
zebra	42	0.090	5	0.190	107
p12wam	3000	3.430	286	3.690	557

Table 1. GNU Prolog compilation evaluation

program [2], the compilation time needed to produce the object, the size of the object code (stripped), the total compilation time (including the link) and the final executable size (stripped). Timings are measured on a Pentium II 400 Mhz with 256 MBytes of memory running Linux RedHat 5.2.

---

[2] neither blank lines nor comments are counted.

The size of (stripped) objects show that this approach really generates small code (less than 10 KBytes for many benchmarks). The size of the whole executable shows the interest of excluding most of unused built-in predicates. Indeed, when all built-in predicates (Prolog+FD) are present the size is at least 596 KBytes (this is the size of the GNU Prolog interactive top-level). Let us recall that we can even further reduce this size with a little reorganization of GNU Prolog libraries (see section 4). The ability of GNU Prolog to produce stand alone small executables is an important feature that makes it possible to use them in many occasions (tools, web CGIs,...). Other Prolog systems cannot produce such standalone executables since they always need the presence of the emulator at run-time (500 KBytes to 2 MBytes).

Compilation timings are rather good and we have reached our initial goal since GNU Prolog compiles 5-10 times faster than wamcc+gcc. Obviously this factor is not constant and the gain is more effective on large programs (and thus it is difficult to give an upper bound of the speedup factor). This is due to the fact that the translation from the WAM to an object is done in linear time (each translation only needs one pass) while a C compiler can need a quadratic time (and even worse) for its optimizations. Table 2 illustrates this comparing compilation times for both systems on some representative benchmarks.

Program	Lines	GNU Prolog	wamcc	Speedup
cal	131	0.320	1.210	3.7
boyer	362	0.650	3.050	4.6
chat_parser	905	1.620	10.120	6.3
pl2wam	3000	3.690	34.210	9.2

Table 2. Compilation speed - GNU Prolog versus wamcc

5.2   Benchmarking Prolog

In this section we compare GNU Prolog with one commercial system: SICStus Prolog emulated and five academic systems: Yap Prolog, wamcc, BinProlog (the last version is now commercialized), XSB-Prolog and SWI-Prolog. Table 3 presents execution times for those systems and the average speedup (or slowdown when preceded by a ↓ sign) of GNU Prolog (the nand program could not be run with XSB-Prolog). For each benchmark, the execution time is the average of 10 consecutive executions.

To summarize, GNU Prolog is 1.6 times slower than Yap Prolog, the fastest emulated Prolog system and also slightly slower than wamcc, mainly because of a richer arithmetic support. On the other hand, GNU Prolog is 1.2 times faster than SICStus emulated, 2.3 times faster than BinProlog, around 2.5 times faster than XSB-Prolog and more than 4 times faster than SWI-Prolog (without taking

Program	GNU Prolog 1.0.5	Yap Prolog 4.2.0	wamcc 2.21	SICStus Prolog 3.7.1	Bin Prolog 5.75	XSB Prolog 1.8.1	SWI Prolog 3.2.8
boyer	0.322	0.187	0.270	0.315	0.576	0.830	1.322
browse	0.410	0.189	0.316	0.409	0.798	0.804	1.217
cal	0.032	0.032	0.030	0.030	0.033	0.031	0.031
chat_parser	0.075	0.055	0.075	0.089	0.103	0.245	0.240
ham	0.293	0.170	0.336	0.329	0.393	0.582	0.723
nand	0.011	0.008	0.010	0.016	0.022	?.???	0.067
nrev	0.042	0.019	0.039	0.037	0.023	0.089	0.192
poly_10	0.023	0.013	0.020	0.024	0.031	0.056	0.097
queens (16)	0.223	0.136	0.126	0.404	0.378	0.751	2.261
queens_n (10)	1.091	0.542	1.011	1.193	1.307	2.143	4.067
reducer	0.021	0.010	0.021	0.022	0.243	0.064	0.077
sendmore	0.026	0.020	0.015	0.047	0.063	0.087	0.166
tak	0.040	0.031	0.029	0.066	0.110	0.156	28.810
zebra	0.026	0.017	0.027	0.021	0.034	0.040	0.057
GNU Prolog speedup	↓ 1.6	↓ 1.2	1.2	2.3	2.5	4.2	

Table 3. GNU Prolog versus other Prolog systems

into account the tak benchmark). To be fair let us mention that had not enough time to exaustively compare with all the Prolog systems and their variants. For instance, SICStus Prolog can compile to native code for some architectures (e.g. under SunOS/sparc but not yet under linux/ix86) and then it will be 2.5 times faster than GNU Prolog on those platforms, BinProlog can partly compile to C and CIAO Prolog seems a bit faster than GNU Prolog,...

Alltogether, this performance evaluation shows that a Prolog system based on a simple, unoptimized WAM engine can nevertheless have good efficiency with this MA-based native compilation scheme. Obviously further improvements could be achieved by integrated all well-known WAM optimizations.

6   Conclusion

GNU Prolog is a free Prolog compiler with constraint solving over finite domains. The Prolog part of GNU Prolog conforms to the ISO standard for Prolog with also many extensions very useful in practice (global variables, OS interface, sockets,...). The finite domain constraint part of GNU Prolog contains all classical arithmetic and symbolic constraints, and integrates also an efficient treatment of reified constraint and boolean constraints. The new compilation scheme of GNU Prolog drastically speeds up compilation times in comparison to compiling to C (5-10 times faster than wamcc+gcc). The MA language can be used by other logic languages as a target language. This choice has been made for the Dyalog system (a logic programming language with tabulation). GNU Prolog produces native binaries and the executable files produced are stand alone. The size of those executable files can be quite small since GNU Prolog can avoid to link the code of most unused built-in predicates. The performances of GNU Prolog are close to commercial systems and several times faster than other popular free systems.

References

1. H. Aït-Kaci. *Warren's Abstract Machine, A Tutorial Reconstruction.* Logic Programming Series, MIT Press, 1991.

2. M. Carlsson. *Design and Implementation of an Or-Parallel Prolog Engine.* PhD dissertation, SICS, Sweden, 1990.

3. J. Chailloux. La machine LLM3. Technical Report RT-055, INRIA, 1985.

4. P. Codognet and D. Diaz. wamcc: Compiling Prolog to C. In *12th International Conference on Logic Programming*, Tokyo, Japan, MIT Press, 1995.

5. P. Codognet and D. Diaz. A Minimal Extension of the WAM for clp(FD). In *Proc. ICLP'93, 10th International Conference on Logic Programming.* Budapest, Hungary, MIT Press, 1993.

6. P. Codognet and D. Diaz. Compiling Constraint in clp(FD). *Journal of Logic Programming*, Vol. 27, No. 3, June 1996.

7. Information technology - Programming languages - Prolog - Part 1: General Core. ISO/IEC 13211-1, 1995.

8. P. Van Roy and A. Despain. High-Performance Logic Programming with the Aquarius Prolog Compiler. IEEE Computer, pp 54-67, 1992.

9. D. H. D. Warren. An Abstract Prolog Instruction Set. Technical Report 309, SRI International, Oct. 1983.

Heap Garbage Collection in XSB:
Practice and Experience

Bart Demoen[1] and Konstantinos Sagonas[2]

[1] Department of Computer Science, K.U. Leuven, Belgium
bmd@cs.kuleuven.ac.be
[2] Computing Science Department, Uppsala University, Sweden
kostis@csd.uu.se

Abstract. Starting from a theoretical understanding of the usefulness logic of a logic programming system with built-in tabling, and from a collector that did not take the characteristics of a tabled abstract machine into account we have build two heap garbage collectors (one mark&slide, one mark&copy) for XSB on top of the CHAT implementation model for the suspension/resumption of consumers. Based on this experience we discuss implementation issues that are general to heap garbage collection for the WAM and also issues that are specific to an implementation with tabling: as such, this paper documents our own implementation and can serve as guidance for anyone attempting a similar feat. We report on the behaviour of the garbage collectors on different kinds of programs. We also present figures on the extent of internal fragmentation and the effectiveness of early reset in Prolog systems with and without tabling.

1   Introduction

In September 1996, we started developing a heap garbage collector for XSB. A mark&slide collector was written, closely following previous experience (see also [1]): it worked as long as tabling was not used. When trying to extend it for tabled programs, we failed to understand the *usefulness logic* (see [2]) of tabling systems. In particular, we could not get a grasp on *early reset* (also known as *virtual backtracking*; see e.g. [12, 2]) in the context of suspended computations. At that point we could have decided to make the garbage collector more conservative — i.e. leave out early reset and just consider everything pointer reachable as useful. This would have been completely acceptable from an engineering perspective but appeared to us very unsatisfactory from a scientific point of view. So we abandoned the work on the garbage collector and concentrated (more than a year later) on alternative ways for implementing suspension/resumption of consumers. This resulted in the 'Copying Approach to Tabling' (abbrv. CAT [7]): this implementation schema lead directly to a better understanding of the usefulness logic of logic programming systems with tabling (see [8]). Armed with this theoretical understanding we resumed work on a more accurate garbage collector in August 1998, finishing the sliding collector and at the same time implementing a copying collector as well: the copying collector uses the same marking phase as

E. Pontelli, V. Santos Costa (Eds.): PADL 2000, LNCS 1753, pp. 93–108, 2000.
© Springer-Verlag Berlin Heidelberg 2000

the sliding one (see [3] for why a copying collector in the WAM needs a marking phase) so it was relatively little additional work. Still, we struggled a lot with technical details and misunderstandings of the invariants of the tabling run time data structures. We finally integrated our garbage collectors in the XSB system in February 1999 and since June 1999 they are part of the XSB release.

This paper reports issues that came up, real problems that occurred, their solutions, decisions we took and why. These are the contents of Sections 3 and 4. Some of these issues may seem trivial (especially in retrospect) but most of them were learned the hard way, i.e. by debugging. We thus think that our experience on the practical aspects of building a garbage collector is of interest and use to other declarative programming language implementors and may even serve as a warning to anyone attempting to write a garbage collector for a system that was not designed to have one, and even more to anyone designing a system without thinking about its proper memory management. We include some performance figures about our collectors in Section 5. Finally, Section 6 discusses memory fragmentation both with and without early reset: to the best of our knowledge, figures related to these issues have never before been published for any Prolog system — let alone a tabled one — and as such they are of independent interest. We start by briefly reviewing the internals of tabled abstract machines.

2   Memory Organization in Tabled Abstract Machines

The implementation of tabling on top of the WAM [19] is complicated by the inherent asynchrony of answer generation and consumption, or in other words the support for a *suspension/resumption* mechanism that tabling requires. The need to suspend and resume computations is a main issue in a tabling implementation because some tabled subgoals, called *generators*, use program clauses to generate answers that go into the tables, while other subgoals, called *consumers*, resolve against the answers from the tables that generators fill. As soon as a generator depends on a consumer, the consumer must be able to suspend and work in a coroutining fashion with the generator, something that is not readily possible in the WAM because it reclaims space on backtracking. In short, in a tabled implementation, the execution environments of suspended computations must somehow be preserved and reinstated. By now, several alternatives for suspension/resumption exist: either by totally sharing the execution environments by interspersing them in the WAM stacks (as in the SLG-WAM [14]), or by a total copying approach (as in CAT [7]), or by a hybrid approach (as in CHAT [9]). In this paper, we stick to a CHAT implementation, and refer the interested reader to the above references for differences between these abstract machines [1].

Independently of the implementation model chosen for the suspension/resumption mechanism, tabling calls for sophisticated memory management. Indeed, tabling systems have inherently more complex memory models and their space requirements are different from (usually bigger than) those of plain Prolog systems. As advocated in e.g. [2], the accuracy of memory management is not related

---

[1] All relevant papers are accessible at http://www.csd.uu.se/~kostis/Papers/.

to the underlying abstract machine or the garbage collection technique; instead it is related to the *usefulness logic* of the run-time system: an abstraction of the operational semantics of the language, or in other words the ability to decide which objects are useful and which are garbage. In [8], we have described the usefulness logic of Prolog systems with tabling and how operations such as early reset can in principle be implemented with equal accuracy in an SLG-WAM or in a CAT-based abstract machine. As our aim is to discuss garbage collection issues in the context of tabled execution of logic programs, we only review information from [8, 9] which is necessary to make this paper reasonably self-contained.

We concentrate on the following typical scenario: The memory management policy has decided that the heap better be garbage collected. The garbage collection process then consists of 1) finding the set of useful data in the heap, and 2) move it appropriately while adapting all pointers to it. The second point is a matter of choosing an appropriate collection algorithm: we have written a sliding collector based on Morris' algorithm [11] and one based on the copying algorithm of Cheney [5]. In the context of Prolog, both need a marking phase and that is precisely the issue of the first point: how to approximate the usefulness of data.

Fig. 1 shows a rough picture[2] of a complete snapshot of the memory areas of a CHAT implementation. The left part of the picture, identified as 'Prolog', shows the usual WAM areas in an implementation that stores environments and choice points separately, such as in SICStus or in XSB; besides this, the only difference with the WAM is that the choice point stack contains possibly more than one kind of choice points: regular WAM ones, P_1, P_2, P_3 for executing non-tabled predicates, choice points for tabled generators, G_1, G_2, and choice points of consumers, C_1. The 'Prolog' part reduces to *exactly* the WAM if no tabled execution has occurred; in particular, the trail here is the WAM trail. The right part of the picture, identified as 'Tabling', shows areas that CHAT adds when tabled execution takes place. The picture shows all memory areas that can possibly point to the heap; areas that remain unaffected by garbage collection such as the Table Space are not of interest here and are thus shown as a black box. For the 'Prolog' part, garbage collection techniques are standard and well-described in the literature; see e.g. [1, 3, 6]. We concentrate on the memory areas of the 'Tabling' part and the choice point stack that differs from the WAM.

As the memory snapshot shows, the evaluation involved consumers, some of which, e.g. $C_2, C_3, \ldots$ are currently suspended (appear only in the CHAT area; see below) and some others, like C_1, have had their execution state reinstalled in the stacks and are part of the active computation. Complete knowledge of CHAT is not required; however, it is important to see how CHAT has arrived in this state and, more importantly, how execution might continue after collection. We thus describe the actions and memory organization of a CHAT-based abstract machine viewed from a heap garbage collection perspective.

---

[2] In figures, relative size of memory areas is not significant. All stacks grow downwards.

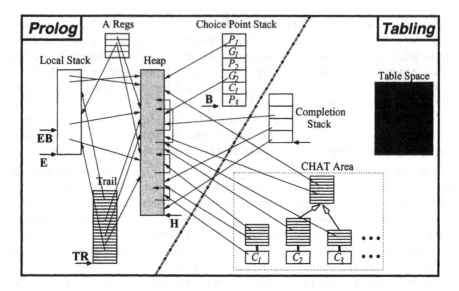

Fig. 1. Memory snapshot of a CHAT-based abstract machine when GC is triggered.

Choice points & Completion stack CHAT, much like the WAM, uses the choice point stack as a scheduling stack: the youngest choice point determines the action to be performed upon failure. A Prolog choice point, P, is popped off the stack when the last program clause of the associated goal is triggered. A generator choice point, G, is always created for a new tabled subgoal and behaves as a Prolog choice point with the following exception: before being popped off the stack, G must resume all consumers with unresolved answers that have their execution state protected by G (as explained below). Only when no more such consumers exist, is G popped off the stack. As far as the choice point stack and the heap are concerned, resumption of a consumer means: 1) re-installation of the consumer choice point C immediately below G and 2) setting $C[H]$ — the H field of C — to $G[H]$ so that C does not reclaim any heap that G protects (e.g. in Fig. 2, G_2 and C_1 protect the same heap: from the top till the dotted line). Finally, a consumer choice point C is pushed onto the stack either when the consumer is reinstalled by a generator, or the first time that the consumer is encountered. The consumer is popped off the stack and gets suspended whenever it has resolved against all answers currently in the table. Besides the H fields of choice points, pointers from the choice point stack to the heap exist in the argument registers stored in choice points used for program clause resolution (the darker areas above G's and P's in Fig. 2).

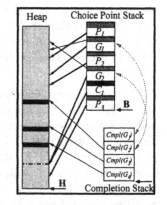

Fig. 2. Detail of choice point & completion stack.

The implementation of tabling becomes more complicated when there exist mutual dependencies between subgoals. The execution environments of the associated generators, $G_1, \ldots, G_n$, which reside in the WAM stacks need to be preserved until all answers for these subgoals have been derived. Furthermore, memory reclamation upon backtracking out of a generator choice point G_i cannot happen as in the WAM; trail and choice point stack can be reclaimed but e.g. the heap cannot: $G_i[H]$ may be protecting heap space of still suspended computations; not just its own heap. To determine whether space reclamation can be performed, subgoal dependencies have to be taken into account. The latter is the purpose of the *Completion Stack*. In Fig. 2, the situation depicted is as follows: subgoals associated with generators G_3 and G_4 cannot be completed independently of that of G_2. G_3 and G_4 have exhausted program clause resolution and the portion of the choice point associated with this operation can be reclaimed; however, there is information about G_3 and G_4 that needs to survive backtracking and this information has been preserved in the completion stack. In other words, generators consist of two parts: one in the choice point stack and one in the completion stack; for G_1 and G_2 that are still in the choice point stack the association between these parts is shown by dotted lines in Fig. 2.

Substitution factors Subgoals and their answers usually share some subterms. For each subgoal only the substitutions of its variables need to be stored in the table to reconstruct its answers. XSB implements this optimization through an operation called *substitution factoring*. On encountering a generator G, the dereferenced variables of the subgoal (found in the argument registers of G) are stored in a substitution factor record SF. For generators, CHAT stores substitution factor records on the heap. The reason: SF is conceptually part of the environment as it needs to be accessed at the 'return' point of each tabled clause (i.e. when a new answer is potentially derived and inserted in the table). Thus, SF needs to be accessible from a part of G that survives backtracking: in CHAT a cell of each completion stack frame points to SF; for consumers the substitution factor can be part of the consumer choice point as described in [13]; see Fig. 2.

CHAT area The first time that a consumer gets suspended, CHAT protects its execution state as follows: a *CHAT freeze* mechanism gets invoked which modifies H and EB fields in some choice points in a way that ensures that parts of the heap and local stack that the consumer might need for its proper resumption are not reclaimed on backtracking (see [9] for further explanation). As it is not possible to protect the consumer choice point C and the trail needed for resumption of the consumer using the same mechanism, these areas are saved using copying to the *CHAT area*. The copying of C (together with its SF record) is immediate, while the relevant entries of the trail (and their values in the heap and local stack) that C requires for

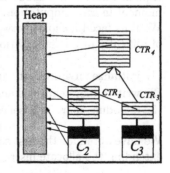

Fig. 3. CHAT area detail.

its resumption are copied incrementally. In this way, trail portions common to a set of consumers are shared between them. For example, consumers C_2 and C_3 in Fig. 3 share the CHAT trail area CTR_4 while they each also have a private part of trail. The same figure shows which are the pointers from the CHAT sub-areas to the heap that need to be followed for marking and possible relocation: they are the trail values of the CTR sub-areas, substitution factors of suspended consumers and the $C[D]$ field (the value of delay register as saved in each choice point; see [15]). The following things are important to note here: 1) the CHAT sub-areas are allocated dynamically and in non-contiguous space; how this influences garbage collection is described in Section 4.3, and 2) in CHAT, suspended computations have parts of their execution state saved in a private area while other parts are either shared or interspersed in the WAM stacks together with the state of the active computation.

3   Implementing Heap Garbage Collection: General Issues

We first discuss issues that are relevant to heap garbage collection in any WAM-based implementation: some or maybe all are folklore, but have not been published before as far as we know [3].

3.1   Dealing with Unitialized Environment Variables

The WAM does not need to initialize permanent variables (in the local stack) on allocation of an environment, because its instruction set is specialized for the first occurrence of a variable. On the other hand, some Prolog systems (e.g. SICStus; see also [4]) do initialize some permanent variables just for the sake of garbage collection. This makes the marking phase more precise; the alternative is a conservative marking schema which follows cautiously all heap pointers from an environment whether from an active permanent variable or not. Indeed, XSB, as most Prolog systems (with MasterProlog a notable exception), have no explicit information about which permanent variables are alive at a particular moment in the computation: this information is only implicit in the WAM code. We thus faced a choice between the following options, given in increasing order of difficulty of implementation:

1. initialize environment variables (e.g. to unbound or to an integer)
2. write a more cautious and conservative marking phase
3. introduce more preciseness about the liveness of permanent variables.

We have opted for the first solution because it was the quickest to implement by extending the allocate instruction: the extra cost is usually quite low.

---

[3] We would be glad to give credit to people who have originally noted similar things.

3.2   The Test for Heap Overflow

XSB, like many other logic programming systems, relies on software tests for overflow of all its stacks: heap overflow was checked on every increase of the **H** register. A more efficient way to check for overflow is at call ports, either by extending the call and execute instructions or by introducing a new instruction, test_heap, which the compiler generates as the entry point of every predicate. Its two arguments are: 1) the arity of the predicate which is needed for the garbage collection marking phase, and 2) the margin of heap that has to be available before proceeding: this margin depends on how much heap the predicate can maximally consume during the execution of its heads and first chunks.

For the first cut of the garbage collector, the XSB compiler was adapted so as to spit out the instruction test_heap with a fixed margin. A related change is needed in the implementation of built-in predicates: they should not commit any changes until they are sure to have enough heap space and if not, call the collector. Also, if built-in predicates that consume heap are inlined, a variant of the test_heap instruction might be needed in the body of clauses; marking needs to have access to the length of the current environment. A similar instruction is needed before inlined built-ins that create choice points. In XSB such an inlined built-in, called **negation_suspend**, was used for the implementation of tabled negation. As its inlining was not time critical, we have simply disabled it.

3.3   H Fields in Choice Points

In a plain Prolog garbage collector, after a segment of computation — starting from the E and CP fields of a choice point — has been marked, as well as the trail, the H field of the choice point can be treated. At that moment, the H field can point to a cell which was marked already and no further action is required. Otherwise, H points to a non-marked cell and then two ways of dealing with this situation are common practice: (1) mark the cell and fill it with an atomic object; (2) decrease the H field until it points to a marked cell. The first method is simple, has constant time cost, and can waste at most a number of heap entries equal to the number of active choice points. The second method wastes no space, but in the worst case adds a time cost to the garbage collection that is linear in the size of the heap. We prefer the first method and in our implementation used the tagged integer 666 as the atomic object. The correctness of this operation in plain WAM is based on the observation that the action if (!marked(B[H])) {*B[H] = tagged_int(666); mark(B[H]);} can be performed as soon as it is sure that *B[H] will not be marked later.

Note that the H fields in the consumer choice points in the CHAT area need not be considered during heap garbage collection: indeed, when the consumer is reinstalled, its choice point will get its H field from the scheduling generator. Following [8] the suspended computations are marked after the active computation. Since the substitution variables are *never* reachable from the active computation (only from the frames in the completion stack), in a CHAT garbage collector the above action needs to be postponed until after the substitution variables are marked. Instead of trying to find the earliest possible moment to perform the action, we have opted for postponing it until the very end of the marking, i.e. to perform it after all other marking has been finished.

3.4 Trail Compaction during Garbage Collection

Trail compaction is possible whenever early reset is performed (cf. Section 4.1). When trail compaction is omitted, one must ensure that trail cells that could have been removed point to something "reasonable". One can reserve a particular cell on the start of the heap for this purpose; i.e. all trail entries that are subject to early reset can be made to point to this heap cell [4]. Since reserving such a cell would involve changes elsewhere in XSB, we have chosen to mark the cell that was reset; i.e. consider it as non-garbage. Although this diminishes somewhat the effect of early reset in the actual implementation, it has no influence on the results of Section 6 as in our measurements we counted these cells as garbage.

3.5 Chain Bits for Dynamically Allocated Root Pointers

The XSB cell representation in one machine word cannot cater for the extra bits needed by the garbage collector. In particular, in the mark&slide collector we were faced with the problem where to store the chain bit for the root pointers: as long as these are in easily recognizable and contiguous areas — like the WAM stacks — one can allocate a parallel bit array and the translation from a root pointer to its corresponding bit is straightforward. For small sets of root pointers, just copying them to the top of the heap (as is the treatment of e.g. the argument registers) is also a good solution, but for a large number of root pointers that are not necessarily in a contiguous area, the solution must be more generic. In CHAT we encounter such a situation as the CHAT trail chunks are allocated dynamically. Section 4.3 discusses in more detail how we dealt with this issue.

3.6 The Copying Collector

The copying collector was implemented following ideas of [3]. We deviate slightly from the usual two-space schema of Cheney [5], since after the marking phase we know exactly how large the *to*-space needs to be to hold the copy so we allocate at that moment just this amount. After having copied the non-garbage to the *to*-space, we copy it as a block back to the original *from*-space and release the allocated *to*-space. This has a principled reason: this scheme uses memory resources more economically because usually, the *to*-space can be quite a bit smaller than the *from*-space. It has however also a pragmatic reason: in the current memory model of XSB, the heap and local stack are allocated contiguously and are growing towards each-other; putting the heap in another region that is not just above the local stack would break some invariants of XSB. Copying back the *to*-space to the original heap has low cost, as was observed already in [6].

---

[4] This trick seems folklore and was once described in comp.lang.prolog by R.A. O'Keefe.

4   Tabling-Specific Issues of Heap Garbage Collection

The usefulness logic of tabled evaluation [8] dictates that both the current computation (together with its backtracking states) and the suspended computations in the CHAT area should be used as a *root set*. As argued in [8] for the SLG-WAM, one can perform the marking phase of garbage collection *without* reinstalling the execution states of the suspended computations on the stacks. The same reasoning applies to CHAT. Moreover, the marking phase of a suspended consumer C does not need to consider the part of the heap that is older than the generator G up to which C has its execution environment CHAT-protected, and neither any choice point between **B** (WAM top of choice point stack) register and G; see [8] on why this scheme is correct in an abstract machine that preserves consumer choice points by copying. It follows that multiple traversal of the same areas is not needed and that garbage collection can be implemented efficiently in the tabled abstract machines we consider here.

Armed with this theoretical understanding, we proceeded with the actual implementation of our garbage collectors only to stumble very quickly on technical issues the theory did not immediately cater for. The remaining part of this section presents these issues, together with their solutions as implemented. The first two issues are related to the order of marking the current and the suspended computations in the presence of early reset. The last two we encountered for the first time in the tabling context, but they are more general.

4.1   Performing Early Reset when Trail Chunks Are Shared

The idea of early reset in the WAM [12, 2] is that a trailed heap or local stack entry which is not reachable for the forward continuation of the active computation (but might be on backtracking) can be set to unbound during garbage collection. The situation is recognized during marking, and it is essential that the continuation is marked before the future alternatives. Early reset in the context of tabling is more complicated: the suspended computations must also be taken into account. [8] describes in detail why it is better to mark the consumers in the CHAT area *after* the marking of the current computation.

However, even the order of marking and performing early reset among suspended consumers matters ! In the WAM, the trail is segmented according to choice points and trail chunks are not shared: the trail is a stack, not a tree. As Fig. 3 shows, in CHAT trail entry chunks are possibly shared between more than one suspended consumer choice points. The same is true in both SLG-WAM and CAT. In such a situation it is wrong to treat suspended consumers separately, i.e. by marking and early resetting from one suspended consumer completely before the other. Instead, the correct treatment of suspended consumers consists in: for each C mark the reachable environments and heap; only *after* this operation is finished for each C mark and early reset the trail of C. This is because it is quite possible to have e.g. two suspended consumers which share some part of the trail (as in Fig. 3) and some trailed variable being reachable in the forward computation of one but not of the other.

4.2 Marking of Substitution Factors & from the Completion Stack

As mentioned, a substitution factor record contains the variables in the subgoal. These variables have to be accessed when a new answer is generated (i.e. at the return point of each clause) in order for the answer substitution to be inserted in the table. Without proper compiler support[5], it is quite easy for substitution factoring to become incompatible with the implementation of the garbage collector. Indeed, the compilation scheme for tabled predicates described in [14, 15] does not reflect the usefulness logic of tabled evaluations and the only alternative to changing it, is to impose strong restrictions on the order of marking. The following example illustrates the issue:

Consider the execution of a query ?- test. w.r.t. the tabled program given below. Here and in the sequel, we use the predicate gc_heap/0 to indicate the point in the computation where garbage collection is triggered. Then marking as performed by a Prolog garbage collector would consider the heap value of variable X as not useful. In a tabled abstract machine, the binding of X to [a] is trailed as tabled predicates always create a choice point (cf. [14]). In such a situation, a Prolog garbage collector would invoke early reset of X. This is correct, as in the usefulness logic of Prolog, X is not used in the forward continuation of the compu-

XSB program	XSB abstract code
test :- t(_).	tabletrysingle 1 ...
	allocate 2 2
:- table t/1.	getVn v2
t(X) :-	call 3 p/1
p(X),	call 3 gc_heap/0
gc_heap.	new_answer 1 r2
	deallocate
p([a]).	proceed

tation. However, note that the usefulness logic of tabled evaluation is different: X also appears in the substitution factor record and its binding needs to be accessed at the return point of the corresponding tabled clause. Otherwise, a wrong answer is inserted in the table. Dealing with this issue by looking at the code in the forward continuation is complicated by the fact that the XSB abstract code for t/1 (as shown above) was not designed to reflect the usefulness logic of tabling: the first argument of the new_answer instruction contains the arity of the procedure and the second a pointer to the subgoal frame in the table space; the substitution factor is accessed only indirectly (cf. [14]).

To overcome this particular problem compiler support is desirable but not strictly required: an alternative is to mark variables in the substitution factor records of all generators *before* marking anything from the active computation. In other words, marking in a CHAT implementation should start by considering as root set pointers to the heap from the completion stack — this is where CHAT keeps a pointer to the substitution factor record of generators (cf. [9] and Fig. 2). In this way, problems caused by this kind of premature early reset are avoided.

---

[5] As a general comment, usually garbage collection requires compiler support: cf. the missing initialization of local variables in the WAM and the story in this subsection.

4.3   A Chain Bit in Cells of the CHAT Area

As Fig. 3 shows, cells in the CHAT area can contain references to the heap. The CHAT areas however, are dynamically allocated and so it is natural to cater for the chain bits in the CHAT sub-areas themselves. We implement a sequence of N words that all need a chain bit, as a number of groups of $(S+1)$ words, where the first S are some of the N words and the $(S+1)^{th}$ word, contains the S chain bits — we actually use a byte for each chain bit. We make sure that each group of $(S+1)$ words is aligned on a $(S+1)$-boundary. S is chosen as `sizeof(Cell *)` that is the size of the pointer type used for cells of the WAM stacks. A pointer p to a CHAT object, can now be translated to a pointer to its chain byte as follows: let $i = ((((\text{int})p)/S)\%(S+1))$, then $pointer\_chain\_byte = (\text{char } *)(p+S-i)+i$.

5   Performance Evaluation

Putting our garbage collectors in perspective Prolog systems have usually opted for a sliding collector since traditionally the order of segments is considered important for cheap reclamation of heap on backtracking and for preserving the semantics of the @-family of compare built-ins. However, the ISO Prolog standard has removed the latter reason, and [3] and [6] argue in different ways against the former reason. So, after having implemented the sliding collector, we implemented a copying collector starting from the marking phase that is common for both collectors and following [3]. The fact that our copying collector is not segment-preserving, makes the interpretation of the results of tests that include backtracking not always clear cut. Few other Prolog systems have more than one garbage collector: [3] reports that Reform Prolog also had a copying and a sliding collector. BinProlog gave up its sliding collector in favor of copying. Touati and Hama report on a partially copying collector (for the most recent segment only) that is combined with a sliding collector: see [18]. In addition, XSB is currently the only system that has tabling implemented at the engine level. So, in tabled programs we can at most compare our collectors with each other and only for plain Prolog execution with collectors from other systems. An extensive comparison of a sliding and a copying collector in the context of a functional programming language can be found e.g. in [16] and its results carry over to Prolog; see also [3]. Two points are worth noting: accurate marking is the difficult part of both collectors and the copying phase is much easier to implement and maintain than the sliding phase. On the other hand, a copying collector may be more difficult to debug due to motion sickness: heap objects can change order.

Performance in programs without tabling We felt that there was no good reason to do lots of testing for programs without tabling as the relative merits of copying and sliding have been discussed in the literature at length. We just present one measurement that places our garbage collectors in context. The test program used (shown as part of Table 1) builds two lists that are interleaved on the heap [6]. Note that length of the second list is 1/10 the length of the first one. The two queries represent the following two situations: either most of the data survives garbage collection, or only a small fraction does. The Prolog systems were started with enough initial heap so that no collection occurred, except the explicitly invoked one. We measured the time (in milliseconds on an Intel 686, 266MHz running Linux) for performing the one garbage collection during the queries ?- q1. and ?- q2. In XSB this was done with the two collectors; in ProLog_by_BIM 4.1 (now named MasterProlog) and SICStus 3.7 using the sliding collector; in BinProlog 6.84 with its segment-preserving copying collector. Table 1 provides some evidence that the collectors of XSB are similar in performance to those of commercially available systems. It also shows that (in the absence of backtracking) copying is a reasonable alternative to sliding.

	gc-q1	gc-q2
XSB slide	1337	316
BIM slide	1270	430
SICStus slide	1426	434
XSB copy	890	126
BinProlog copy	974	214

```
mklists(0,L1,L2) :- !, L1 = [], L2 = [].
mklists(N,[1,2,3,4,5,6,7,8,9,0|R1],[1|R2]) :-
         M is N - 1, mklists(M,R1,R2).
q1 :- mklists(100000,L1,L2),gc_heap,use(L1,L2).
q2 :- mklists(100000,L1,L2),gc_heap,use(_,L2).
use(_,_).
```

Table 1. Performance of sliding and copying GC on an artificial Prolog program.

Performance in programs with tabling To get an idea of how our garbage collectors perform on programs with tabling, we took the programs from the benchmarks in [9] and gave them just enough heap and local stack so that expansion of these areas was not necessary: in all cases this meant that the garbage collection was called at least once. In Table 2, we indicate, for each test the -m option for XSB (-m13 allocates an area of 13000 cells of heap and local stack), the number of times garbage collection was called and the number of garbage cells reclaimed (both using copying and sliding), the time spent in garbage collection, and this time as a percentage of the total time for the benchmark. The runtime without garbage collection is given in the last row of the table. All times are again in milliseconds but this time on a Ultra Sparc 2 (168 MHz) under Solaris 5.6. We also note that in XSB a cell is represented using one machine word.

In all cases the sliding collector gets invoked less frequently than the non segment-preserving copying collector and collects less garbage. In some cases the sliding collector can spend less time than the copying collector. The reason for this last behavior could be that the effect of the loss of reclamation on backtracking can be much worse when tabling is used and several consumers have frozen the heap than when using plain Prolog code. However, this effect is not uniformly visible in the tested programs. Also, in a backtracking system, a copying collector can be called arbitrarily more often than a sliding collector. On the other hand, note that because most data remains useful (this can be deduced

---

[6] The particular form of mklists/3 was chosen so as not to disadvantage BinProlog because of its binarization.

	cs_o	cs_r	disj_o	gabriel	kalah_o	peep	pg	read_o
−m	11	12	11	15	17	110	39	187
copying GC #	183	107	10	77	17	11	8	4
cells collected	43951	33100	4113	18810	9680	13519	8802	14462
GC time	90	77	0	77	21	800	179	439
% GC time	29	16	0	34	15	67	64	44
sliding GC #	86	57	3	40	5	8	5	2
cells collected	12143	11644	1050	16332	5265	12288	8138	13584
GC time	66	62	0	150	22	1319	129	410
% GC time	23	13	0	50	15	77	56	42
runtime (no GC)	219	400	130	151	121	400	100	560

Table 2. Performance of sliding and copying GC on a set of benchmarks with tabling.

from the low figures of collected garbage) the copying collector is disadvantaged in this benchmark set. A generational schema can in all cases improve the figures.

6 Measuring Fragmentation & Effectiveness of Early Reset

Prolog implementors have paid little attention to the concept of internal fragmentation: as far as we know, measurements of internal fragmentation have never been published before for any Prolog system. Still this notion is quite important, as it gives a measure on how effectively the total occupied space is used by the memory allocator, and in the memory management community it is a recurring topic (see e.g. [10]). It is also surprising that although early reset is generally implemented in Prolog garbage collectors, its effectiveness has not been reported in the literature with [17] being a notable exception. We will combine both measurements. Once one has a collector, these figures can in principle be obtained quite easily. It is important to realise that the results tell something about the memory allocator, not about the collector !

According to [10], internal fragmentation can be expressed in several possible ways. To us, the most informative seems the one that compares the maximal space required by the allocator (i.e. the minimal heap size required if no garbage collection were present) with the minimal amount of dead memory during the running of the program. In contrast to [10], we prefer to express fragmentation as the ratio of these quantities: it represents the percentage of wasted memory. E.g. a fragmentation of 75% means that without garbage collection the allocator uses four times more heap space than minimally needed to run the program.

To this effect, we have conducted two experiments: one using a set of typical Prolog benchmarks and another using the same set of tabled programs as before (as well as tboyer: a tabled version of the boyer program). To measure fragmentation reasonably accurately, we have forced the marking phase to be invoked every 100 predicate calls. At each such moment, the number of marked (useful) cells is recorded. Garbage is not collected at these moments. After the run, the two quantities above are computed and their ratio is reported in Tables 3 and 4 with and without performing early reset. Additionally, the tables contain the number of times there was an opportunity for early resetting a cell, the number of predicate calls (in K) and the maximum heap usage (in K cells). Note that one early reset operation can result in more than one cell becoming garbage.

fragmentation	boyer	browse	chat_parser	reduce	simple_analyser	zebra
with early reset	61.2	46.4	11.7	91.17	49.9	41.9
without early reset	61.2	46.3	6.4	91.15	47.9	16.5
# early resets	6	9	64	7	60	38
predicate calls (K)	865	599	74	30	16	14
maximum heap (K)	144	11	1	20	5	0.2

Table 3. Fragmentation in a set of Prolog programs with and without early reset

In most cases, the figures show a surprisingly high fragmentation: remember that the fragmentation gives an upper limit for the amount of *avoidable* waste given a perfect allocator. The fragmentation would be even higher if XSB would trim its environments and have a more sophisticated determinism detection.

The fragmentation with early reset is higher than without, because when performing early reset fewer cells are marked as useful. The effect of early reset can of course be very much dependent on the characteristics of a program, but given the range of programs here, it seems safe to conclude that one should not expect more than 10% gain in memory efficiency for most realistic programs. We also note that the experience reported in [17] is similar. On the other hand, the cost of early reset is extremely small: the test whether a trail cell points to a marked heap cell happens anyway, and the extra cost consists in resetting the (unmarked) heap cell and redirecting the trail entry. So it appears that early reset is worth its while both in Prolog as well as in tabled execution.

7   Concluding Remarks

In this paper we bridged the usual gap between the theoretical understanding of a memory management principle and its actual implementation. We addressed

fragmentation	cs_o	cs_r	disj_o	gabriel	kalah_o	peep	pg	read_o	tboyer
with early reset	52.3	51.7	63.4	62.9	83.6	67.3	73.8	53.9	0.44
without early reset	41.4	41.1	57.4	58.3	77.7	65.9	69.8	53.4	0.15
# of early resets	21.5	19.2	12.9	18.9	31.8	40.0	124.6	49.1	123
predicate calls (K)	72	138	40	47	45	134	34	169	6.6
maximum heap	1.1	1.2	0.8	2.1	4.8	28	12	43	67

Table 4. Fragmentation in a set of programs with tabling with and without early reset

the practical aspects of heap garbage collection in Prolog systems with or without tabling and reported our experience and the main lessons learned from implementing two garbage collectors in XSB. Furthermore, we addressed methodological issues of implementing and benchmarking garbage collectors: this is only rarely reported in the literature. We hold that by making implementation choices concrete and documented — even those that are considered folklore — this paper can be of significant value to implementors that consider garbage collection in a system with tabling or in a system that is similar in certain respects.

It is the case that relatively little has been published on garbage collection in logic programming systems. The WAM — on which many logic programming systems are based — has the reputation of being very memory efficient; still, it provides no support (in the instruction set for instance) for doing precise garbage collection. Also, the WAM has a fixed allocation schema for data structures (allocation on the top of the heap), about which there is relatively little empirical knowledge: the figures we presented show a high fragmentation and thus suggest that the WAM is not particularly good at using the heap very efficiently. Finally, most often people have been interested almost solely in the efficiency of *garbage collection-less* execution. Consequently, implementors have not been inclined to give up some efficiency for better memory management and some Prolog systems have even lived for quite a while without garbage collection at all. For sure research in logic programming implementation has not focussed on considering alternative memory management schemas, neither on *accurate* identification of useful data. This contrasts sharply with the attention that the functional programming community has given to memory management. Similarly to the story of fragmentation about which there seem no figures available in literature, no one has hard data on the effectiveness of early reset: our admittedly small set of benchmarks indicates how effective one can expect it to be in realistic programs. It is clear that a continuous follow-up on such issues is needed as new allocation schemas and extensions of the WAM emerge: such new allocation schemas will be the subject of our future research. More directly practical, we will also investigate incremental and generational variants of the current collectors in the XSB system.

Acknowledgements

We are grateful to members of the XSB implementation team for helping us understand code they designed or wrote ages ago: in particular, we thank David S. Warren, Terrance Swift, and Prasad Rao. The second author was supported by a K.U. Leuven fellowship.

References

[1] K. Appleby, M. Carlsson, S. Haridi, and D. Sahlin. Garbage collection for Prolog based on WAM. *Communications of the ACM*, 31(6):719–741, June 1988.

[2] Y. Bekkers, O. Ridoux, and L. Ungaro. Dynamic memory management for sequential logic programming languages. In *IWMM'92: International Workshop on Memory Management*, number 637 in LNCS, pages 82–102, Sept. 1992. Springer.

[3] J. Bevemyr and T. Lindgren. A simple and efficient copying garbage collector for prolog. In M. Hermenegildo and J. Penjam, editors, *Proceedings of the 6th PLILP*, number 844 in LNCS, pages 88–101, Madrid, Spain, Sept. 1994. Springer-Verlag.

[4] M. Carlsson. *Design and Implementation of an Or-Parallel Prolog Engine*. PhD thesis, The Royal Institute of Technology (KTH), Stokholm, Sweden, Mar. 1990.

[5] C. J. Cheney. A nonrecursive list compacting algorithm. *Communications of the ACM*, 13(11):677–678, Nov. 1970.

[6] B. Demoen, G. Engels, and P. Tarau. Segment preserving copying garbage collection for WAM based Prolog. In *Proceedings of the 1996 ACM Symposium on Applied Computing*, pages 380–386, Philadelphia, Feb. 1996. ACM Press.

[7] B. Demoen and K. Sagonas. CAT: the Copying Approach to Tabling. In C. Palamidessi, H. Glaser, and K. Meinke, editors, *Principles of Declarative Programming*, number 1490 in LNCS, pages 21–35, Pisa, Italy, Sept. 1998. Springer.

[8] B. Demoen and K. Sagonas. Memory management for Prolog with tabling. In *Proceedings of ISMM'98: ACM SIGPLAN International Symposium on Memory Management*, pages 97–106, Vancouver, B.C., Canada, Oct. 1998. ACM Press.

[9] B. Demoen and K. Sagonas. CHAT: the Copy-Hybrid Approach to Tabling. In G. Gupta, editor, *Practical Aspects of Declarative Languages (PADL)*, number 1551 in LNCS, pages 106–121, San Antonio, Texas, Jan. 1999. Springer.

[10] M. S. Johnstone and P. R. Wilson. The memory fragmentation problem: Solved? In *Proceedings of ISMM'98: ACM SIGPLAN International Symposium on Memory Management*, pages 26–36, Vancouver, B.C., Canada, Oct. 1998. ACM Press.

[11] F. L. Morris. A time- and space-efficient garbage compaction algorithm. *Communications of the ACM*, 21(8):662–665, Aug. 1978.

[12] E. Pittomvils, M. Bruynooghe, and Y. D. Willems. Towards a real time garbage collector for Prolog. In *Proceedings of Symp. on Logic Progr.*, pages 185–198, 1985.

[13] I. V. Ramakrishnan, P. Rao, K. Sagonas, T. Swift, and D. S. Warren. Efficient access mechanisms for tabled logic programs. *J. of Logic Progr.*, 38(1):31–54, 1999.

[14] K. Sagonas and T. Swift. An abstract machine for tabled execution of fixed-order stratified logic programs. *ACM Trans. Prog. Lang. Syst.*, 20(3):586–634, May 1998.

[15] K. Sagonas, T. Swift, and D. S. Warren. An abstract machine for computing the well-founded semantics. In *Proceedings of JICSLP'96*, pages 274–288, Sept. 1996.

[16] P.M. Sansom. Combining copying and compacting garbage collection or Dual-mode garbage collection. In *Functional Programming*, Glasgow, Aug. 1991. Springer.

[17] J. Schimpf. Garbage collection for Prolog based on twin cells. In *Proceedings of the 1990 NACLP Implementation Workshop*, pages 16–25, Austin, Texas, 1990.

[18] H. Touati and T. Hama. A light-weight Prolog garbage collector. In *Proceedings of FGCS'88*, pages 922–930, Tokyo, Japan, Nov./Dec. 1988. OHMSHA and Springer.

[19] D. H. D. Warren. An abstract Prolog instruction set. Technical Report 309, SRI International, Menlo Park, U.S.A., Oct. 1983.

Implementation of a Linear Tabling Mechanism

Neng-Fa Zhou[1], Yi-Dong Shen[2], Li-Yan Yuan[3], and Jia-Huai You[3]

[1] Department of Computer and Information Science, Brooklyn College
The City University of New York
New York, NY 11210-2889, USA
zhou@sci.brooklyn.cuny.edu
[2] Department of Computer Science, Chongqing University,
Chongqing, 400044, P.R.China
ydshen@cqu.edu.cn
[3] Department of Computing Science, University of Alberta
Edmonton, Alberta, Canada T6G 2H1
{yuan,you}@cs.ualberta.ca

Abstract. Delaying-based tabling mechanisms, such as the one adopted in XSB, are non-linear in the sense that the computation state of delayed calls has to be preserved. In this paper, we present the implementation of a linear tabling mechanism. The key idea is to let a call execute from the backtracking point of a former variant call if such a call exists. The linear tabling mechanism has the following advantages over non-linear ones: (1) it is relatively easy to implement; (2) it imposes no overhead on standard Prolog programs; and (3) the cut operator works as for standard Prolog programs and thus it is possible to use the cut operator to express negation-as-failure and conditionals in tabled programs. The weakness of the linear mechanism is the necessity of *re-computation* for computing fix-points. However, we have found that re-computation can be avoided for a large portion of calls of directly-recursive tabled predicates. We have implemented the linear tabling mechanism in B-Prolog. Experimental comparison shows that B-Prolog is close in speed to XSB and outperforms XSB when re-computation can be avoided. Concerning space efficiency, B-Prolog is an order of magnitude better than XSB for some programs.

1 Introduction

Tabling [11,13] in Prolog is a technique that can get rid of infinite loops for bounded-term-size programs and possible redundant computations in the execution of Prolog programs. The main idea of tabling is to memorize the answers to some calls and use the answers to resolve subsequent variant calls. Tabling has found useful in many applications including program analysis, parsing, deductive databases, theorem proving, model checking, and problem solving [13]. It is not impossible to do tabling on top of Prolog [5]. Doing so, however, is a burden to the programmers and can hardly achieve satisfactory performance. For this reason, it is mandatory that tabling be supported at the abstract machine level.

E. Pontelli, V. Santos Costa (Eds.): PADL 2000, LNCS 1753, pp. 109–123, 2000.

Currently, XSB is the only well-known Prolog system that supports tabling. The SLG [2] resolution adopted in XSB relies on the suspend/resume mechanism to do tabling. When a call (consumer), which is a variant of a former call (producer), has used up the results in the table, it will be suspended. After the producer adds answers to the table, the execution of the consumer will be resumed. In contrast to the *linear* SLD resolution [6] where a new goal is always generated by extending the latest goal, SLG resolution is *non-linear*. The non-linearity of the suspend/resume mechanism considerably complicates the implementation and the handling of the cut operator. In SLG-WAM [8], the abstract machine adopted by XSB, the state of a consumer is preserved by freezing the stacks, i.e., by not allowing backtracking to reclaim the space on the stacks as is done in the WAM [12]. CHAT [4] preserves the state by copying part of it to a separate area and copying it back when the execution of the consumer needs to be resumed. In XSB, tabled calls are not allowed to occur in the scope of a cut.

Shen et al [9] proposed a strictly linear tabulated resolution, called SLDT in this paper, for Prolog. The main idea is as follows: Each tabled call can be a producer and a consumer as well. When there are answers available in the table for the call, the call consumes the answers; otherwise, it, like a usual Prolog call, produces answers by using clauses until a call that is a variant of some former call occurs. In this case, the later call steals the choice point from the former call and turns to produce answers by using the remaining clauses of the former call. After a call produces an answer, it also consumes one. Answers in a table are used in a *first-generated-first-used* fashion. Backtracking is strictly chronological. The later call will be re-executed after all the available answers and clauses have been exhausted. Re-execution will stop when no new answer can be produced, i.e., when the fix-point is reached.

To implement SLDT, we have extended the ATOAM [14], the abstract machine of B-Prolog. The extension of the abstract machine is straightforward thanks to the linearity of SLDT . Since no modification of the existing instructions and data areas is required, programs that do not use tabling are not affected. The implementation will be described in Section 3. While re-computation is necessary in general, we show in Section 4 that it can be avoided for a class of tabled calls. Most calls of predicates in deductive databases, such as *transitive closure* and *same generation*, belong to this class.

We have implemented the linear-tabling mechanism in B-Prolog. For the CHAT benchmark suite [4] for which re-computation is necessary, B-Prolog is about 20% slower than XSB. Nevertheless, for another benchmark suite for which re-computation is avoidable, B-Prolog is faster than XSB. The experimental results will be presented in Section 5.

2   An Introduction to SLDT

In this section, we give a brief introduction to SLDT. The reader is referred to [9] for a formal description and a formal proof of the soundness and completeness of SLDT, and to [6] for definitions of SLD and related concepts.

Predicates in a tabled Prolog program are divided into *tabled* and *non-tabled* ones. Tabled predicates are explicitly declared by declarations in the following form:

$$\text{:-table } p_1/n_1, \ldots, p_k/n_k$$

where each p_i(i=1,...,k) is a predicate symbol and n_i is an integer that denotes the arity of p_i. A call of a tabled predicate is called a *tabled call*. Tabled calls are resolved by using SLDT, and non-tabled calls are resolved by using SLD. A tabled call that occurs first in an SLD tree is called a *pioneer*, and all subsequent calls that are variants of a pioneer are called *followers* of the pioneer. There is a table associated with every pioneer and its followers. Initially, the table is empty.

The SLDT resolution takes a tabled Prolog program and a goal, and constructs an SLD tree in the same left-to-right and depth-first fashion as the SLD resolution except when the selected call is a variant of some former call. In this case, we first use the answers in the table to resolve the call. After we exhaust all the answers, we resolve the call by using the remaining clauses of the latest former call. We say that the current call *steal* the choice point from the latest former call.

Backtracking is done similarly as in Prolog. When we backtrack to a tabled call, we use an alternative answer or a clause to resolve the call. After we exhaust all the answers and clauses, however, we cannot simply fail it since doing so we may risk loosing answers. Instead, we decide whether it is necessary to re-execute the call starting from the first clause of the predicate. Re-execution will be repeated until no new answers can be generated, *i.e.*, when the fix-point is reached.

In the following, we illustrate the behavior of SLDT using three examples.

Example 1

Consider resolving the query ?-reach(a,Y0) against the following tabled program:

```
:-table reach/2.
reach(X,Y):-reach(X,Z),edge(Z,Y).    (C1)
reach(X,X).                          (C2)
reach(X,d).                          (C3)

edge(a,b).                           (C4)
edge(d,e).                           (C5)
```

We first apply the clause C1 to the call reach(a,Y0) and obtain a new goal
N1: reach(a,Z1),edge(Z1,Y0) where the subscripts are added to indicate the
effects of variable renaming (see Figure 1). As the call reach(a,Z1) is a follower
of reach(a,Y0), we choose C2, the backtracking point of reach(a,Y0), and
apply it to reach(a,Z1), which results in a new child goal N2:edge(a,Y0). As
reach(a,a) is an answer to the call reach(a,Z1), it is memorized in the table
for reach(a,Y0). We then resolve the call edge(a,Y0) by using the clause C4,
which leads to an empty goal. So the answer reach(a,b) is added into the table
for reach(a,Y0). After these steps, we finish the leftmost branch of the tree as
shown in Figure 1.

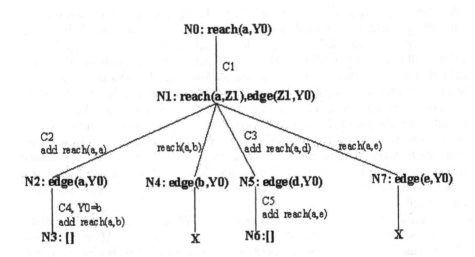

Fig. 1. The SLD tree for the example.

Now consider backtracking. We first backtrack to the call reach(a,Z1) at
node N1. This call has consumed reach(a,a) in the table. So, we use the next
answer reach(a,b) to resolve it, which derive the goal to N4:edge(b,Y0). Obviously, this goal will fail. So, we backtrack to the call reach(a,Z1) again. This
time, as all answers in the table have been used, we use C3 to resolve the call and
obtain a new answer reach(a,d), which is added to the table. After this step,
the goal becomes N5:edge(d,Y0). By using C5 to resolve the call, we obtain
another new answer reach(a,e), which is added into the table. The goal now
becomes empty, and the second answer reach(a,b) is returned to the top-level
goal.

When more answers are required, we backtrack again to the call reach(a,Z1)
at node N1. At this time, there is only one answer, reach(a,e), remaining for
the call. By using the answer to resolve the call, we obtain a goal N7:edge(e,Y0)
which will fail immediately. By now, reach(a,Z1) has consumed all the answers

and executed all the clauses. We re-execute the call but fail to produce any new answers. So, we fail it and backtrack to the pioneer reach(a,Y0), which will consume the two remaining answers: reach(a,d) and reach(a,e).

Example 2

In the previous example, re-computation produces no new answers. This example illustrates the necessity of re-computation. Consider the query ?-p(X0,Y0) against the following program [9]:

```
:-table p/2.
p(X,Y):-q(X,Y).

q(X,Y):-p(X,Z),t(Z,Y).
q(a,b).

t(b,c).
```

There are two answers, namely, p(a,b) and p(a,c), to the query. Without re-computation, the second answer p(a,c) would be lost.

Example 3

Before a call steals the choice point (call it C1) from a former variant call, the former call might have created some other choice points (call them C2) which locate to the left of C1 in the SLD tree[1]. If this is the case, the order of solutions will differ from that found by SLD resolution since C1 will be explored before C2. Consider the query ?-p(X),p(Y) against the following program:

```
:-table p/1.
p(V):-t(V).
p(c).

t(a).
t(b).
```

First, we use the clause p(V):-t(V) to rewrite the subgoal p(X) to t(X), and the fact t(a) to resolve the subgoal and bind X to a. Then, we turn to execute p(Y). Since p(Y) is a variant of p(X), the choice point of p(X) is stolen by p(Y). We use the first answer in the table, i.e., p(a), to resolve p(Y). At this point, we get the first answer (X=a,Y=a). To obtain the next answer, we backtrack to p(Y). Since there is no answer remaining, we use the clause p(c), which lead to the second solution (X=a,Y=c). Note that if SLD resolution is used, the second answer obtained will be (X=a,Y=b).

---

[1] To say it more precisely, the corresponding branches of C2 locate to the left of the corresponding branches of C1 in the SLD tree.

The order issue would not happen if we only allowed a call to steal a choice point from one of its ancestors. To do so, however, we have to check the ancestor/descendant relationship between two variant calls, which is expensive. It is acceptable in practice to avoid this test because fix-points are usually required for tabled predicates and thus the order of answers is not important.

3   Extending the ATOAM for Tabling

In the ATOAM [14], unlike in the WAM, arguments are passed through stack frames and only one frame is used for each predicate call. Frames for different types of predicates have different structures. Currently, predicates are classified into the following types: *flat*, *nonflat*, *nondeterminate*, and *delayed* [14].

To implement SLDT, we introduce a new data area, called *table area*, for memorizing tabled calls and their answers, a new frame structure for tabled calls, and several new instructions for encoding the basic operations on tabled calls and the table area. We illustrate the instructions by examples. The reader is referred to the Appendix for their complete definitions.

3.1   The Table Area

For each pioneer and its followers, there is an entry in the *subgoal table* that contains the following four fields:

Call: the predicate symbol and the arguments of the call.
AR: the pointer to the frame of the latest variant call.
Answers: list of available answers
Revised: whether or not new answers have been added

The subgoal table is a hashing table that uses Call as the key. The AR field points to the frame of the latest variant call. It may take either of the following two values if it is not a pointer to a frame:

NULL: the corresponding frame has been cut off by a cut
COMPLETE: the frame has been discarded after completion

For a follower call, if the AR field of its table entry is NULL, then the call will have no choice point to steal from and the execution will start from the beginning of the predicate. If the AR field is COMPLETE, then all the answers of the call must have been produced in the table and thus no clause in the predicate need be executed.

The Answers field, which is called the *answer table* for the variant calls, stores the list of answers that are currently available for the calls. The answer table is also a hashing table, but the order of answers is preserved. The Revised is used to check whether or not re-computation needs to be continued. It is set to be **false** whenever the tabled predicate is executed or re-executed, and set to be **true** whenever an answer is added into the answer table. After the execution of the tabled predicate, Revised is checked. If it is **true**, then the predicate needs to be re-executed; otherwise, not.

3.2   Frames for Tabled Calls

The frame for a tabled call contains the following three slots in addition to the arguments, a copy of the arguments and the information stored in a choice point frame[2]:

Table	pointer to the table entry for the call
CurrA	pointer to the answer that has just
Pioneer	Pointer to the frame of the pioneer

If the tabled call is a pioneer, then an entry is added into the table , the Table slot of its frame is made to point to the entry, and the Pioneer slot is made to point to itself. If the call is a follower for which there is already an entry in the subgoal table, then the Table slot is made to point to the entry and the Pioneer slot is made to point to the frame of the pioneer. The first answer in an answer table is a dummy answer and CurrA is initialized to be a pointer to this dummy answer.

3.3   New Instructions

There are four newly introduced instructions for tabled programs without cuts. The following example illustrates their meanings and how they are used.

```
:-table p/2.
p(X,Y):-q(X,Y).
```

The generated code is as follows:

```
      table_allocate 2,13,p/2,L2
  L1: table_use_answer
      fork L2
      para_value y1
      para_value y2
      call q/2
      table_add_use_answer
  L2: table_use_answer
      table_check_completion L1
```

where the instructions starting with table_ are new. A new clause, called *completion-checking clause*, is added into the predicate. The two instructions at L2 encode this clause.

---

[2] A choice point frame has the following slots: AR (parent frame), CP (continuation program point), TOP (top of the control stack), B (parent choice point), CPF (backtracking point), H (top of the heap), and T (top of the trail stack).

table_allocate 2, 13, p/2, L2 The instruction `table_allocate` is the first instruction in a tabled predicate. The operands are as follows: 2 is the arity, 13 is the size of the frame, p/2 is the predicate symbol, and L2 is the address to go to after all the clauses have been tried. For each call to the predicate, this instruction copies the arguments and allocates a frame for the call. Besides bookkeeping operations needed for backtracking, this instruction also does the following:

- If the call is a pioneer, then create an entry in the table, let the `Table` slot of the frame point to the table entry, and let the `AR` field in the table entry point to the frame. The backtracking point `CPF` of the frame is set to point to the next instruction.
- If the call is a follower for which that there is already an entry in the subgoal table, then let the `Table` slot of the frame point to the table entry and take the following different actions according to the `AR` field in the table entry.
  - If the `AR` field is `NULL`, meaning that its frame has been discarded by a cut operator (see below), then treat the call as a pioneer, letting the `AR` field point to the current frame.
  - If the `AR` field is `COMPLETE`, meaning that all the answers have been produced for the call, then jump to L2 and let the call consume the answers.
  - If the `AR` field points to a frame which must be the frame of the latest variant call, then we execute from the backtracking point stored in the frame and reset the backtracking point to be L2. This operation is what we call *stealing a choice point*.

table_use_answer The `table_use_answer` instruction tries to use the next answer. If there are answers available, it unifies the original arguments of the call with the next answer and returns control to the continuation program point; otherwise, it does nothing before turning to execute the clause following the instruction.

The `fork L2` instruction resets the backtracking point `CPF` to be L2. So, q/2 will not be executed on the next backtracking. The next three instructions following `fork L2` passes the arguments to the callee and starts the execution of q/2.

table_add_use_answer The `table_add_use_answer` instruction adds the current call into the answer table if the call is not yet there and tries to use the next answer. If there is an answer in the table, then it does the same thing as `table_use_answer`, returning the answer to the caller. Otherwise, if no answer is available, then it triggers backtracking. Note that this situation is possible since the answer being added may have been in the table and may have already been consumed by the call.

table_check_completion L1 As we mentioned above, L2 is the address to go to after all the clauses have been executed. The **table_use_answer** instruction at L2 returns all remaining answers. After that, the **table_check_completion L1** instruction determines whether or not the current predicate need be re-executed. If the AR field in the table entry for the call is COMPLETE, then discard the current frame and fail; if there was some new answers added into the table during the last round of execution, then re-execute the predicate starting from L1; otherwise, if no new answer was added into the table during the last round of execution, then set the AR field to be COMPLETE, discard the current frame, and fail.

3.4   Cut

The cut operator '!' in SLDT behaves in strictly the same way as that in the SLD resolution. Consider a cut in the clause

        H:-L,!,R.

The cut ! discards the choice points created for H and L. With tabling, however, we cannot just discard the choice points. We have also to cut the connection between the tabled calls in L and their table entries by properly updating the AR fields in the table entries. Otherwise, the AR fields in some table entries may become dangling pointers pointing to frames that no longer exist. We handle the cut in three different ways depending on the context in which the cut appears:

- If H and all those called (directly or indirectly) by L are non-tabled, then we just treat the cut as a cut in a standard program, letting it discard the choice points created for H and L.
- If H is not tabled but there is at least one tabled predicate call in L, then we let the cut discard the choice points and cut the relationship between the tabled calls and their table entries by resetting the AR fields in the entries to be NULL. We introduce a new instruction, called **table_cut_outside**, to encode this type of cuts, where **outside** means that the cut does not reside in a tabled predicate.
- If H is tabled predicate, then we let the cut discard the choice points created by L, cut the relationship between the tabled calls and their table entries, and set the backtracking point to be the address of the completion-checking clause. So, when the calls to the right of the cut fail, the **table_use_answer** and **table_check_completion** instructions will be executed. We introduce another new instruction, called **table_cut_inside**, to encode this type of cuts, where **inside** means that the cut resides in a tabled predicate.

After the AR field in a subgoal table entry becomes NULL, the next variant call will be treated as a pioneer (see the **table_allocate** instruction).

Consider, as an example, a cut that does not reside in a tabled predicate but has tabled calls in its scope:

```
:- table q/1.
p(X,Y):-q(X),!,q(Y).
q(Z):-q(Z).
q(a).
q(b).
```

The call q(X) produces one answer, namely q(a), and binds X to a. After that, the cut discards the choice point for q(X) and disconnects q(X) and its table entry by setting the AR field of the entry to be NULL. Because the relationship was cut off, q(Y) will be executed like a pioneer. The answers returned to the query ?-p(X,Y) will be p(a,a) and p(a,b).

Consider, as another example, a cut that resides in a tabled predicate:

```
:- table q/1.
q(X):-!,q(X).
q(a).
```

Since there is no call appearing to the left of the cut, the cut just sets the backtracking point to be the address of the ending clause. When the call following the cut, which is a follower of the head, is executed, it will execute from the ending clause. Since no answer exists in the table, the follower will fail, which will cause the pioneer to fail too.

There is a case that we have not considered yet: what should we do if the AR field of the table entry of the current call is NULL when we execute the completion-checking clause? The following example illustrates this situation:

```
:- table p/1.
p(X):-q(X).
p(a).
p(b).
q(Y):-p(Y),!.
```

Consider the query p(X0). It is reduced to q(X0), which is re-written to p(X0),! by the last clause. The later p(X0) steals the choice point of the pioneer and execute from the second clause, i.e., p(a). After that, the cut sets the AR field of the table entry to NULL. Upon backtracking, the completion-checking clause will be executed for the pioneer. If the original table_check_completion instruction is used, we will lose the solution p(b)!

The above-mentioned case is very special and can seldom occur in real programs. We have not found a method for handling this special case. In the current implementation, the system just displays a warning message saying that possible solutions may be lost because a cut is used inappropriately.

4 Direct-Recursion Optimization (DRO)

Re-computation should be avoided if it is known to produce no new answers. It is an open problem to decide the exact class of predicates and calls for which re-computation is avoidable. In this section, we define a class of predicate calls for which re-computation is unnecessary and show how to optimize it.

Definition 1. A predicate is said to be *table-irrelevant* if it is not tabled and all the predicates it calls directly or indirectly are table-irrelevant.

Definition 2. A clause in a tabled predicate p is said to be *directly-recursive* if all the calls in the body either call p or call table-irrelevant predicates.

Definition 3. A tabled predicate is called a *DRO (Directly-Recursive Optimizable)* predicate that consists of one directly-recursive clause and possibly several clauses whose bodies are table-irrelevant.

Theorem 4. *For a DRO predicate, re-computation is unnecessary for ancestor/descendant variant calls of the predicate.*

Let the following be the directly-recursive clause in a DRO predicate:

$$P : -Q_1, ..., Q_i, P, Q_{i+1}, ..., Q_n$$

In database terms, the relation P is defined as a join of P and Q_is. In deductive databases where rules are evaluated bottom-up, re-evaluation of recursive rules is needed to reach a fix-point [1]. In SLDT, however, since the relations are joined tuple by tuple and a newly generated tuple is added into the relation P immediately, no re-execution is necessary. As long as a follower has no answer to be used in the join, no new answer can be produced for its pioneer. This guarantees that we can fail a follower safely after it exhausts all its answers and clauses.

Note that re-computation is still required if the follower is not a descendant but a sibling of the former variant call. Consider the following program:

```
:-table p/2.
q(A,B,C,D):-p(A,B),p(C,D).

p(X,Z):-p(X,Y1),p(Y2,Z),Y1=Y2.
p(X,Y):-t(X,Y).

t(a,b). t(b,c). t(c,a).
```

Without re-computation of p(C,D), the solution q(a,b,a,a) and many others would be lost. The readers are encouraged to check the reason.

We introduce another new instruction, called **table_end** L, which substitutes **table_check_completion** L instruction in the completion-checking clauses in DRO predicates. This instruction first checks whether the parent call and the pioneer of the current call are the same. If so, it behaves just like **table_check_completion** as though the fix-point has been reached. Otherwise, if the parent and the pioneer are different, then **table_end** L behaves exactly the same as `table_check_completion`. Note that what offered by the theorem is not fully exploited here. We only avoid re-computation for parent/child calls but not ancestor/descendant calls because we want to avoid the more expensive test of the ancestor/descendant relationship.

5   Performance Evaluation

Tables 1 and 2 compare the time efficiency of B-Prolog (version 3.5) with that of XSB (version 2.0) for two benchmark suites: a suite of 6 small programs [5] and the CHAT benchmark suite [4]. The numbers show the times taken by B-Prolog assuming that the times taken by XSB are 1. The comparison was done on a SPARC-2 workstation.

For the suite of small programs, B-Prolog has a time performance that is comparable with or better than that of XSB (see Table 1). The programs in this suite are mostly datalog (i.e., function-free) programs and do not require re-computation. For `tcl` (*transitive-closure left-recursion*), `tcr` (*tc right-recursion*), and `sg` (*same generation*) where fix-points are required, the execution times would almost double without DRO.

For the CHAT suite, B-Prolog is on average about 20% slower than XSB. Two factors contribute to this result: First, DRO is applicable to none of the predicates in the suite and thus re-computation is necessary; and second, arguments of the tabled calls are complex terms for which the decision-tree data structure, called *trie*, adopted in XSB [10] is much faster than hash tables adopted in B-Prolog. It is difficult to draw a consistent conclusion from the figures. On the one hand, B-Prolog is on average twice as fast as XSB for standard programs, and on the other hand the trie data structure used in XSB is far more advanced than hash tables used in B-Prolog for managing the table area[3]. But, we at least understand from this comparison that linearity is not a feature for which we would have to severely sacrifice the performance.

Table 1. Comparing time efficiency(small programs).

Progs	fib	water	farmer	tcl	tcr	sg
B/XSB	0.24	0.68	0.76	0.95	1.00	0.47

Table 3 compares the amounts of space required by B-Prolog and XSB to run the CHAT suite. Program and table areas are not included since they are irrelevant to the methods compared. For XSB, the chat area, which is used to preserve computation status, is included. Except for `cs_o`, B-Prolog consumes less space than XSB. For some programs such as **peep** and **read**, B-Prolog consumes an order of magnitude less memory than XSB.

---

[3] The trie data structure is just like a hash table for the small programs in the first suite.

Table 2. Comparing time efficiency(CHAT).

Progs	cs_o	cs_r	disj	gabriel	kalah	peep	pg	read
B/XSB	1.09	1.09	1.30	1.50	1.33	1.21	1.27	1.12

Table 3. Comparing space efficiency(CHAT).

Progs	cs_o	cs_r	disj	gabriel	kalah	peep	pg	read
B/XSB	1.318	0.241	0.734	0.599	0.685	0.028	0.124	0.045

In both B-Prolog and XSB, tabled predicate calls take more stack space than non-tabled ones. In B-Prolog, arguments of each tabled call are copied twice, one copy being stored in the table area and the other copy being stored on the stack for producing answers. In XSB, arguments only need to be copied once. This may explain why B-Prolog consumes more memory than XSB for cs_o.

6 Concluding Remarks

The need to extend Prolog to narrow the gap between declarative and procedural readings of programs has been urged long before [7]. Tabling is a technique that eliminates infinite loops and reduces redundant computations. With tabling, Prolog becomes more friendly to beginners, and even for professional programmers, tabling can alleviate their burden to cure infinite loops and redundant computations. Unfortunately, by now, tabling has not gained wide acceptance. Currently, there is basically only one Prolog system, namely XSB, that supports tabling. There are several possible reasons. One primary reason is the lack of an easy-to-implement tabling mechanism. The SLG-WAM [8] adopted in XSB is complicated and imposes about 10% overhead on standard Prolog programs, which is obviously unacceptable to Prolog vendors and implementers.

To simplify the implementation of tabling in XSB, Demoen and Sagonas proposed two alternative schemes for preserving the choice points of consumers and the related stacks [3,4]. The new schemes are simpler than SLG-WAM and impose less overhead on the execution of standard Prolog programs, but the implementation is still complicated and the cut operator is left unhandled. In addition, the new schemes have a new problem that SLG-WAM does no have: the garbage collector becomes more complicated because of the copying of some stack segments.

In this paper, we presented the implementation of a linear tabling mechanism. The linear feature makes it possible for us to handle the cut operator easily and work out a simple and overhead-free implementation. Our implementation has a better performance than XSB for programs that do not require re-computation, and is still slower than XSB for programs that require re-computation and/or manipulate complex terms. We believe that the gap will be gone after more efficient data structures are adopted for tables and more techniques are invented for eliminating re-computation.

Acknowledgement

This work was started while the first author visited University of Alberta in the summer of 1998 and most of the implementation work was done while the first author was with Kyushu Institute of Technology. The first author is supported in part by ONR grant N00014-96-1-1057, and the second author is supported in part by Chinese NNSF and Trans-Century Training Programme Foundation for the Talents by the Chinese Ministry of Education. We are grateful to Bart Demoen and Kostis Sagonas for kindly sharing with us the CHAT benchmark suite.

References

1. Bancilhon, F. and Ramakrishnan, R.: An Amateur's Introduction to Recursive Query Processing Strategies, *SIGMOD'86*.
2. Chen, W. and Warren, D.S.: Tabled Evaluation with Delaying for General Logic Programs, *J. ACM*, Vol.43, No.1, 20-74, 1996.
3. Demoen, B. and Sagonas, K.: CAT: The Copying Approach to Tabling, *Proceedings of PLILP'98*, 1998.
4. Demoen, B. and Sagonas, K.: CHAT: The Copy-Hybrid Approach to Tabling, *Proceedings of PADL'99, LNCS 1551*, pp.106-121, 1999.
5. Fa, C.G. and Dietrich, S.W. : Extension Table Built-ins for Prolog, *Software Practice and Experience*, Vol.22, No.7, 573-597, 1992.
6. Lloyd, J.W.: *Foundations of Logic Programming*, Springer-Verlag, 1987.
7. Parker, D.S., Carey, M. Jarke, M. Sciore, E. and Walker, A.: Logic Programming and Databases, *Expert Database Systems*, Kersobberg Larry, Ed., The Benjamin/Cummings Pub., 1986.
8. Sagonas, K. and Swift, T.: An Abstract Machine for Tabled Execution of Fixed-Order Stratified Logic Programs, *ACM Transactions on Programming Languages and Systems*. Vol.20, No.3, 1998.
9. Shen, Y.D., Yuan, L., You, J.H. and Zhou, N.F.: Linear Tabulated Resolution Based on Prolog Control Strategy, *submitted for publication*.
10. Ramakrishnan, I.V., Rao, P., Sagonas, K., Swift, T., and Warren, D.S.: Efficient Access Mechanisms for Tabled Logic Programs, *J. Logic Programming*, vol. 38, pp.31-54, 1998.
11. Tamaki, H. and Sato, T.: OLD Resolution with Tabulation, *Proc. of the Third ICLP*, LNCS 225, 84-98, 1986.
12. Warren, D.H.D.: An Abstract Prolog Instruction Set, Technical Report 309, SRI International, 1983.
13. Warren, D.S.: Memoing for Logic Programs, *CACM*, Vol.35, No.3, pp.93-111, 1992.
14. Zhou, N.F.: Parameter Passing and Control Stack Management in Prolog Implementation Revisited, *ACM Transactions on Programming Languages and Systems*, Vol.18, No.6, 752-779, 1996.

Appendix I: Tabling Instructions

```
table_allocate Arity, Size, p, L:
    copy the arguments;
    allocate Size slots;
    tableEntry = lookupTable(AR,p,Arity);
    if (tableEntry == NULL){ /* AR is a pioneer */
        AR->Table = tableEntry = add a new table entry;
        AR->Pioneer = AR;
        P = NextInstruction;
    } else {
        AR->Table = tableEntry;
        if (tableEntry->AR==NULL){ /* treat AR as a pioneer */
            AR->Pioneer = AR;
            tableEntry->AR = AR;
            P = NextInstruction;
        } else if (tableEntry->AR==COMPLETE){
            P = L;
        } else {
            AR->Pioneer = tableEntry->AR->Pioneer;
            P = tableEntry->AR->CPF; /* steal backtracking point */
            tableEntry->AR->CPF = L;
            tableEntry->AR = AR;
        }
    }
    AR->CurrA = first answer in tableEntry;
    AR->CPF = P;
    do bookkeeping operations for backtracking;

table_add_use_answer:
    add the current answer to the table if it is not there
    if (AR->CurrA->Next!=NULL){
        goto consume_answer;
    } else fail.

table_use_answer:
    if (AR->CurrA->Next!=NULL){ /* answer available */
    consume_answer:
        unify the answer with the original arguments
        AR->CurrA = AR->CurrA->Next;
        P = AR->CP; /* return control to the caller */
        AR = AR->AR;
    } else P = NextInstruction;

table_check_completion L:
    if (AR->Table->AR==COMPLETE){
        cut_fail;
    } else if (AR->Table->Revised==true){
        P = L;
    } else {
    fix_point_reached:
        AR->Table->AR = COMPLETE;
        B = AR->B; /* discard the current choice point frame */
        fail;      /* provoke backtracking */
    }

table_end L:
    if (AR->Pioneer == AR->AR){ /* AR is a child of the pioneer */
        goto fix_point_reached;
    } else goto table_check_completion;
```

How to Incorporate Negation
in a Prolog Compiler*

Juan José Moreno-Navarro and Susana Muñoz-Hernández

Universidad Politécnica de Madrid
Dpto. LSIIS - Facultad de Informática.
Campus de Montegancedo s/n, 28660, Madrid, SPAIN.
voice: +34-91-336-7458, fax: +34-91-336-7412
jjmoreno@fi.upm.es,susana@lml.ls.fi.upm.es

Abstract. Knowledge representation based applications require a more
complete set of capabilities than those offered by conventional Prolog
compilers. Negation is, probably, the most important one. The inclusion
of negation among the logical facilities of LP has been a very active
area of research, and several techniques have been proposed. However,
the negation capabilities accepted by current Prolog compilers are very
limited. In this paper, we discuss the possibility to incorporate some of
these techniques in a Prolog compiler in an efficient way. Our idea is to
mix some of the existing proposals guided by the information provided
by a global analysis of the source code.
Keywords: Semantics of Negation, Global Analysis, Implementation of
Negation.

1 Introduction

Knowledge representation based applications are a natural area for logic programming. However, this kind of applications requires a more complete set of
capabilities than those offered by conventional Prolog compilers. As the knowledge about any subject contains positive as well as negative information, the
possibility to include negation in goals is crucial for knowledge representation.

For these reasons, the research community on negation in LP has made a lot
of efforts to propose different ways to understand and incorporate negation into
logic programming languages. Most of the interesting proposals rely on semantics, and a considerable amount of papers in logic programming conferences is
devoted to these subjects. Surprisingly, only a small subset of these ideas has
arrived to the field on implementation and has produced modifications to Prolog
compilers. In fact, the negation capabilities incorporated by current Prolog compilers are rather limited. To our knowledge, the only negation techniques that
are present in a (commercial) Prolog compiler are:

- The (unsound) negation as failure rule, that is present in most Prolog compilers (Sicstus, Bin Prolog, Quintus, etc.).

---

* This research was partly supported by the Spanish CICYT project TIC96.1012-C02-
02.

E. Pontelli, V. Santos Costa (Eds.): PADL 2000, LNCS 1753, pp. 124–140, 2000.

- The sound (but incomplete) delay technique of the language Gödel [14], or Nu-Prolog [21] which applies negation as failure when the variables of the negated goal are ground. It is well known that it has the risk of floundering.
- The constructive negation of Eclipse, which was announced in earlier versions but has been removed from recent releases.

There are some direct approaches to implement negation (as the implementation of stable models or bottom-up computation style like XSB). However our goal is to study the possibility to go a bit further than these experiences, and to design the steps needed to extend a Prolog compiler with a negation subsystem. Notice that this allows us to keep the very advanced Prolog current implementations based on the WAM technology as well as to reuse thousands of Prolog code lines.

Our work does not try to propose any new method, but to combine existing techniques to make some negation techniques useful for practical application. The novelty appears in some implementation oriented improvements of existing techniques, the uniform presentation, and, mainly, in the techniques used for the combination and the combination strategy.

We are interested in techniques with a single and simple semantics. For this reasons we adopt the most simple possibility: Closed Word Assumption (CWA) [9] by program completion and Kunen's 3-valued semantics [15]. These semantics will be the basis for soundness results.

Therefore, the techniques we are interested in need to share these semantics. Another important issue is that they must be "constructive", i.e. the program execution need to search for the values that make false a negated goal. One can argue that Chan's constructive negation [7, 8] fulfills both points, but it is quite difficult to implement and expensive in terms of execution resources. Therefore, our idea is to try to use the simplest technique as possible in any particular case. To help on this distinction, we need to use some tests to characterize the situation. To avoid the execution of these tests during the execution of the program, the results of a global analysis of the source code are used. The program analyses includes groundness detection, elimination of delays, and the determination of the finiteness of the number of solutions.

All these analyses are incorporated in the CIAO development system [13], an extension of Sicstus Prolog, which will be used as the testbed for our implementation work.

Our goal is to write a paper more expositive than technical, although some details about the techniques used and the soundness of the method are provided.

The rest of the paper is organized as follows. Section 2 presents some preliminaries: we discuss the negation techniques to be used, and briefly enumerate the characteristics of the program analyses. In order to present how the techniques can be introduced in a Prolog compiler, we start with the management of disequality constraints (Section 3), then we discuss the implementation of (a part of) constructive negation (Section 4). Intensional negation as well as the computation of universal quantified goals are studied in Section 5. Section 6 explains how to combine all the techniques and Section 7 shows some experimental results. Finally, we conclude.

2   Preliminaries

In this section we introduce some previous work on negation and program analysis that will be used along the paper.

2.1   Treatment of Negation

Among the techniques that have been proposed to implement the computation of negated goals of the form $\neg Q$ in a program P based on the CWA, the most accepted are the following:

- The negation as finite failure rule of Clark [9], which states that $\neg Q$ is a consequence of a program P if a finitely failed SLD tree for the query Q with respect to P exists, (in short, if Q finitely fails). The implementation provided by Prolog compilers is the following:

      naf (Q) :- Q, !, fail.
      naf (Q).

  that is unsound except when the free variables of Q are not constrained (for instance, if Q has no free variables).
- There are many works related to the program completion of Clark [9], (see [16, 1]), some of them ([2, 3]) oriented to obtain a program that is a transformation of a original program P which introduces also the "only if" part of the predicate definitions (i.e., interpreting implications as equivalences).
- The constructive negation proposed by Chan [7, 8], and formalized in the context of CLP by Stuckey [25].

2.2   Information Obtained by Global Analysis

In order to provide some heuristics to guide the computation of the negation process we will use some information provided by a global analysis of the source program. Along the paper we assume that a part of the Prolog compiler produces with an acceptable level of accuracy, the following information. At least this is true for the CIAO system:

- Groundness: The groundness analysis tries to identify those variables that are bound to a ground term in a certain point of the program. There are several papers and implementation of groundness analysis (see [20]).
- Elimination of delays: In the presence of delays (or waits) the analysis tries to identify which of them are useless (so, removing them), or if there is a reordering of the goals that does not need the delay directive (see [11, 23]).
- Finiteness of the number of solutions: The analysis is based on complexity and execution cost to determine if a goal has a finite number of solutions (even none) or there are a potential infinite number of answers. The interested reader can consult [17, 4].

3   Management of Disequality Constraints

The first step in our management of negation is to handle disequalities between terms $t_1 \neq t_2$. Most Prolog implementations can work with disequalities if both terms are ground (built-in predicate /==). However, they cannot work in the presence of free variables. The "constructive" behavior must allow the "binding" of a variable with a disequality: the solution to the goal X /== t is the constraint $X \neq t$. In fact, what we need is an implementation of CLP $(\mathcal{H})$ (constraints over the Herbrand Universe with equality and disequality). This capability is present in several CLP Prolog extensions (Prolog III for instance), but is not available in usual Prolog compilers. As we are going to prove, the inclusion of disequalities and constrained answers has a very low cost.

First of all, we need a representation for constraint answers. The disequation $c(X, a) \neq c(b, Y)$ introduces a disjunction $X \neq b \vee Y \neq a$. For this reason, we use conjunctions of disjunctions of disequations as normal forms. On the other hand, we will produce disequations by means of the negation of an equation $X = t(\overline{Y})$. This fact produces the universal quantification of the free variables in the equation, unless a more external quantification affects them. The negation of such equation is $\forall \overline{Y} \, X \neq t(\overline{Y})$. Also, universally quantified disequations are allowed in the constraints. More precisely, the normal form of constraints is:

$$\underbrace{\bigwedge_i (X_i = t_i)}_{\text{positive information}} \wedge \underbrace{\bigvee_j \forall \overline{Z}_j^1 \, (Y_j^1 \neq s_j^1) \wedge \ldots \wedge \bigvee_l \forall \overline{Z}_l^n \, (Y_l^n \neq s_l^n)}_{\text{negative information}}$$

where each X_i appears only in $X_i = t_i$, none s_k^r is Y_k^r and the universal quantification could be empty (leaving a simple disequality).

Using some normalization rules we can obtain a normal form formula from any initial formula. It is easy to redefine the unification algorithm to manage constrained variables.

This very compact way to represent a normal form was firstly presented in [18] and differs from Chan's representation where only disjunctions are used[1].

Therefore, in order to include disequalities into a Prolog compiler we need to reprogram unification. It is possible if the Prolog version allows attributed variables [6] (e.g. in Sicstus Prolog, or in Eclipse where they are called meta-structures). These variables let us keep associated information with each variable during the unification what can be used to dynamically control the constraints.

Attributed variables are variables with an associated attribute, which is a term. We will associate to each variable a data structure containing a normal form constraint. Basically, a list of list of pairs (variable, term) is used. They behave like ordinary variables, except that the programmer can supply code for unification, printing facilities and memory management. In our case, the printing facility is used to show constrained answers. The main task is to provide a new unification code.

---

[1] Chan treats the disjunctions by means of backtracking. The main advantage of our normal form is that the search space is drastically reduced.

Once the unification of a variable X with a term t is triggered, there are three possible cases (up to commutativity):

1. if X is a free variable and t is not a variable with a negative constraint, X is just bound to t,
2. if X is a free variable or bound to a term t' and t is a variable Y with a negative constraint, we need to check if X (or, equivalently, t') satisfies the constraint associated with Y. A conveniently defined predicate `satisfy` is used for this purpose,
3. if X is bound to a term t' and t is a term (or a variable bound to a term), the classical unification algorithm can be used.

The predicate `=/=`, to check disequalities, is defined in a similar way than unification. The main difference is that it incorporates negative constraints instead of bindings and the decomposition step can produce disjunctions.

As an example, let us show the constraints produced in certain situations. The attribute/ constraint of a variable is represented as a list of list of pairs (variable, term) using a constructor /, i.e. the disequality $X \neq 1$ is represented as `X / 1`. When an universal quantification is used in a disequality (e.g. $\forall Y\ X \neq c(Y)$) the new constructor `fA/2` is used (the previous constraint is represented as `fA (Y, X =/= c (Y))`). The first list is used to represent disjunctions while the inside list represents the conjunction of disequalities. We focus on the variable X.

SUBGOAL	ATTRIBUTE	CONSTRAINT
`not_member (X,[1,2,3])`	$[[X/1, X/2, X/3]]$	$X \neq 1 \wedge X \neq 2 \wedge X \neq 3$
`member (X,[1]), X=/=1`	fail	$false$
`X =/= 4`	$[[X/4]]$	$X \neq 4$
`X =/= 4; X=/=5`	$[[X/4],[X/5]]$	$X \neq 4 \vee X \neq 5$
`X =/= 5; (X=/=6, X=/=Y)`	$[[X/4],[X/6, X/Y]]$	$X \neq 4 \vee (X \neq 6 \wedge X \neq Y)$
`member (X,[0,s(0),s(s(0))]),`		
`fA (Y, X =/= s (Y))`	0	$X = 0$

4   Constructive Negation

The second technique we are going to implement is constructive negation. Constructive negation was proposed by Chan [7, 8] and it is widely accepted as the "most promising" method to handle negation with Kunen's 3-valued semantics (up to some extensions and modifications proposed by other authors). Although the first Chan's paper is credited as the presentation of the idea, but a "mistake" in the development of the technique (solved in the second one), it has still some interesting results from the implementation point of view. The main idea of constructive negation is easy to describe: in order to obtain the solutions for $\neg Q$ we proceed as follows:

1. Firstly, the solutions for Q are obtained getting a disjunction: $Q \equiv S_1 \vee S_2 \vee \ldots \vee S_n$. Each component S_i can be understood as a conjunction of equalities: $S_i \equiv S_i^1 \wedge S_i^2 \wedge \ldots \wedge S_i^{m_i}$

2. Then the formula is negated and a normal form constraint is obtained:

$$\neg Q \equiv \neg(S_1 \vee S_2 \vee \ldots \vee S_n) \qquad \equiv$$
$$\neg S_1 \wedge \neg S_2 \wedge \ldots \wedge \neg S_n \qquad \equiv$$
$$\neg(S_1^1 \wedge \ldots \wedge S_1^{m_1}) \wedge \ldots \wedge \neg(S_n^1 \wedge \ldots \wedge S_n^{m_n}) \qquad \equiv$$
$$(\neg S_1^1 \vee \ldots \vee \neg S_1^{m_1}) \wedge \ldots \wedge (\neg S_n^1 \vee \ldots \vee \neg S_n^{m_n})$$

The formula can be obtained in different ways depending on how we negate a solution. It can also be arranged into a disjunction of conjunctions according to the variables in each S_i^j.

Of course, the solution is not valid in general, because a goal (Q in the previous description) can have an infinite number of solutions. [7] offers a technique to negate a solution and to normalize the previous formula. [18], working on a CLP framework as proposed by [25], adapted the idea (in a different but equivalent context) using our notion of constraint normal form. Given a constraint

$$\bigwedge_{i=1}^{m}(X_i = t_i) \wedge \bigwedge_{j=1}^{n} \bigvee_{k=1}^{n_j} \forall \overline{Z}_k^j \ (Y_k^j \neq s_k^j)$$

the negation will produce the following constraints:

- $\bigvee_{i=1}^{m} \forall \overline{Z}_i \ (X_i \neq t_i)$, where $\overline{Z}_i$ are the variables of t_i not quantified outside.
- $\bigwedge_{i=1}^{m}(X_i = t_i) \wedge \bigwedge_{k=1}^{n_l}(Y_l^k = s_l^k) \wedge \bigwedge_{j=1}^{l-1}\bigvee_{k=1}^{n_j} \forall \overline{Z}_k^j \ (Y_k^j \neq s_k^j)$, for all $l \leq n$.

Note, again, that we are using a much more compact representation for the negated constraints than that proposed in [7].

Once we have explained how to negate a constraint, the rest is easy: for each solution, each possibility of the negation is combined with one of the others. All these different solutions are obtained by backtracking.

We implement $\neg Q$ by the Prolog predicate cneg (Q), and it works as follows:

1. First of all, all variables V of the goal Q are obtained.
2. Secondly, all Q's solutions for variables in V are computed using setof/3. Each solution is a constraint in normal form.
3. The negation of each solution is computed and combined to obtain the answers of $\neg Q$ one by one.

This implementation is only valid when it is detected that the goal has a finite number of solutions. The full code ([19]) is available from the authors on request.

Some examples were the technique is useful are the following. They are extracted from a running session.

```
| ?- cneg (X =/= Y).                    | ?- cneg (X =/= X).
     X = Y                                   true
| ?- cneg (X=/=Y, member(Y,[1,2])).     | ?- cneg (cneg (X =/= X)).
     Y /= 1, Y /= 2 ?;                       no
     X = 1, Y = 1 ?;                     | ?- cneg(member(X,[1,2,3])).
     X = 2, Y = 2                            X /= 1, X /= 2, X /= 3
| ?- cneg(member(Y,[X]),member(Y,[2])). | ?- cneg ([1,X] =/= [Y,2]).
     X /= 2; Y /= 2                          Y = 1, X = 2
```

5   Intensional Negation and Universal Quantification

Intensional negation [2, 3] uses a different approach to handle negation. A program transformation technique is used to add new predicates to the program in order to express the negative information. Informally, the *complement* of head terms of the positive clauses are computed and they are used later as the head of the negated predicate.

For example, the transformation of a program (from [2]):

```
even (0).
even (s(s(X))) :- even (X).
```

yields a new predicate not__even that succeeds when even fails.

```
not__even (s(0)).
not__even (s(s(X))) :- not__even (X).
```

There are two problems with this technique. The first one is that in the presence of logical variables in the rhs of a clause, the new program needs to handle some kind of universal quantification construct. The second trouble affects the outcomes of the program: while the new program is semantically equivalent to the completed program, the operational behavior can differ. In the presence of logical variables, the new predicate can generate all the possible values one by one, even when a more general answer can be given. The predicate P defined by the single clause $p(X, X)$. is negated by:

```
not__p (X, Y) :- not__eq (X, Y).
not__eq (0, s(Y)).
not__eq (s(X), 0).
not__eq (s(X), s(Y)) :- not__eq (X, Y).
```

if the program only contains natural numbers with 0 and succ. The query not__p (X,Y) will generate infinitely many answers, instead of the more general $X \neq Y$. An answer like $X \neq Y$ can only be replaced by an infinite number of equalities.

Our approach to manage this problem is to use constraints instead of concrete terms. All what we need is to have disequality constraints, which are included yet. Therefore, the negated predicates of the previous examples, with our transformation, are the following:

```
not__even (X) :- X =/= 0, fA (Y, X =/= s(s(Y))).
not__even (s(s(X))) :- not__even (X).
not__p (X, Y) :- X =/= Y.
```

Note that if the program only contains natural numbers, the first clause is equivalent to the one obtained above.

A bit more complicate is the first problem. For this purpose we have implemented a predicate for_all/4 that tries to detect if a goal Q is valid for all possible values of a list of variables $[X_1, \ldots, X_n]$ with a call to the goal for_all ([X1, ..., Xn], Q, ...).

Roughly speaking, the implementation, explained in more detail later, generates incrementally all possible instantiations of the variables $X_1, \ldots, X_n$ by terms $t_1(\overline{Y}), \ldots, t_n(\overline{Y})$ and tries to make true the goal Q, for all these possibilities, without instantiating the variables $\overline{Y}$ at all. The idea was sketched in [3] but many important details where ignored and no concrete implementation was supplied.

5.1 Program Transformation

Our transformation approach basically follows the ideas of [3], but differs in some significant points. Barbuti and his coauthors apply the transformation to a restricted class of programs. Then they show that any program can be translated into a program of that class. However, while both programs are semantically equivalent, they are not operationally equivalent (infinitely many answers can appear as shown above). Our transformation applies to all kind of programs and maintains compact outcomes.

In order to formally define the negated predicate not_p for p we proceed step by step. First of all we need the definition of the complement of a term t. Without using constraints, the only way to represent the complement of a term is a set of terms. However, this set can be expressed by means of a constraint on a variable X that does not appear in the term (i.e. the constrained values for X are exactly the terms that have not t's shape).

Definition: *Complement of a term*
The complement of a term t (not using the variable X) on the variable X (in symbols $Comp(t)$) is a constraint value for X, defined inductively as follows:

- $Comp(Y) = fail$
- $Comp(c) = (X \neq c)$, with c constant.
- $Comp(c(t_1, \ldots, t_n)) = \forall \overline{Z}(X \neq c(t_1, \ldots, t_n))$, with c a constructor and $\overline{Z}$ the variables of $t_1, \ldots, t_n$.

Without loss of generality we can consider that all the predicates has one argument, taking the tuple construction as a constructor. Given a set of clauses for a predicate p:

C_1: $p(t^1) :- G_1$.
...
C_m: $p(t^m) - G_m$.

we say that the **complement clause** of p is

$not\_p(X)$ $:- Comp(t^1), \ldots, Comp(t^m)$.

assuming, by adequate renamings, that the terms do not share variables (i.e. $var(t^i) \cap var(t^j) = \emptyset$ for $i \neq j$).

This clause covers the cases where there is no definition for the predicate in the original program, and it must be included in the new program. For the rest of the clauses of the negated predicates some additional concepts are needed:

Definition: *Critical pair*

We say that a program has a critical pair t in $\{l_1, \ldots, l_r\} \subseteq \{1, \ldots, m\}$ if $m.g.u.(t^{l_1}, \ldots, t^{l_r}) = \sigma$ and $t = t^{l_j}\sigma, \quad \forall\, j \in \{1, \ldots, r\}$

The definition is well know in term rewriting and, intuitively, detects those terms for which there are more than one applicable clause. In those cases, all the *rhs*s of the applicable clauses must be negated together.

For each critical pair t of the program in $\{l_1, \ldots, l_r\}$ we generate the following clause:

$$not\_p(t) \; : - \; negate\_rhs(var(t), (G_{l_1}; \ldots; G_{l_r})).$$

where the *negate_rhs* function negates a clause rhs (see below). There is no rule if all the G_{l_j} are empty. Note that the formula $p(t) \longleftrightarrow \exists \overline{X} G_{l_1} \vee \ldots \vee G_{l_r}$ ($\overline{X} = var(G_{l_1} \cup \ldots \cup var(G_{l_r}))$) is part of the completed program.

Now, we are in a position to transform each of the clauses of the program. Each clause $p(t^i) : - G_i$. generates one of the following clauses for not_p:

- $not\_p(t^i) : -t^i = / = t, negate\_rhs(var(t^i), G_i)$.

  if there is a critical pair t involving clause i and t^i is not strictly identical to t ($t^i/ == t$).

- $not\_p(t) : -negate\_rhs(var(t^i), G_i)$.

  otherwise. There is no clause if G_i is empty.

The effect of *negate_rhs* is easy to explain. It just negates the rhs and introduces universal quantifications when they are needed:

- $negate\_rhs(V, G) = negate(G)$ if $var(G) \subset V$
- $negate\_rhs(V, G) = \texttt{for\_all}([Y_1, \ldots, Y_k], negate(G))$ if $var(G) - V = \{Y_1, \ldots, Y_k\} \neq \emptyset$.

The function *negate* can be defined inductively: it moves conjunction $(,)$ into disjunction $(;)$, equality into disequalities and vice versa.

The effect of *negate* over a single predicate call needs a further discussion. In principle it is possible to define $negate(q(s))$ by any of the methods to handle negation: negation as failure (`naf (q (s))`), constructive negation (`cneg (q (s))`) or the transformed predicate (`not_q (s)`). The last one will be used in case of recursive calls. The decision will be fixed by the negation strategy of the compiler that will be discussed in the next section.

The transformation has some similarities with the transformation proposed in [5], but there are still some differences. The transformation of [5] has a much more simple formulation and some optimization covered by our detection of critical pairs are not taken into account. The result is that much more universally quantified goals are generated and the programs contains a lot of trivial constraints (i.e. they are trivially true or false, as $X = a \land X \neq a$, $X = a \lor X \neq a$).

Let us discuss the application of the method in a couple of examples. Consider the fragment of the program:

```
less (0, s(Y)).
less (s(X), s(Y)) :- less (X, Y).
```

First of all, we need to compute the complements of the terms in the lhs of the clauses, with respect to the variable pair (W, Z). We have:

– $Comp(0, s(Y)) = (W \neq 0, \forall Y(Z \neq s(Y)))$
– $Comp(s(X), s(Y)) = (\forall X(W \neq s(X)), \forall Y(Z \neq s(Y)))$

The complement clause is:

```
not_less (W, Z) :- W =/= 0,
                   fA (X, W =/= s (X)),
                   fA (Y, Z =/= s (Y)).
```

There are no critical pairs and the first clause has no rhs, so the transformed clause is:

```
not_less (s (X), s (Y)) :- not_less (X, Y).
```

The second example, *family*, is also well known, and includes free variables in the rhs:

```
parent (john, mary).     ancestor (X, Y) :- parent (X, Y).
parent (john, peter).    ancestor (X, Y) :- ancestor (X, Z),
parent (mary, joe).                         parent (Z, Y).
parent (peter, susan).
```

The transformation of the predicate **ancestor** has no complement clause. The first and the second clause have an obvious critical pair (X, Y). The associated clause is:

```
not_ancestor (X, Y) :- cneg (parent (X,Y)),
                       for_all ([Z], (not_ancestor (X, Z);
                                      cneg (parent (Z,Y)))).
```

Note that we have used **cneg** as the way to negate the predicate **parent**. It is safe because **parent** has always a finite number of solutions. In the case we can infer that a call to $\neg parent(Z, Y)$ is ground, we can use **naf** instead of **cneg**. Also, the call inside the **for_all** goal has the first argument ground for sure.

In principle, we need to transform each of the clauses of the predicate, including the constraint $(X, Y) \neq (X, Y)$ in their bodies, but it is trivially unsatisfiable and we can omit the clauses.

5.2   Implementation of Universal Quantification

The efficient implementation of universally quantified goals is not an easy task. In fact it is an undecidable problem. However, we are not interested in a complete implementation but a implementation powerful enough to resolve the quantifications that we obtain from the previous transformation. There are other approaches to implement some kind of universal quantification:

1. Nu-Prolog [21] and Gödel [14] include universally quantified goals, but they are executed when all the variables are ground. Obviously it has the risk of floundering.
2. Voronkov [26] has studied the use of bounded quantifications over finite sets.

But both are rather limited. Our implementation is based on two ideas:

1. A universal quantification of the goal Q over a variable X succeeds when Q succeeds without binding (or constraining) X.
2. A universal quantification of Q over X is true if Q is true for all possible values for the variable X.

The second point can be combined with the first one in order to get an implementation. Instead of generating all possible values (which is not possible in the presence of a constructor of arity greater than 0) we can generate all the possible skeletons of values, using new variables. The simplest possibility is to include all the constants and all the constructors applied to fresh variables. Now, the universal quantification is tested for all this terms, using the new variables in the quantification.

In order to formalize this concept, we need the notion of **covering**.

Definition: *Covering of the Herbrand Universe* A covering is any set of terms $\{t_1, \ldots, t_n\}$ such that:

- For every i, j with $i \neq j$, t_i and t_j do not superpose, i.e. there is no ground substitution σ with $t_i \sigma = t_j \sigma$.
- For all ground term s of the Herbrand Universe there exists i and a ground substitution σ with $s = t_i \sigma$.

The simplest covering is a variable $\{X\}$. If the program uses only natural numbers, the following sets of terms are coverings:

- $\{0, s(X)\}$
- $\{0, s(0), s(s(X))\}$
- $\{0, s(0), s(s(0)), s(s(s(X)))\}$

The example also gives us the hint about how to incrementally generate coverings. We depart from the simplest covering X. From one covering we generate the next one choosing one term and one variable of this term. The term is removed and then we add all the terms obtained replacing the variable by all the possible instances of that element.

In order to fix a strategy to select the term and the variable we use a Cantor's diagonalization[2] to explore the domain of a set of variables. It is a breadth first

---

[2] This is the method to enumerate $I\!N^m$. It ensures that all elements are visited in a finite number of steps.

strategy to cover every element of the domain. The previous concepts extend trivially in the case of tuple of elements of the Herbrand Universe, i.e. several variables.

We implement the universal quantification by means of the predicate for_all ([X1,...,Xn], Q,D,S), where $X1,...,Xn$ are the universal quantified variables, Q is the goal or predicate, D is the depth until we want to generate coverings, and S is an output parameter indicating the success of the evaluation. We start with the initial covering $\{(X_1,...,X_n)\}$ of depth 1.

The current covering is checked with the predicate Q. This means that for each element $\bar{t}$ in the covering we execute Q replacing the variables $(X_1,...,X_n)$ by $\bar{t}$. We have three possibilities:

1. Q succeeds in all the cases without any bind of the variables introduced by the covering, then the universal quantification is true.
2. Q fails for a ground case, then the universal quantification is false for sure.
3. Q fails in at least one of the cases. The next covering is generated and the process continues recursively.

There are two important details that optimize the execution. The first one is that in order to check if there are bindings in the covering variables, it is better to replace them by new constants that do not appear in the program. In other words, we are using "Skolem constants".

The second optimization is much more useful. Notice that the coverings grow up incrementally, so we only need to check the most recently included terms. The other ones have been checked before and there is no reason to do it again.

As an example, consider a program which uses only natural numbers: the sequence of coverings for the goal $\forall\ X,Y,Z\ p(X,Y,Z)$ will be the following (where Sk (i), with i a number, represents the ith Skolem constant).

$C_1 = [(Sk(1), Sk(2), Sk(3))]$
$C_2 = [(0, Sk(1), Sk(2)), (s(Sk(1)), Sk(2), Sk(3))]$
$C_3 = [\underline{(0, 0, Sk(1))}, \underline{(0, s(Sk(1)), Sk(2))}, (s(Sk(1)), Sk(2), Sk(3))]$
$C_4 = [\underline{(0, 0, 0)}, \underline{(0, 0, s(Sk(1)))}, (0, s(Sk(1)), Sk(2)), (s(Sk(1)), Sk(2), Sk(3))]$
$C_5 = [(0, 0, 0), \underline{(0, 0, s(0))}, \underline{(0, 0, s(s(Sk(1))))}, (0, s(Sk(1)), Sk(2)),$
$\qquad (s(Sk(1)), Sk(2), Sk(3))]$
$C_6 = \ldots$

In each step, only two elements need to be checked, those that appear underlined. The rest are part of the previous covering and they do not need to be checked again. Again, the authors can supply details of the code (or see [19]).

Let us show some examples of the use of the for_all predicate, indicating the covering found to get the solution. We are still working only with natural numbers and we are going to consider a maximal depth of 5:

```
| ?- for_all ([X], even (X), 5, S).
     S = fail
```

with the covering of depth 3 $\{0, \underline{s(0)}, s(s(Sk(1)))\}$.

```
| ?- for_all ([X], X =/ a, 5, S).
    S = true
```

with the covering of depth 1 $\{Sk(1)\}$.

```
| ?- for_all ([X], less (0, X) -> less (X, Y), 5, S).
    Y = s (s(_A)), S = true
```

with the covering of depth 2 $\{0, s(Sk(1))\}$.

The general solution does not guarantee completeness of the query evaluation process. There are some cases when the generation of coverings does not find one which is correct or incorrect. Nevertheless, this solution fails to work properly in very particular cases. Remember that we are not interested in giving the user an universal quantification operator, but just to implement the code coming from the transformation of a negated predicate. In order to have a practical use of the method, we limite the depth of the coverings to some (user defined) constant d. If the *for_all/4* predicate is not able to achieve a solution at this depth, the predicate informs that it is not possible to know the result of the computation at that depth d (S = unknown).

5.3   Behavior of the Application of the Technique

Here we have some examples coming from a running session that show the behavior of the transformation technique:

```
|?- not__even (s(s(0))).
    no
|?- not__even (s(s(s(0)))).
    yes
|?- not__even(X).
    X =/= 0,fA(_A,X=/=s(s(_A))) ?;
    X=s(s(Y)),Y=/=0,fA(_A,Y=/=s(s(_A))) ?;
    :
    :
|?- not__less (0, s(X)).
    no
|?- not__less (s(X), 0).
    true
```

```
|?- not__less(s(X),X).
    unknown
|?- not__ancestor(mary,peter).
    yes
|?- not__ancestor(john,X).
    no
|?- not__ancestor(peter,X).
    X = john ? ;
    X = mary ? ;
    X = joe ? ;
    X = peter
```

The divergence of the goal not__less(s(X), X) is of the same nature of the divergence of less (X, s (X)) and is related to the incompleteness of Prolog implementations.

In any case, our implementation provides only sound results, although there are cases where we cannot provide any result.

6   The Compiler Strategy

Once we have described the main implemented methods, we can discuss the most important part: the combination of these techniques in order to get a system to handle negation.

What we need is a strategy that the compiler can use to generate code for a negated goal. The strategy is fixed by the information of the different program analyses. Notice that the strategy also ensures the soundness of the method: if the analysis is correct, the precondition to apply a technique is ensured, so the results are sound. Given a (sub)goal of the form $\neg G(\overline{X})$ the compiler produces one of the following codes:

1. If the analysis of the program ensures that $G(\overline{X})$ is ground then simple negation as failure is applied, i.e. it is compiled to naf $(G(\overline{X}))$. Since floundering is undecidable, the analysis only provides an approximation of the cases where negation as failure can be applied safely. This means that maybe we are avoiding to use the technique even in cases that it could work properly.
2. Otherwise, the compiler generates a new program replacing the goal by $G(\overline{X})$ and adding a delay directive to get ground variables in $\overline{X}$ before the call. Then, the compiler applies the elimination of delays technique. If the analysis and the program transformation are able to remove the delay (maybe moving the goal), use the outcoming program but replace $G(\overline{X})$ by naf $(G(\overline{X}))$ as before. Again, the approximation of the analysis could forbid us to apply constructive negation in cases it should give a sound result.
3. Otherwise, look for the result of the finiteness analysis. If it ensures that $G(\overline{X})$ has a finite number of solutions, then the compiler can use simple constructive negation, transforming the negated goal into cneg $(G(\overline{X}))$.
4. Otherwise, the compiler uses the intensional negation approach. Some negated predicates are generated and the goal is replaced by $negate(G(\overline{X}))$.
   During this process new negated goal can appear and the same compiler strategy is applied to each of them.
5. If the intensional negation cannot compute a result, full constructive negation is used.

The weakest point of this strategy appears in the last two steps. The decision to use intensional negation or full constructive negation is dynamic. We are trying to statically identify when the universal quantification can be used (this is related with the *negation as instantiation* property of [22]). On the other hand, we have not yet an implementation of full constructive negation.

The strategy is complete and sound with respect to Kunen 3-valued semantics, what is deduced from the soundness of the negation techniques, the correctness of the analysis and the completeness of constructive negation. This result is obtained as a straightforward composition of the corresponding soundness and correctness theorems.

Let us conclude showing a small example. The static analysis studies each negated goal in the input program and the strategy applies the simplest technique in each case.

SOURCE PROGRAM   TRANSFORMED PROGRAM

```
p(X):- member(X,[0,s(0),s(s(0))]),    p(X):- member(X,[0,s(0),s(s(0))]),
       ¬ less(X,s(s(0))).                     naf(less(X,s(s(0)))).


q(X):- ¬ less(X,s(s(0))),             q(X):- member(X,[0,s(0),s(s(0))]),
       member(X,[0,s(0),s(s(0))]).            naf(less(X,s(s(0)))).

r(X):- ¬ less(X,s(s(0))).             r(X):- cneg(less(X,s(s(0)))).

t(X):- ¬ less(s(0),Y).                t(X):- not_less(s(0),Y).
```

6.1   Experimental Results

Up to now, we have applied this strategy manually (using the real results of
the analyzers) and a good collection of programs (found in the literature about
negation) has been checked. They are small and medium size examples, but
this is the usual kind of problems where negation is applied. As a future work,
we plan to modify the CIAO compiler in order to implement our strategy. To
report the results, we have selected a small number of examples to show how
our strategy works. A summary of the techniques that our compiler chooses to
solve each negation goal appears in the following table where we use the short
names: naf (negation as failure), delay (elimination of delays technique), cneg
(simple constructive negation), and intneg (intensional negation).

EXAMPLE	NEGATION USED	REFERENCE
free	cneg	[24]
ordered	cneg/naf	[8]
different digits	delay	[8]
greater	intneg	[2]
family	intneg/cneg	[16]
disconnected	intneg	[12]

free constructs natural numbers and checks if they do not belong to a given list.
ordered deduces if a list is sorted by checking if there are not two consecutive
unsorted elements. *different digits* detects if a list contains only different numbers (if there are not duplicates). *greater* is implemented as the negation of less
or equal. *family* is the example presented in section 5 (with *parent/2* and *an-
cestor/2*). *disconnected* indicates that two vertices of a graph are disconnected if
one of them is not reachable from the other.

7   Conclusion

Prolog can be more widely used for knowledge representation based applications
if negated goals can be included in programs. We have presented a collection

of techniques, more or less well known in logic programming, that can be used together in order to produce a system that can handle negation efficiently. Although we do not claim to invent any "new method" to implement negation, to our knowledge it is one of the first serious attempts to include such proposals on the incorporation of negation into a Prolog compiler.

Our main contribution is the use of the information of a program analyzer to define a strategy to organize the use of the negation components. The strategy is designed to be a good trade-off between complexity and generality.

Some other contributions of the paper are the management of disequality constraints using attributed variables and the new compact way to handle constraint normal forms, which has a number of advantages.

The transformation approach in term of disequality constraint is another important point, because it solves some of the problems of intensional negation [3] in a more efficient way than [5].

Finally, the approach to compute universally quantified goals was sketched in [3], but the concrete implementation needs to solve a lot of technical difficulties, what makes our implementation more than a student exercise.

The results of the practical experimentation are quite acceptable on time (although some of the involved algorithms are exponential). We can provide a table of runtime on request. However, we have not included them because of the lack of space and, mainly, because they are not significative due to the fact that we cannot compare with other existing implementations; they do not exist.

As a future work, we plan to modify the compiler in order to produce a version of CIAO with negation. It will give us a real measure of what important is the information of the analyzer to help our strategy. On the other hand, there are still some unsolved problems. The most important is the detection of the cases where the universal quantification does not work in order to avoid the overhead of the for_all predicate when it cannot find a solution. Of course, we will need to use full constructive negation, hard to implement and, probably, not very efficient. The work of [10] could help on this task. In any case, it will be the last resource to be used and will ensure the completeness of the method.

References

[1] K. R. Apt. Logic programming. In J. van Leeuwen, editor, *Handbook of Theoretical Computer Science*, volume 3, pages 493–574, Elsevier, New York, 1990.

[2] R. Barbuti, D. Mancarella, D. Pedreschi, and F. Turini. Intensional negation of logic programs. *Lecture notes on Computer Science*, 250:96–110, 1987.

[3] R. Barbuti, D. Mancarella, D. Pedreschi, and F. Turini. A transformational approach to negation in logic programming. *JLP*, 8(3):201–228, 1990.

[4] C. Braem, B. Le Charlier, S. Modart, and P. Van Hentenryck. Cardinality analysis of Prolog. In *I. S. on Logic Programming*, pages 457–471. The MIT Press, 1994.

[5] P. Bruscoli, F. Levi, G. Levi, and M.C. Meo. Compilative Constructive Negation in Constraint Logic Programs. In Sophie Tyson, editor, *Proc. of the Nineteenth International Colloquium on Trees in Algebra and Programming, CAAP '94*, volume 787 of *LNCS*, pages 52–67, Berlin, 1994. Springer-Verlag.

[6] M. Carlsson. Freeze, indexing, and other implementation issues in the wam. In *I. Conference on Logic Programming*, pages 40–58. The MIT Press, 1987.

[7] D. Chan. Constructive negation based on the complete database. In *Proc. Int. Conference on Logic Programming'88*, pages 111–125. The MIT Press, 1988.

[8] D. Chan. An extension of constructive negation and its application in coroutining. In *Proc. NACLP'89*, pages 477–493. The MIT Press, 1989.

[9] K. L. Clark. Negation as failure. In J. Minker H. Gallaire, editor, *Logic and Data Bases*, pages 293–322, New York, NY, 1978.

[10] W. Drabent. What is a failure? An approach to constructive negation. *Acta Informatica.*, 33:27–59, 1995.

[11] M. García de la Banda, K. Marriott, and P. Stuckey. Efficient analysis of constraint logic programs with dynamic scheduling. In *1995 International Logic Programming Symposium*, pages 417–431. The MIT Press, 1995.

[12] A. Van Gelder, K.A. Ross, and J.S. Schlipf. The well-founded semantics for general logic programs. *J. of the ACM*, 38(3):620–650, 1991.

[13] M. Hermenegildo, F. Bueno, D. Cabeza, M. García de la Banda, P. López, and G. Puebla. The CIAO Multi-Dialect Compiler and System: An Experimentation Workbench for Future (C)LP Systems. In *Parallelism and Implementation of Logic and Constraint Logic Programming*. Nova Science, Commack, NY, USA, April 1999.

[14] P.M. Hill and J.W. Lloyd. *The Gödel Programming Language*. The MIT Press, 1994.

[15] K. Kunen. Negation in logic programming. *J. of Logic Programming*, 4:289–308, 1987.

[16] J. W. Lloyd. *Foundations of Logic Programing, 2nd edition*. Springer, 1987.

[17] P. López-García, M. Hermenegildo, S. Debray, and N. W. Lin. Lower bound cost estimation for logic programs. In *1997 International Logic Programming Symposium*. MIT Press, 1997.

[18] J.J. Moreno-Navarro. Default rules: An extension of constructive negation for narrowing-based languages. In *Proc. ICLP'94*, pages 535–549. The MIT Press, 1994.

[19] S. Munoz. Algunas técnicas para el tratamiento de información negativa en Prolog. Master's thesis, Facultad de Informática, UPM, 1997.

[20] K. Muthukumar and M. Hermenegildo. Compile-time derivation of variable dependency using abstract interpretation. *JLP*, 13(2/3):315–347, July 1992.

[21] L. Naish. Negation and quantifiers in NU-Prolog. In *Proc. 3rd ICLP*, 1986.

[22] A. Di Pierro, M. Martelli, and C. Palamidessi. Negation as instantiation. *Information and Computation*, 120(2):263–278, 1995.

[23] G. Puebla, M. García de la Banda, K. Marriott, and P. Stuckey. Optimization of Logic Programs with Dynamic Scheduling. In *1997 International Conference on Logic Programming*, pages 93–107, Cambridge, MA, June 1997. MIT Press.

[24] R. F. Stark. Cut-property and negation as failure. *International Journal of Foundations of Computer Science*, 5(2):129–164, 1994.

[25] P. Stuckey. Constructive negation for constraint logic programming. In *Proc. IEEE Symp. on Logic in Computer Science*, volume 660. IEEE Comp. Soc. Press, 1991.

[26] A. Voronkov. Logic programming with bounded quantifiers. In A. Voronkov, editor, *First Russian Conference on Logic Programming*, volume 592, pages 486–514, Irkutsk, Rusia, September 1990. Springer 1992.

A Logic-Based Information System

Salvador Pinto Abreu

Departamento de Informática, Universidade de Évora and
CENTRIA (FCT/UNL)
Portugal
spa@di.uevora.pt

Abstract. In this article we present the University of Evora's Integrated Information System (SIIUE), which is meant to model most of the information necessary for the management and day-to-day operation of an institution such as a public University. SIIUE is centered around a logic-based representation of all intervenients and processes, which is used to generate the more efficient and specific representations for the actual use. This includes extended SQL, PHP3 and Java code generation. SIIUE also interacts with an etherogenous set of partial information systems, both to supply and collect information.

Keywords: Information Systems, Logic Programming, Object-Relational Databases, Deductive Databases, Web Interfaces.

1 Introduction

With the increasing pervasiveness of networked computing resources, people come to expect that a growing number of services be available on-line. This applies to all sorts of usages from prospective and actual students, researchers, faculty and staff.

The existing information repositories at our university were very scattered, hiding many inconsistencies and redundancies. These problems were exacerbated because of the lack of network-awareness of these systems. This situation becomes painfully obvious when, for instance, faculty members are asked by several different sectors of the administration for the same piece information, albeit with slight variations. This particular situation was at the source of much institutional dis-functionality, as faculty members would frequently fail to produce the information that was required of them, purporting that they had already given it out.

From the decision-support point of view, the availability of a general-purpose information repository is desirable, structured so that that complex queries can be made pertaining to the whole system. The full benefits of the availability of the information can only be reaped if it is integrated.

Having a Logic Programming representation for an information system goes a long way in allowing for maximal flexibility in expressing concepts as well as in

E. Pontelli, V. Santos Costa (Eds.): PADL 2000, LNCS 1753, pp. 141–153, 2000.

providing a natural specification language for complex queries, as the full power of first-order logic may be employed.

It is our belief that, in an actual implementation, the benefits of Logic Programming can indeed be made effective, by allowing incremental extensions to be developed with relatively little work, when compared with other methods.

In section 2 we introduce the overall system architecture, of which some components are further detailed in section 3. In section 4 some applications of SIIUE are briefly described. In section 5 compares the approaches used in SIIUE to others. In sections 6 and 7 we discuss our experience of actually using this system in the day-to-day operation of our University and propose directions for on-going and future development.

2   Architecture

The main goals for the development of SIIUE are:

1. To promote a declarative approach to the definition and manipulation of the structure and data in the information system.
   This need, together with the requirement that the system be easily prototyped, led to the use of a Prolog-based system both as a modeling language and as the source for the generation of further components.
2. While allowing for multiple forms of access to the information, a single canonical representation should be maintained for all items to be represented, in order to ensure consistency.
   An implication of this approach is that, while there may be several representations for some piece of information, each suited for one specific use, SIIUE must provide mechanisms to ensure consistency and guarantee that every change maps back to the canonical representation.
3. Provide means to represent both structured and unstructured information, tying them up when appropriate.
   The structured information component itself has two classes of information: that which is essentially immutable (for instance the departmental structure of the University) and the information that is subject to change, for instance the students' grades, the researchers' publications or the registry of scientific and cultural events.

We now proceed with a description of the main components of SIIUE, namely the Logic Programming dialect DL in section 2.1, some features of the generated SQL in section 3.2, the generated PHP3 code in section 3.3 and the Java code in section 3.4.

2.1   The Logic Description Language DL

To describe the system's classes, a modeling language can be used. Instead of resorting to an existing modeling language such as UML [1], we decided to implement a new such language, based on a first-order logic description of classes and inheritance, attributes and the values used to populate the classes. We feel that this approach provides more flexibility at the meta-level than would be feasible with other tools. Presently the only form of programming is textual but there is on-going work geared towards developing a visual programming language to satisfy the same design goals (see in section 6).

The approach chosen involves a stylized logic program where the relation between the entities is described, in an object-oriented fashion. The entity taxonomy used for the information system are introduced as a type system with inheritance.

For example, suppose we want to model the hierarchy described by figure 1.[1] The (simplified) correspondig DL syntax could be that given in figure 2. As can be gathered from this example, the DL syntax is fairly simple and can be expressed as Prolog terms with a few operator definitions.

Fig. 1. Sample hierarchy

From the logic description (DL) specification, several processings can be made to generate different types of derived operating components:

1. An SQL file with all the instructions necessary to construct an object-relational database which corresponds to the information described in the DL source. This can map to several database backends, but is currently only implemented for PostgreSQL [6] as it already provides the necessary concepts, namely built-in inheritance. Future versions may interface to another database such as Oracle 8, which also has object-relational features.
2. A set of PHP3 [5] class definitions, to be used for web page construction. PHP3 (PHP Hypertext Processor) is an embedded scripting language for web servers.

---

[1] This example is a fragment of the hierarchy actually used in SIIUE.

```
class individuo: entidade.
 field nome. attr unique.
 field bi.

class vinculo.
 abstract.
 field id: int. domain individuo.id.

class funcionario: vinculo.
 field numero: int.
 field unidade. domain unidade.sigla.

class docente: funcionario.
 field carreira.

class aluno: vinculo.
 field numero: int. attr unique.
```

Fig. 2. DL syntax for the hierarchy from figure 1

3. A Java package, basically a collection of Java classes which mirror the DL hierarchy. These are fitted with constructors which interface to the SQL database previously generated using JDBC. The goal is to simplify the construction of applications which make use of the information system.
4. A document describing the class hierarchy, with comments on every class' usage, on the attributes that are used as external keys, etc. This is especially useful in describing the actual system to non-technical persons.

The derived components are detailed in sections 3.2 through 3.4, with particular emphasis on the "programming components".

2.2 Organization

In order to meet its stated goals, the design for SIIUE makes the following assumptions:

1. The authoritative representation is the Logic (DL) one.
2. Updates to data (instances of classes) are performed through any interface to the (object-)relational database.
3. Changes in the schema can only be performed at the DL level, possibly through the use of more sophisticated tools such as structural editors.

3 Implementation

This section describes some of the issues involved in implementing SIIUE. These have mostly to do with translating one representation into another.

Section 3.5 addresses the issue of ensuring the global coherence of all representations and section 3.7 deals with the aspect of coordinating the information held within SIIUE with external representations thereof, contained in other, more specialized, systems which do not directly rely on SIIUE's information.

3.1 Preprocessing

All the derived components are generated from the DL representation with a translator written in Prolog. This approach provides a large degree of freedom at a stage where the exact syntax and semantics of DL are still in a state of flux.

The logic description language is preprocessed into several operational forms, targeted at different uses:

- An SQL database. This will subsequently be used in the actual applications to perform the work of accessing the information.
- Components for other programming languages. These will mimic some of the information described in DL, but in a form more suitable for specific usages, namely the construction of WWW interfaces. This issue is further discussed in sections 3.3 through 3.4.

This process is presently carried out statically: the DL source is loaded into a Prolog processor which then runs several different queries which will produce the different derived programs.

3.2 SQL Generation

The classes introduced in section 2.1 are preprocessed into some dialect of SQL. In the implemented prototype, we're using PostgreSQL because of its object-oriented features, basically inheritance.

PostgreSQL, as of version 6.4, has some restrictions as to the subset of SQL92 it implements, in particular it does not allow foreign keys. This and a few other restrictions can be worked around by generating the appropriate domain-checking functions and constraints.[2]

The approach of using a logic description pays off especially well in the situation of having to generate SQL because:

- Classes may be directly translated to tables with inheritance in an object-relational database such as PostgreSQL but, should we opt for a traditional relational database without inheritance, the accessibility of the Prolog description of the hierarchy can be used to produce a flattened version of the tables, possibly using views to (artificially) simulate superclasses.

---

[2] This approach could be kept even in the situation where the database can provide foreign keys, because it allows for a very fine-grained control over what is actually performed as an SQL constraint.

- Issues such as dependencies between otherwise unrelated classes (eg. by means of integrity constraints) which may require a given class to be defined *before* it is referenced, may be dealt with by performing a topological sort on the *references* relation between attributes of different classes. This approach is particularly simple to implement in a language such as Prolog. A class A (which will map to an SQL table) is said to depend on another class B if either one of the following conditions is true:
  - A has an attribute whose domain is in the range of an attribute from any superclass of B, provided A is itself not a subclass of B.
  - A is a subclass of B.

This information can then be used to initialize the database but is also important when it is necessary to rebuild it partially or entirely.

3.3   PHP Code Generation

Universidade de Évora adopted PHP3 [5] as a scripting language for its dynamic web pages. PHP is used extensively to construct server-side applications with access to the data and structures available through the information system.

As the structure of the information system is described as a class hierarchy which can be altered, it is important to keep this form of access synchronized with the definitions actually in effect.

From each class declared in DL, a corresponding PHP3 class is created which follows the DL inheritance structure, provides each attribute as an instance variable and defines a few automatically configured methods, which include:

- A constructor method, which can optionally behave as a query to the underlying database in which the query result is used to initialize the class instance. Access to the database is performed using the corresponding PHP library, for PostgreSQL it's the pg_* functions.

  The constructor method may be directed to perform the database query over the set of all subclasses of the given class or to stick to the instances of the class itself only.

  The queries performed are restricted to simple ones, in which all the attributes of the table are fetched, allowing for an optional where clause.[3]
- Traversal methods (more() and next()), which provide an interator construct for use in PHP scripts, similar to a cursor. These are useful for instance to produce listings or selection lists.
- Update methods (update() and insert()). These map to their SQL counterparts and are used to alter the data in the underlying database.

The generated PHP code relies upon the availability of database access functions. In the prototype implementation, the database is PostgreSQL but PHP3 provides access functions which allow for other database engines to be used.

---

[3] In fact it's a suffix of the SQL select query which may be specified, thereby allowing slightly more complex queries to be constructed.

Another category of PHP code that is generated are components for the construction of user interfaces. Initially this includes methods which generate a list-box (or a pop-up menu or two list-boxes) for selecting one or more items from a set, defined by the instances of a given class.

3.4 Java Code Generation

Generating Java classes is not much different from generating PHP classes. The advantage of these is to allow for more client-side work to be performed, thereby relieving the server system from the duty of having to parse long declarations for each page, as happens with the PHP code.

The access to the database component is acheived through JDBC.

Besides creating a Java class for each DL class, the java code base includes classes which use the Swing [3] toolkit in order to create interface components which can be used throughout a wide range of different applications.

With the perspective of having a Java constraint solver, [4] it will be increasingly interesting to utilize the Java interfaces as these will be endowed with a powerful computational mechanism, akin to what can be done in DL.

3.5 Synchronisation

The issue of maintaining the information in its various representations (the database as well as the Logic Programming versions) coherent has to be addressed carefully because the information system (both its schema and the data therein) can be updated frequently.

The main form of updates is to the database, with incidence on a limited set of relations. Each update made must be reflected on the logic representation. This goal can be acheived in one of two ways:

1. An "off-line" method, where the database is periodically queried for changes and these are translated by an external program into logic form, to be subsequently integrated into the logic representation.
2. An "on-line" method which requires a direct SQL/Prolog interface.

In either case, and considering that the updates are performed exclusively on the database[5] it is reasonable to have the updates at the logic level initiated from updates and insertions and deletions at the database level.

The relations which can be updated are explicitly marked as such at the DL level. For these, the SIIUE engine will generate SQL statements which ensure that:

---

[4] We are presently developing such a system.
[5] The logic representation is presently used to rebuild the database and construct the operational interfaces described in sections 3.3 through 3.4. Changes at this level are not tought of as "updates" because they may be arbitrary.

- The tables may be updated.
- Changes get propagated back to the DL level.

With PostgreSQL this can be implemented via the trigger mechanism, in which auxiliary tables can be used to indicate what changes were made. These can then be read back to DL in order to guarantee that both representations are consistent with each other.

With the on-line approach, the trigger-based architecture remains applicable but the method used to convey the changes to the Logic Programming representation can be different: the DL system is made to appear as a *procedural language* in the PostgreSQL database, thereby allowing us to specify actions at the Prolog level from the database specification.

3.6   Authentication

Given the diverse nature of the information contained within SIIUE, it is crucial to ensure that it is correct. To enable this we constructed an authorization system which:

- Encodes within SIIUE itself the access rights to mutable data. The entities that can change information are themselves represented as data.
- Defines validation paths which are required in order for a change to a relation to become effective. This models the workflow process insofar as certain types of information may be provided by one entity, but require an approval by other entities before becoming effective.

At present, the entire authentication mechanism lies within SIIUE. We plan on integrating this with the Kerberos servers within the University.

3.7   Interface to Other Systems

SIIUE is not planned to be a stand-alone information system. It must allow for the interaction with legacy applications which will act as both producers and consumers of information.

This goal is presently satisfied through ad-hoc solutions, programs which import the definitions from SIIUE and interact with the external programs.

4   Applications

The goal of SIIUE is to provide a framework in which several applications can be developed. The main characteristic of the SIIUE-based applications is that the data they rely on is permanently kept up-to-date.

In this section we briefly describe some of the applications presently in use or in development.

4.1   The Academic Services System

The Academic Services at Universidade de Évora provide access to academic information and records for the whole university, namely for students and faculty. The present system was developed before SIIUE came into being, but has been reworked to integrate into SIIUE: the technology used is essentially compatible (relational database).

At present, the Academic Services application feeds SIIUE with information related to student performance as well as the academic calendar. It relies on SIIUE to provide it with the present constitution of the University, in terms of its institutional structure (eg. departments) and its personnel, especially faculty.

4.2   The ECTS Guides

The European Credit Transfer System (ECTS) establishes rules whereby the academic performance of undergraduate students in any adhering University may be assessed in any other such academic institution. The requirements are that the guides provide information — in at least two languages — to a prospective student on the courses offered for any undergraduate program.

The mechanisms that were provided to meet the ECTS guides requirements are such that the information on specific courses, provided by the faculty members, may be used for other purposes. Such is the case with the on-line course descriptions presented on the University's web site. This issue is further exemplified in section 4.5.

4.3   Institutional Evaluation

Portuguese public Universities are currently undergoing an external assessment process, which requires that much information (esp. academic) be available in a timely and flexible manner. This process focusses on specific graduation programs, which usually share many courses with other programs, and requires that all manner of statistics be gathered from the academic data provided in SIIUE.

The course and staff descriptions used for the evaluation is shared with the ECTS guides, thereby achieving one of the stated goals of SIIUE, ie. non-redundancy at the user level.

4.4   Computing Services User and System Support

One of the most obvious users of SIIUE are the University's computing services, who make use of the information contained within SIIUE to manage accounts for faculty, staff and students. This circumvents the previous requirement imposed upon users that they fill in a (paper) form with their personal information. This information is then used to automate the process of creating user profiles, covering aspects such as e-mail, personal web pages, remote access, etc.

A branch in SIIUE's type hierarchy which is currently being developed deals with all the information pertaining to hardware and networks: the goal is to be able to describe the University's network and produce the various configuration files needed for DNS, routing configurations and SNMP, among others. This work is currently well under way and will be the subject of another article.

It is also in our plans to use SIIUE to describe the University's network and maintain information on installed hardware and software. SIIUE will also be used in the next version of the Computing Services' helpdesk system.

4.5   The University's Web Site

One of the driving goals was to be able to provide up-to-date information on the University's web site, whilst avoiding the duplication of such efforts. The new web site relies heavily upon the information contained within SIIUE to refer to such concepts as Departments, faculty and staff, courses and their contents, graduation programs, research activities, etc.

From the SIIUE perspective, the web site (http://www.uevora.pt/) is a consumer-only application. It draws on the information provided by SIIUE to present a highly-connected set of pages, where just about every mention of a term that has a representation within SIIUE is also a hyperlink.

5   Related Work

The University of Porto's Faculty of Engineering has developed a similar information system [7]. However, their approach seems to be restricted to academic and personnel information, lacking the open nature of SIIUE.

At Universidade Nova de Lisboa, a system sharing some aspects with SIIUE is currently being developed: both SIIUE and UNL's system rely on a logic-based description of the type hierarchies involved and generate SQL for the actual application.

6   Future Directions

To promote SIIUE's development and general usefulness, we plan on extending its functionality along the following lines:

- Wider coverage of issues and concepts in an organization such as Universidade de Évora.
  The purpose is to extend the hierarchy described by SIIUE in order to cover concepts such as spaces (building, classrooms, etc.), timetables, research activities, internal document circulation, inventory-related information, network topology information, etc.
  This kind of development is continuously being made, as the system's use reaches further into the organization's structures.

- Further refinements of DL language.
  DL is presently very incomplete insofar as its ability to describe properties of the data model are concerned. We plan on revamping the DL language itself, so as to include abstract types, some form of modular design mechanism (such as contexts [4]).
- Implementation of the on-line DL.
  The present implementation of SIIUE ties the DL and SQL representations off-line only, with the updates performed on the database being propagated to the DL representation in batch and at periodic intervals. It is our goal to ensure that the synchronization is performed on-line, as described in section 3.5.
  To carry this out, we plan on using a lightweight implementation of Prolog such as GNU-Prolog [2], as the basis for our extensions to PostgreSQL. Ironically, Prolog will appear as a *procedural language* from the SQL point of view.
- Mapping of some SQL types as Finite Domains.
  The point is to be able to rely on a CLP system's ability to compute solutions for CSPs. This is highly desirable in an environment such as ours, where many problems may be formulated as CSPs; class schedules are only one such example.
- Higher level interface components on the generated (Java and PHP) code.
  The components presently being generated are fairly low-level; further experience with building applications with SIIUE suggests that more complex components may be constructed.
- Natural language interface.
  One of the most challenging issues when constructing database applications is the ability to automatically generate useful queries from a specification created by a non-technical user.
  It is within our plans to provide support for queries specified in a simplified natural language (we will be targeting Portuguese, obviously), with concepts and vocabulary appropriate for the information contained within SIIUE.
- Visual Programming language to edit the class hierarchy and other aspects of SIIUE.
  With grounds similar to those that motivate a natural language interface, to which we can add the desire to ease the definition process for the concepts which underlie SIIUE (ie. the class hierarchy), SIIUE may prove a fertile ground on which to experiment with visual programming. Work is presently underway to explore this line of research.

7   Conclusions

SIIUE is actively being used at Universidade de Évora; its flexibility has allowed us to address a variety of problems on relatively short notice. Even with a restricted subset of its applications, SIIUE has already gathered enough momentum to prove useful as exhibited by, for instance, the reuse of information between the ECTS guides (see section 4.2) and the Institutional Evaluation (see section 4.3).

When compared to a previous experience we had using the same lower-level tools (PHP3 and PostgreSQL) this approach has proved itself able to cope with the many incremental changes which are bound to happen when dealing with this kind of problem. In particular, changes to the database which can be quite chaotic when directly using the DBMS, tend to be much more controlled if they have to be performed at the DL level. This contrasts clearly with the previous experience we had when designing and implementing a web-based system for the University's Academic Services [8].

It is noteworthy that, so far, only two people have been involved part-time in the design and implementation of all of SIIUE, one of these dealt exclusively with user interface issues. The entire process of design and implementation has nevertheless led to a production release in about a year, even with such limited human resources. This would certainly not have been feasible if not for the expressiveness of the logic programming tools, as witness the related academic services system which required two full-time programmers to develop and maintain during a similar time period.

The system encompasses about 2500 lines of Prolog code, these concern the preprocessing, PHP, SQL and documentation generation as well as the DL source for SIIUE's classes. There are about 100 different classes in the present state of the implementation, these deal with only a fraction of the intended coverage of SIIUE (see the section on future work). The generated SQL schema amounts to approximately 2000 lines of PostgreSQL, including table definitions and various sorts of integrity constraint support functions. The generated PHP support code amounts to about 6000 lines, this is slightly larger than the size of the whole of the hand-written interface code for about 10 different applications, which is also in PHP3.

The issue that, so far, has proved the most troublesome relates to making changes in the schema which apply to information already in the database. The situation seems unavoidable in the incremental development of a system such as this, because the specification is not fully known or even understood by anyone beforehand. The issue has been dealt with manually (painfully so) but we are working towards automating the process: the ability to specify rewrite rules relating different versions of the schema will hopefully highlight our option of using a higher-level description tool such as DL.

As a concluding remark, it must be said that in a traditional university with little CS tradition such as ours, the implementation of a system such as SIIUE has led to a moderate culture-shock situation. Most users of the system (Faculty and Staff, but mostly the former as they constitute a more vocal group) initially failed to grasp the benefits of the electronic fulfillment of their academic duties, and took this requirement as yet another request to provide the information they already had supplied in the recent past. As of this writing and as the second "production" year begins, these misunderstandings are starting to clear up as much information which is common from one year to the next doesn't have to be provided anew.

8 Acknowledgements

The author would like to thank Luis Quintano (Universidade de Évora Computing Services) for his cooperation in the construction of the user interfaces for SIIUE. Universidade de Évora's administration is also acknowledged for the support they provided during the early stages of the project's deployment, without which the work described in this article would have remained a purely academic exercise.

References

[1] Grady Booch, Jim Rumbaugh, and Ivar Jacobson. *Unified Modeling Language User Guide*. Addison Wesley, December 1997. ISBN: 0-201-57168-4. See URL http://www.awl.com/cp/uml/uml.html.

[2] Daniel Diaz. GNU prolog. URL http://pauillac.inria.fr/~diaz/gnu-prolog/, 1999.

[3] Sun Microsystems. The Java Foundation Classes. URL http://java.sun.com/products/jfc/tsc/index.html.

[4] Luís Monteiro and António Porto. A Language for Contextual Logic Programming. In K.R. Apt, J.W. de Bakker, and J.J.M.M. Rutten, editors, *Logic Programming Languages: Constraints, Functions and Objects*, pages 115–147. MIT Press, 1993.

[5] PHP hypertext processor. URL http://www.php.net/.

[6] PostgreSQL www site. URL http://www.postgresql.org/.

[7] Lígia Maria Ribeiro, Gabriel David, Ana Azevedo, and José Marques dos Santos. Developing an information system at the engineering faculty of porto university. In *Proceedings of the EUNIS'97 – European Cooperation in Higher Education Information Systems*, 1997.

[8] Ana Graça Silva and Mário Filipe. O Sistema Informático dos Serviços Académicos da Universidade de Évora. Technical Report, Universidade de Évora, 1998. (in Portuguese).

HIPPO – A Declarative Graphical Modelling System

Chris J.Hinde

Department of Computer Science, Loughborough University, Loughborough, Leics,
LE11 3TU, UK

Richard J.Reader & Kath Phelps

Horticulture Research International, Wellesbourne, Warwick, CV35 9EF, UK

Abstract. The software tool HIPPO allows biologists to produce models that
are realistic biologically without having to write complex computer programs.
Specification of models is simplified by using a graphical user interface and
distribution of models to both scientific and commercial users is expedited by
generating platform independent C code that can be linked to a variety of
interfaces. Individual based and life cycle models, which are relevant to many
biological problems, are easily represented. Some relevant features of HIPPO
are described and an example of a prey-predator-plant interaction is
demonstrated.

Unlike many comparable modellers the graphical representation of the models
is declarative and the whole system has been written in Prolog.
Key words: model, declarative, interaction, integrate, software

Introduction

Most modelling systems are aimed at the research scientists who construct and study
models rather than at the end-users of models. Thus, distribution of dynamic models
within the agri-food chain often requires considerable extra programming effort. A
modelling system, GRaphical Integrated Modelling Environment has been developed
to assist with efficient transfer of simulation models to farmers and growers. The
GRIME system consists of two parts: the development environment and the target
environment. The first comprises a tool „HIPPO" (Hinde *et al,* 1996) and associated
modules to support scientists in the construction, inter-linking and execution of
models based on appropriate sub-models. The second is a grower/advisor system
which can be tailored to each user's particular needs, such as MORPH, the delivery
framework used by Horticulture Research International and GUICS, freely available
from USDA-ARS. The grower advisor systems are generically referred to as the
RHINO system. This paper describes and demonstrates the capabilities of HIPPO for
modelling very diverse systems.

Software such as MATLAB and Mathematica can be used for biological modelling
and are powerful enough to represent the various types of knowledge. However,
without a suitable interface they do not allow biologists to express problems in terms
with which they are familiar. Therefore, much of the work on the HIPPO system has

E. Pontelli, V. Santos Costa (Eds.): PADL 2000, LNCS 1753, pp. 154–168, 2000.

focused on developing a graphical language that would allow biologists to encode knowledge in their own terms. It was not the priority in the design to follow other modelling techniques, but rather to follow the concepts central to biological models and build a graphical description from them. Central to the modelling paradigm, derived from examining many horticultural models and interviewing biologists, is the description of systems in terms of life cycles. An innovative feature of the software is that it uses entity relationship modelling to allow different models to be totally inter-linked. An essential adjunct to the modelling tool is a facility for inclusion of one or more libraries of models. These library models are text based and can be read by the HIPPO modeller and incorporated into a developing model, they also form the basis of a model interchange system and as such allow researchers to access existing models, arising from both their own work and that of their colleagues. Help facilities allow all components of models to be extensively documented.

The system consists of a modelling tool, HIPPO, and a set of support libraries. The latter allow HIPPO to be interfaced to a range of grower/advisor systems for example MORPH (Lucey *et al*, 1999), DESSAC (Henderson *et al*, 1999). The original motivation for HIPPO was to support scientists in constructing, inter-linking and executing models. However experience with the prototype suggested that HIPPO could play an important role in model formulation and a project was initiated to explore this role whilst continuing with model development. This paper describes aspects of HIPPO that distinguish it from other modellers.

A Brief Overview of GRIME

The original objective of the HIPPO system was to integrate already existing and newly developed models associated with Horticulture. Many models existed in a variety of languages with a strong leaning towards Fortran. A few models existed in modelling system such as MATLAB though these were relatively rare. Incorporating „legacy" models would require multi language compilation and linking facilities that could be found within language development environments such as CODE WARRIOR but were not generally part of modelling systems. It therefore seemed sensible to use the multi language facilities available and generate a suitable source language that would be platform independent. GRIME therefore consists of two main parts, HIPPO and RHINO; HIPPO is the subject of this paper.

HIPPO enables a modeller to concentrate on the description of the model rather than its implementation as a simulation. It has a graphical user interface (GUI) which allows the modellers to encode knowledge in their own terms. No knowledge of programming languages is needed and typing is kept to a minimum. To facilitate exchange of models extensive library facilities are available and models are self-documenting. When a model is completed the HIPPO system checks it for logical flaws and, if none are found, C code is generated from the graphical specification. This code is compiled and linked with the relevant libraries for a range of specific interfaces. The ability to link a new model into an existing interface is facilitated by HIPPO generating an executable symbol table that allows the interface to access any variables required to populate the graphical displays. The part of the system responsible for execution of the models is known as RHINO.

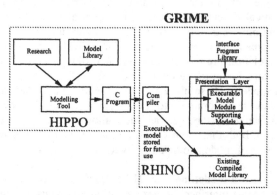

Figure 1. The relationship between HIPPO model denotation system and the RHINO execution system operating as two parts of the GRIME system.

The major features of HIPPO have been designed to relate closely to biological systems, however this does not preclude its use for other models and several other applications have been explored; a current project uses HIPPO to model sustainability indicators for inter-modal transport hubs. Initial investigations focused on the concepts used by biologists rather than the processes they used to generate models. Many biological models and modelling systems had been written by biologists whose efforts had been heavily directed to the programming of their model rather than a description of the biology. As such the goal of HIPPO was to enable the biologists to model using biological terms and to insulate them as far as possible from any kind of implementation issues. In this sense HIPPO may be regarded as a graphical specification language. The biologists interviewed stated that they thought about their systems in terms of life cycles rather than differential equations and flows. Modellers available, such as STELLA (Doyle, 1988), encourage the model designer to express their ideas in terms of rates of change from the beginning of the design of the model. HIPPO encourages the modeller to decide on the participants in the model, the life cycles of those participants, and finally the detailed changes that occur at the various life cycle stages. Other models were examined to establish whether they could be used to model simple life cycles and motivated the research and development leading to the current HIPPO system. Entity relationship modelling (Chen, 1976) is used to denote the connections between models at the top level. At the top level the existence of the entities and the presence of named relationships is all that is denoted, at this stage no direction exists or is implied. Because any interaction generally affects each party to the interaction direction is often inappropriate. Thus the main elements are collections of entities, or objects, containing models that define their behaviour and their relationships. An instance is a single copy of an entity that can interact with other instances of the same or different entities. Each instance exists in one of several states at any given time; these states along with the conditions for transition between states are defined inside each entity. Instances of an entity can create or interact with other instances of the same or different entities in the same or different states. Within a state, details of differential equations and other calculations are described using elementary objects. A range of mathematical functions is available along with random number generators for a wide range of distributions. Support for both deterministic and stochastic modelling is provided but writing additional functions in traditional programming languages can readily extend it. Unlike many modelling systems HIPPO does not animate the model but passes it to RHINO. RHINO has access to a range of pre compiled modules which otherwise would have to be built into HIPPO. Modellers have access to any extra functionality they care to define.

HIPPO

HIPPO is the part of the GRIME system responsible for generating the model and provides the interface for the modeller to specify the model. It is on three layers, the top layer specifies the Entities that make up the model together with the Entity Relationships that specify the relationships between the Entities. The second layer specifies the states that these entities can exist, the transitions between those states and beneath the Entity Relationships, the relations between the Entities in their respective states. The final layer deals with the intra relationships of the properties of the States of the Entities and also the inter relationships. Models of entities and other objects developed within the HIPPO system and stored as HIPPO library object can be re-used as part of other models.

Entity and Entity Relationships

Examples of entities are insect, plant, spore and weather, or train and plane in a transport system. Instances of these entities are individual insects, plants or spores. Usually there would only be one instance of the entity weather but this may be related to any of the other entities. Examples of relationships are; weather warms aphid shown in figure 2 or aphid defines aphid_population as shown in figure 3. These relationships are not intentionally directional at this level and so although the aphid may be unable to affect the weather, the aphid instances making up the entity aphid define the attributes of the aphid_population and in turn the properties of the aphid_population may affect each aphid. In a reflexive relationship, instances of the same entity interact. A common form of same entity interaction is reproduction; here, the interaction may be between the same states as in bacterial multiplication or between different states as in insects laying eggs. The population entity usually consists of one instance of a population that is defined by all the constituent members of the population.

Figure 2. Two entities „weather and „aphid" are related via the relationship „warms".

Figure 3. The details of the „aphid_popn" entity are defined by the collection of individual aphids. At this level all that is defined is that there is an interaction between „aphid" and „aphid_popn".

Entity Relationships

The entities are linked at the top level by entity relationships. It is straightforward to add another entity to the overall system and to link it to the existing entities; the project was initially concerned with integrating sub models. The top level of an early aphid model is as shown below for illustration.

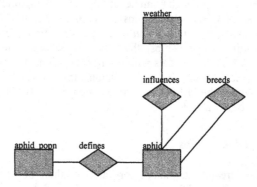

Figure 4. A model of an aphid population with a simple weather model linked in.

A new entity is link into the model the additional variation caused by seasonal fluctuations. It is then populated either by creating the requisite states and underlying equations, or including them from the library. The top level of the resultant system is illustrated in figure 5.

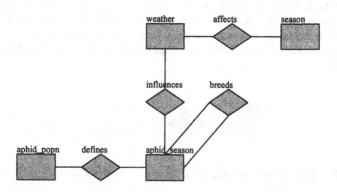

Figure 5 a new entity has been introduced called season which affects the weather model.

It might be convenient to include the seasonal model within the weather model but the separation of the two makes the model more explicit and has no effect on the final numerical result. It is consistent with the idea that the modelling system should reflect the ideas of the modeller rather than the underlying executable code.

An example of a tightly coupled model and a loosely coupled model illustrates the differences. An example from (Froberg 1966) is presented, (figure 6) which shows the components split over several entities and linked together. The execution and animation system reaches the same answers for both the distributed system and an equivalent tightly coupled system that consists of only one entity. Because the denotation of the entities tells the system what is and how it is connected it is then up to the HIPPO/RHINO system to resolve any differences. In particular as the details of implementation are left to HIPPO, the details of integration methods are left to the RHINO system. The modeller needs only to address the model itself.

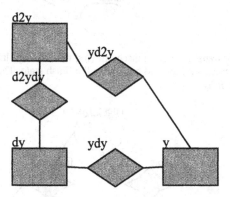

Figure 6. A differential equation modelled over several entities. The entities are „y", „dy" and „d2y", related by $d^2y = (x^2 - y^2)/(1+dy^2)$ with initial values x=0, y=1, dy=0.

The integration scheme obtains answers that are within 5 decimal places of one another depending on the underlying integration method used, this is the responsibility of the RHINO system but HIPPO outputs code which enables the choice to be delayed until execution time. Details of the integration methods and the strategy used to ensure correct integration are dealt with elsewhere.

States and State Transitions

States are used to define life cycles; where appropriate states can be connected by state transition boxes to provide life cycle diagrams. Thus an entity 'insect' may exist in 3 states: egg_larva, nymph and fly. The transition diagram shown in figure 7 describes the order in which an insect passes through the states and the conditions when transitions occur, for example, accumulation of a certain amount of thermal time. A special finish state allows a given instance of 'insect' to be removed from the system when it has completed the 'adult' state. Prior to that a female insect will have created several new instances when she lays a batch of eggs. Some state changes are reversible; for instance a leaf might alternate between a dry state and a wet state according to the time of day. A pond may alternate between a frozen state and a liquid state going through two stages responsible for the process of freezing or melting where latent heat is either released or absorbed, figure 8.

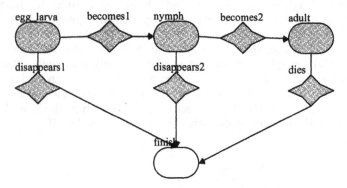

Fig 7 States and state transitions of an insect moving from the egg larva state to the adult state. At each stage the insect could die and transfer to the finish state. These are the states and state transitions of *P.persimilis*

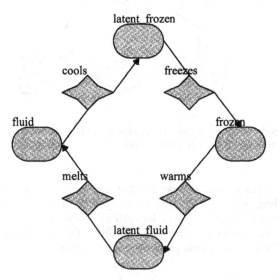

Fig 8 States and state transitions of an body of liquid moving from the frozen state to the liquid state and back again through a state which models the latent heat of freezing and melting showing that transitions may be bi-directional. This sort of bi-directional transition enables hysteresis to be modelled.

Following through the earlier aphid model the states in different entities are connected together underneath the entity relationship. The example used is that of the weather affecting the pre adult aphids and also the adult aphids. The weather affects the different states differently; the pre adult matures given thermal energy whereas the adult aphid produces young.

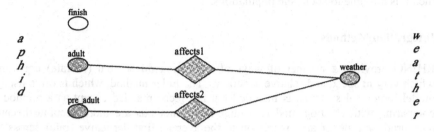

a
p
h
i
d

w
e
a
t
h
e
r

Figure 9. The weather affects the pre adult aphid in a different manner to the adult aphid; the pre adult matures given thermal energy whereas the adult aphid produces young.

Differential Equations

Many horticultural models involve the influence of weather on rates of progress of disease or insect attack. These may be coupled with models for crop growth and phenology. Simulation of these systems involves the numerical integration of a set of differential equations over time. These integration processes are often disguised by basing predictions on concepts such as thermal time or hours of leaf wetness but the underlying differential equations remain. For instance a requirement for d units of thermal time above a base b is based on integrating the equation: rate = $(T-b)/d$ where T ($>b$) is hourly temperature. The transition condition is that the integral of rate (the thermal time) is greater than d. Likewise a requirement for h units of leaf wetness can be expressed as rate=1/h with a transition condition that the integral of rate is greater than 1.

Many other modelling systems support solution of differential equations, perhaps one of the simplest to use is STELLA (Doyle 1988), MATLAB has a strong following in engineering and Model Maker is popular in agriculture. Horticulture requires state transition modelling and it proved difficult to model those aspects in the modellers examined. There are typically radically different sets of equations in the various states of an insect's life.

Types of Integration

Often in crop protection the amounts accumulated within a time step need to be calculated and passed to another entity. For instance in an aphid model the number born (or new instances created) within a time step are calculated and added to the total number in the population. A special zeroed accumulator is provided for this type of situation. Normally rates are modelled by 'taps' but for events a 'sluice' is used. Several taps or sluices can drive a single integration concurrently. Sluices are also used to count populations independently of the time step used. In the „aphid" model one is added to an integrator/accumulator within the population entity for every interaction between that entity and the aphid entity. As interactions have conditions then it is possible to count sub populations.

Integration Methods

RHINO provides a number of ways of evaluating differential (or rate) equations, which vary in speed and relative accuracy. The Euler method, which is often used to model biological systems, is included but not recommended except as a method of comparing with existing models. Runge-Kutta methods are more accurate because they produce a better approximation to the average first derivative (rate) across the whole time step. Adaptive methods save time but retain accuracy by allowing long step lengths to be used during periods of little change (Press et al. 1992). RHINO incorporates functions that allow determination of the step length to be based on prior knowledge of catastrophic events that would not normally be predictable using the standard error measure; these can be defined using the HIPPO system. This is highly relevant in disease forecasting where a sudden violent rainfall may have profound effects.

Interactions

Instances of entities can interact with each other in a variety of ways. In life cycle modelling the most elementary form of interaction is that one instance gives birth to another, figure 10. However instances may also kill one another. This can happen directly as in predator-prey systems or indirectly where population density gets too high and different instances are competing for food. Less dramatic forms of interaction occur where an instance of one entity has a direct effect on an instance of another entity. For instance spores landing on a plant will increase the spore population and ultimately the disease level on that plant. As introduced above it is often useful to incorporate a population entity into a model, properties of the population such as density and structure can then be updated by interactions with other entities.

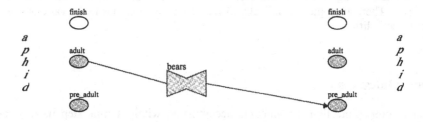

Figure 10. The interaction shown above is a special type that creates another instance. In this case an „adult" „aphid" is responsible for creating another „aphid" in the „pre-adult" state.

Example

Skirvin et al (1999) developed an individual-based stochastic simulation model to investigate the effect of crop type on the biological control of spider mites, *Tetranychus urticae,* by the predatory mite, *Phytoseiulus persimilis.* This model has been reprogrammed in HIPPO to illustrate some of the features of HIPPO that are relevant to crop protection. HIPPO has a graphical user interface which allows models to be specified and modified using icons which are appropriate to each level of the model. The contents of each model component are specified or inspected by double clicking the objects on the screen. For clarity in this paper we show just the parts of the screen that are relevant to the model. In the text quotation marks denote names supplied by the user and underline denotes the first mention of HIPPO objects.

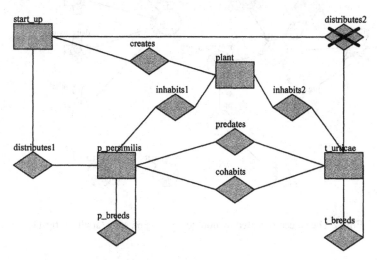

Fig 11 The Entity Relationship Diagram

The model (Fig 11) describes the behaviour of 3 <u>entities</u> denoted by rectangles; the plant, the predator 'p.persimilis' and the prey 't.urticae'. The diamonds represent <u>interactions</u>, here a single instance of the 'start-up' entity creates 100 plants arranged on a square grid and distributes 100 prey and predators randomly and uniformly respectively. The tritrophic predator, prey, plant interaction is described in the <u>diamonds</u> connecting the 3 entities. The prey and predator are connected by 2 diamonds, double clicking on either of these reveals how each instance of the prey and predator interact: 'cohabits' describes the effect on the growth rate of the adult predator of eating different stages egg, nymph or adult of the prey; 'predates' shows which <u>states</u> of the predator predate on each state of the prey. Double clicking on the connection between these states produces a list of the objects in each of the states of the 2 entities, a condition diamond showing that they only interact if they are in the same position on the grid and an addition of a single instance of the prey to the predator's daily food consumption. The diagram also indicates the existence of an error in the distributes relation. Opening this relationship will indicate in more detail where the error lies.

In Fig 12 the oval shapes define the egg/larvae, nymph and adult states. Double clicking on the <u>transition diamonds</u> 'becomes1' or 'becomes2' (not shown) would reveal that transition occurs when egg/larvae and nymphs reach a certain age. Adults die when they reach a certain age. 'dies1' and 'dies2' allow survival rates to be incorporated by comparing known failure rates with a random number. The diagram for the prey entity is very similar whereas, in this system, the plant entity exists in just one state called 'growing'.

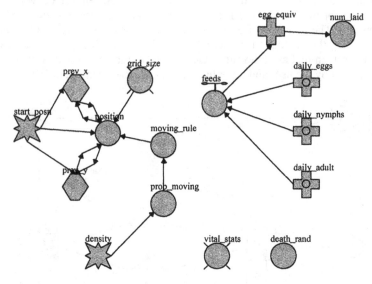

Fig 12 The screen revealed by double clicking on state 'adult' in fig 11.

The left-hand side of fig 12 is concerned with movement, the right hand side with feeding behaviour. The <u>tap</u> 'feeds' converts daily intakes to a rate based on egg equivalents so that the <u>integral</u> 'egg-equiv' holds the size of the mite. The <u>node</u> 'num_laid' uses this size to calculate the number of eggs that it will lay. During the time step (daily, in this case) the values held in the node 'position' change when and if the adult moves. To specify this, <u>delay nodes</u> 'prev_x' and 'prev_y' are used to find the position at the end of the last time step. In practice, a more elegant, non time-step dependant, formulation of movement is obtained by generating a random distance and direction of travel and calculating the position of the mites by integration. The <u>constant node</u> 'vital_stats' stores information which is set up when an individual mite enters the adult state and remains constant for the whole time that it remains in that state; it contains the time of birth, the longevity of the mite and the probability of death within a daily time step. The node 'death_rand' compares that probability with a random number from a uniform (0,1) distribution. The dialogue box used for specifying all calculations allows the modeller to click in parts of the expression and thus avoid simple errors.

Double clicking on the ' p_breeds' reflexive <u>relationship</u> in fig 11 produces a diagram (not shown) of the states involved in breeding: 'adult' 'lays' 'egg'. Double clicking on 'lays' gives rise to lists of objects (fig 13) pertaining to the 'adult' and 'egg_larvae' states along with a <u>condition diamond</u> for specifying whether eggs will be laid at that time step. The <u>quantity rectangle</u> holds the actual number laid which is defined via the node 'num_laid' (fig 13).

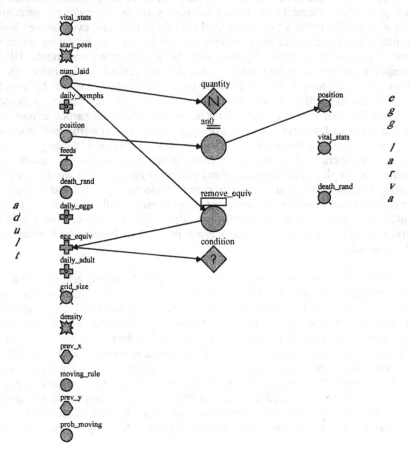

Fig 13 Details of the breeding behaviour of p.persimilis

Implementation

Implementation of the HIPPO modeller has been done almost entirely in MacProlog32 (Johns 1994a) using the graphics primitives provided on a Macintosh computer. A few extra routines that provide added capability to manage the filing system were written but no other extras were required. Although the user has no perception of the underlying implementation Prolog provides an ability to construct/ delete and manage complex models which is unusual in other languages. The modeller consists of around 800K of source code and has taken some years to reach the current state.

Discussion

This paper has given a brief introduction to using HIPPO and its implementation. The biological example used provides a good example of the problems encountered by biologists when attempting to model complex systems. To make the simulation Skirvin et al (1999) wrote a very complex FORTRAN program; even so they had to make many compromises in order to produce results without taking an excessive amount of programming time. By removing the programming constraints, HIPPO encourages modellers to set up models so that they are realistic biologically. Thus a more natural way to program a predator-prey relationship may be by coupled differential equations that mimic the continuous nature of the predation process. Stochastic behaviour is also important; for instance by chance a particular prey may avoid predation and survive to lay many eggs. Such deterministic and stochastic models can easily be combined in HIPPO. Renshaw (1991) says 'the tragedy is that too few researchers realise that both deterministic and stochastic models have important roles to play in the analysis of any particular system'. We would argue that the average applied biologist is all too aware of stochasticity but has neither the mathematical awareness nor the computer programming skills to consider it either separately or combined with deterministic models. Our experience with HIPPO is that users quickly begin to formulate models that are in keeping with Renshaw's (1991) approach.

HIPPO allows complex simulations to be set up relatively quickly and in such a way that the processes are readily understood by other biologists. Anecdotally, some biologists are now using HIPPO to help them to understand the underlying mechanisms reported in research papers. By including checks for logical consistency and referring to variables by pointing and clicking rather than by typing it reduces the likelihood of errors in program code. One compromise made by Skirvin *et al* (1999), in common with many other modellers, was to use a fixed daily time step. In this example this meant that mite movement was restricted to once per day and that a set number of prey were consumed in a day. HIPPO encourages the modeller to specify models independently of the time step to be used. The time step is specified at run-time allowing the scientific user to investigate different integration methods and time steps.

How does HIPPO differ from other software? This paper demonstrates that it allows models to be constructed by users with no knowledge of programming languages. HIPPO is a parsimonious language and the instructions can be learned very quickly. However these few instructions allow an enormous variety of models to be programmed. Some of its most notable advantages over other specialist systems are: finished models can be connected to any interface; systems of individuals can be modelled efficiently because models are dynamically resized; state changes are a fundamental part of the system; models from different sources are easily integrated. In summary, HIPPO offers the exciting prospect of completely new ways of addressing old problems. Perhaps the most significant advantage HIPPO offers to the modellers is the speed at which a prototype model can be produced and also the ease with which models can be connected together, something that was very difficult to do in hard coded models. The model reported above took a mere fraction of the time to construct and debug.

The first prototype, used to demonstrate the principles which were to underpin the HIPPO, was written in a matter of days and although it lacked many of the features of the HIPPO today it served to elicit more information from the biologists and biometricians interviewed and also convinced them of the validity of the approach. Although it lacked many of the features it now sports, it was able to generate executable code which could again demonstrate the ability to deliver models to users without the explicit model definition and which could run stand alone. The original code generator produced Prolog that could then be executed in the MacProlog environment to demonstrate the principles.

Using the HIPPO modeller written in Prolog as an executable specification a student project was initiated to rewrite the modeller in C as this was likely to have substantial effects on size and speed of the modeller. In practice the Prolog HIPPO was sufficiently reactive to user commands that the improved speed of the partial C implementation was of no value.

The reduction in size would have been of value but the ease of modification and introduction of new elements and aspects of the modeller eclipsed any likely benefits. The original author and the students were all proficient in C so it is likely that the gains in the flexibility and ability to modify the system are real.

Acknowledgements

HIPPO is funded by the Ministry of Agriculture, Fisheries and Food.   We thank Dr D.J. Skirvin for making details of his model available to us, and other members of the project team for advice.

References

Booch G. 1986. Object-Oriented Development. IEEE Trans. on Software Eng., Vol. SE12 No 2 Feb. 1986, pp. 211-221.

Chen P P. 1976. The Entity-Relationship Model - Toward a Unified View of Data. *ACM Trans. on Database Systems, Vol. 1, No 1 March 1976,* pp. 9-36.

Doyle J. 1988. Stella, *High Performance Systems Inc.*

Froberg C.-E. 1966. Introduction to Numerical Analysis. Addison Wesley.

Henderson D, Anthony S. 1999. Component Technologies for Support of Agricultural Consultancy and Research A Case Study : MANNER. *Aspects of Applied Biology 55, Information Technology for Crop Protection.*

Hinde C J, Reader R J, Phelps K, Parker C G. 1996. GRIME-A Graphical Integrated Modelling Environment for transferring inter-linked research models to commerce. *Aspects of Applied Biology 46, Modelling in applied biology: Spatial aspects*

Johns N. 1994a. MacProlog32 User Guide, *Logic Programming Associates Ltd.*
  London.

Johns N. 1994b. MacProlog32 Graphics Guide, *Logic Programming Associates Ltd.*
  London.

Lucey S. 1999. MORPH - Decision Support Systems in practice. *Aspects of Applied*
  Biology 55, Information Technology for Crop Protection

Press W H, Teukolsky S A, Vetterling W T, Flannery B P. 1992. Numerical
  Recipes in C. Cambridge University Press.

Reader R J, Hinde C J, Phelps K, Jones J E, Lynn J R. 1998 A Graphical
  Integrated Modelling Environment for Transferring Interlinked Research Models
  to Commerce. *Acta Horticulturae 476, Proceedings of the International*
  Symposium on Applications of Modelling as an Innovative Technology in the Agri-
  Food-Chain

Renshaw E. 1993 Modelling Biological Populations in Space and Time. Cambridge
  University Press. 403pp

Skirvin D J, de Courcy Williams M, Sunderland K D, 1999. Models for
  biocontrol in ornamentals: the importance of spatial population dynamics. *Aspects*
  of Applied Biology 53, Challenges in applied population biology

Calculating a New Data Mining Algorithm for Market Basket Analysis

Zhenjiang Hu[1], Wei-Ngan Chin[2], and Masato Takeichi[1]

[1] Department of Information Engineering
University of Tokyo
7-3-1 Hongo, Bunkyo-ku, Tokyo 113, Japan
{hu,takeichi}@ipl.t.u-tokyo.ac.jp
[2] Department of Computer Science
National University of Singapore
Lower Kent Ridge Road, Singapore 119260
chinwn@comp.nus.edu.sg

Abstract. The general goal of data mining is to extract interesting correlated information from large collection of data. A key computationally-intensive subproblem of data mining involves finding frequent sets in order to help mine association rules for market basket analysis. Given a bag of sets and a probability, the frequent set problem is to determine which subsets occur in the bag with some minimum probability. This paper provides a convincing application of program calculation in the derivation of a completely new and fast algorithm for this practical problem. Beginning with a simple but inefficient specification expressed in a functional language, the new algorithm is calculated in a systematic manner from the specification by applying a sequence of known calculation techniques.

1 Introduction

Program derivation has enjoyed considerable interests over the past two decades. Early work concentrated on deriving programs in imperative languages, such as Dijkstra's Guarded Command Language, but now it has been realized that functional languages offer a number of advantages over imperative ones.

- Functional languages are so abstract that they can express the specifications of problems in a more concise way than imperative languages, resulting in programs that are shorter and easier to understand.
- Functional programs can be constructed, manipulated, and reasoned about, like any other kind of mathematics, using more or less familiar known algebraic laws.
- Functional languages can often be used to express both clear specification and its efficient solution, so the derivation can be carried out within a single formalism. In contrast, the derivation for imperative languages often rely on a separate (predicate) calculus for capturing both specification and program properties.

E. Pontelli, V. Santos Costa (Eds.): PADL 2000, LNCS 1753, pp. 169–184, 2000.

Such derivation in a single formalism is often called *program calculation* [Bir89, BdM96], as opposed to simply program derivation. Many attempts have been made to apply the program calculation for the derivation of various kinds of efficient programs [Jeu93], and for the construction of optimization passes of compilers [GLJ93, TM95]. However, people are still expecting more *convincing* and *practical* applications where program calculation can give a better result, while other approaches could falter.

This paper aims to illustrate a practical application of program calculation, by deriving a completely new algorithm to solve the problem for finding frequent sets - an important building block of data mining applications [AIS93, MT96]. In this problem, we are given a set of items and a large collection of transactions which are essentially subsets of these items. The task is to find all sets of items that occur in the transactions frequently enough - exceeding a given threshold. More concrete explanation of the problem can be found in Section 2.

The most well-known classical algorithm for finding frequent set is the Apriori algorithm [AIS93] (from which many improved versions have been proposed) which relies on the property that a set can only be frequent if and only if all of its subsets are frequent. This algorithm builds a tree of frequent sets in a level-wise fashion, starting from the leaves of the tree. Firstly, it counts all the 1-item sets (sets with a single item), and identifies those counts which exceed the threshold, as frequent 1-item sets. Then it combines these to form candidate (potentially frequent) 2-item sets, counts them in order to determine the frequent 2-item sets. It continues by combining the frequent 2-item sets to form candidate 3-item sets, counting them before determining which are the frequent 3-item sets, and so forth. The Apriori algorithm stops when there are no more frequent n-set found.

Two important factors, which govern the performance of this algorithm, are the number of passes made over the transactions, and the efficiency of each of these passes.

- The database that records all transactions is likely to be very large, so it is often beneficial for as much information to be discovered from each pass, so as to reduce the total number of passes [BMUT97].
- In each pass, we hope that counting can be done efficiently and less candidates are generated for later check. This has led to the studies of different pruning algorithms as in [Toi96, LK98].

Two essential questions arise; what is the least number of passes for finding all frequent sets, and could we generate candidates that are so necessary that they will not be pruned later? Current researches in data mining, as far as we are aware, have not adequately address both these issues. Instead, they have been focusing on the improvement of the Apriori algorithm, while taking for granted that database of transactions should only be traversed transaction by transaction.

We shall show that program calculation indeed provides us with a nice framework to examine into these practical issues for data mining application. In this framework, we can start with a straightforward functional program that solve the problem. This initial program may be terribly inefficient or practically infeasible. We then try to improve it by applying a sequence of calculations such as fusion, tabulation, and accumulation, in order to reduce the number of passes and to avoid generating unnecessary candidates. As will be shown later in this paper, our program calculation can yield a completely novel algorithm for finding frequent sets, which uses only a single pass of the transactions, and generates only necessary candidates during execution. Furthermore, the new algorithm is guaranteed to be correct with respect to the initial straightforward program due to our use of correctness-preserving calculation.

The rest of this paper is organized as follows. We begin by giving a straightforward functional program for finding frequent sets in Section 2. We then go to apply the known calculation techniques of fusion, accumulation, base-case filter promotion and tabulation to the initial functional program to derive an efficient program in Section 3. Discussion on the features of our derived program and the conclusion of the paper are given in Section 4 and 5 respectively.

2   Specification

Within the area of data mining, the problem of deriving associations from data has received considerable attention [AIS93, Toi96, BMUT97], and is often referred to as the "market-basket" problem. One common formulation of this problem is finding association rules which are based on *support* and *confidence*. The support of an itemset (a set of items) I is the fraction of transactions that the itemset occurs in (is a subset of). An itemset is called *frequent* if its support exceeds a given threshold σ. An association rule is written as $I \to J$ where I and J are itemsets. The confidence of the rule is the fraction of the transaction I that also contains J. For the association rule $I \to J$ to hold, $I \cup J$ must be frequent and the confidence of rule must exceed a given confidence threshold, γ. Two important steps for mining association rules are thus:

– Find frequent itemsets for a given support threshold, σ.
– Construct rules that exceed the confidence threshold, γ, from the frequent itemsets.

Of these two steps, finding frequent sets is the more computationally-intensive subproblem, and have received the lion share of data mining community's attention. Let us now formalize a specification for this important subproblem.

Suppose that a shop has recorded the set of objects purchased by each customer on each visit. The problem of finding frequent sets is to compute all subsets of objects that appear frequently in customers' visits with respect to a specific threshold. As an example, suppose a shop has the following object set:

$$\{1, 2, 3, 4, 5, 6, 7, 8, 9, 10, 11\}$$

and the shop recorded the following customers' visits:

$$
\begin{array}{ll}
\text{visit 1:} & \{1, 2, 3, 4, 7\} \\
\text{visit 2:} & \{1, 2, 5, 6\} \\
\text{visit 3:} & \{2, 9\} \\
\text{visit 4:} & \{1, 2, 8\} \\
\text{visit 5:} & \{5, 7\}
\end{array}
$$

We can see that 1 and 2 appear together in three out of the five visits. Therefore we say that the subset $\{1, 2\}$ has frequency ratio of 0.6. If we set the frequency ratio threshold to be 0.3, then we know that the sets of

$$\{1\}, \{2\}, \{5\}, \{7\} \text{ and } \{1, 2\}$$

pass this threshold, and thus they should be returned as the result of our frequent set computation.

To simplify our presentation, we impose some assumption on the three inputs, namely object set *os*, customers' visits *vss*, and threshold *least*. We shall represent the objects of interest using an ordered list of integers without duplicated elements, e.g.,

$$os = [1, 2, 3, 4, 5, 6, 7, 8, 9, 10, 11]$$

and represent customers' purchasing visits by a list of the sublists of *os*, e.g.,

$$vss = [[1, 2, 3, 4, 7], [1, 2, 5, 6], [2, 9], [1, 2, 8], [5, 7]].$$

Furthermore, for threshold, we will use an integer, e.g.,

$$least = 3$$

to denote the *least* number of appearances in the customers' visits, rather than using a probability ratio.

Now we can solve the frequent set problem straightforwardly by the following pseudo Haskell program[1]

$$
\begin{array}{ll}
fs & :: [Int] \rightarrow [[Int]] \rightarrow Int \rightarrow \{[Int]\} \\
fs \ os \ vss \ least = (fsp \ vss \ least) \triangleleft (subs \ os).
\end{array}
$$

It consists of two passes that can be read as follows.

1. First, we use *subs* to enumerate all the sublists of the object list *os*, where *subs* can be defined by

$$
\begin{array}{ll}
subs & :: [a] \rightarrow \{[a]\} \\
subs \ [] & = \{[\,]\} \\
subs \ (x : xs) & = subs \ xs \cup (x :) * subs \ xs.
\end{array}
$$

---

[1] We assume that the readers are familiar with the Haskell notation in this paper. In addition, we say that our Haskell programs are "pseudo" in the sense that they include some additional notations for sets.

We use the infix $*$ to denote the map function on sets. Similar to the *map* function on lists, it satisfies the so-called *map-distributivity* property (we use $\circ$ to denote function composition):

$$(f*) \circ (g*) = (f \circ g) * .$$

2. Then, we use the predicate fsp to filter the generated sublists to keep only those that appear frequently (exceeding the threshold *least*) in customers' visits vss. Such fsp can be easily defined by

$$
\begin{aligned}
fsp &\quad :: \; [[Int]] \to Int \to [Int] \to Bool \\
fsp \; vss \; least \; ys &= \#((ys \; `isSublist`) \lhd vss) \geq least
\end{aligned}
$$

Note that for ease of program manipulation, we use the shorten notation: $\#$ to denote function *length*, and $p\lhd$ to denote *filter p*. The filter operator enjoys the *filter-element-map* property (that is commonly used in program derivation e.g. [Bir84]):

$$(p\lhd) \circ ((x :)*) = ((x :)*) \circ ((p \circ (x :))\lhd)$$

and the *filter-pipeline* property:

$$(p\lhd) \; \circ \; (q\lhd) = (\lambda x.(p \; x \; \wedge \; q \; x)) \lhd .$$

In addition, $xs \; `isSublist` \; ys$ is true if xs is a sublist of ys, and false otherwise:

$$
\begin{aligned}
[] \; `isSublist` \; ys &= True \\
(x : xs) \; `isSublist` \; ys &= xs \; `isSublist` \; ys \; \wedge \; x \; `elem` \; ys \; \wedge
\end{aligned}
$$

So much for our specification program which is simple, straightforward, and easy to understand. No attention has been paid to efficiency or to implementation details. In fact, this initial functional program is practically infeasible for all but the very small object set, because the search space of potential frequent sets consists of $2^{\#os}$ sublists.

3 Derivation

We shall demonstrate how the exponential search space of our initial concise program can be reduced dramatically via program calculation. Specifically, we will derive an *efficient* program for finding frequent sets from the specification

$$fs \; os \; vss \; least = (fsp \; vss \; least) \lhd (subs \; os)$$

by using the known calculation techniques of fusion [Chi92], generalization (accumulation) [Bir84, HIT99], base-case filter promotion [Chi90], and tabulation [Bir80, CH95].

3.1   Fusion

Fusion is used to merge two passes (from nested recursive calls) into a single one, by eliminating intermediate the data structure passing between the two passes. Notice that our fs has two passes, and the intermediate data structure is huge containing all the sublists of os. We shall apply the fusion calculation to eliminate this huge intermediate data structure by the following calculation via an induction on os.

$$
\begin{aligned}
& fs \; [] \; vss \; least \\
=\;\; & \{ \text{ def. of } fs \} \\
& (fsp \; vss \; least) \lhd (subs \; []) \\
=\;\; & \{ \text{ def. of } subs \} \\
& (fsp \; vss \; least) \lhd \{[]\} \\
=\;\; & \{ \text{ def. of } \lhd \text{ and } fsp \} \\
& \text{if } \#(([] \; `isSublist`) \lhd vss) \geq least \text{ then } \{[]\} \text{ else } \{ \} \\
=\;\; & \{ \; isSublist \; \} \\
& \text{if } \#((\lambda ys.True) \lhd vss) \geq least \text{ then } \{[]\} \text{ else } \{ \} \\
=\;\; & \{ \text{ simplification } \} \\
& \text{if } \# vss \geq least \text{ then } \{[]\} \text{ else } \{ \}
\end{aligned}
$$

And

$$
\begin{aligned}
& fs \; (o:os) \; vss \; least \\
=\;\; & \{ \text{ def. of } fs \} \\
& (fsp \; vss \; least) \lhd (subs \; (o:os)) \\
=\;\; & \{ \text{ def. of } subs \} \\
& (fsp \; vss \; least) \lhd (subs \; os \cup (o:) * (subs \; os)) \\
=\;\; & \{ \text{ def. of } \lhd \} \\
& (fsp \; vss \; least) \lhd (subs \; os) \cup \\
& (fsp \; vss \; least) \lhd ((o:) * (subs \; os)) \\
=\;\; & \{ \text{ by } \textit{filter-element-map} \text{ property } \} \\
& (fsp \; vss \; least) \lhd (subs \; os) \cup \\
& (o:) * ((fsp \; vss \; least \circ (o:)) \lhd (subs \; os)) \\
=\;\; & \{ \text{ calculation for equation (1) } \} \\
& (fsp \; vss \; least) \lhd (subs \; os) \cup \\
& (o:) * ((fsp \; ((o \; `elem`) \lhd vss) \; least) \lhd (subs \; os))
\end{aligned}
$$

To complete the above calculation, we need to show that

$$
fsp \; vss \; least \circ (o:) \;=\; fsp \; ((o \; `elem`) \lhd vss) \; least. \tag{1}
$$

This can be easily shown by the following calculation.

$$
\begin{aligned}
& fsp \; vss \; least \circ (o:) \\
=\;\; & \{ \text{ def. of } fsp \} \\
& (\lambda ys.(\#((ys \; `isSublist`) \lhd vss) \geq least)) \circ (o:) \\
=\;\; & \{ \text{ function composition } \} \\
& \lambda ys.(\#(((o:ys) \; `isSublist`) \lhd vss) \geq least) \\
=\;\; & \{ \text{ def. of } isSublist \} \\
& \lambda ys.(\#((\lambda xs.(ys \; `isSublist` \; xs \; \wedge \; o \; `elem` \; xs)) \lhd vss) \geq least) \\
=\;\; & \{ \text{ by } \textit{filter-pipeline} \text{ property } \} \\
& \lambda ys.(\#((ys \; `isSublist`) \lhd ((o \; `elem`) \lhd vss)) \geq least) \\
=\;\; & \{ \text{ def. of } fsp \} \\
& fsp \; ((o \; `elem`) \lhd vss) \; least
\end{aligned}
$$

To summarize, we have obtained the following program, in which the intermediate result used to connect the two passes have been eliminated.

$$fs\ []\ vss\ least \qquad = \text{if } \#vss \geq least \text{ then } \{[]\} \text{ else } \{\ \}$$
$$fs\ (o:os)\ vss\ least = fs\ os\ vss\ least\ \cup$$
$$\underline{(o:)*}(fs\ os\ ((o\ 'elem')\lhd vss)\ least)$$

3.2   Generalization/Accumulation

Notice that the underlined part in the above program for insert o to every element of a list will be rather expensive if the the list consists of a large number of elements. Fortunately, this could be improved by introducing an accumulating parameter in much the same spirit as [Bir84, HIT99]. To this end, we generalize fs to fs', by introducing an accumulating parameter as follows.

$$fs'\ os\ vss\ least\ r = (r\ +\!\!+\ )*(fs\ os\ vss\ least)$$

And clearly we have

$$fs\ os\ vss\ least = fs'\ os\ vss\ least\ [].$$

Calculating the definition for fs' is easy by induction on os, and thus we omit the detailed derivation. The end result is as follows.

$$fs'\ []\ vss\ least\ r \qquad = \text{if } \#vss \geq least \text{ then } \{r\} \text{ else } \{\ \}$$
$$fs'\ (o:os)\ vss\ least\ r = fs'\ os\ vss\ least\ r\ \cup$$
$$fs'\ os\ ((o\ 'elem')\lhd vss)\ least\ (r\ +\!\!+\ [o])$$

The accumulation transformation has successfully turned an expensive map operator of $(o:)*$ into a simple operation that just appends o to r. In addition, we have got a nice side-effect from the accumulation transformation in that fs' is defined in an *almost* tail recursive form, in the sense that each recursive call produces independent part of the resulting list. This kind of recursive form is used by the base-case filter promotion technique of [Chi90].

3.3   Base-Case Filter Promotion

From the second equation (inductive case) of fs', we can see that computation of

$$fs'\ os\ vss\ least\ rs$$

will need $2^{\#os}$ recursive calls to $(fs'\ []\ ...)$ after recursive expansion. In fact, not all these recursive calls are necessary for computing the final result, because the first equation (base case) of fs' shows that those recursive calls of $fs'\ []\ vss\ least\ r$ will not contribute to the final result if

$$\#vss < least.$$

The base-case filter promotion [Chi90] says that the base case condition could be promoted to be a condition for the recursive calls, which is very helpful in pruning unnecessary recursive calls. Applying the base-case filter promotion calculation gives the following program:

$$
\begin{aligned}
fs'\ [\,]\ vss\ least\ r\quad &= \text{if } \#vss \geq least \text{ then } \{r\} \text{ else } \{\,\} \\
fs'\ (o:os)\ vss\ least\ r &= (\text{if } \#vss \geq least \\
&\quad\quad \text{then } fs'\ os\ vss\ least\ r \text{ else } \{\,\}) \ \cup \\
&\quad (\text{if } \#((o\ `elem`) \lhd vss) \geq least \\
&\quad\quad \text{then } fs'\ os\ ((o\ `elem`) \lhd vss)\ least\ (r + [o]) \\
&\quad\quad \text{else } \{\,\})
\end{aligned}
$$

and accordingly fs changes to

$$
fs\ os\ vss\ least = \text{if } \#vss \geq least \text{ then } fs'\ os\ vss\ least\ [\,] \text{ else } \{\,\}.
$$

Now propagating the condition of $\#vss \geq least$ backwards from the initial call of fs' to its recursive calls, we obtain

$$
\begin{aligned}
fs'\ [\,]\ vss\ least\ r\quad &= \{r\} \\
fs'\ (o:os)\ vss\ least\ r &= fs'\ os\ vss\ least\ r \text{ else } [\,] \ \cup \\
&\quad (\text{if } \#((o\ `elem`) \lhd vss) \geq least \\
&\quad\quad \text{then } fs'\ os\ ((o\ `elem`) \lhd vss)\ least\ (r + [o]) \\
&\quad\quad \text{else } \{\,\})
\end{aligned}
$$

in which any recursive call $fs'\ os\ vss\ least\ r$ that does not meet the condition of $\#vss \geq least$ would be selectively pruned.

3.4   Tabulation

Although much improvement has been achieved through fusion, accumulation, and base-case filter promotion, there still remains a source of serious inefficiency because the inductive parameter os is traversed multiple times by fs'. We want to share some computation among all recursive calls to fs', by using the tabulation calculation [Bir80, CH95].

The purpose of our tabulation calculation is to exploit the relationship among recursive calls to fs' so that their computation could be shared. The difficulty in such tabulation is to determine which values should be tabulated. Now, taking a close look at the derived definition for fs'

$$
\begin{aligned}
fs'\ (o:os)\ \underline{vss}\ least\ \underline{r} &= fs'\ os\ \underline{vss}\ least\ \underline{r}\ \cup \\
&\quad (\text{if } \#((o\ `elem`) \lhd vss) \geq least \\
&\quad\quad \text{then } fs'\ os\ \underline{((o\ `elem`) \lhd vss)}\ least\ \underline{(r + [o])} \\
&\quad\quad \text{else } \{\,\})
\end{aligned}
$$

reveals some dependency of the second and the fourth arguments of fs' among the left and the right recursive calls to fs', as indicated by the underlined parts.

Moreover these two arguments will be used to produce the final result, according to the base case definition of fs'. This hints us to keep (memoize) all *necessary* intermediate results of the second and the fourth parameters:

$$(r_1, vss_1), (r_2, vss_2), \ldots.$$

According to base-case filter promotion, each element (r_i, vss_i) meets the *invariant* property

$$\#vss_i \geq least.$$

We could store all these pairs using a list. But a closer look at the second equation of fs' reveals that along with the extension of r, the corresponding number of vss decreases with each filtering. More precisely, for any two intermediate results of (r_i, vss_i) and (r_j, vss_j), $r_i \subseteq r_j$ implies $vss_i \subseteq vss_j$. This observation suggests us to organize all these pairs into a tree. To do so, we define the following tree data structure for memoization:

$$Tree = Node\ ([Int], [[Int]])\ [Tree].$$

In this tree, each node, tagged with a pair storing (r_i, vss_i), can have any number of children.

Now we apply the tabulation calculation to fs' by defining

$$tab\ os\ least\ (Node\ (r, vss)\ [\,]) = fs'\ os\ vss\ least\ r$$
$$tab\ os\ least\ (Node\ (r, vss)\ ts) = fs'\ os\ vss\ least\ r\ \cup$$
$$flattenMap\ (tab\ os\ least)\ ts$$

where $flattenMap$ is defined by

$$flattenMap\ f = foldr\ (\cup)\ \{\}\ \circ\ map\ f.$$

Clearly fs' is a special case of tab:

$$fs'\ os\ vss\ least\ r = tab\ os\ least\ (Node\ (r, vss)\ [\,])$$

We hope to synthesize a new definition that defines tab inductively on os where os is traversed only once (it is now traversed by both fs' and tab). The general form for this purpose should be

$$tab\ [\,]\ least\ t \quad\ = select\ least\ t$$
$$tab\ (o : os)\ least\ t = tab\ os\ least\ (add\ o\ least\ t)$$

where $select$ and add are two newly introduced functions that are to be calculated. We can synthesize $select$ by induction on tree t. From

$$
\begin{aligned}
&tab\ [\,]\ least\ (Node\ (r, vss)\ [\,]) \\
=\ &\{\ \text{def. of } tab\ \} \\
&fs'\ [\,]\ vss\ least\ r \\
=\ &\{\ \text{def. of } fs'\ \} \\
&\{r\}
\end{aligned}
$$

and

$$tab \; [] \; least \; (Node \; (r, vss) \; ts)$$
$=$ { relation between tab and fs', the invariant tells: $\#vss \geq least$ }
$$fs' \; [] \; vss \; least \; r \cup flattenMap \; (tab \; [] \; least) \; ts$$
$=$ { def. of fs', and the above invariant }
$$\{r\} \; \cup \; flattenMap \; (tab \; [] \; least) \; ts$$
$=$ { relation between tab and $select$ }
$$\{r\} \; \cup \; flattenMap \; (select \; least) \; ts$$

we soon have

$$select \; least \; (Node \; (r, vss) \; []) = \{r\}$$
$$select \; least \; (Node \; (r, vss) \; ts) = \{r\} \; \cup \; flattenMap \; (select \; least) \; ts.$$

The definition of add can be inferred in a similar fashion. For the base base:

$$tab \; (o : os) \; least \; (Node \; (r, vss) \; [])$$
$=$ { def. of tab }
$$fs' \; (o : os) \; vss \; least \; r$$
$=$ { def. of fs' }
$$fs' \; os \; vss \; least \; r \; \cup$$
$$(if \; \#((o \; `elem`) \lhd vss) \geq least$$
$$then \; fs' \; os \; ((o \; `elem`) \lhd vss) \; least \; (r \mathbin{+\!\!+} [o])$$
$$else \; \{\})$$
$=$ { by if property }
$$if \; \#((o \; `elem`) \lhd vss) \geq least$$
$$then \; fs' \; os \; vss \; least \; r \; \cup \; fs' \; os \; ((o \; `elem`) \lhd vss) \; least \; (r \mathbin{+\!\!+} [o])$$
$$else \; fs' \; os \; vss \; least \; r$$
$=$ { relation between tab and fs' }
$$if \; \#((o \; `elem`) \lhd vss) \geq least$$
$$then \; tab \; os \; least \; (Node \; (r, vss) \; [Node \; ((r \mathbin{+\!\!+} [o]), (o \; `elem`) \lhd vss) \; []])$$
$$else \; tab \; os \; least \; (Node \; (r, vss) \; [])$$
$=$ { by if property }
$$tab \; os \; least$$
$$(if \; \#((o \; `elem`) \lhd vss) \geq least$$
$$then \; Node \; (r, vss) \; [Node \; ((r \mathbin{+\!\!+} [o]), (o \; `elem`) \lhd vss) \; []]$$
$$else \; Node \; (r, vss) \; [])$$

we thus get:

$$add \; o \; least \; (Node \; (r, vss) \; []) =$$
$$if \; \#((o \; `elem`) \lhd vss) \geq least$$
$$then \; Node \; (r, vss) \; [Node \; ((r \mathbin{+\!\!+} [o]), (o \; `elem`) \lhd vss) \; []]$$
$$else \; Node \; (r, vss) \; [].$$

Similarly, for the inductive case, we can derive the following result, whose detailed derivation is omitted.

$$add \; o \; least \; (Node \; (r, vss) \; ts) =$$
$$if \; \#((o \; `elem`) \lhd vss) \geq least$$
$$then \; Node \; (r, vss)$$
$$(Node \; ((r \mathbin{+\!\!+} [o]), (o \; `elem`) \lhd vss) \; [] \; : \; map \; (add \; o \; least) \; ts)$$
$$else \; Node \; (r, vss) \; ts$$

$$
\begin{aligned}
&fs\ os\ vss\ least \quad\ = fs'\ os\ vss\ least\ [\,] \\
&fs'\ os\ vss\ least\ r = tab\ os\ least\ (Node\ (r, vss)\ [\,]) \\
&tab\ [\,]\ least\ t \quad\ = select\ least\ t \\
&tab\ (o:os)\ least\ t = tab\ os\ least\ (add\ o\ least\ t)
\end{aligned}
$$

where

$$
\begin{aligned}
&select\ least\ (Node\ (r, vss)\ [\,]) = \{r\} \\
&select\ least\ (Node\ (r, vss)\ ts) = \{r\}\ \cup\ flattenMap\ (select\ least)\ ts
\end{aligned}
$$

and

$$
\begin{aligned}
&add\ o\ least\ (Node\ (r, vss)\ [\,]) = \\
&\quad \text{if } \#((o\ \text{`elem`})\triangleleft vss) \geq least \\
&\quad \text{then } Node\ (r, vss)\ [Node\ (r \mathbin{+\!\!+} [o], (o\ \text{`elem`})\triangleleft vss)\ [\,]] \\
&\quad \text{else } Node\ (r, vss)\ [\,] \\
&add\ o\ least\ (Node\ (r, vss)\ ts) = \\
&\quad \text{if } \#((o\ \text{`elem`})\triangleleft vss) \geq least \\
&\quad \text{then } Node\ (r, vss) \\
&\qquad (Node\ ((r \mathbin{+\!\!+} [o]), (o\ \text{`elem`})\triangleleft vss)\ [\,]\ :\ map\ (add\ o\ least)\ ts) \\
&\quad \text{else } Node\ (r, vss)\ ts
\end{aligned}
$$

Fig. 1. Our Final Program for Finding Frequent Sets

Comparing the two programs before and after tabulation calculation, we can see that the latter is more efficient in that it shares the computation for checking the invariant conditions; when an object o is added to the tree, it checks from the root and if it fails at a node, it does not check its descendants. Now putting all together, we get the final result in Figure 1.

4 Discussion

We shall clarify three features of the derived algorithm, namely correctness, simplicity, efficiency and inherited parallelism, and highlight how to adapt the algorithm to practical use.

Correctness

The correctness follows directly from the basic property of program calculation. Our derived algorithm is *correct* with respect to the initial straightforward specification, because the whole derivation is done in a semantics-preserving manner. In contrast, the correctness of existing algorithms, well summarized in [Toi96], are often proved in an ad-hoc manner.

Simplicity

Our derived algorithm is surprisingly *simple*, compared to the existing algorithms which pass over the database many times and use complicated and costly manipulation (generating and pruning) of candidates of frequent sets. A major difference is that our algorithm traverse the database only once, object by object (i.e., item by item) rather than the traditional processing of transaction by transaction. Put it in another way, our algorithm traverses the database vertically while the traditional algorithms traverse the database horizontally, if we assume that the database is organized by transactions.

The vertical traversal of database comes naturally from our initial straightforward specification, where we were not at all concerned with efficiency and implementation details. In comparison, traditional algorithms were designed with an implicit assumption that database should be scanned horizontally, which we believe is not essential. We can preprocess the database to fit our algorithm by transposing it through a single pass. This preprocessing can be done in an efficient way even for a huge database saved in external storage (see [Knu97]). In fact, as such preprocessing need only be done once for a given transaction database, we can easily amortize its costs over many data mining runs for the discovery of interesting information/rules.

Efficiency

To see how efficient our algorithm is in practice, we shall not give a formal study of the cost. Such a study needs to take account of both the distribution as well as the size of data sample. Rather we use a *simple* experiment to compare our algorithm with an existing improved Apriori algorithm [MT96], one of the best algorithms used in the data mining community.

We start by considering the case of a small database which can be put in the memory. We tested three algorithms in Haskell: our initial specification program, the functional coding of the existing improved Apriori algorithm in [HLG+99], and our final derived program. Our initial and final algorithms can be directly coded in Haskell by representing sets using lists.

The input sample data was extracted from the Richard Forsyth's zoological database, which is available in the UCI Repository of Machine Learning Databases [BM98]. It contains 17 objects (corresponding to 17 boolean attributes in the database) and 101 transactions (corresponding to 101 instances). We set the threshold to be 20 (20% of frequency), and did experiment with Glasgow Haskell Compiler and its profiling mechanism. The experimental result is as follows.

	total time (secs)	memory cells (mega bytes)
Our Initial Specification	131.2	484.1
An Apriori Algorithm	10.88	72.0
Our Final Algorithm	0.44	2.5

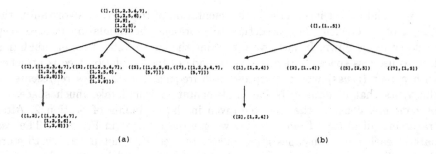

Fig. 2. Tree Structure for Tabulation

It shows that our final algorithm has been dramatically improved comparing to our initial one, and that it is also much more efficient than the functional coding of an existing algorithm (about 20 times faster but using just 1/30 of memory cells).

What if the database is so huge that only part of database can be read into memory at one time? Except for the preprocessing of the database to match our algorithm (to be done just once as discussed above), our algorithm can deal with the partitioning of database very well. If the database has N objects (items), our algorithm allow it to be partitioned into N smaller sections. We only require that each of these sections be read into memory, one at a time, which poses no problem practically.

Parallelism

Our algorithm is quite suitable for parallel computation, which can be briefly explained as follows. Suppose that we have objects from 1 to N, and M processors of $P_1, \ldots, P_M$. We can decompose the objects into M groups, say 1 to N/M, $N/M + 1$ to $2N/M$, ..., and use P_i to compute the tabulation tree for items from $(i-1)N/M + 1$ to iN/M. Certainty all the processors can do this in parallel. After that, we may propagate information of the single-item frequent sets from processor P_{i+1} to P_i for all i, to see whether these single-item frequent sets in P_{i+1} could be merged with frequent sets computed in P_i. Note that this parallel algorithm can be obtained directly from the sequential program *tab* in Figure 1 by parallelization calculation [HTC98], which is omitted here.

Practical Issues

The derived algorithm can be used practically to win over the existing algorithms. To be able to compare our results more convincingly with those in data mining field, we are mapping the algorithm to a C program and testing it on the popular benchmark of sample database. The detailed results will be summarized in another paper. Here, we only highlight one practical consideration.

A crucial aspect in practical implementation of the derived algorithm is the design of an efficient data structure to represent the tabulation tree to keep memory usage down. In fact, we can refine the current structure of tabulation tree to use less space. Notice that each node of the tabulation tree is attached with a pair (r, vss) where r represents a frequent set, and vss represents all the visits that contain r. Naive implementation would take much space. To be concrete, consider the example given in the beginning of Section 2. After traversing all objects from 1 to 11, we get the tree (a) in Figure 2. The vss part in each node consumes much space. In fact, it is not necessary to store the detailed visit content in each node. Instead, it is sufficient to store a list of indices to the visits, as shown in tree (b) in Figure 2. Practically, the number of indices in each node is not so big except for the root where we use the range notation to represent it cheaply, and this would become smaller with each step down from parent to its children.

We can do further in many ways to reduce the size of the tabulation tree. (1) In preprocessing phase, we may sort the objects of the database by decreasing frequency, which should allow subrange notation of indices to be used in a maximized fashion. (2) If the size of vss is within twice of the threshold $least$ at a particular node, we may keep negative information at the children nodes, as these lists would be shorter than the threshold. (3) As nodes for 1-itemset take the most memory and these should perhaps be kept offline in virtual memory and be paged in when required.

5   Conclusion

In this paper, we have addressed a practical application of program calculation of functional programs by deriving novel algorithms that are also practically fast. We have chosen an important subproblem of finding frequent sets as our target. This problem is of practical interest, and have been extensively researched by the data mining community in the last six years. Many researchers have devoted much time and energy to discover clever and fast algorithms. By program calculation of functional programs, we have successfully obtained a completely new algorithm that is also practically fast.

Our derivation of a new frequent set algorithm did not depend on new tricks. Instead, it is carried out using a sequence of standard calculation techniques such as fusion, accumulation, filter promotion and tabulation. These calculation techniques are quite well-known in the functional programming community.

Acknowledgments

This paper owes much to the thoughtful and inspiring discussions with David Skillicorn, who argued that program calculation should be useful in derivation of data mining algorithms. He kindly explained to the first author the problem as well as some existing algorithms. We would also like to thank Christoph Armin

Herrmann who gave us his functional coding of an existing (improved) Apriori algorithm, and help test our Haskell code with his HDC system.

References

[AIS93]   R. Agrawal, T. Imielinski, and A. Swami. Mining association rules between sets of items in large databases. In *1993 International Conference on Management of Data (SIGMOD'93)*, pages 207–216, May 1993.

[BdM96]   R.S. Bird and O. de Moor. *Algebras of Programming*. Prentice Hall, 1996.

[Bir80]   R. Bird. Tabulation techniques for recursive programs. *ACM Computing Surveys*, 12(4):403–417, 1980.

[Bir84]   R. Bird. The promotion and accumulation strategies in transformational programming. *ACM Transactions on Programming Languages and Systems*, 6(4):487–504, 1984.

[Bir89]   R. Bird. Constructive functional programming. In *STOP Summer School on Constructive Algorithmics, Abeland*, 9 1989.

[BM98]   C.L. Blake and C.J. Merz. UCI repository of machine learning databases, 1998. http://www.ics.uci.edu/~mlearn/MLRepository.html.

[BMUT97] S. Brin, R. Motwani, J. Ullman, and S. Tsur. Dynamic itemset counting and implication rules for market basket data. In *1997 International Conference on Management of Data (SIGMOD'97)*, pages 255–264, AZ, USA, 1997. ACM Press.

[CH95]   W. Chin and M. Hagiya. A transformation method for dynamic-sized tabulation. *Acta Informatica*, 32:93–115, 1995.

[Chi90]   W.N. Chin. *Automatic Methods for Program Transformation*. Phd thesis, Department of Computing, Imperial College of Science, Technology and Medicone, University of London, May 1990.

[Chi92]   W. Chin. Safe fusion of functional expressions. In *Proc. Conference on Lisp and Functional Programming*, pages 11–20, San Francisco, California, June 1992.

[GLJ93]   A. Gill, J. Launchbury, and S. Peyton Jones. A short cut to deforestation. In *Proc. Conference on Functional Programming Languages and Computer Architecture*, pages 223–232, Copenhagen, June 1993.

[HIT99]   Z. Hu, H. Iwasaki, and M. Takeichi. Caculating accumulations. *New Generation Computing*, 17(2):153–173, 1999.

[HLG+99] C. Herrmann, C. Lengauer, R. Gunz, J. Laitenberger, and C. Schaller. A compiler for HDC. Technical Report MIP-9907, Fakultat fur Mathematik und Informatik, Universitat Passau, May 1999.

[HTC98]   Z. Hu, M. Takeichi, and W.N. Chin. Parallelization in calculational forms. In *25th ACM Symposium on Principles of Programming Languages*, pages 316–328, San Diego, California, USA, January 1998.

[Jeu93]   J. Jeuring. *Theories for Algorithm Calculation*. Ph.D thesis, Faculty of Science, Utrecht University, 1993.

[Knu97]   D. Knuth. *The Art of Computer Programming: Volume 3 / Sorting and Searching*. Addison-Wesley, Longman, 1997. Second Edition.

[LK98]   D. Lin and Z. Kedem. Princer Search: A new algorithm for discovering the maximum frequent set. In *VI Intl. Conference on Extending Database Technology*, Valencia, Spain, March 1998.

[MT96]   H. Mannila and H. Toivonen. Multiple uses of frequent sets and condensed representations. In *2nd International Conference on Knowledge Discovery and Data Mining (KDD'96)*, pages 189 – 194, Portland, Oregon, August 1996. AAAI Press.

[TM95]   A. Takano and E. Meijer. Shortcut deforestation in calculational form. In *Proc. Conference on Functional Programming Languages and Computer Architecture*, pages 306–313, La Jolla, California, June 1995.

[Toi96]   H. Toivonen. *Discovery of Frequent Patterns in Large Data Collections*. Ph.D thesis, Department of Computer Science, University of Helsinki, 1996.

A Toolkit for Constraint-Based Inference Engines

Tee Yong Chew, Martin Henz, and Ka Boon Ng

National University of Singapore, Singapore 117543,
{henz,ngkaboon}@comp.nus.edu.sg,
http://www.comp.nus.edu.sg/

Abstract. Solutions to combinatorial search problems can benefit from custom-made constraint-based inference engines that go beyond depth-first search. Several constraint programming systems support the programming of such inference engines through programming abstractions. For example, the Mozart system for Oz comes with several engines, extended in dimensions such as interaction, visualization, and optimization. However, so far such extensions are monolithic in their software design, not catering for systematic reuse of components.

We present an object-oriented modular architecture for building inference engines that achieves high reusability and supports rapid prototyping of search algorithms and their extensions. For the sake of clarity, we present the architecture in the setting of a C++ constraint programming library. The SearchToolKit, a search library for Oz based on the presented architecture, provides evidence for the practicality of the design.

1 Introduction

Finite domain constraint programming (CP(FD)) grew out of research in logic programming. The first programming systems for CP(FD), including earlier versions of Ilog Solver [Pug94], had Prolog's depth-first search built-in as their only inference engine.

The language CLAIRE [CL96] and the most recent version of Ilog Solver [ILO99a] (see discussion in [LP99]) support the programming of backtracking-based inference engines. Oz [Smo95] allows the programming of copying-based engines [Sch97b] through a a built-in data type called space.

Mozart [Moz99], the most recent implementation of Oz, provides engines for depth-first search (with or without branch-and-bound), limited discrepancy search [HG95] and parallel search. The Oz Explorer [Sch97a] is a graphical tool that allows to visualize and to interactively explore search trees.

The programming of new tree search algorithms can be a complex task. A true software engineering problem arises when several design dimensions need to be considered. Such dimensions include for example user interaction with the inference engine during search, visualization of the search tree, and optimization via a constraint-based cost function (branch-and-bound).

E. Pontelli, V. Santos Costa (Eds.): PADL 2000, LNCS 1753, pp. 185–199, 2000.
© Springer-Verlag Berlin Heidelberg 2000

The engines included in the Mozart search libraries are monolithic in that they combine a basic inference engine with a fixed set of extensions. For example, the class `Search.object` combines depth-first search with interaction on the level of solutions, memory utilization based on recomputation and branch-and-bound optimization. The Oz Explorer [Sch97a] adds to these visualization and interaction on the level of nodes. Due to the monolithic design, the effort spent on implementing extensions of previous engines to support for example visualization of search trees is virtually lost for programming a new search algorithm. In practice, the monolithic structure discourages experimenting with application-specific engines, because it becomes a major effort to implement such a new engine and equip it with useful facilities like visualization of search trees.

The question that is addressed in this work is how to overcome this situation. The answer is to modularize inference engines in such a way that the basic engines and the various design dimensions can be implemented separately, using well-defined interfaces between them. We shall present a design that allows to plug together search algorithms with modules for optimization, interaction, visualization, etc. If a search algorithm is constructed following the outlined guidelines, it becomes trivial to equip it with branch-and-bound optimization, node-level tracing, Oz-Explorer-like branch-and-bound optimization or visualization of the search tree, and other features. Modules for individual dimensions can be developed independently and employed by all search algorithms.

2   Scripts, Stores, Engines

Finite domain problems are problems of assigning integer values to variables such that all given constraints are satisfied. A simple example is

$$x \in \{5, \ldots, 10\}, y \in \{1, \ldots, 7\}, x < y, x + y = 11$$

In finite domain constraint programming, the domains of variables, i.e. the set of its possible values, are kept in a store. Initially, the domains are unrestricted. Simple constraints such as $x \in \{5, \ldots, 10\}$ and $y \in \{1, \ldots, 7\}$ can be directly entered in the store by restricting the domains of the variables in the store. More complex constraints such as $x < y$ and $x + y = 11$ are operationalized using propagators, which are connected to the store. Propagators observe the domains of their variables and strengthen the store according to a propagation algorithm. For example, the propagator for $x < y$ may eliminate from the domain of x all values that are greater than or equal to the biggest value in the domain of y.

Systems that support the programming of inference engines provide abstractions that represent the store. Ilog Solver [ILO99a] represents stores by C++ objects of class `IlcManager`, and Oz represents stores by data of a built-in datatype `Space`. To allow a concise presentation of our results, we present them in the setting of a C++ constraint programming library, assuming the reader to be familiar with C++ syntax. Stores are represented by objects of class `store`. The member function

---

Program 1 Representing Variables and Propagators

```
void main(int argc, char * argv[]) {
    store * s = new store();
    var x = s->newvar(5,10);
    var y = s->newvar(1,7);
    LessThan(s,x,y);
    Sum(s,x,y,11);
    ...
}
```

```
var store::newvar(int low, int high);
```

introduces a new variable in a given store and returns an identifier by which the variable can be referred to. Propagators are represented by instances of propagator classes, whose creation leads to installation of a propagator in a store. For example, the following function installs a less-than propagator in a given store s.

```
void LessThan(store * s, var left, var right);
```

A store that represents the above constraints can be created as shown in Program 1.

The member function `tell` of stores is used by propagators and allows to narrow the domain d_1 of a given variable such that it contains only values from the domain d_2 passed to `tell`.

```
store::tell(var v, int lo, int hi);
```

If the intersection of d_1 and d_2 is empty, a failure occurs. Such failures are crucial for constraint programming, since they allow to prune the search tree. As a generic way to indicate failure to search algorithms, failing `tell` operations raise the C++ exception `Failure()`. The design and implementation algorithms for propagators is well developed in systems such as Ilog Solver [ILO99a] and the Oz Constraint Programming Interface [Moz99]. In this work, we concentrate on the design of tree search algorithms.

3   Search Trees

Usually propagation alone does not suffice to solve constraint problems. Thus, after exhaustive propagation, a distribution step is done, i.e. a constraint c is chosen and search is performed recursively with two stores to which c and, respectively, $\neg c$ are added. An algorithm that systematically generates suitable constraints for distribution is called a distributor, and the constraints c and $\neg c$ define a choice point. Distributors are represented in our library by extension of an abstract class `choice`.

Program 2 Naive Variable Enumeration

```
class naive : public choice {
private:
    vector<var> vars; // variables to be enumerated
    int idx;          // index of variable to be enumerated
    choice * cont;    // continuation for further distribution
public:
  naive(vector<var> vs,int i,choice * c ) : vars(vs), idx(i), cont(c) {}
  choice * choose(store * s, int i) {
    int l = s->getlo(vars[idx]); int h = s->gethi(vars[idx]);
    if (i==0) {
      s->tell(vars[idx],l,l);
      return (idx+1==vars.size() ? cont : new naive(vars,idx+1,cont));
    }
    else {
      s->tell(vars[idx],l+1,h);
      return new naive(vars,idx,cont);
    }
  }
}
```

```
class choice {
public:
  virtual choice * choose(store *, int)=0;
};
```

The member function **choose** of **choice** is given an integer i and returns its ith alternative. Often, distributors fix one variable v of a given set of variables to a value x in the left child ($i = 0$) and exclude x from the domain of v in the right child ($i = 1$). Such distributors are called enumerators. Program 2 represents naive enumeration, where the variables of a given vector are enumerated from left to right, starting with the smallest values in their domains.

Note that **choose** returns new objects of class **naive**, until all variables in **vars** are fixed, in which case the continuation choice **cont** is returned. The continuation can be used to continue distribution with other constraints after all variables in **vars** are fixed, or to collect information from the encountered solutions. For example, if the continuation choice is an instance of the class **print** in Program 3, the lower bounds of the components of a given variable vector are displayed each time a choice is performed. The return value **NULL** indicates that the search is done.

4   Search

A technical difficulty in searching for solutions is that changes on a store done in one branch of the search tree may not affect the exploration of other branches.

Program 3 A Node Class for Printing Variables

```
class print : public choice {
private: vector<var> vars;
public:
  print(vector<var> vs) : vars(vs) {}
  node * choose(store * s, int i) {
    for (int j = 0; j < vars.size(); j++)
      cout<<"col: "<<vs[i]<<"\nrow: "<<s->getlo(vars[i])<<"\n";
    return NULL;
}
}
```

Two solutions to this problem are in use for this. The most common approach—following Prolog implementation tradition—is to mark a store and record all changes done after a mark. A backtrack operation allows to undo changes that were done since a given mark. The following operations on stores support this concept.

```
mark store::mark();
void store::backtrack(mark m);
```

A depth-first inference engine that employs backtracking is given in Program 4.

Using this engine, the first solution to the constraint problem of the previous section can be displayed by extending Program 1 as follows.

```
void main(int argc, char * argv[]) {
   store * s = new store();
   ...
   vector<var> vars(2);
   vars[1]=x; vars[2]=y;
   solve_one(s,new naive(vars,0,new print(vars)));
}
```

Program 4 Backtracking Depth-First Search

```
choice * solve_one(store * s,choice * c) {
  if (c == NULL) return c;
  mark m = s->mark();
  try {return solve_one(s,c->choose(s,0));}
  catch (Failure) {
   s->backtrack(m);
    return solve_one(s,c->choose(s,1));
  }
}
```

An alternative approach to backtracking is to copy stores at each node and start from the copy when a different branch needs to be explored. This technique is described by Schulte in [Sch97b]. In [Sch99], Schulte analyses recomputation, a method for reducing the space consumption of copying-based search, and compares several variants of recomputation with backtracking-based search. In order to support copying/recomputation, we allow to copy stores through the following operation.

```
store * store::copy();
```

The implementation of depth-first search using the memory policy of copying unfortunately requires a re-implementation of depth-first search using copy instead of mark and backtrack. This hinders the reuse of algorithms. We would like to keep the aspects of exploration and memory policy independent from each other.

5   Memory Policy

The first step towards a modular search library is to separate the memory policy from the basic search algorithm. To this aim, we introduce a level of abstraction between engines and stores. This level is represented by abstract stores. An abstract store abstracts away how a store at a particular node in the search tree is represented.

```
class a_store {
public:
  virtual store * get_store()=0;
  virtual a_store * new_store(store);
}
```

A class representing an abstract store for backtracking is given in Program 5. Its instances keep a reference to a store. Initialization marks the store. Each time the store is retrieved via get_store, backtracking is performed and a new mark created. The member function new_store is a virtual constructor needed to create an abstract store of the same class as a given abstract store (see next section).

6   Search Trees

In order to describe tree search algorithms, it is useful to have a data structure for representing nodes of search trees. A node in a search tree is determined by an abstract store together with a distributor. The service provided by a node is to navigate to a child node. Assuming binary choices, a corresponding node class is given in Program 6. The creation of a child node needs to be protected from Failure exceptions arising from corresponding choose operations on choices. We represent leaf nodes of the search tree by the special nodes success_node and failure_node.

Program 5 Abstract Store with Backtracking Policy

```
class backtrack_store : public a_store {
  mark m;
  store * s;
public:
  backtrack_store(store * st) : s(st) {
    mark = st->mark(); }
  store * get_store() {
    s->backtrack(mark);
    mark = s->mark();
    return s;
  }
  // virtual constructor
  a_store * new_store(store * st) {
    return new backtrack_store(st);
  }
}
```

7 Exploration

The engine in Program 4 tightly integrates two aspects of a search engine, namely the exploration—the *order* in which nodes are visited—and the interaction—the *way* in which the exploration proceeds. The interaction is fixed to a straight first-solution search. Other possibilities are all-solution search, last-solution search (e.g. useful in combination with optimization); tools such as the Oz Explorer allow to interactively explore the search tree. Our aim is to separate these modes of interaction from the basic exploration algorithm. To this aim, we represent the basic exploration algorithm by a function `one_step` that says how to perform one step in the search. An interaction performs `one_step` as needed by the desired mode of interaction.

Program 7 shows a depth-first exploration class. A stack of nodes keeps track of the path from the root to the current node in the tree. Initially the stack contains the root node of the tree. If the stack becomes empty, NULL is returned. Otherwise, we pop the stack. If the top of stack is a non-leaf node, we check whether the left child was visited before. If not, we push the node back and create the left child. If it was visited before, we know that depth-first search explored the left subtree and thus create the right child. In both cases, the new node is pushed on the stack and returned.

An exploration can keep a representation of the tree in the state of the engine object. For depth-first search, we only need to keep the path from the current node to the root. This path is kept in a stack. Breadth-first search would keep instead of a stack a queue, representing the current fringe of the breadth-first tree.

Program 6 Nodes in Search Trees

```
class node {
private:
  choice * c;
  a_store * as;
public:
  node * left, * right;
  node(choice * ch, a_store * ast) :
    left(NULL), right(NULL), c(ch), as(ast) {};
  node * make_left_child() {
    store * s = as->get_store();
    try {
      choice * c0 = c->choose(s,0);
      left = c0 ? new node(c0,as->new_store(s)) : success_node;
    }
    catch (Failure) left = failure_node;
    return left;
  }
  node * make_right_child() {
    store * s = as->get_store();
    try {
      choice * c1 = c->choose(s,1);
      right = c1 ? new node(c1,as->new_store(s)) : success_node;
    }
    catch (Failure) right = failure_node;
    return right;
  }
}
node * success_node = new node(NULL,NULL);
node * failure_node = new node(NULL,NULL);
```

8   Interaction

Given an exploration, search can be conducted by repeatedly calling `one_step` and examining the resulting nodes. This task is performed by interaction functions. In the simplest case, an interaction searches for the first, the last or all solution nodes. For example, search for the first solution can be done as shown in Program 8.

Thus, putting it all together, the first solution to the problem given in Section 2 can be displayed by calling

```
void main(int argc, char * argv[]) {
  store * s = new store();
  ...
  first(new depth_first(new backtrack_store(s),
                  new naive(vars,0,new print(vars))));
}
```

Program 7 Depth-first Exploration

```
class depth_first : public exploration {
private:
  Stack<node *> stack;
public:
  depth_first(a_store * s,choice * c) {
    stack.push(new node(c,s));
  }
  node * one_step() {
    if (stack.empty()) return NULL;
    node * n = stack.pop();
    if (n == success_node || n == failure_node) return n;
    node * n2;
    if (!n->left) {         // there's a no left child yet
      stack.push(n);        // go left
      n2 = s->make_left_child();
    }
    else
      n2 = s->make_right_child();  // go right
    stack.push(n2);
    return n2;
  }
};
```

Program 8 First-solution Search

```
node * first(exploration * e) {
  node * n;
  while (n = e->one_step()) if (n==success_node) break;
  return n;
}
```

9   STK: A Search Toolkit for Oz

The presented architecture allows to develop classes for memory policy, classes for exploration and interaction functions independently from each other. We used the presented concepts to develop a modular search toolkit, STK, for the constraint programming language Oz. STK is available in [HC99] and documented in [Che99]. In addition to the dimensions of memory policy, exploration and interaction, STK supports the design dimensions optimization, information and visualization, which are briefly described below.

9.1   Optimization

Modules of dimension "optimization" allow to modify an engine such that a pruning behavior is achieved. A well-known method for pruning is branch-and-bound.

After a solution is found, a constraint is added to every subsequent node that the next solution should be better than the one already found, where "better" is defined using a given optimization function. In addition to branch-and-bound, STK provides a module for restart optimization, where the constraint is added to the root node and search restarts from the root.

Optimization modules rely on interaction modules to indicate that a solution has been found.

9.2   Information

When designing constraint-based solutions, it is often useful to inspect the search tree in detail. The dimension "information" provides modules for accessing the information in a given node in the tree. Using an information module, interaction modules and a visualization modules can be enhanced by the facility of application-specific display of the information in a node, which is passed to the information module in form of an Oz procedure.

In addition, STK provides an information module `edgeInformation` to display information on the distribution step that leads to a given node. For example, it is possible to display which variable was enumerated and to which value it was bound. To achieve this behavior, distributors communicate with the STK engine to annotate choice points with information that is then stored in nodes and displayed on demand. STK provides a suitably modified version of Mozart's distributor library `FD.distribute`.

9.3   Visualization

The visualization of search trees is a dimension orthogonal to exploration and interaction. In a corresponding module, the creation of the root node leads to opening of a display area in which the root node is graphically represented. Similar to the Oz Explorer, this module uses an incremental tree drawing algorithm inspired by [Ken96]. Figure 1 shows the display of an engine that combines breadth-first search with visualization.

STK provides two visualization modules. The first, `standardDisplay`, requires the `tracer` interaction and allows to interactively explore the search tree, whereas the second, `simpleDisplay` only displays the search tree as it is being explored, but works with any interaction module.

9.4   Generating Inference Engines

Figure 2 shows the currently available modules for each dimension available in STK.

In STK, each module is described by two classes; a node class that specifies the local effect of the module and an engine class that specifies its global effect. In order to achieve generation of custom-made search engines at runtime, we need to build two inheritance graphs containing the desired node and engine

Fig. 1 Visualization of Breadth-First Search. Choice nodes are represented by circles, solutions by diamonds and failure nodes by squares.

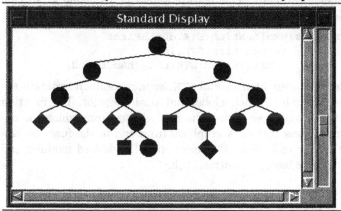

Fig. 2 Dimensions and Modules of STK

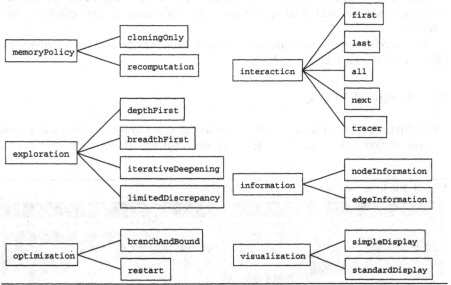

classes for each dimension. This results in different inheritance graphs for every
desired combination of search algorithm with extension modules. Here, we are
making use of Oz's advanced object-oriented features [Hen98]. Classes are first-
class citizen in Oz, which means that we can decide at runtime from which
parent class a class should inherit. This feature allows us to define a function
MakeEngine to which we pass the desired modules as arguments.

```
E={STK.makeEngine dims(exploration:STK.depthFirst
                       interaction:STK.last
                       optimization:STK.branchAndBound)}
```

Here the modules STK.depthFirst and STK.branchAndBound contain engine and node classes, describing their global and local behavior. The function
MakeEngine constructs from these classes the final classes from which the desired inference engine is constructed. A graphical front-end to the function MakeEngine as shown in Figure 3 allows the selection of the desired modules and
creates a corresponding engine upon button click.

9.5 Example

Through engine generators, STK supports experiments with different combinations of search algorithms and extensions. Figure 4 shows a snapshot of an
engine constructed by the engine generator in Figure 3, which combines limited
discrepancy search [HG95] with recomputation, node-level tracing, edge information, visualization, recomputation and branch-and-bound optimization. The
tracer tool on the left displays the edge information of the three edges leading to
the left-most solution of a crypto-arithmetic problem. Using STK, engines can
be tailor-made for individual applications and embedded in their graphical user
interface.

New modules such as application-specific explorations and search tree visu-
alizers can be easily added to STK.

10 Related Work

Individual aspects of this work are addressed by other systems. The most recent
version of Ilog Solver [ILO99a] provides object-oriented abstractions for pro-

Fig. 3 An Interface for an Engine Generator

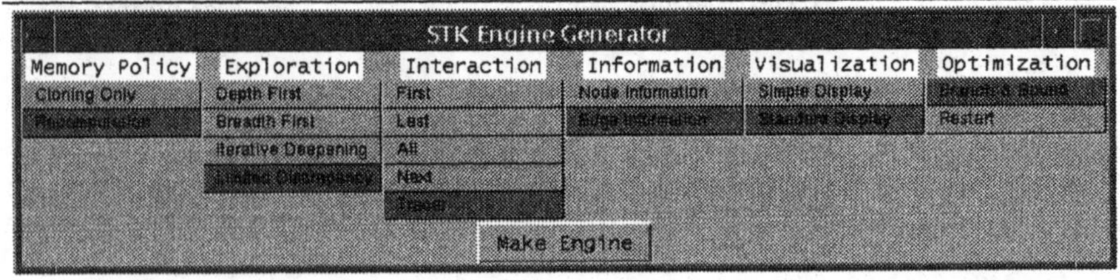

Fig. 4 A Custom-made Engine

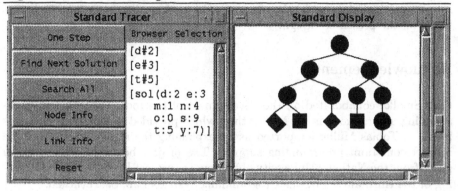

gramming search engines. Tracing facilities for constraint-based search are investigated by [Mei95] and provided by the tool OPL Studio [ILO99b]. Visualization of search trees together with tracing is provided by the Oz Explorer [Sch97a], where earlier tools are also discussed. The Mozart system provides several different search engines, including limited discrepancy search and parallel search. None of these systems address the question how to systematically reuse components of search engines.

Compared to the engines provides by the Mozart system, our modular approach carries a certain overhead, due to late binding and extra member function calls. However, since for typical applications, the majority of the overall runtime is spent on propagation and cloning/recomputation, this overhead is usually negligible. Benchmarks given in [Che99] show that STK is competitive in performance with the Oz search libraries except for the search tree visualization, where the Oz Explorer is currently significantly faster.

The facility of annotating choice points and display the annotation on demand provided by the module edgeInformation in Section 9.2 is not available in the Oz Explorer, but could be supported with few changes.

11   Conclusion

We identified the following dimensions for designing constraint-based inference engines: memory policy, exploration (defining the search algorithm), interaction, information, visualization and optimization. This structure provided the base for an object-oriented software design that supports flexible reuse and recombination of components. Evidently, we do not claim that this list of dimensions is exhaustive. We argued, however, that it is useful to identify such dimensions in order to obtain a modular design of search libraries.

We outlined how a constraint programming library or language can utilize the secribed design. The toolkit STK [HC99] for search engines in Oz provides evidence for the practicality of the approach.

Besides improving the performance of STK for visualization of search trees, future work includes the development of a C++ constraint programming library based on the presented design.

Acknowledgements

Gert Smolka collaborated on the development of the room concept and corresponding abstractions in an ML setting, which provided a blueprint for stores in C++. Tobias Müller supported us by explaining the implementation of the Mozart constraint programming support. The project benefited from a travel grant from the National University of Singapore (project ReAlloc) and the hosting of the third author by the Programming Systems Lab, Saarbrücken.

References

[Che99]   Tee Yong Chew. A toolkit for constraint-based tree search. Honours Year Project Report, School of Computing, National University of Singapore, available at **http://www.comp.nus.edu.sg/ henz/projects/toolkit/**, March 1999.

[CL96]   Yves Caseau and François Laburthe. CLAIRE: Combining objects and rules for problem solving. In *Proceedings of the JICSLP'96 workshop on multi-paradigm logic programming*. TU Berlin, 1996.

[HC99]   Martin Henz and Tee Yong Chew. SearchToolKit: A toolkit for constraint-based tree search. Oz code available via WWW at **http://www.comp.nus.edu.sg/~henz/projects/stk**, 1999.

[Hen98]   Martin Henz. *Objects for Concurrent Constraint Programming*. The Kluwer International Series in Engineering and Computer Science, Volume 426. Kluwer Academic Publishers, Boston, 1998.

[HG95]   William D. Harvey and Matthew L. Ginsberg. Limited discrepancy search. In Chris S. Mellish, editor, *Proceedings of the International Joint Conference on Artificial Intelligence*, pages 607–615, Montréal, Québec, Canada, August 1995. Morgan Kaufmann Publishers, San Mateo, CA.

[ILO99a]   ILOG Inc., Mountain View, CA 94043, USA, **http://www.ilog.com**. *ILOG Solver 4.4, Reference Manual*, 1999.

[ILO99b]   ILOG Inc., Mountain View, CA 94043, USA, **http://www.ilog.com**. *OPL Studio User Manual*, 1999.

[Ken96]   Andrew J. Kennedy. Functional pearls: Drawing trees. *Journal of Functional Programming*, 6(3):527–534, May 1996.

[LP99]   Irvin J. Lustig and Jean-François Puget. Program ! = program: Constraint programming and its relationship to mathematical programming. white paper of Ilog Inc., Mountain View, CA 94043, USA, available at **http://www.ilog.com**, 1999.

[Mei95]   Micha Meier. Debugging constraint programs. In *Proceedings of the First International Conference on Principles and Practice of Constraint Programming*, Lecture Notes in Computer Science 976, pages 328–344, Cassis, France, September 1995. Springer-Verlag, Berlin.

[Moz99]   Mozart Consortium. The Mozart Programming System. Documentation and
          system available from http://www.mozart-oz.org, Programming Systems
          Lab, Saarbrücken, Swedish Institute of Computer Science, Stockholm, and
          Université catholique de Louvain, 1999.
[Pug94]   Jean-François Puget. A C++ implementation of CLP. In *Proceedings of
          the Second Singapore International Conference on Intelligent Systems (SPI-
          CIS)*, pages B256–B261, Singapore, November 1994.
[Sch97a] Christian Schulte. Oz Explorer: A visual constraint programming tool. In
          Lee Naish, editor, *Proceedings of the International Conference on Logic
          Programming*, pages 286–300, Leuven, Belgium, July 1997. The MIT
          Press, Cambridge, MA.
[Sch97b] Christian Schulte. Programming constraint inference engines. In Gert
          Smolka, editor, *Principles and Practice of Constraint Programming—CP97,
          Proceedings of the Third International Conference*, Lecture Notes in Com-
          puter Science 1330, pages 519–533, Schloss Hagenberg, Linz, Austria, Octo-
          ber/November 1997. Springer-Verlag, Berlin.
[Sch99]   Christian Schulte. Comparing trailing and copying for constraint program-
          ming. In *Proceedings of the International Conference on Logic Programming*,
          1999. to appear.
[Smo95]   Gert Smolka. The Oz programming model. In Jan van Leeuwen, editor,
          Computer Science Today, Lecture Notes in Computer Science 1000, pages
          324–343. Springer-Verlag, Berlin, 1995.

CLIP: A CLP(Intervals) Dialect
for Metalevel Constraint Solving

Timothy J. Hickey

Michtom School of Computer Science, Brandeis University, USA,
tim@cs.brandeis.edu

Abstract. CLIP is an implementation of CLP(Intervals) built on top of
Prolog. It has been developed using the simplest model of constraint solving in which constraints are decomposed into sets of primitive constraints
and a simple constraint queue is used to repeatedly apply primitive constraint contractions until some termination condition applies (e.g. no significant change occurs, or a preset limit on the number of contractions
is reached). The simple semantics and implementation make it relatively
straightforward to prove that the system is sound. In this paper we show
how to implement more complex constraint solvers in CLIP. In particular, we demonstrate that several of the box-narrowing algorithms from
the Newton and Numerica systems can be easily implemented in CLIP.
The principal advantages of this approach are (1) the resulting solvers
are relatively easy to prove correct, (2) new solvers can be rapidly prototyped since the code is more concise and declarative than for imperative
languages, and (3) contractors can be implemented directly from mathematical formulae without having to first prove results about interval
arithmetic operators.

1 Introduction

Historically, there have been two approaches to implementing Interval Arithmetic constraint solvers, represented by the two systems: CLP(BNR) and Newton. In CLP(BNR), [5,21,20,4,2], each constraint is decomposed into primitive
constraints (similar to compiling to 3-address code), and then a general constraint solving engine is invoked to repeatedly contract each primitive constraint
until some termination condition is satisfied. In Newton, Numerica, and similar
systems [3,23,22,9,8] the constraint solver is much more powerful than the underlying CLP(BNR) solver, but in some cases it can take hours to solve a single
constraint.

We argue the merits of the CLP(BNR) approach where one first implements
a fast CLP(BNR) system and then builds a Newton/Numerica-style constraint
solver in this system. The main benefits of such a two step approach are

- it is relatively straightforward to provide a convincing proof of the correctness of the combined system, whereas proving the correctness of a Newton
  solver implemented in traditional languages such as C or Java would be much
  more difficult

E. Pontelli, V. Santos Costa (Eds.): PADL 2000, LNCS 1753, pp. 200–214, 2000.
© Springer-Verlag Berlin Heidelberg 2000

- new solvers can be rapidly prototyped since the necessary code is much simpler and more concise in CLP(Intervals) than in imperative or functional languages (e.g. C, Java, Scheme).
- contractors can be implemented directly from the corresponding mathematical formulae without having to detour through the language of interval arithmetic. In particular, one does not need to consider interval extensions of functions.

We have successfully used this approach to build constraint solvers for a large class of Ordinary Differential Equation (ODE) constraints [10,12]. Here we show that some of the Newton/Numerica style contractors can be easily and efficiently implemented in a CLP(Intervals) system.

In this paper, we first describe our implementation of CLIP, a CLP(Intervals) system using a simple queue method for applying sound primitive constraint contractors [11]. We then give some benchmarks on its performance, illustrate the use of CLIP in implementing Newton/Numerica contractors with several concrete examples. Finally, we discuss directions for future research.

2   CLIP Syntax and Semantics

Syntactically, CLIP is an extension of GNU prolog [7] in which arithmetic constraints are enclosed in curly brackets and are separated by commas. Each constraint is an atom in a particular first order theory of the reals. This theory contains some specified set of relation, function, constant, and variable symbols. In CLIP the currently allowable symbols include those in Fig. 1.

Semantically, CLIP constraints are interpreted as relations among real numbers. If a CLIP constraint $C(X_1, \ldots, X_n)$ fails, then there is implicitly a proof that there are no real numbers X_i which make the constraint true. CLIP is designed so that the solver is powerful enough to be able to always solve constraints that require only simple propagation, e.g.,

```
?- {2*log(Z+1) = 5, Z*exp(X-1)=Y+3/Z, Z*Y^3=cos(Z)}.
   X = -2.06163426224723...
   Y =  0.2551887203100...
   Z = 11.18249396070347...
```

Moreover, the solver will make a limited attempt to solve more complex constraints which require iterative constraint propagation, e.g.,

```
| ?- {X*Y=1, Y=sin(X), pi/2 >= X, X >= 0}.
   X = 1.1141571408719...
   Y = 0.89753946128048...
```

(See [1], p. 77 for a classical approach to this problem, or [13] for a comparable constraint contraction approach.)

The user is allowed to set parameters which put a limit on how much work the CLIP solver will invest each time it is called. This allows one to write CLIP programs knowing that each time the constraint solver is invoked (by writing a constraint in curly braces), control will always return to the Prolog engine in time at most T, where T is implicitly determined by setting various constraint engine parameters. These parameter are discussed in more detail below. There is also (quite importantly) a method to add all constraints back onto the queue and reinvoke the constraint solver. This guarantees that constraint narrowing which was prematurely halted by the constraint engine can be resumed at a later time.

```
Relations:  X=Y, X<Y, X=<Y, X>Y, X>=Y, X\==Y, integer(X), boolean(X)
Constants:  0, -1, 1.23, 1.0E100, '1.10000*', '1.123...', pi,
Functions:  X+Y, X-Y, X*Y, X/Y, -X, abs(X),
            exp(X), log(X), X^n, X^(p/q), X**Y,
            sin(X), cos(X), tan(X), asin(X), acos(X), atan(X),
Variables:  (capitalized identifiers)
```

Fig. 1. CLIP constraint language

2.1 I/O Syntax

The difference between base 2 and base 10 representations of numbers requires most decimal constants to be represented by non-point floating point intervals. If this is not done carefully, logically incorrect results can follow. Consider, for example, the following query:

```
?- {X = 1.1, (X-1)*10=1+Z, Z=0}.
```

If X were represented by the nearest floating point number to 1.1, then the query would fail because $Z = (X - 1) * 10 - 1$ would be about $2^{-50} \neq 0$, when clearly it should succeed if the semantics are really given by the real numbers. To avoid these problems, we follow CLP(BNR)[2,5] and let the floating point constants denote the smallest floating point intervals which contain them. Since this introduces a small loss of precision which the user may wish to avoid, CLIP allows the use of the quoted constants listed below to give the user more flexibility in deciding how to interpret constants. Thus,

- {X = 1.1} or {X = '1.1'} will bind X to the smallest interval with floating point bounds which contains X.
- {X = '1.1#'} or {X = '#1.1'} will bind X to the floating point number which is closest to 1.1. This is useful when the user really does want a point interval close to a decimal number.
- {X = '1.100*'} will specify that X is only known to four digits of accuracy, i.e., the asterisk indicates that the number X is in [1.0995,1.1005].

- {X='1.1000...'} where the "..." notation indicates that all of the decimal digits listed so far are correct, so, in this case, X represents a number in [1.1000,1.1001).

Similar conventions are used for printing intervals.

2.2 CLIP Semantics as Generalized Contraction

Let P be a CLIP program and let $Q(X)$ be a CLIP query (where X is a vector of interval variables). Suppose the CLIP interpreter returns with a finite number of interval boxes $B_1, B_2, \ldots, B_k$, and then fails. The soundness of the general CLP semantics [17] implies that

$$ T \cup P^* \models \forall x. \left(Q(x) \Rightarrow x \in \bigcup_i B_i \right) $$

where P^* is Clark's completion of P and T is the theory of real constraints (i.e. T is the set of all first order sentences in the CLIP constraint language which are true for the real numbers.) Thus, the set $\bigcup_i B_i$ contains all solutions of the query $Q(x)$. It may not be the case, however, that each box B_i contains some solution of Q.

This semantic property of CLIP allows us to view a CLIP interpreter as a sound contractor for a generalized constraint language. Indeed, given a set X of variables, initially bound to $[-\infty, \infty]$, and a query $Q(X)$ to a program P, the interpreter contracts the intervals associated to X without removing any solutions to the query.

This simplicity of the CLIP semantics and the fact that it is defined in terms of contraction, greatly simplifies the implementation of sound contractors, since CLIP will automatically contract the intervals of variables in mathematical formulae, without removing any solutions.

3 The Implementation of CLIP

CLIP is implemented as a foreign file extension to Prolog. It consists of two parts: a Prolog program clip.pl which defines the constraint predicate {}/1 and a C program clip.c which implements a simple interval arithmetic constraint solver. The Prolog interface code is about 1500 lines of Prolog (700 to translate constraints to primitives and 800 to implement various split solvers). The constraint engine is about 10000 lines of C code (6000 for for the primitive narrowing and interval arithmetic and 4000 for the constraint solver).

3.1 Prolog Interface Code

CLIP currently interprets constraints by translating them, at runtime, into primitive constraints and invoking the constraint engine's solver. The constraint engine maintains its own choice stack and the interface code is responsible for sending commands to push and pop that stack appropriately. The toplevel predicates of clip.pl are shown in Fig. 2. The main idea is that a constraint $\{C1, \ldots, Cn\}$ is handled by pushing a choice point in the constraint stack (and popping it on backtracking), converting the constraints into primitive constraints which are stored in the constraint engine, and invoking the constraint engine narrowing loop. The loop succeeds (with A=1) or fails (with A=0), or overflows a resource bound (with A=2), in the latter case the execution is aborted.

```
{C} :- set_cp,!(add_constraints(C)),narrow.

set_cp :- clip_push_cp(C),reset_cp(C).
reset_cp(_).
reset_cp(C) :- clip_pop_cp(C),fail.
narrow:-clip_narrow(A),(A=1;(A=2,abort)).
!(G) :- G,!.
```

Fig. 2. Toplevel of clip.pl

3.2   Constraint Engine in C

The core of the constraint engine is the narrow_loop which repeatedly

- takes a constraint off of the queue of active constraints,
- contracts the constraint and determines which of the variables have changed values significantly
- adds constraints to the active queue if they contain variables which have changed significantly

This loop is repeated until the queue is empty or unsatisfiability is detected.

The system also keeps track of how many constraints have been narrowed and when that number exceeds a user selected bound, the definition of significant change is made much more stringent so that the queue will rapidly be emptied. Typically this max_narrow parameter is set at 1000. The engine can also be told to add all constraints to the active queue. Thus one useful strategy is to set the max_narrow parameter to a low value while the constraint set is being built up and then just before printing the answer, add all the constraints back into the queue and set max_narrow to a large value.

The primitive constraint contractors (shown in Fig 3) are based on an interval arithmetic library which has been designed with careful attention to soundness. The underlying interval arithmetic algorithms have been proved correct [15,14], and we are preparing a proof of the correctness of the contractors for the special functions (exp, log, sin, etc.).

```
nar_add(X,Y,Z)      nar_mul(X,Y,Z)      nar_u_minus2(X,Y)
nar_exp2(X,Y)       nar_square2(X,Y)
nar_eq2(X,Y)        nar_lt2(X,Y)        nar_le2(X,Y)        nar_ne2(X,Y)
nar_integer1(X)     nar_bool1(X)        nar_abs2(X,Y)       nar_sgn2(X,Y)
nar_max(X,Y,Z)      nar_min(X,Y,Z)      nar_flr2(X,Y)       nar_ceil2(X,Y)
nar_or(X,Y,Z)       nar_and(X,Y,Z)      nar_xor(X,Y,Z)      nar_not2(X,Y)
nar_imp(X,Y,Z)      nar_if(X,Y,Z)
nar_sin2(X,Y)       nar_cos2(X,Y)       nar_tan2(X,Y)
nar_sin2pi2(X,Y)    nar_cos2pi2(X,Y)    nar_tan2pi2(X,Y)
nar_lessfn(X,Y,Z)nar_leqfn(X,Y,Z)      nar_eqfn(X,Y,Z)     nar_subset2(X,Y)
nar_pow_even(X,Y,Z) nar_pow_odd(X,Y,Z)
```

Fig. 3. Primitive narrowing routines used by the constraint engine

4 Higher Level Contractors

Next we look at the problem of implementing the Newton contraction algorithms in CLIP. We will examine closely the Taylor contractor and will describe not only its implementation but its correctness proof as well. The advantage of using CLIP as the implementation language for the solver is that the correctness of the contractors is equivalent to a corresponding mathematical property of the function being contracted. Making this correspondence explicit provides a methodology for proving the correctness as part of the implementation rather than as a separate analysis.

4.1 The Taylor Formula

The first contraction we implement is the simple Taylor contraction. It is based on the Taylor formula, which states that any function f, continuously differentiable on an interval I must satisfy the following property:

$$\forall a, x \in I, \exists t \in [0,1], \xi \in \mathcal{R} \, . \, f(x) = f(a) + f'(\xi)(x-a) \, \wedge \, \xi = a + t * (x-a)$$

Observe that the second equation states that ξ is a point which lies between a and x. The idea behind the Taylor contraction is to solve a constraint of the form

$$f(x_1, \ldots, x_n) = 0$$

by adding, for each i, a redundant constraint of the form

$$0 = f_i(a_i) + (x_i - a_i)f_i'(\xi_i), \quad \xi_i = a_i + t_i * (x_i - a_i)$$

where t_i and ξ_i are new interval variables and

$$f_i(z) = f(x_1, \ldots, x_{i-1}, z, x_{i+1}, \ldots, x_n)$$

is f viewed as a function of x_i, and where $(a_1, \ldots, a_n)$ can be any point in the domain of f. One usually gets the best convergence however by selecting a_i be the midpoint of the current value of x_i.

Observe that the Taylor constraint differs from the standard interval Newton operator in that the latter evaluates f' on x_i not on $a_i + t_i * (x_i - a_i)$. Indeed, the standard Interval Newton contraction is

$$x_i \leftarrow x_i \cap (a_i - (f_i(a_i)/f_i'(x_i)))$$

In the constraint context, the extra complexity of adding t_i is necessary, because the constraint variables represent real numbers not real sets. Note also that the Taylor constraint has the advantage that as x_i is contracted toward a_i this is reflected in the smaller active domain for f_i'. Thus, one Taylor constraint contraction can perform more narrowing than one Interval Newton contraction.

An Example   Consider the case of the Broyden Banded Function example (the first example cited in [23]) which is to solve the following system of n equations in $\{x_1, \ldots, x_n\}$

$$x_i(2 + 5x_i^2) + 1 = \sum_{i-5 \leq j \leq i+1, j \neq i, j \in [1,n]} x_j(x_j + 1)$$

For example, when $n = 2$, the Broyden problem is to solve

$$2x_1 + 5x_1^3 + 1 = x_2 + x_2^2$$
$$2x_2 + 5x_2^3 + 1 = x_1 + x_1^2$$

The simple Taylor contraction for this system consists of the following constraint, which is true assuming that (x_1, x_2) is a solution to the two Broyden equations above

$\forall a_1, a_2 \; \exists t_1, t_2, t_3, t_4, z_1, z_2, z_3, z_4$ s.t.

$$0 = 2a_1 + 5a_1^3 + 1 - (x_2 + x_2^2) + (2 + 15z_1^2)(x_1 - a_1),$$
$$0 = 2x_1 + 5x_1^3 + 1 - (a_2 + a_2^2) + (1 + 2z_2)(x_2 - a_2),$$
$$0 = 2a_2 + 5a_2^3 + 1 - (x_1 + x_1^2) + (2 + 15z_3^2)(x_2 - a_2),$$
$$0 = 2x_2 + 5x_2^3 + 1 - (a_1 + a_1^2) + (1 + 2z_4)(x_1 - a_1),$$
$$z_1 = a_1 + t_1(x_1 - a_1), 0 \leq t_1 \leq 1$$
$$z_2 = a_2 + t_2(x_2 - a_2), 0 \leq t_2 \leq 1$$
$$z_3 = a_2 + t_3(x_2 - a_2), 0 \leq t_3 \leq 1$$
$$z_4 = a_1 + t_4(x_1 - a_1), 0 \leq t_4 \leq 1$$

To get good convergence, we select a_1 and a_2 to be the midpoints of x_1 and x_2 and the standard CLIP solver will then narrow the bounds of the x_i.

There are two strategies for applying such a contractor. One is to create new redundant constraints with different a_i each time the contraction is called. This tends to add many constraints to the constraint store and those corresponding to older values of a_i usually contribute very little to the contractions. Our approach is to use these constraints to compute contracted bounds for the x_i

using a forward checking operator (implemented with `findall`) as described below. This has the advantage of only storing the constraints in the constraint store temporarily while the bounds are being contracted. The soundness of the contraction follows from the soundness of the CLIP semantics, but the forward checking approach allows us to keep the set of active constraints bounded even with a large number of Taylor contractions.

Invoking Contractions The CLIP implementation of simple Taylor contractions described below is already powerful enough to solve the Broyden Banded Function examples. Syntactically we define two predicates one to create a contractor and another to apply the contractor. Thus, to solve the 20 variable instance of the Broyden problem we would give the following query:

```
?- broyden(20,Vs,Es), make_contractor(taylor,Es,Vs,T),
    iterate(T,10,allsmall(Vs,1.0e-6)).
```

where the predicate `broyden(N,Vs,Es)` constructs (symbolically) the Broyden system Es on the N variables Vs, the `make_contractor` predicate creates a contractor as described below, and the `iterate(T,N,C)` operator calls T at most N times or until C is true.

The CLIP system solves this 20 variable Broyden problem and returns an answer for Vs with 6 decimal digits of accuracy in about 4 seconds (on a 500 Mhz Gateway 2000). The Taylor contractor T gets transformed into about 7K primitive constraints on 6K variables. A total of about 1.1 million primitive constraint narrowings are invoked. We suspect that the 7K primitive constraints could be significantly reduced by using a smarter differentiation routine and by making use of common subexpression optimizations. Fig. 4 shows the statistics for various values of N. We also include the Numerica times, as listed in [22] for some unspecified machine, for solving the Broyden problems.

It is interesting to note that this CLIP query is able to solve the Broyden problem using only Taylor contraction. In [23], the authors state that Interval Newton alone is not able to solve this problem, and they use this to argue the importance of the (fairly complex) box-consistency operators they employ. It appears that the Taylor constraint method offers an alternative approach, which at least for this problem is simpler and comparably efficient. In the final remarks we describe various strategies for improving the performance of the Taylor (and other) contractors.

Implementing Contractions We will now show how to define the general predicates

```
make_contractor(taylor,Es,Vs,taylor(Vs,As,T))
taylor(Vs,As,T)
```

which will create and apply the Taylor contraction to a list Es of constraints on a list Vs of variables. The contractor consists in applying the Taylor constraint

$$0 = f(a) + (x - a)f'(b), \quad b = a + t * (x - a)), \quad t \in [0,1]$$

N	5	10	20	40	80
prim constraints	851	2720	6905	16835	42815
variables	756	2415	5998	14109	34001
prim contractions	0.4M	0.6M	1.1M	2.2M	4.6M
CPU time	1.0s	1.9s	3.9s	9.4s	25.3s
Numerica CPU time	--	0.5s	1.6s	4.2s	9.8s

Fig. 4. Taylor Contractions for the Broyden Example

for each equation in $f = 0$ in Es, and each variable x in Vs, where the (partial) derivatives f' are computed using a combination of symbolic differentiation and interval contraction.

To illustrate the techniques needed to implement this contractor in CLIP we show in Fig. 5 the predicates to create and apply the Taylor contractor for a single variable X and a single expression $Exp1 = Exp2$. Observe that the contractor is defined directly in terms of the Taylor formula and so its correctness depends only on the correctness of the underlying constraint solver. The auxiliary procedures used in the figure are not shown but are discussed in the next paragraphs.

The procedure copyExpr(E,X,A,F) is a meta-level predicate which makes a copy F of the expression E, but replaces every occurrence of X by A.

The diff(F,D,DF,DEs) predicate produces both a variable DF representing the value of the derivative of F at X, and a set DEs of equations which relate DF to the other variables and constants in F, using rules of the form:

```
diff(X*Y,D,DF,(DF=X1*Y+X*Y1,E1,E2)) :-
    diff(X,D,X1,E1), diff(Y,D,Y1,E2).
```

This provides a very simple approach to automatic numerical differentiation. Observe that the derivative DF is computed both symbolically (as a solution to a symbolic set of equations) and numerically (as an interval resulting from the contraction of those equations). This versatile approach allows one to solve $F'(X) = 0$ for X using the same diff predicate. Finally, the forward_check(X,G) predicate finds upper and lower bounds on X for each solution to the query G, and then forms the union U and then contracts X by intersecting it with U. Here X can be a list of variables and the union finds the smallest box U which contains all of the boxes in Bs.

```
forward_check(X,G) :-
    findall(B,(G,get_bounds(X,B)),Bs), union(Bs,U), bind(X,U).
```

Note that forward checking in this manner temporarily adds constraints to the constraint store to compute the bounds B of each solution to G. The temporary constraints are then removed from the constraint store (by backtracking through a findall) and the remembered bounds are used to contract X.

```
make_contractor(taylor,[Exp1=Exp2],[X], taylor([X],[A],C)) :-
  C= (Exp1=Exp2, 0 = FA + DFB*(X-A),
      B = A + T*(X-A), 1 >= T, T >= 0,
      DEs),
  Expr = Exp1 - Exp2,
  copyExpr(Expr,X,A,FA),   copyExpr(Expr,X,B,FB),
  diff(FB,B,DFB,DEs).

taylor([X],[A],C) :-
  forward_check([X],(midpoint(X,M),{A=M,C})).
```

Fig. 5. Implementation of the Taylor Contraction

4.2   Multivariate Taylor Contractions

The mathematical formula for multivariate contractions is very similar to the univariate formula. Assuming that f is a continuously differentiable map from a convex subset U of $\mathcal{R}^m$ to $\mathcal{R}$, the multivariable Taylor formula states that:
$\forall a, x \in U, \exists t \in [0,1], \exists \xi \in U:$

$$f(x) = f(a) + Df(\xi) \cdot (x - a)$$
$$\xi = a + t * (x - a), \quad t \in [0,1]$$

where $Df(z) = \left(\frac{\partial f}{\partial x_j}(z) \right)$ is the derivative of f at z. This formula can be deduced from the univariate formula applied to

$$g(s) = f(a + s * (x - a))$$

Straightforward translation of this formula into CLIP yields the "centered form" contraction of the equation $f(x) = 0$. For example, the centered form contraction constraint for the 2 variable Broyden problem is as follows:
$\forall a_1, a_2 \; \exists t_1, t_2, z_{11}, z_{12}, z_{21}, z_{22}$ s.t.

$$0 = 2a_1 + 5a_1^3 + 1 - (a_2 + a_2^2) + (2 + 15z_{11}^2)(x_1 - a_1) - (1 + 2z_{12})(x_2 - a_2),$$
$$0 = 2a_2 + 5a_2^3 + 1 - (a_1 + a_1^2) + (2 + 15z_{22}^2)(x_2 - a_2) - (1 + 2z_{21})(x_1 - a_1),$$
$$z_{11} = a_1 + t_1(x_1 - a_1), \quad z_{12} = a_2 + t_1(x_2 - a_2),$$
$$z_{21} = a_1 + t_2(x_1 - a_1), \quad z_{22} = a_2 + t_2(x_2 - a_2),$$
$$t_1, t_2 \in [0,1]$$

The performance data for the centered form contraction is shown in Fig. 6. Again, we have included the Numerica times, as listed in [22] for some unspecified machine, for solving the Broyden problems. The current implementation is completely unoptimized, and we suspect that the time and space requirements will decrease significantly after applying some simple optimizations.

N	5	10	20	40	80
prim constraints	678	2083	6528	21658	77118
variables	609	1864	5829	19416	69393
prim contractions	0.2M	0.4M	1.0M	1.9M	4.1M
CPU time	0.5s	1.2s	3.2s	7.9s	24.9s
Numerica CPU time	---	0.5s	1.6s	4.2s	9.8s

Fig. 6. Centered Taylor Contractions for the Broyden Example

4.3 Absolving

We are currently implementing several other contractors described in [23], including NARROW_BOX_XX, with XX in {NE, DE, TE}. Each of these contractors makes use of a well-known general contraction strategy which has gone by many names. It is the main idea behind box-consistency of Newton/Numerica, and has been called the squash algorithm in the RIA solver of the ECLiPSe CLP system, and was called **absolving** in early implementations of CLP(BNR) [20]. For the purpose of this paper, we will call this method **absolving**.

The absolve method contracts the interval for a variable by removing small subsets of the current solution interval near the endpoints in which it can prove there are no solutions. This algorithm can be easily expressed in CLIP as shown in Fig. 7.

```
% absolve(Vars,Choose,Constraints,
%         Percent,NumIter,Termination)
  absolve(_Vs,_Ch,_Co,_P,_N, Terminate) :-    Terminate,!.
  absolve(_Vs,_Ch,_Co,_P, N,_Te) :-    {N=<0},!.
  absolve( Vs, Ch, Contract, P, N, Te) :-    {N>0, N1 = N-1},
    choosevar(Ch,V,Vs,NewVs),
    forward_chk(Vs,(multisplit(V,P,Contract))),
    Contract,
    absolve(NewVs,Ch,Contract,P,N1,Te).

multisplit(V,P,C) :- get_bounds_clip(V,L,H),
    D is (H-L)*P,    ms(V,C,L,D,H).

ms(V,C,L,D,_) :- {V=<L+D},C.
ms(V,C,_,D,H) :- {V>=H-D},C.
ms(V,_,L,D,H) :- {L+D =<V, V =< H-D}.
```

Fig. 7. Implementing Absolve

For example, the following query will solve the 20 variable Broyden problem using the absolve algorithm where the simple Taylor contractor is applied at each step and termination occurs when all variables have relative or absolute width at most 10^{-6} or when a limit of 10 iterations has been exceeded:

```
?-  broyden(20,Vars,Eqns),
    make_contractor(taylor,Eqns,Vars,T),
    absolve(Vars,roundrobin,T,
            0.125,10,allsmall(Vars,1.0e-6)).
```

This query finds a solution in 5 seconds after performing about 1.2 million primitive constraint contractions on a constraint set of about 7K primitive constraints.

5 Depth First Split Solving

Sometimes a constraint may have multiple solutions and a solver must use some sort of domain splitting to return each answer. The are several strategies that one might employ. The simplest is the `splitsolve` method [5], which repeatedly selects a variable, splits it into two or more parts and uses backtracking to look for solutions in each partition.

```
splitsolve(Vars,Choose,Contract,Terminate) :-     Terminate,!.
splitsolve(Vars,Choose,Contract,Terminate) :-
    choosevar(Choose,V,Vars,NewVars),split(V),
    Contract,
    splitsolve(NewVars,Choose,Contract,Terminate).
choosevar(roundrobin,Vs,Ws)  :- dequeue(V,Vs,Tmp),enqueue(V,Tmp,Ws).
split(V) :- midpoint(V,M), {V>=M}.
split(V) :- midpoint(V,M), {V<M}.
dequeue(V,[V|Vs],Vs).
enqueue(V,Vs,Ws) :- append(Vs,[V],Ws).
```

For example, to apply the Taylor contractor for the 20 variable Broyden example using a splitsolve search for possible solutions with 6 decimal digits of precision, we can pose the following query:

```
?-  broyden(20,Vars,Eqns),make_contractor(taylor,Eqns,Vars,Taylor),
    forward_check(Vars,
        splitsolve(Vars,roundrobin,Taylor,allsmall(Vars,1.0e-6))).
```

This finds a solution box in 6 seconds after performing 1.7 million primitive narrowings on a constraint set containing about 7K primitive constraints on 6K variables.

6 Specifying Compound Contractions

We are currently developing a language for specifying compound contractions. For example, the following query

```
?-  broyden(20,Vs,B),
    solve(absolve(cftaylor(B),0.10,20,1.0e-10)).
```

applies an approximation to the NARROW_BOX_NE operator of [23] to the 20 variable Broyden problem. It first constructs the centered form taylor contraction for the 20 variable Broyden problem, and then repeatedly applies an "absolve" contraction which attempts to trim 10% off of each end of the interval. This continues at most 20 times or until the interval widths are below 10^{-10}. More complex queries such as the following can also be made

```
?- broyden(20,Vs,B),
   solve(iterate( (absolve(cftaylor(B),0.1,5,1.0e-10),
                   taylor(B),2,1.0e-10)
                   10,1.0e-10)).
```

This iterates a compound contraction up to 10 times. The compound contraction first applies up to 5 iterations of the absolve strategy with the centered form contraction, and then applies a simple taylor contraction.

7   Future Work

Multivariate Taylor contractions. We have shown that the simple Taylor contractors can be implemented in a declarative style using CLIP. The convergence of multivariable Interval Newton contraction is widely reported to be greatly improved by preconditioning the equations using an approximate inverse to the Jacobian. In Newton/Numerica and in Interval Arithmetic algorithms, this involves proving the correctness of a multidimensional interval arithmetic function operating on sets of reals (see, e.g. [19], p. 177). Using CLIP, this contraction can be expressed as the following mathematical constraint, which holds whenever $f(x) = 0$:

$$\forall a \in U, \; \forall B \in M_n, \; \exists t \in [0,1]^n, \; \exists \xi \in (\mathcal{R}^n)^n \; \text{s.t.,}$$

$$x = a - (B \cdot f)(a) - M(\xi) \cdot (x - a)$$
$$\xi_i = a + t_i * (x - a)$$
$$M(\xi) = B * Df(\xi) - I_n$$
$$Df(\xi) = \left(\frac{\partial f_i}{\partial x_j}(\xi_i) \right)$$

where M_n is the space of $n \times n$ real matrices, and $I_n \in M_n$ is the $n \times n$ identity matrix.

We are currently extending CLIP to allow us to implement preconditioned multivariate contractors in the same declarative style. This will require adding vector and matrix operations to the CLIP constraint language, but the same approach used for the univariate contractor should extend to the multivariate case.

To get good convergence one generally lets a be the midpoint of x and selects B to be an approximate inverse to the Jacobian of f at a, then $M(\xi)$ is a matrix of small norm applied to an interval $x - a$ of small width. Thus the right hand side will generally have much smaller width than the left hand side (x) and so substantial contractions are often possible.

Note however that this formula holds for any matrix B and any point $a \in U$ and correctness does not rely on any special properties of these parameters. Thus, this contraction formula is really a family of sound contractors.

In order to declaratively express more complex constraints we will also need to adopt a summation syntax. One interesting approach would be to use the finite domain solver of GNU prolog to generate the indices for complex summations which would then be evaluated in CLIP. Adding such a syntax for expression summation in which the indices would be specified and determined using CLP(FD) could be an interesting and powerful feature. Newton and Numerica both have a summation syntax, but to our knowledge they do not use a solver as sophisticated as CLP(FD) to evaluate the indices.

We also plan to look for a constraint version of the Moore-Penrose Newton contractor used in Cucker and Smale's sound constraint solver [6].

Existence Proofs. Another powerful feature of the Newton system is that it is able to prove that certain boxes contain solutions to a given constraint set. This type of proof requires more sophisticated techniques than we have used in this paper since it deals explicitly with properties of *sets* of reals, whereas to define contraction constraints we only needed to specify properties of real numbers themselves. We have developed a theory of "functional constraints" in CLIP in another context [12] and we are currently working on expressing existence proofs as functional constraint problems. Such an extension would allow CLIP to solve global optimization constraints as in Newton and Numerica.

Efficiency. The current CLIP implementation offers many opportunities for significant optimization at every level. At the lowest level, the primitive Interval Arithmetic operations and contractors are written in C, but since they make use of directed rounding operators, they cannot, to our knowledge, be safely compiled on any currently available C compiler with the C optimization switches set. There are plans to incorporate directed rounding into a dialect of Java (see, e.g., Joseph Darcy's Borneo project at Stanford), but for now the only way to attain efficient code containing directed rounding operations is hand compilation. At the level of translating constraint expressions into primitive constraints, the natural optimization would be to compile the constraints to assembly language just as Dìaz has done with the Finite Domain constraints in GNU Prolog.

At the level of implementing the high level constraint contractors in CLIP, no attempt was made at this stage to minimize the number of constraints generated. We have made a preliminary investigation into the use of a minimal sequence of Taylor contractions for solving particular constraints efficiently and to maximal accuracy [13]. In particular, making use of symbolic algebra techniques to compute normal forms for the derivatives would probably both lessen the number of constraints generated and improve the precision of the underlying interval arithmetic routines.

References

1. Forman S. Acton, Real computing made real: Preventing Errors in Scientific and Engineering calculations, Princeton University Press, Princeton, New Jersey 1996.
2. Applied Logic Systems. CLP(BNR) manual. www.als.com 1999.
3. Frédéric Benhamou and David McAllister and Pascal Van Hentenryck CLP(Intervals) Revisited Proceedings of ILPS'94, 1994.
4. Frédéric Benhamou and William J. Older. Applying interval arithmetic to real, integer, and Boolean constraints. *Journal of Logic Programming*, 32:1–24, 1997.
5. Bell Northern Research. CLP(BNR) Reference and User Manuals. 1988
6. Cucker, F. and Smale, S. Complexity Estimates Depending on Condition and Round-Off Error, Journal of the ACM, 46:1, pp. 113-184, 1999.
7. Daniel Dìaz. GNU Prolog. www.gnu.org/software/prolog 1999.
8. L. Granvilliers. A Symbolic-Numerical Branch and Prune Algorithm for Solving Non-linear Polynomial Systems. Journal of Universal Computer Science vol. 4(2):125-146, 1998. Springer Science Online.
9. F. Benhamou and L. Granvilliers. Automatic Generation of Numerical Redundancies for Non-Linear Constraint Solving. Reliable Computing, vol 3(3):335-344, 1997. Kluwer Academic Publishers.
10. T. Hickey, CLP(F) and Constrained ODEs, in the Workshop on Constraint Languages and their use in Problem Modeling, ECRC Tech. Report (defunct), 1994.
11. T. Hickey, CLIP: an implementation of CLP (Intervals), www.cs.brandeis.edu/~tim/clip, 1999.
12. T. Hickey, Analytic Constraint Solving and Interval Arithmetic, to appear in the Proceedings of POPL'00, Boston, MA, Jan. 2000.
13. T. Hickey and D. Wittenberg, Validated Constraint Compilation Brandeis University, Tech Rep. CS-99-201, April, 1999.
14. T. Hickey, H. Wu, and M.H. van Emden, A Unified Framework for Interval Constraints and Interval Arithmetic, in Principles and Practice of Constraint Programming – CP98, M. Maher and J-F. Puget (eds.), Springer-Verlag, LNCS v. 1520, pp. 250-264, 1998.
15. T. Hickey, Q. Ju, and M.H. van Emden, Interval Arithmetic: from Principles to Implementation, Brandeis University Tech Report. CS-99-202, July, 1999.
16. R. Hammer, M. Hocks, U. Kulisch, and D. Ratz. *Numerical Toolbox for Verified Computing I.* Springer-Verlag, 1993.
17. Jaffar, J. and Lassez, J. L., Constraint Logic Programming. in Proceedings of the 14th ACM Symposium on the Principles of Programming Languages, 1987.
18. Moore, R. E., Interval Analysis. Prentice-Hall, 1966.
19. A. Neumaier. Interval Methods for Systems of Equations. Cambridge University Press. 1990.
20. William Older and Frédéric Benhamou. Programming in CLP(BNR). Proceedings of PPCP'93, 1993.
21. Older, W. and Vellino, A., Constraint Arithmetic on Real Intervals, in Constraint Logic Programming: Selected Research. Colmerauer, A. and Benhamou, F. (eds), MIT Press 1993.
22. Pascal Van Hentenryck, Laurent Michel, and Yves Deville. *Numerica: A Modeling Language for Global Optimization.* MIT Press, 1997.
23. Pascal Van Hentenryck, David McAllester, Dipak Kapur. *Solving Polynomial Systems Using a Branch and Prune Approach*, SIAM Journal on Numerical Analysis, 34(2), 1997.

Programming Deep Concurrent Constraint Combinators

Christian Schulte

Programming Systems Lab, Universität des Saarlandes
Postfach 15 11 50, 66041 Saarbrücken, Germany
schulte@ps.uni-sb.de

Abstract. Constraint combination methods are essential for a flexible constraint programming system. This paper presents deep concurrent constraint combinators based on computation spaces as combination mechanism. It introduces primitives and techniques needed to program constraint combinators from computation spaces. The paper applies computation spaces to a broad range of combinators: negation, generalized reification, disjunction, and implication. Even though computation spaces have been conceived in the context of Oz, they are mainly programming language independent. This point is stressed by discussing them here in the context of Standard ML with concurrency features.

1 Introduction

It is widely acknowledged that applications require a constraint programming system to be flexible. Regardless of how many primitive constraints a system offers, combination of primitive constraints into more complex application-specific constraints remains a must. This makes mechanisms for constraint combination key components of a constraint programming system.

Desirable properties of a constraint combination mechanism include that it is *compositional* and *conservative*. Compositional means that constraints obtained by combination can be combined again. Conservative means that the mechanism can be applied to existing constraints without changing them.

This paper's focus is on *deep concurrent constraint combinators* as combination mechanism. The paper introduces primitives from which constraint combinators can be programmed. It presents techniques that are characteristic in programming combinators. As underlying primitives *computation spaces* are proposed. Computation spaces offer two important features: they encapsulate arbitrary, that is *deep*, computations involving constraints and allow for concurrent control of computations. Combinators based on computation spaces are fully compositional: they can be nested arbitrarily. In particular, the constraints that can be combined are not limited to built-in constraints.

Computation spaces and combinator programming techniques are applied to a broad range of combinators, including negation, generalized reification, disjunction, and conditional (implication). In the same way as combinators allow to program new constraints, computation spaces allow to program new combinators: they provide flexibility on the constraint and on the combinator level. The paper introduces and refines the very

E. Pontelli, V. Santos Costa (Eds.): PADL 2000, LNCS 1753, pp. 215–229, 2000.
© Springer-Verlag Berlin Heidelberg 2000

few operations on computation spaces as the presentation of the paper proceeds. This is complemented by an overview over all operations at the end of the paper in Sect. 7.

Computation spaces are the basic concept that underlies deep-guard combinators found in programming languages like AKL [3,4] and Oz [11]. Even though computation spaces were conceived in the context of Oz, they are a general mechanism independent from the underlying programming language. To stress this point (and to make the paper's program fragments more accessible to a broader audience) this paper chooses Standard ML extended by threads and logic variables as host language [12].

Our experience shows that applications of constraint combinators in finite domain programming are not frequent. They turn out to be of great importance for other constraint domains, like feature or finite set constraints. In particular, they have turned out to be essential in the area of computational linguistics [1], where constraints from different domains are combined naturally.

A second area of application is prototyping new constraints. Starting from already implemented constraints new constraints can be developed by combining them at a high level. After experiments have shown that they are indeed the right constraints, a more efficient implementation can be attempted. This motivation is similar to the motivation for constraint handling rules (CHR) [2]. The difference is that this paper is concerned with primitives to combine constraints, a feature that an implementation of CHRs already requires.

Combinators for constraint programming is not a new idea. Previous approaches include Saraswat's concurrent constraint programming framework [8,7], the cardinality operator by Van Hentenryck and Deville [13], and cc(FD) [14]. The approaches have in common that the combinators considered are not "deep": the constraints that can be combined must be either built-in, or allow a simple reduction to built-in constraints (cardinality combinator). Another difference to the approach taken in this paper is that these approaches offer a fixed set of combinators. This paper's focus is on the primitives and techniques to program combinators. For all combinators but constructive disjunction (as available in cc(FD)) it is shown how to encode them with computation spaces.

A different approach to combining constraints are *reified* constraints (also known as metaconstraints). Reified constraints reflect the validity of a constraint into a 0/1-variable. Constraints can then be combined by using the 0/1-variable in other constraints. Computation spaces are not intended as a replacement for reified constraints. As is discussed in detail in Sect. 4, a reification combinator based on computation spaces can offer better propagation in cases where reified constructions propagate poorly. And, since the reification combinator is deep, it offers reification for all expressions, including propagators for which the constraint programming system itself does not offer a reified version.

Plan of the Paper. Section 2 outlines the computation model and introduces some terminology. The following section introduces computation spaces by discussing a negation combinator. Sections 4 to 6 discuss a generic reification combinator, a disjunction combinator, and a conditional combinator. Section 7 provides a complete overview of computation and relates computation spaces presented in this paper to computation spaces available in Oz. The paper is concluded by Sect. 8.

2   Prerequisites

This section introduces the model of computation and notions used in the remainder of the paper.

Computation is performed in a *computation space*. A computation space consists of propagators and threads (to be explained later) connected to a constraint store:

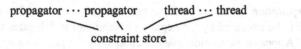

The *constraint store* holds information about values of variables expressed by a conjunction of basic constraints. *Basic constraints* are logic formulae interpreted in a fixed first-order structure. For the purpose of this paper we restrict ourselves to finite domain constraints. A basic finite domain constraint has the form $x \in D$ where D is a finite subset of the positive integers. Other relevant basic constraints are $x = y$ and $x = n$, where n is a positive integer.

More expressive constraints, e.g., $x + y = z$, are not written to the constraint store. Instead, they are imposed by propagators. A *propagator* is a concurrent agent that tries to amplify the store by *constraint propagation*: The propagator amplifies the store by telling new basic constraints to it. A propagator imposing P disappears as soon as it detects that P is entailed by the store's constraints. A propagator imposing P becomes *failed* if it detects that P is inconsistent with the constraints hosted by the store.

In addition to propagators, the computation space contains threads. A thread is a functional evaluator operating on the store. As programming language that defines the set of expressions threads can evaluate, we use Standard ML extended by threads and logic variables. This extension of SML is due to Smolka, for more information we refer the reader to [12].

Threads are used to provide the concurrent execution needed by concurrent constraint combinators. Logic variables are used for synchronization. For example, the evaluation of an application x () might block since x can be a logic variable. The application blocks until x is bound to a value (in this particular case, a function).

3   Getting Started: A Concurrent Negation Combinator

This section familiarizes the reader with computation spaces by showing how to program a concurrent negation combinator from them.

For a given constraint C the negation combinator provides an implementation for the constraint $\neg C$. The negation combinator $\neg C$ executes the propagator for C and:

- disappears, if the propagator for C becomes failed.
- fails, if the propagator for C becomes entailed.

Execution of C by the negation combinator requires *encapsulation* of the computation performed by C. Basic constraints that are told by propagation of C must be hidden from any other computation. On the other hand, basic constraints that are told by other computations must be visible to C.

We are looking for a method to build a *compositional* negation combinator:

- It must be general enough to deal with statements that post propagators rather than with a single propagator. This supports modularity. Typically, several constraints are composed together by some expression E.
- Execution for both expressions and propagators should remain unchanged.

Local Computation Spaces. *Local computation spaces* are used as primitives. The expression E to be executed by the negation combinator is delegated to a local computation space. A local computation space is created by the primitive operation

```
space : (unit -> unit) -> space
```

To execute an expression E in a computation space, the application

```
space(fn () => E)
```

is evaluated which returns the newly created space.

Variables, propagators, and threads are now situated in exactly one space S, which we call the entity's *home*. If an expression E is being executed by a thread T whose home is S, we refer to T as the *current thread* and to S as the *current space*.

Evaluation of space e in the space S_1 returns a newly created space S_2, which is initialized as follows. The constraint store of S_2 contains all constraints of S_1's constraint store. A new thread is spawned in S_2 to evaluate e (). We refer to this thread as S_2's *root thread*. S_1 is called the *parent (space)* of S_2.

This construction naturally leads to a tree of computation spaces. The root of the tree we refer to as *toplevel (space)*. Spaces that occur in the subtree rooted at space S (not including S) are called subordinated to S. A space S_1 is superordinated to a space S_2, if S_2 is subordinated to S_1.

With the exception of telling a basic constraint ϕ, both threads and propagators compute in the same way as in the toplevel space. Telling a basic constraint ϕ in a space S means to tell ϕ to S's store and to all stores in spaces subordinated to S.

Status of a Space. In addition to starting an encapsulated computation, the negation combinator needs access to the *status* of the encapsulated computation.

A space S is called *blocked*, if all threads and propagators within S and within spaces subordinated to S cannot reduce. A space S is *stable*, if it is blocked and remains blocked regardless of any tell operations performed in a space superordinated to S.

A space becomes *failed* by an attempt to tell a basic constraint to the store that would make it inconsistent. Failing a space S discards all threads and propagators in S and also fails all spaces subordinated to S. Note that a space S can be failed by a tell issued by a thread whose home is S, as well as by a tell issued in a space superordinated to S. Further note that a failed space is also stable.

A space is *solved*, if it is stable, not failed, and does not contain any propagators or threads. Note that the constraint store of a solved space S is entailed by the constraint store of S's parent. This justifies why we sometimes refer to a solved space as *entailed*.

A space that is stable, but neither failed nor solved, is *stuck*. If a space S becomes stuck, it has arrived at a state where it contains propagators or threads that block on variables that are local to S (otherwise S would be blocked, but not yet stable). This means that constraint propagation within S has not been strong enough to completely drive reduction of all threads and propagators. In other words, a stuck space is usually the result of a programming error.

The operation

```
datatype status = Failed | Solved | Stuck
status : space -> status
```

takes as input a space S and if S is stable, returns S's status. If S is not stable there are two alternative designs: either status blocks until S becomes stable, or behaves asynchronously. We choose the asynchronous behavior: if S is not stable, status returns a logic variable that is bound to S's status when S becomes stable. Subsequent examples clarify that the asynchronous design is preferable.

The Combinator. The concurrent negation combinator takes an expression (as a first-class function e of type unit -> unit) and creates a space running e.

To make the combinator concurrent, a new thread is created that blocks until the created space becomes stable and then takes the appropriate action. For thread creation we use the function

```
spawn : (unit -> unit) -> unit
```

It spawns a new thread for execution of an expression E, which is passed as function fn () => E. Taking this together, we arrive at:

```
fun not c =
    let val s = space c
    in  spawn(fn () => case status s of
                           Failed => ()
                         | Solved => fail()
                         | Stuck  => raise Error) end
```

Here fail is a function that fails the current space (e.g., by attempting to tell the constraint $1 = 2$ to the store).

4 A Generic Reification Combinator

As it has been argued in the introduction, reification of constraints is a powerful and natural way to combine constraints. This section presents a generic reification combinator. The reification combinator is shown to sometimes provide stronger constraint propagation than constructions that use reified propagators alone.

Reification. The reification of a constraint C with respect to a 0/1-variable b (a finite domain variable with domain $\{0, 1\}$) is the constraint $C \leftrightarrow b = 1$. The idea behind reification is to reflect whether C holds into whether the *control variable b* is 0 or 1.

Operationally, it is important that reification is bidirectional:

"$\Rightarrow$" If C holds, $b = 1$ must hold; and if $\neg C$ holds, $b = 0$ must hold.
"$\Leftarrow$" If $b = 1$ holds, C must hold; and if $b = 0$ holds, $\neg C$ must hold.

Having 0/1-variables b that reflect validity of constraints allows for powerful means to combine constraints. Common examples for combination are boolean connectives expressed by propagators (see Sect. 5 for an example).

Direction "$\Rightarrow$" can be programmed along the lines of the negation combinator of Sect. 3. Suppose that s refers to the space running the expression E to be reified and b refers to the 0/1-variable. Then Direction "$\Rightarrow$" is as follows:

```
⟨"⇒"⟩ := case status s of
              Failed => tell(b, 0)
            | Solved => tell(b, 1)
            | Stuck  => raise Error
```

Here tell(b, i) is used to tell the basic constraint b = i to the constraint store.

Let us consider the case of Direction "$\Leftarrow$" where b is determined to 0. In this case, if the space s becomes solved, the current space must be failed. Otherwise, if the space s becomes failed, nothing has to be done. This behavior is already realized by the above encoding of Direction "$\Rightarrow$".

Committing a Space. Let us consider the case of Direction "$\Leftarrow$" for $b = 1$. The required operational behavior includes two aspects. Firstly, a computation state must be established as if execution of E had not been encapsulated. Secondly, if E has not yet been completely evaluated, its further execution must perform without encapsulation.

These two aspects are dealt with by the operation

```
commit : space -> unit
```

It takes a computation space S_2 and merges S_2 with the current space S_1 (which is S_2's parent) as follows. If S_2 is failed, also S_1 becomes failed. Otherwise:

1. All constraints of S_2's constraint store are told to S_1's constraint store. By this, the effects of computations performed in S_2 are made available in S_1.
2. All propagators and threads situated in S_2 now become situated in S_1. From now on, they execute as if they had been created in S_1 in the first place.

Using commit, Direction "$\Leftarrow$" of the reification combinator is encoded as follows:

```
⟨"⇐"⟩ := if value b = 1 then commit s else ()
```

Here the function value takes a finite domain variable, blocks until it becomes determined, and returns its integer value.

The Combinator. The reification combinator is obtained from the implementation of both directions, which must execute concurrently. Concurrent execution is achieved by spawning a thread for each direction.

Taking the two directions together we arrive at a function reify that takes a function that specifies the expression to reify as input and returns a 0/1-variable:

```
fun reify e =
    let val s = space e  val b = fdvar(0, 1)
    in spawn(fn () => ⟨"⇒"⟩) ;
       spawn(fn () => ⟨"⇐"⟩) end
```

Comparison with Propagator-based Reification. It is instructional to compare space-based reification with propagator-based reification. Suppose we are interested in reifying the conjunction of the two constraints $x + 1 = y$ and $y + 1 = x$ with respect to the variable b, where both x and y are finite domain variables. Similar reified constraints occur in computing Hamiltonian paths.

Ideally, the reification mechanism should determine b to 0, since the conjunction is unsatisfiable. Posting the constraints without reification exhibits failure.

Let us first study reification with propagators alone. In order to obtain a reified conjunction, we have to reify each of the conjuncts by introducing two control variables b_1 and b_2. Altogether we arrive at

$$b_1 = (x + 1 = y) \wedge b_2 = (y + 1 = x) \wedge b \in \{0, 1\} \wedge b_1 + b_2 = b$$

Neither b_1 nor b_2 can be determined, thus b cannot be determined.

Let us now study the behavior of the reification combinator developed in this section. It is applied as

```
b = reify(fn () => (x+1=y ; y+1=x))
```

Both constraints are posted in the same local space S. Exactly like posting them in the toplevel space, constraint propagation leads to failure of S. Indeed, the reification combinator determines b to 0.

This shows that using spaces for reification can yield better constraint propagation than using per propagator reification. Per propagator reification encapsulates the propagation of each propagator. This in particular *disables* constraint propagation in reified conjunctions. This is a major disadvantage, since reified conjunctions occur frequently as building block in other reified constructions as for example disjunction.

On the other hand the generic reification combinator offers weak propagation in case the control variable is determined to be 0. Instead of propagation, constraints told by other propagators are tested only. Whenever a reified propagator is available, it is preferable to use it directly.

So the reification combinator can be best understood as offering additional techniques but not as a replacement of reified propagators.

5   Disjunction

This section shows how to program disjunctive combinators that resolve their alternatives by propagation rather than by search. Disjunctive combinators occur frequently in a variety of application domains, a well-known example is scheduling. For examples that use disjunctive combinators in the domain of computational linguistics see [1].

Let us consider a disjunction

$$E_1 \vee \cdots \vee E_n$$

that is composed of n expressions E_i. We refer to the E_i as the disjunction's *alternatives*. A straightforward operational semantics is as follows:

1. Discard failed alternatives ($\bot \vee C$ is logically equivalent to C).
2. If a single alternative E remains, reduce the disjunction to E (a disjunction with a single alternative C is equivalent to C).
3. If all alternatives have failed, fail the current space (a disjunction with no alternatives is equivalent to $\bot$).

This operational semantics can be directly encoded by the reification operator as introduced in Sect. 4. The well-known encoding reifies each alternative E_i with respect to a 0/1-variable b_i. The disjunction itself is encoded by

$$b_1 + \cdots + b_n \geq 1$$

The suggested operational semantics is driven by failure only. However, it can be beneficial to also take entailment of alternatives into account. As an example consider the placement of two squares s_1 and s_2 such that they do not overlap. A well known modeling of this constraint is

$$x_1 + d_1 \leq x_2 \vee x_2 + d_2 \leq x_1 \vee y_1 + d_1 \leq y_2 \vee y_2 + d_2 \leq y_1$$

where the meaning of the variables x_i, y_i, and d_i is sketched to the right. The squares do not overlap, if the relative position of s_1 with respect to s_2 is either left, right, above, or below. As soon as one of the relationships is established, the squares are guaranteed to not overlap.

Suppose s_1 is placed left to s_2. Since the first and second alternatives are mutually exclusive (so are the third and fourth), the first and second reified propagator disappears. However, the third and fourth remain.

Assume a constraint store C and a disjunction $C_1 \vee C_2$ where C_1 is entailed by C (that is, $C \rightarrow C_1$ is valid). Under this condition, $C_1 \vee C_2$ is logically equivalent to $\top \vee C_2$, which in turn is equivalent to $\top$. This justifies extending the operational semantics of the disjunctive combinator as follows:

4. If an alternative is entailed, reduce by discarding all alternatives.

Taking entailment into account has the following advantages: execution can be more efficient since computations that cannot contribute are discarded early. The computation space in which the disjunctive combinator is executed can possibly become solved sooner. In our compositional setup this might allow for earlier reduction of other combinators and by this provide better propagation.

Discarding a Space. For programming a disjunctive combinator with entailment we need to discard a computation space. The primitive

```
discard : space -> unit
```

discards a computation space *S* by failing it. The operational semantics is exactly as if creating a new thread in *S* that executes `fail ()`.

The implementation of the disjunctive combinator can be simplified by the following observation: it is sufficient to discard all failed alternatives but the last one. If a single alternative remains, commit to it, regardless of whether the alternative is failed or not. Committing a failed space fails the current space (see Sect. 4). In the following the discussion is limited to a binary disjunctive combinator only. Generalization to the *n*-ary case is straightforward.

A function `or` that takes two alternatives `a1` and `a2` (again encoded as first-class functions) decomposes naturally into three parts: space creation for encapsulated execution of the alternatives, a concurrent controller, and last but not least the part that implements the reduction rules as discussed before. This yields the following encoding:

```
fun or(a1, a2) =
    let val (s1, s2) = (space a1, space a2)
        fun reduce(s1, s2) = ⟨Reduction⟩
    in ⟨Controller⟩ end
```

The concurrent controller blocks until either `s1` or `s2` becomes stable. This indeterminate choice is encoded by:

```
first : 'a * 'b -> bool
```

The application `first(x,y)` takes logic variables `x` and `y` as input and blocks until at least one of `x` and `y` becomes determined. If it returns `true` (`false`), `x` (`y`) is determined. Now the concurrent controller can be programmed from `first` which is applied to the status of both `s1` and `s2` as follows:

```
⟨Controller⟩ := if first(status s1, status s2)
                then reduce(s1, s2) else reduce(s2, s1)
```

The concurrent controller guarantees the invariant that the first space to which `reduce` is applied, is stable.

Finally, reduction is programmed as follows:

```
⟨Reduction⟩ :=
if failed s1 then commit s2
else if solved s1 then (discard s1 ; discard s2)
else if failed s2 then commit s1
        else if solved s2 then (discard s1 ; discard s2)
        else raise Error
```

where `failed` (`solved`) returns `true`, if applied to a failed (solved) space. Both `failed` and `solved` can be obtained straightforwardly from `status`. The part of `reduce` that does not have a gray background executes immediately, since the concurrent controller ensures that `s1` is stable. The gray part synchronizes on stability of `s2`.

Without the nested `if`-statements that test whether `s1` or `s2` are solved, the programmed disjunctive combinator implements the reduction rules 1 to 3. As it has been argued, this simplified version of disjunction can be expressed by the reification combinator introduced in Sect. 4.

The other direction, that is programming `reify` by using `or`, is also possible with the additional use of `not` as introduced in Sect. 3. The reification of expression E with respect to b can be programmed as follows:

```
or (fn () => (tell(b,1) ; E),
    fn () => (tell(b,0) ; not(fn () => E)))
```

Programming reification from disjunction has the disadvantage that the expression E is executed twice. This points out a deficiency in the designs of AKL and early versions of Oz, where neither spaces nor reification but disjunction was provided.

6   Conditional

This section shows how to program conditionals that use arbitrary expressions as conditions (so-called *deep guards*). In particular it presents how to use continuations that allow to share variables between the condition and the body of a conditional. We also study how to apply the same ideas to parallel conditionals and disjunctions.

A conditional consists of three constituents, all of which are expressions: a guard G, a body B, and an else-constituent E. A common suggestive syntax would be

```
cond G then B else E
```

The part G `then` B is called the *clause* of the conditional.

Programming a conditional from computation spaces is straightforward. The program used for programming `not` (see Sect. 3) can be adapted as follows:

```
fun cond(g,b,e) =
    let val s = space g
    in  case status s of
            Failed => e()
          | Solved => b()
          | Stuck  => raise Error end
```

where g, b, and e are functions that specify the guard, body, and else-constituent of the conditional. In contrast to the concurrent negation combinator, the conditional is sequential. It does not spawn a new thread to synchronize on stability of the guard's space.

A common desire is to introduce variables $\bar{x}$ locally in the guard G of the conditional and use them in the body. Thus the conditional should synchronize on entailment of $\exists \bar{x} G$. In our current setup, the bindings computed for $\bar{x}$ in G are not accessible. An inefficient and thus unsatisfactory solution would be to execute the guard expression again together with the body.

A more satisfactory solution is to let the guard pass the variables to the body. This can be accommodated by extending computation spaces as follows. The root thread in a space computes a result (of some type 'a). Committing the space gives access to that result. That is, space creation and committing of spaces is extended as follows:

```
space   : (unit -> 'a) -> 'a space
commit  : 'a space -> 'a
```

Note that this extension of space and commit does not require a modification of the programs presented so far in this paper (in these cases 'a is just unit).

A space can be committed before the root thread has terminated and has computed the result. Therefore commit returns a logic variable that is bound to the root thread's result as soon as it terminates.

In the context of a programming language with first-class functions the sharing of variables between guard and body is achieved straightforwardly by letting the guard return as result a function for the body:

```
let x̄ in (G ; fn () => B) end
```

Here B can refer to variables declared in the let-expression. Without first-class functions, the variables would be stored in an appropriate data structure.

Programming the conditional from the extended primitives is now straightforward.

```
fun cond(c, e) =
    let val s = space c
    in case status s of
            Failed => e()
          | Solved => let val b = commit s in b() end
          | Stuck  => raise Error end
```

Parallel Conditional. A common combinator is a *parallel* conditional that features more than a single clause with a committed choice operational semantics: As soon as the guard of a clause becomes entailed, commit the conditional to that clause (that is, continue with reduction of the clause's body). Additionally, discard all other guards. If the parallel conditional also features an else-constituent E, reduce the conditional with E if all guards have failed.

Encoding the parallel conditional from computation spaces follows closely the program for the disjunction presented in Sect. 5. In fact, the setup of the computation spaces for guard execution and the concurrent controller can remain unchanged. The function that implements the reduction rules is as follows:

```
⟨Reduction⟩ :=
let val b = if solved s1 then
                (discard s2 ; commit s1)
            else if solved s2 then
                (discard s1 ; commit s2)
            else raise Error
in b() end
```

The encoding is simplified in that it does not consider the straightforward handling of an else-constituent.

Clauses for Disjunction. The disjunctive combinator presented in Sect. 5 can be extended to employ clauses as alternatives. This extension is straightforward but two issues require some consideration. Firstly, when to start execution of a clause's body? Secondly, for which clause employ reduction by entailment?

Execution of the parallel conditional evaluates a clause's body B only after the clause's guard G has become entailed. This in particular ensures that the root thread has terminated and has computed B as its result. A disjunctive combinator, in contrast, can already commit to a clause C if its guard G is not yet stable, provided the clause is the last remaining.

Nevertheless, it is desirable that evaluation of the C's body B starts only after G has been completely evaluated. The semantics of commit ensures this: It returns a logic variable that is bound to the root thread's result as soon it terminates. Since function application synchronizes (see Sect. 2), evaluation of the body synchronizes on termination of the root thread.

As discussed in Sect. 5 it is beneficial to consider both failure and entailment of alternatives for the disjunctive combinator. Reduction by entailment is justified by the fact that if an alternative A is entailed it becomes logically equivalent to $\top$. This justification does apply to a clause only if its body is known to be logically equivalent to $\top$ as well. A possible solution is to tag clauses appropriately (as $\top$-clause). Reduction by entailment is then applied to $\top$-clauses only.

7   Computation Spaces: Summary and Comparison

The signature of all space operations that are necessary to program concurrent constraint combinators is as follows:

```
type 'a space
datatype status = Failed | Solved | Stuck

val space   : (unit -> 'a) -> 'a space
val status  : 'a space -> status
val commit  : 'a space -> 'a
val discard : 'a space -> unit
```

Search Engines. A different use of computation spaces is to use them for programming search engines. Search requires two further concepts: cloning and choice points.

A search engine takes a specification of the search problem (as function) and runs it in a computation space. The primitive

```
val choose : unit -> int
```

creates a choice point. A thread that executes choose() blocks. If a stable space contains a thread blocking on choose(), the status-operation is extended to return Choice. The search engine uses

```
val select : 'a space -> unit
```

to select whether 1 or 2 is returned by the blocking choose operation. The last additional primitive

```
val clone : 'a space -> 'a space
```

creates a copy of stable space. A search engine can use clone to implement backtracking. The programming of search engines from computation spaces is detailed in [9,10].

Spaces in Oz. As has already been argued in the introduction, the choice of SML as host language for spaces is mostly to stress language independence. In the following we relate the computation spaces as presented in this paper to computation spaces in Oz, where they have been originally conceived.

Spaces as presented here are almost identical to spaces in Oz with the exception of the additional concept of a *root variable*. Each space in Oz is created initially with a logic variable as root variable. The function supplied with space creation is applied to that root variable. Thus the root variable in Oz roughly corresponds to the result computed by the root thread in this paper. This paper does not introduce the root variable since it is not needed for programming combinators.

Combinators in Oz. The latest Mozart implementation of Oz (version 1.1.0) switched from a native C⁺⁺-based implementation of combinators to a space-based implementation. Information on techniques for native implementation of combinators can be found in [4,6,5]. The main motivation to switch was to simplify the implementation. The goal is to decrease the necessary maintenance effort which has been considerable with the native implementation.

First experiments suggest that the space-based implementation is competitive to the native C⁺⁺-implementation as it comes to runtime and memory requirements. Space consumption of both approaches is approximately the same. Native combinators are approximately twice as fast for programs where execution time is dominated by reduction of combinators (for example, appending two lists, where a deep guard conditional is used to decide whether the first input list is empty or not). For examples where the runtime is dominated by constraint propagation, both approaches offer approximately the same execution speed.

8 Conclusion

In this paper, we have presented computation spaces as primitives for deep concurrent constraint combinators. We have shown how to program negation, generalized reification, disjunction, and conditional from computation spaces.

The paper displays the simplicity of the approach: all combinators are obtained from a single concept with very few (four) primitive operations. By the choice of Standard ML with concurrency extensions as host language we have demonstrated that our approach is mainly language independent.

Computation spaces are provided by the Mozart implementation of Oz, which is available from www.mozart-oz.org.

Acknowledgements

Thanks to Denys Duchier, Tobias Müller, and Gert Smolka for fruitful discussions on combinators and computation spaces. Leif Kornstaedt, Tobias Müller, Andreas Rossberg, Gert Smolka, and the anonymous referees provided helpful comments. Tobias brought to my attention that the example in Sect. 4 occurs in computing Hamiltonian paths.

References

1. Denys Duchier and Claire Gardent. A constraint-based treatment of descriptions. In H. C. Bunt and E. G. C. Thijsse, editors, *Third International Workshop on Computational Semantics (IWCS-3)*, pages 71–85, Tilburg, NL, January 1999.
2. Thom Frühwirth. Constraint handling rules. In Andreas Podelski, editor, *Constraint Programming: Basics and Trends*, volume 910 of *Lecture Notes in Computer Science*, pages 90–107. Springer-Verlag, 1995.
3. Seif Haridi, Sverker Janson, and Catuscia Palamidessi. Structural operational semantics for AKL. *Future Generation Computer Systems*, 8:409–421, 1992.
4. Sverker Janson. *AKL - A Multiparadigm Programming Language*. PhD thesis, SICS Swedish Institute of Computer Science, SICS Box 1263, S-164 28 Kista, Sweden, 1994. SICS Dissertation Series 14.
5. Michael Mehl. *The Oz Virtual Machine: Records, Transients, and Deep Guards*. Doctoral dissertation, Universität des Saarlandes, Im Stadtwald, 66041 Saarbrücken, Germany, 1999.
6. Michael Mehl, Ralf Scheidhauer, and Christian Schulte. An abstract machine for Oz. In Manuel Hermenegildo and S. Doaitse Swierstra, editors, *Programming Languages, Implementations, Logics and Programs, Seventh International Symposium, PLILP'95*, volume 982 of *Lecture Notes in Computer Science*, pages 151–168, Utrecht, The Netherlands, September 1995. Springer-Verlag.
7. Vijay A. Saraswat. *Concurrent Constraint Programming*. ACM Doctoral Dissertation Awards: Logic Programming. The MIT Press, Cambridge, MA, USA, 1993.
8. Vijay A. Saraswat and Martin Rinard. Concurrent constraint programming. In *Proceedings of the 7th Annual ACM Symposium on Principles of Programming Languages*, pages 232–245, San Francisco, CA, USA, January 1990. ACM Press.
9. Christian Schulte. Oz Explorer: A visual constraint programming tool. In Lee Naish, editor, *Proceedings of the Fourteenth International Conference on Logic Programming*, pages 286–300, Leuven, Belgium, July 1997. The MIT Press.
10. Christian Schulte. Programming constraint inference engines. In Gert Smolka, editor, *Proceedings of the Third International Conference on Principles and Practice of Constraint Programming*, volume 1330 of *Lecture Notes in Computer Science*, pages 519–533, Schloß Hagenberg, Linz, Austria, October 1997. Springer-Verlag.
11. Gert Smolka. The Oz programming model. In Jan van Leeuwen, editor, *Computer Science Today*, volume 1000 of *Lecture Notes in Computer Science*, pages 324–343. Springer-Verlag, Berlin, 1995.
12. Gert Smolka. Concurrent constraint programming based on functional programming. In Chris Hankin, editor, *Programming Languages and Systems*, volume 1381 of *Lecture Notes in Computer Science*, pages 1–11, Lisbon, Portugal, 1998. Springer-Verlag.

13. Pascal Van Hentenryck and Yves Deville. The cardinality operator: A new logical connective for constraint logic programming. In Frédéric Benhamou and Alain Colmerauer, editors, *Constraint Logic Programming: Selected Research*, pages 383–403. The MIT Press, Cambridge, MA, USA, 1993.
14. Pascal Van Hentenryck, Vijay Saraswat, and Yves Deville. Design, implementation, and evaluation of the constraint language cc(FD). *The Journal of Logic Programming*, 37(1–3):139–164, October 1998.

Labeling and Partial Local Consistency for Soft Constraint Programming

Stefano Bistarelli[1], Philippe Codognet[2], Yan Georget[3], and Francesca Rossi[4]

[1] Università di Pisa, Dipartimento di Informatica, Corso Italia 40, 56125 Pisa, Italy.
bista@di.unipi.it
[2] University of Paris 6, LIP6, case 169, 4, Place Jussieu, 75 252 Paris Cedex 05, France.
Philippe.Codognet@lip6.fr
[3] INRIA Rocquencourt, BP 105, 78153 Le Chesnay, France
Yan.Georget@inria.fr
[4] Università di Padova, Dipartimento di Matematica Pura ed Applicata, Via Belzoni 7, 35131 Padova, Italy.
frossi@math.unipd.it

Abstract. In this paper we generalize to soft constraints the approximation techniques usually used for local consistency in classical constraint satisfaction and programming. The theoretical results show that this is indeed possible without loosing the fundamental properties of such techniques, and the experimental results (on partial arc-consistency) show that this work can help develop more efficient implementations for logic-based languages working with soft constraints.

1 Introduction

In [4,5,6,11,12], a new constraint solving framework (called SCSP) has been defined and implemented where classical CSPs, fuzzy CSPs, hierarchical CSPs and others can be easily cast. The framework simply adds a semiring structure to a constraint system, in order to represent preferences among the variable instantiations, and thus also among constraints and solutions. The aim of this paper is to extend the local consistency algorithms, defined in [4,5] for SCSPs, in order to capture some approximated algorithms which have been proved useful for classical constraints, so much that they are widely used in current constraint programming systems like clp(FD)[7], Ilog Solver [14] and CHIP[1].

The SCSP framework comes with a class of local consistency (LC) algorithms, that are useful to perform a simplification of the problem, cutting away some tuples of domain values that are shown to be useless w.r.t. the solutions of the problem.

This scheme is in theory very useful but experiments show that even the simplest non-trivial LC algorithm (which corresponds to Arc-Consistency [16,3] extended to SCSPs) has a heavy complexity for most applications. Moreover, one has to apply it several times if used during the labeling phase. Hence, the reduction of its complexity is a crucial point.

E. Pontelli, V. Santos Costa (Eds.): PADL 2000, LNCS 1753, pp. 230–248, 2000.

To go in this direction, we define a class of Partial Local Consistency (PLC) algorithms, which perform less pruning that (complete) local consistency but can nevertheless be rather useful in reducing the search. Some instances of these algorithms are able to reduce the domains of the variables in constant time, and can work with a convenient representation of the domains of the variables. Using PLC together with labeling, the aim is to find the solutions of a problem with a better practical complexity bound.

From this point of view, our work is related to the one of K. Apt [2]. Infact, he studied a class of filtering functions for classical CSPs which can express both local consistency and also less pruning notions.

Summarizing, here are our results:

1. the extension of the definitions and properties of the labeling procedure from classical CSPs to SCSPs;
2. a general scheme for approximating local consistency in SCSPs, and properties that are sufficient for the correctness of the approximations;
3. some implementations issues in the particular case of arc-consistency;
4. experimental results for partial arc-consistency.

The rest of the paper is organized as follows. In Section 2 we recall the basic notions of the soft contraint framework based on semirings. In Section 3 we introduce some properties about labelings, we describe their interaction with usual filtering algorithms, and we define the generalization of the labeling procedure to SCSPs. Then, we introduce the notion of rule approximations and study the correctness of such rules in Section 4, we discuss some implementations issues in Section 5, and we give experimental results in Section 6. Finally, we conclude and give some perspectives for future work in Section 7. For reasons of space, we had to leave out some of the proofs of our statements, which however are contained in [10].

2   Soft Constraints

In the literature there have been many formalizations of the concept of *soft constraints*. Here we refer to a specific one [4,5], which however can be shown to generalize and express many of the others. In a few words, a soft constraint is just a constraint where each instantiation of its variables has an associated value from a partially ordered set. Combining constraints will then have to take into account such additional values, and thus the formalism has also to provide suitable operations for combination ($\times$) and comparison ($+$) of tuples of values and constraints. This is why this formalization is based on the concept of semiring, which is just a set plus two operations.

Semirings and SCSPs. A *semiring* is a tuple $\langle A, +, \times, 0, 1 \rangle$ such that: A is a set and $0, 1 \in A$; $+$ is commutative, associative and 0 is its unit element; $\times$ is associative, distributes over $+$, 1 is its unit element and 0 is its absorbing element.

In reality, we will need some additional properties, leading to the notion of c-semiring (for "constraint-based"): a *c-semiring* is a semiring $\langle A, +, \times, \mathbf{0}, \mathbf{1} \rangle$ such that $+$ is idempotent with $\mathbf{1}$ as its absorbing element and $\times$ is commutative.

Let us consider the relation $\leq_S$ over A such that $a \leq_S b$ iff $a + b = b$. Then it is possible to prove that: $\leq_S$ is a partial order; $+$ and $*$ are monotone on $\leq_S$; $\mathbf{0}$ is its minimum and $\mathbf{1}$ its maximum; $\langle A, \leq_S \rangle$ is a complete lattice and $+$ is its lub. Moreover, if $\times$ is idempotent, then: $+$ distribute over $\times$; $\langle A, \leq_S \rangle$ is a complete distributive lattice and $\times$ its glb. The $\leq_S$ relation is what we will use to compare tuples and constraints: if $a \leq_S b$ it intuitively means that b is better than a.

A *constraint system* is a tuple $CS = \langle S, D, V \rangle$ where S is a c-semiring, D is a finite set (the domain of the variables) and V is an ordered set of variables.

Given a semiring $S = \langle A, +, \times, \mathbf{0}, \mathbf{1} \rangle$ and a constraint system $CS = \langle S, D, V \rangle$, a *constraint* is a pair $\langle def, con \rangle$ where $con \subseteq V$ and $def : D^{|con|} \to A$. Therefore, a constraint specifies a set of variables (the ones in con), and assigns to each tuple of values of these variables an element of the semiring.

Given a constraint $c = \langle def, con \rangle$, we call $type(c)$ the set con of the variables of c. Given a constraint set C, $type(C) = \{type(c)/c \in C\}$ and $V(C) = \bigcup_{c \in C} type(c)$ is the set of all the variables appearing in the constraints of C.

Consider two constraints $c_1 = \langle def_1, con \rangle$ and $c_2 = \langle def_2, con \rangle$, with $|con| = k$. Then $c_1 \sqsubseteq_S c_2$ if for all k-tuples t, $def_1(t) \leq_S def_2(t)$. The relation $\sqsubseteq_S$ is a partial order.

An SCSP *constraint problem* is a pair $\langle C, con \rangle$ where $con \subseteq V$ and C is a set of constraints: con is the set of variables of interest for the constraint set C, which however may concern also variables not in con.

Combining and projecting soft constraints. Given two constraints $c_1 = \langle def_1, con_1 \rangle$ and $c_2 = \langle def_2, con_2 \rangle$, their *combination* $c_1 \otimes c_2$ is the constraint $\langle def, con \rangle$ defined by $con = con_1 \cup con_2$ and $def(t) = def_1(t \downarrow_{con_1}^{con}) \times def_2(t \downarrow_{con_2}^{con})$, where $t \downarrow_Y^X$ denotes the tuple of values over the variables in Y, obtained by projecting tuple t from X to Y. In words, combining two constraints means building a new constraint involving all the variables of the original ones, and which associates to each tuple of domain values for such variables a semiring element which is obtained by multiplying the elements associated by the original constraints to the appropriate subtuples.

Given a constraint $c = \langle def, con \rangle$ and a subset I of V, the *projection* of c over I, written $c \Downarrow_I$ is the constraint $\langle def', con' \rangle$ where $con' = con \cap I$ and $def'(t') = \sum_{t/t \downarrow_{I \cap con}^{con} = t'} def(t)$. Informally, projecting means eliminating some variables. This is done by associating to each tuple over the remaining variables a semiring element which is the sum of the elements associated by the original constraint to all the extensions of this tuple over the eliminated variables.

Summarizing, combination is performed via the multiplicative operation of the semiring, and projection via the additive operation.

Examples. Classical CSPs are SCSPs where the chosen c-semiring is $Bool = \langle \{false, true\}, \vee, \wedge, false, true \rangle$. In fact, by using this semiring we mean to associate to each tuple a boolean value, and then to combine constraints via the logical and operation.

Fuzzy CSPs [9] can instead be modeled by choosing the c-semiring $Fuzzy = \langle[0,1], max, min, 0, 1\rangle$. In fact, here each tuple has a value between 0 and 1, and constraints are combined via the min operation, and compared via the max operation. Figure 1 shows a fuzzy CSP. Variables are inside circles, constraints are represented by undirected arcs, and semiring values are written to the right of the corresponding tuples. Here we assume that the domain of the variables contains only elements a and b.

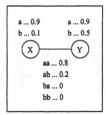

Fig. 1. A fuzzy CSP.

Solutions. The *solution* of an SCSP problem $P = \langle C, con \rangle$ is the constraint $Sol(P) = (\bigotimes C) \Downarrow_{con}$. That is, we combine all constraints, and then project over the variables in con. In this way we get the constraint over con which is "induced" by the entire SCSP.

For example, each solution of the fuzzy CSP of Figure 1 consists of a pair of domain values (that is, a domain value for each of the two variables) and an associated semiring element. Such an element is obtained by looking at the smallest value for all the subtuples (as many as the constraints) forming the pair. For example, for tuple $\langle a, a \rangle$ (that is, $x = y = a$), we have to compute the minimum between 0.9 (which is the value for $x = a$), 0.8 (which is the value for $\langle x = a, y = a \rangle$) and 0.9 (which is the value for $y = a$). Hence, the resulting value for this tuple is 0.8.

Consider two problems P_1 and P_2. Then $P_1 \sqsubseteq_P P_2$ if $Sol(P_1) \sqsubseteq_S Sol(P_2)$. If $P_1 \sqsubseteq_P P_2$ and $P_2 \sqsubseteq_P P_1$, then they have the same solution, thus we say that they are equivalent and we write $P_1 \equiv P_2$.

Sometimes it may be useful to find the semiring value of the optimal solutions. This is called the *best level of consistency* of an SCSP problem P and it is defined by $blevel(P) = Sol(P) \Downarrow_\emptyset$. We also say that: P is α-consistent if $blevel(P) = \alpha$; P is consistent iff there exists $\alpha >_S \mathbf{0}$ such that P is α-consistent; P is inconsistent if it is not consistent.

Another operation. Besides combination and projection, we need in this paper another operator, which we will call the *disjunction* operator. Given two constraints $c_1 = \langle def_1, con_1 \rangle$ and $c_2 = \langle def_2, con_2 \rangle$ over CS, their *disjunction* $c_1 \oplus c_2$ is the constraint $c = \langle def, con \rangle$ with $con = con_1 \cup con_2$ and $def(t) = def_1(t \downarrow^{con}_{con_1}) + def_2(t \downarrow^{con}_{con_2})$.

The informal meaning of the disjunction operator is to give more possibility to (or to enhance the level of preference of) certain instantiations. If we consider the semiring *Bool* which corresponds to classical CSPs, the meaning of having the disjunction of two constraints C_1 and C_2 is to have the possibility of choosing not only the tuples permitted by C_1 but also those permitted by C_2. Figure 2 shows an example using the semiring Fuzzy, where, we recall, the operation $+$ is the maximum.

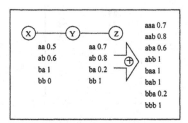

Fig. 2. Disjunction example.

Using the properties of $\times$ and $+$, it is easy to prove that: $\otimes$ is associative and commutative; $\oplus$ is associative, commutative and idempotent; $\otimes$ distributes over $\oplus$; $\otimes$ and $\oplus$ are monotone over $\sqsubseteq_S$. Moreover, if $\times$ is idempotent: $\oplus$ distributes over $\otimes$ and $\otimes$ is idempotent.

Local consistency. SCSP problems can be solved by extending and adapting the techniques usually used for classical CSPs. For example, to find the best solution we could employ a branch-and-bound search algorithm (instead of the classical backtracking), and also the successfully used propagation techniques, like arc-consistency, can be generalized to be used for SCSPs.

Instead of deleting values of tuples, in SCSPs obtaining some form of local consistency means changing the semiring values associated to some tuples or domain elements. In particular, the change always brings these values towards the worst value of the semiring, that is, the **0**.

In the following of this section, we recall the basic formal notions and properties of local consistency over SCSPs.

First, we need the notion of *local inconsistency*. We say that the SCSP problem $P = \langle C, con \rangle$ is *locally inconsistent* if there exist $C' \subseteq C$ such that $blevel(C') = \mathbf{0}$.

Consider a set of constraints C and $C' \subseteq C$. If C is α-consistent then C' is β-consistent with $\alpha \leq_S \beta$. As a corollary: if a problem is locally inconsistent, then it is inconsistent.

Now, in order to define local consistency algorithms, we use the notion of *typed location*, which is just a set of variables, that will be used to identify a subproblem of a given SCSP.

A *typed location* l is a set of variables. Given a problem $P = \langle C, con \rangle$, if there is a constraint $c = \langle def, l \rangle$ in C, then the value $[l]_P$ of the location l in P is $\langle def, l \rangle$; otherwise it is $\langle 1, l \rangle$. The value $[\{l_1, \cdots, l_n\}]_P$ of the set of locations $\{l_1, \cdots, l_n\}$ is the set $\{[l_1]_P, \cdots, [l_n]_P\}$.

An *assignment* is a pair $l := c$ where $c = \langle def, l \rangle$. Given a problem $P = \langle C, con \rangle$, the result of the assignment $l := c$ is defined as $[l := c](P) = \langle \{\langle def', con' \rangle \in C / con' \neq l\} \cup c, con \rangle$. In words, the assignment $l := c$ in P produces a new problem P' which is the same as P, except that it has an additional constraint, c, over the variables in l, and that the old constraints over l are removed.

A *local consistency rule* is written as $l \leftarrow L$, where l is a location, L a set of locations and $l \notin L$. The result of applying the rule $l \leftarrow L$ to the problem P is:

$$[l \leftarrow L](P) = [l := Sol(\langle [L \cup \{l\}]_P, l \rangle)](P).$$

In words, the application of $l \leftarrow L$ to P adds to P the constraint $Sol(\langle [L \cup \{l\}]_P$ over the variables in l. This constraint, by definition of Sol (see previous section), is obtained by combining all constraints identified by $L \cup \{l\}$ and then projecting over l.

The application of a sequence of rules $r; R$ is defined by $[r; R](P) = [R]([r](P))$. It is important to observe at this point that, given a problem P and a rule r, we have that $P \equiv [r](P)$.

Given a problem P and a set R of rules for P, P is said to be *stable* w.r.t R if, for each $r \in R$, $[r](P) = P$. Given a set R of rules, a *strategy* for R is an infinite sequence of rules, that is, a value from R^∞. A strategy T is *fair* if each rule of R occurs in T infinitely often.

We are now ready to define *local consistency algorithms*. Given a problem P, a set of rules R and a fair strategy T for R, a *local consistency algorithm* applies to P the rules in R in the order given by T. The algorithm stops when the current problem is stable w.r.t R. In that case, we write $lc(P, R, T)$ to denote the resulting problem.

Any local consistency algorithm satisfies the following properties [5]:

- it terminates (even when the semiring is infinite, provided that the set of semiring elements occurring in the problem is contained in a finite set over which the semiring operations are closed);
- if $\times$ is idempotent and $P' = lc(P, R, T)$, then $P \equiv P'$;
- if $\times$ is idempotent, then $lc(P, R, T)$ does not depend on T, so we will write $lc(P, R)$ instead of $lc(P, R, T)$;
- given a problem P and a value v assigned to a tuple in a constraint of P, consider $P' = lc(P, R)$ and the value v' assigned to the same tuple of the same constraint in P', then $v' \leq_S v$.

Notice the importance of the condition that the $\times$ operator be idempotent. This means that, if it is not idempotent, like for example in the semiring $\langle \mathcal{R} \cup$

$+\infty, min, +, 0, +\infty\rangle$ for constraint optimizations (where we have to minimize the sum of the costs, and thus $\times$ is the sum), we cannot be sure that the local consistency algorithms have the above desirable properties. Since in this paper we will heavily need such properties, our results are applicable to SCSPs over semirings with an idempotent $\times$ operation.

Arc consistency. Arc-consistency [16,3] (AC) is an instance of local consistency where one propagates only the domains of the variables. With our notations, this type of algorithm deals only with rules of the form $\{x\} \leftarrow \{\{x, y_1, \ldots, y_n\}, \{y_1\}, \ldots, \{y_n\}\}$. In fact, an arc-consistency rule considers a constraint, say over variables $x, y_1, \ldots, y_n$, and all unary constraints over these variables, and combines all these constraints to get some information (by projecting) over one of the variables, say x^1. Let us call AC this set of rules. In the following, we will write $ac(P)$ to denote $lc(P, AC, T)$.

3   Labeling in SCSPs

Local consistency algorithms, when applied to an SCSP P, can reduce the search space to find its solutions. However, solving the resulting problem P' is still NP-hard. This scenario is similar to what happens in the classical CSP case, where, after applying a local consistency algorithm, the solution is found by replacing P' with a set of subproblems $\{P_1, \ldots, P_n\}$ where some of the variables have been instantiated and such that P' is "equivalent" to $\{P_1, \ldots, P_n\}$, in the sense that the set of solutions of P' coincides with the union of the sets of solutions of $P_1, \ldots, P_n$. Usually, problems P_i are obtained by choosing a variable, say x, and instantiating it to its i-th domain value. Then, the local consistency (usually arc-consistency) algorithm is applied again [15]. By doing this, one hopes to detect the inconsistency of some of the subproblems by detecting their local inconsistency (via the local consistency algorithm). When all the variables of the initial problem are instantiated, arc-consistency becomes complete in the sense that if the problem is not consistent then it is not arc-consistent. Therefore at that point arc-consistency implies global consistency.

Let us consider, for example, the following problem:

$$X \in [1, 3], Y \in [1, 2], Z \in [1, 2], X \neq Y, Y \neq Z, Z \neq X.$$

Figure 3 shows the interaction between AC and the labeling procedure, since each node of the search tree (except the root) shows the CSP obtained after the application of an arc-consistency algorithm. In this particular case we have two solutions (the dashed line indicates the second solution found by the labeling).

We will now study the properties of the labeling procedure when applied to SCSPs.

---

[1] Actually, this is a generalized form of arc-consistency, since originally arc-consistency was defined for binary constraints only [13].

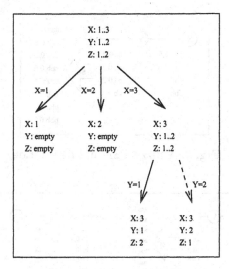

Fig. 3. AC and labeling.

In the following we assume to work with a constraint system $CS = \langle S, D, V \rangle$, where $S = \langle A, +, \times, \mathbf{0}, \mathbf{1} \rangle$.

Given a set $\mathcal{P} = \{P_1, \cdots, P_n\}$ of SCSPs, the *solution of* $\mathcal{P}$ is the constraint defined as $Sol(\mathcal{P}) = Sol(P_1) \oplus \cdots \oplus Sol(P_n)$.

Given $x \in V$, $d \in D$ and $v \in A$, we call $c_{x,d,v}$ the unary constraint $\langle def, \{x\} \rangle$ where $def(d) = v$ and $def(d') = \mathbf{0}$ if $d' \neq d$. In practice, $c_{x,d,v}$ instantiates x to d with semiring value v. We call this constraint a *simple instantiation constraint*.

Given a total order $\prec$ on V, let $W = \{x_1, \ldots, x_n\}$ be a subset of V, and assume that $x_1 \prec \cdots \prec x_n$. Given an n-tuple of domain values $d = \langle d_1, \ldots, d_n \rangle$ and an n-tuple of semiring values $v = \langle v_1, \ldots, v_n \rangle$, we define: $I_W^{d,v} = \{c_{x_i,d_i,v_i}/i \in [1,n]\}$. We write I_W^d for $I_W^{d,\mathbf{1}}$, and we call it a *W-instantiation set*. In practice, I_W^d gives the best semiring value ($\mathbf{1}$) to the assignment of d_i to variable x_i. Instead, $I_W^{d,v}$ gives semiring value v_i to the assignment of d_i to variable x_i.

Given a problem $P = \langle C, con \rangle$, let W be a subset of $V(C)$ and t be a $|W|$-tuple. We call a *W-labeling* of the problem P the problem $P_W^t = \langle C \cup I_W^t, con \rangle$. In words, a *$W$-labeling* of P adds to P some additional constraints which identify a specific partial labeling for P (partial because it involves only the variables in W). A *complete labeling* of P is thus written $P_{V(C)}^t$. Also, $\mathcal{L}_W(P) = \{P_W^t/t \in D^{|W|}\}$ is the set of all W-labelings of P. We call it *the* W-labeling of P.

Figure 4 presents a fuzzy SCSP and shows its solution, while Figure 5 shows the $\{x, y\}$-labeling corresponding to the original problem and the set of possible partial solutions, whose disjunction gives rise to the complete solution. Notice that the problem set solution coincides with the solution of the problem in Figure 4.

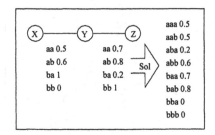

Fig. 4. A fuzzy CSP and its solution.

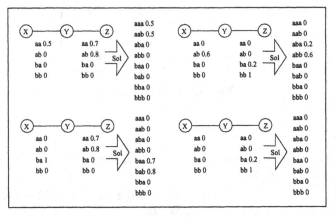

Fig. 5. The set of the $\{x, y\}$-labelings corresponding to the problem.

This is true also in general; therefore, we can compute the solution of an SCSP by computing the disjunction of the solutions associated to the labeling. This is important, since it means that we can decompose an SCSP and solve it by solving its sub-problems. The following theorem formalizes this informal statement.

Theorem 1 (disjunction correctness). *Given a SCSP $P = \langle C, con \rangle$, a subset W of $V(C)$, and a set $\{c_1, \ldots, c_n\}$ of constraints over W such that $\bigoplus_i c_i = \langle \mathbf{1}, W \rangle$, we have that $Sol(P) = \bigoplus_i Sol(\langle C \cup \{c_i\}, con \rangle)$. Moreover, $P \equiv \mathcal{L}_W(P)$.*

Proof. By the assumptions, and by the distributivity of $\times$ over $+$, for any tuple t of domain values for all the variables, we get:

We note V the set $V(C)$ and p the size of W. We assume $\bigotimes C = \langle def_C, V \rangle$, $c_i = \langle def_i, W \rangle$ and $\bigoplus_i Sol(\langle C \cup c_i, con \rangle) = \langle def, con \rangle$. We have:

$$def(t) = \sum_i \sum_{\{t'/t' \downarrow_{con}^{V \cup W} = t\}} def_i(t' \downarrow_W^{V \cup W}) \times def_C(t' \downarrow_V^{V \cup W})$$

Since $W \subseteq V$, we have:

$$def(t) = \sum_i \sum_{\{t'/t' \downarrow_{con}^V = t\}} def_i(t' \downarrow_W^V) \times def_C(t')$$

Now, by distributivity of $\times$ over $+$, we get:

$$def(t) = \sum_{\{t'/t' \downarrow_{con}^V = t\}} def_C(t') \times (\sum_i def_i(t' \downarrow_W^V))$$

Since $\bigoplus_i c_i = \langle 1, W \rangle$, we have $\sum_i def_i(t' \downarrow_W^V) = 1$. Thus:

$$def(t) = \sum_{\{t'/t' \downarrow_{con}^V = t\}} def_C(t')$$

that coincides with $Sol(P)$.   □

This result allows us to compute the solution of a SCSP using the labeling procedure. Moreover, if all the variables are instantiated, i.e. when the labeling $\mathcal{L}$ is complete ($W = V(P)$), then the values found for the variables contain all the informations needed to compute (very easily) the exact solution of the problem:

Theorem 2 (solution of a complete labeling). *We suppose given a problem* $P = \langle C, con \rangle$ *where* $C = \{c_i/i \in [1,n]\}$ *and* $\forall i \in [1,n], c_i = \langle def_i, con_i \rangle$. *Let* $P_{V(C)}^t = \langle C \cup I_{V(C)}^t, con \rangle$ *be a complete labeling of* P. *Then* $Sol(P_{V(C)}^t) = \langle def, con \rangle$ *with:*

- $def(t \downarrow_{con}^{V(C)}) = \prod_{i \in [1,n]} def_i(t \downarrow_{con_i}^{V(C)})$,
- $def(t') = 0$ *if* $t' \neq t \downarrow_{con}^{V(C)}$.

Moreover, $blevel(P_{V(C)}^t) = \prod_{i \in [1,n]} def_i(t \downarrow_{con_i}^{V(C)})$.

Proof. We denote by p the size of $V(C)$. By definition of a complete labeling problem:

$$Sol(P_{V(C)}^t) = ((\bigotimes_{j \in [1,n]} c_j) \otimes (\bigotimes_{k \in [1,p]} c_{x_k,t_k,1})) \Downarrow_{con}$$

By associativity and idempotence of $\otimes$, we have:

$$Sol(P_{V(C)}^t) = (\bigotimes_{j \in [1,n]} (c_j \otimes (\bigotimes_{k \in [1,p]} c_{x_k,t_k,1})) \Downarrow_{con}$$

Let $\langle def', V(C) \rangle = c_j \otimes (\bigotimes_{k \in [1,p]} c_{x_k,t_k,1})$. Then:

- $def'(t) = def_j(t \downarrow_{con_j}^{V(C)})$,
- $def'(t') = 0$ *if* $t' \neq t$.

The statement of the theorem easily follows.   □

As in the CSP case ([16]), it is sufficient to maintain AC during the labeling procedure to completely solve the problem (after a complete labeling has been obtained).

Theorem 3 (correctness of AC). *Given a SCSP $P = \langle C, con \rangle$ and a total order $\prec$ between the variables, assume that $V(C) = \{x_1, \ldots, x_p\}$ with $x_1 \prec \cdots \prec x_p$, and let $P^t_{V(C)} = \langle C \cup I^t_{V(C)}, con \rangle$ be a complete labeling of P. Also, let $P' = ac(P^t_{V(C)})$ be the arc-consistent problem obtained starting from $P^t_{V(C)}$. Then:*

- *for each i in $[1, p]$, the value $[\{x_i\}]_{P'}$ of location x_i in problem P' is a simple instantiation constraint c_{x_i, t_i, v_i},*
- *$blevel(P^t_{V(C)}) = \prod_{i \in [1,p]} v_i$.*

4 Partial Local Consistency

In this section we introduce the notion of *approximate local consistency algorithms*, and we give some sufficient conditions for such algorithms to terminate and be correct.

Notice that a local consistency algorithms is already an approximation in itself. In fact, because of its incompleteness, it approximates a complete solution algorithm. However, usually local consistency algorithms (as we have defined them in this paper and as they are usually used in practice) replace a constraint by the *solution* of a set of other constraints. Here we want to approximate this aspect of such algorithms, by allowing them to replace a constraint by a *superset of the solution* of a set of other constraints. However, to preserve the nice properties of local consistency, we must assure that such superset is not too big, so not to introduce any additional solution of the whole problem.

4.1 Approximated Rules

The idea of an approximation function is to replace the real computation (that is, the solution of the subproblem defined by a rule) with a simpler one. The following definition states that a "correct" and "complete" approximation function should not enlarge the domains and also it should not loose any solution. Given a rule $r = l \leftarrow L$, an *approximation function* ϕ for r is a function from $type^{-1}(L) \times type^{-1}(l)$ to $type^{-1}(l)$ such that:

- for all constraint set C of type L, for all constraint c of type l, $Sol(\langle C \cup \{c\}, l \rangle) \sqsubseteq_S \phi(C, c) \sqsubseteq_S c$,
- for all constraint sets $\{c_1, \ldots, c_p\}$, $\{c'_1, \ldots, c'_p\}$ of type L, for all constraints c, c' of type l, $(\forall i \in [1, p], c_i \sqsubseteq_S c'_i, c \sqsubseteq_S c') \Rightarrow (\phi(\{c_1, \ldots, c_p\}, c) \sqsubseteq_S \phi(\{c'_1, \ldots, c'_p\}, c'))$.

As trivial examples, one can consider the approximation function that does no approximation (let us call it ϕ_{best}) and also the one that does no domain reduction (ϕ_{worst}).

Example 1. Let $r = l \leftarrow L$ be a rule. Let ϕ_{best} such that $\forall C \in type^{-1}(L), \forall c \in type^{-1}(l)$, $\phi_{best}(C, c) = Sol(\langle C \cup \{c\}, l \rangle)$, It is easy to see that ϕ_{best} is an approximation function for r. It is the "best" approximation function (in fact, there are no rule that compute an approximation closer to the solution).

Example 2. Let $r = l \leftarrow L$ be a rule. Let ϕ_{worst} such that $\forall C \in type^{-1}(L), \forall c \in type^{-1}(l), \phi_{worst}(C, c) = c$, It is easy to see that ϕ_{worst} is an approximation function for r. It is the "worst" approximation function (in fact, the rule does not change any information over the constraints).

Given a rule $r = l \leftarrow L$ and an approximation function ϕ for r, the *approximation of rule r by function ϕ* is defined as $r_\phi = l \leftarrow_\phi L$. Given an approximated rule $r_\phi = l \leftarrow_\phi L$, the application of r_ϕ to problem P is defined by $[l \leftarrow_\phi L](P) = [l := \phi([L]_P, [l]_P)](P)$. That is, we apply to P the approximated rules instead of the original ones.

This notion of rule approximation can be used to modify the definition of a constraint without changing the solution of the problem. In fact, as the following theorem states, applying the approximated rule leads to a problem which has better values that the problem obtained by applying the rule. Thus, we cannot loose any solution, since we obtain an SCSP which is "between" the original problem and the problem obtained by using the non-approximated rules, which we know by definition of local consistency that they do not change the solution set.

Theorem 4. $[l \leftarrow L](P) \sqsubseteq_P [l \leftarrow_\phi L](P) \sqsubseteq P$.

It is easy to verify that ϕ_{best} computes the same problem as the rule itself while ϕ_{worst} does not change the problem.

Theorem 5 (equivalence for rules). *Given a problem P and an approximated rule r_ϕ, $P \equiv [r_\phi](P)$.*

Example 3. Let $r = l \leftarrow L$ be a rule. We have $[l \leftarrow_{\phi_{best}} L](P) = [l \leftarrow L](P)$ and $[l \leftarrow_{\phi_{worst}} L](P) = P$.

We recall to the reader that in order to fruitfully apply the local consistency scheme the $\times$ operation of the semiring has to be idempotent ([4,5]) so in every statement regarding local consistency in the following we assume to have an idempotent $\times$ operation.

Since the application of an *approximated rule* does not change the solution of the problem, we can define a correct and complete semiring-based *partial local consistency* algorithm, by applying, following a given strategy, several approximated rules to a given SCSP.

Given a set of rules R, an *approximation scheme* Φ for R associates to each rule $r = l \leftarrow L$ of R an approximation $\Phi(r) = l \leftarrow_\phi L$. Given a problem P, a set R of local consistency rules, an approximation scheme Φ for R, and a fair strategy

S for R, a local consistency algorithm applies to P the Φ-approximations of the rules in R in the order given by S. Thus, if the strategy is $S = s_1 s_2 s_3 \ldots$, the resulting problem is $P' = [\Phi(s_1); \Phi(s_2); \Phi(s_3); \ldots](P)$. The algorithm stops when the current problem is stable w.r.t. R. In that case, we denote by $plc(P, R, S, \Phi)$ the resulting problem.

Proposition 1 (equivalence). $P \equiv plc(P, R, S, \Phi)$.

Theorem 6 (termination). *Consider a SCSP P over a finite semiring. Then the application of a partial local consistency algorithm over P terminates in a finite number of steps.*

Proof. Trivially follows from the intensivity of $\times$ and finiteness of A. $\qquad \square$

Theorem 7 (order-independence). *Consider a SCSP P and two different applications of the same partial local consistency algorithm to P, producing respectively the problem $P' = plc(P, R, S, \Phi)$ and $P'' = plc(P, R, S', \Phi)$. Then, $P' = P''$. Thus, we will write $P' = plc(P, R, \Phi)$.*

Proof. It is easy to verify that $[\Phi(r)]$ is intensive and monotone which is sufficient to apply the chaotic iteration theorem [8]. $\qquad \square$

4.2   Partial Arc-Consistency

Given a SCSP P and an approximation scheme Φ for AC, we will write $pac(P, \Phi)$ instead of $plc(P, AC, \Phi)$.

Let ϕ be an approximation function for $r = \{x\} \leftarrow \{\{x, y_1, \ldots, y_n\}, \{y_1\}, \ldots, \{y_n\}\}$ (which, we recall, is the scheme for the AC rules). Let $Y = \{y_1, \ldots, y_n\}$ and $V = \{x\} \cup Y$. We say that ϕ is *instantiation-correct* if, for all constraints c of type V, for all $I_V^{d,v} = \{c_x\} \cup I_Y^{d',v'}$, we have

$$\phi(\{c\} \cup I_Y^{d',v'}, c_x) = Sol(\langle \{c\} \cup I_V^{d,v}, \{x\}\rangle).$$

Informally, ϕ is instantiation-correct if the rule $\Phi(r)$ performs an exact computation as soon as all the variables appearing in such a rule are instantiated. For example, ϕ_{best} is instantiation-correct, but ϕ_{worst} is not.

For approximation functions satisfying the previous definition, partial AC performs the same domain reductions as AC, as soon as all the variables of the problem are instantiated.

Theorem 8 (correctness of PAC). *Given a SCSP $P = \langle C, con \rangle$, and an approximation scheme Φ for AC that is instantiation-correct, assume that $V(C) = \{x_1, \ldots, x_p\}$ with $x_1 \prec \cdots \prec x_p$. Let $P_{V(C)}^t = \langle C \cup I_{V(C)}^t, con \rangle$ be a complete labeling of P. Let $P'' = pac(P_{V(C)}^t, \Phi)$ and $P' = ac(P_{V(C)}^t)$. Then, for each i in $[1, p]$, $[\{x_i\}]_{P'} = [\{x_i\}]_{P''}$.*

Proof. We will study the computation of the two algorithms (ac and pac). Because of the property of order-independence, we can assume that the rules are applied with the same strategy. Φ is correct w.r.t. to the instantiation. Hence, for each step (rule application and approximation of a rule application), the two algorithms compute the same domains (since all the variables are instantiated). Finally, for each i in $[1, p]$, $[\{x_i\}]_{P'} = [\{x_i\}]_{P''}$. □

Corollary 1. *With the notations of Theorem 8, for each i in $[1, p]$, the value $[\{x_i\}]_{P''}$ of location x_i in problem P'' is a simple instantiation constraint c_{x_i, t_i, v_i}. Moreover, $blevel(P^t_{V(C)}) = \prod_{i \in [1, p]} v_i$.*

5 Domains

We have seen that it is possible to approximate the computation of AC. We are now going to restrict our attention to certain kinds of approximations for AC, for which there exists a "good" representation for the variable domains. Then, we will adapt the computation of the approximations to these representations.

In the following we will always assume to have a constraint system $CS = \langle S, D, V \rangle$ where D is totally ordered. This means that there must be a way to compare any two elements of the domain D.

We call a *domain* any unary constraint. Given a set of domains E, we are looking for approximations schemes that build domains in E. Because of the properties of approximations, the set E has to satisfy the following three properties:

- for each domain, there must be a bigger domain in E;
- for each domain, there must be a smaller domain in E;
- E has to contain instantiation constraints (by instantiation-correctness); or, equivalently: $E \supseteq \{\langle 1, \{x\}\rangle / x \in V\} \cup \{c_{x,i,v} / x \in V, i \in D, v \in S\}$.

We will call an *approximation domain set* a set satisfying the above properties. The following proposition states that the notion of approximation domain is sufficient for the purpose of this work.

Proposition 2. *Given an approximation domain set E, there exists an approximation scheme Φ such that the application of an approximation function (corresponding to Φ) builds domains in E.*

The choice of an approximation domain set is very open. However, the approximation domains should have a fixed memory requirement. Here we will consider some generalizations of the min-max scheme usually used in current constraint programming.

An *up-down-stair* is a domain $d = (d(1), \ldots, d(n))$ such that there exists $k \in [1, n]$ s.t. $d(1) \leq_S \ldots d(k) \geq_S \ldots d(n)$. We call *m-up-down-stair* any *up-down-stair* domain such that $|d(D)| - 1 \leq m$. We note $S(m)$ the set of *m*-up-down-stairs.

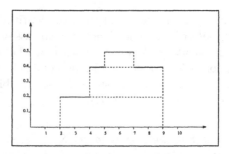

Fig. 6. A 3-up-down-stair.

Note that the 1-up-down-stair corresponds exactly to the min-max scheme in the case where the semiring is the boolean one. Figure 6 presents an example of a 3-up-down-stair in the case of the fuzzy semiring.

Proposition 3. *For each $m > 0$, $S(m)$ is an approximation domain set.*

Note that an m-up-down-stair can be stored using $2m$ integers and m semiring values. A m-up-down-stair is made of m rectangles of decreasing width. Then, for each k between 1 and m, one has to store the interval $[inf_k, sup_k]$ that defines the kth rectangle and the total height of the k first rectangles. For the example of Figure 6, we get: $([2,9], 0.2); ([4,9], 0.4); ([5,7], 0.5)$.

Let us now slightly restrict our definition of approximation functions in order to give some hints for their construction. We suppose m given and we will focus on m-up-down-stair domains. Let us consider a constraint c over $V = \{x\} \cup Y$ where $Y = \{y_1, \ldots, y_n\}$ and $y_1 \prec \cdots \prec y_n$. Let us also consider one of the associated AC rules: $\{x\} \leftarrow \{V, \{y_1\}, \ldots, \{y_n\}\}$. We are looking for an approximation function $\phi : type^{-1}(\{V, \{y_1\}, \ldots, \{y_n\}\}) \times type^{-1}(\{x\}) \to type^{-1}(\{x\})$.

Since we do not consider general local consistency but only AC, only the domains can change; this is the reason why the approximation function should not take the constraint as a parameter. Moreover, because of their presence in many applications, and also for implementation issues, we will focus on approximations functions that intersect the new domain with the old one (more precisely, we will consider the case of a unique intersection function).

Hence, we will focus on the case where ϕ is defined by:

$$\phi(\{c, c_{y_1}, \ldots, c_{y_n}\}, c_x) = \chi(\psi(c_{y_1}, \ldots, c_{y_n}), c_x)$$

where:

- $\psi : S(m) \times \ldots \times S(m) \to S(m)$ computes a new domain (m-up-down-stair) for variable x;
- $\chi : S(m) \to S(m)$ intersects[2] the new domain and the old one.

---

[2] In the general case, $\otimes$ is not a function from $S(m) \times S(m)$ to $S(m)$ (this is true only in the case where $m = 1$), hence we have to use χ instead.

In the following, we will assume that the domain of the variable D has the form $[0, \infty]$ where ∞ is the maximal value an integer can take. As a practical and simple example, let us consider the case where $m = 1$. Here $\otimes$ is stable over $S(m)$, hence we take $\chi = \otimes$, which can be implemented by:

$$\chi(([i_1, s_1], v_1), ([i_1', s_1'], v_1')) = ([\max(i_1, i_1'), \min(s_1, s_1')], v_1 \times v_1').$$

Using 1-up-down-stairs, it is also easy to implement the rules for usual constraints.

Example 4 (constraint $X \leq Y$). For example, the two rules corresponding to constraint $x \leq y$ can be implemented by:

$$\psi_x(([i_y, s_y], v_y)) = ([0, s_y], v_y)$$

and

$$\psi_y(([i_x, s_x], v_x)) = ([s_x, \infty], v_x).$$

Example 5 (contraint $X = Y + C$). As another example, the two rules corresponding to constraint $x = y + c$ can be implemented by:

$$\psi_x(([i_y, s_y], v_y)) = ([i_y + c, s_y + c], v_y)$$

and

$$\psi_y(([i_x, s_x], v_x)) = ([i_x - c, s_x - c], v_x).$$

In the case where $m > 1$, it is also possible to implement χ and the rules associated to usual constraints. This implementation is more complicated since there are different representations corresponding to the same up-down-stair. Hence, one has to define a function that chooses a representation among all the possible ones.

6   Implementation

The clp(FD, S) system [7,11] contains a logic-based language for semiring-based constraint solving, developed at INRIA[3]. Our implementation of partial AC in the clp(FD, S) system uses a unique constraint of the form X in r (see [7,11]). In this notation, X is a variable and r is a range, and the meaning of this constraint is that r denotes the set of possible values for X.

A range r can be as simple as 1..10, meaning all integers between 1 and 10, but it can also include references to other variables, such as in min(Y) .. max(Z)+1, meaning all integers between the minimum element in the current range of Y and the maximum element in the current range of Z plus 1. Those

---

[3] clp(FD, S) is freely available by http at
   loco.inria.fr/~georget/clp_fds/clp_fds.html.

terms like min(X), which require an evaluation of the current range of a variable (in this case X), are called *indexicals*.

The language of ranges has been extended to deal with our new definition of domains: Table 1 presents the set of operators and indexicals needed for writing ranges that will be in $S(1)^4$. An indexical that may need explanations in this table is sigma(X), which is defined to be $\sum_i X_i$, that is, the least upper bound of all values in the domain of X.

$r ::= sing(it)$	(singleton)	
$it .. it$	(interval)	
$r + r$	(union)	
$r * r$	(intersection)	
$r + at$	(+ operation)	
$r * at$	(× operation)	
$it ::= n$	(integer ($< \infty$))	
$infinity$	(∞)	
$min(Y)$	(indexical)	
$max(Y)$	(indexical)	
$add(it, it)$	(addition)	
$sub(it, it)$	(subtraction)	
$mul(it, it)$	(multiplication)	
$floor\_div(it, it)$	(division, rounded down)	
$ceil\_div(it, it)$	(division, rounded up)	
$at ::= a$	(element of the semiring)	
$at + at$	(+ operation)	
$at * at$	(× operation)	
$sigma(Y)$	(indexical)	

Table 1. Operators and indexicals needed for partial AC.

Some examples on how to encode arithmetic constraints using this set of indexicals and operators:

- the constraint $x \geq y$ can be encoded by:
  ```
  X in (min(Y)..infinity)*sigma(Y),
  Y in (0..max(X))*sigma(X)
  ```

- the constraint $x = y + c$ can be encoded by:
  ```
  X in (add(min(Y),C) .. add(max(Y),C))*sigma(Y),
  Y in (sub(min(X),C) .. sub(max(X),C))*sigma(X)
  ```

---

[4] We recall that S(1) is the set of 1-up-down-stair.

In order to measure the efficiency of our implementation, we have first compared the execution times of AC and partial AC (PAC) in clp(FD, S) on the well-known problem alpha (coming from the newsgroup rec.puzzle). The results (obtained on a **PII, 400 Mhz**) are as follows: AC takes 175200 ms, while PAC takes just 4590 ms. This comparison shows that PAC is much faster than AC on problems that use a lot of arithmetic constraints, like the alpha problem does. Notice that the problem alpha is not soft. Thus in this case we have used PAC over the semiring *Bool*.

We have also compared the execution times of PAC in clp(FD, S) [11] and PAC in clp(FD) [7] on a set of classical benchmarks which do not strictly require soft constraints. Note that the purpose of these experiments was not to solve the benchmarks as quick as possible but to compare the two systems, hence, we did not use heuristics or sophisticated methods. The results (obtained on a **PII, 400 Mhz**) are given in Table 2.

Name	clp(FD, S) (ms)	clp(FD) (ms)	$\frac{clp(FD,S)}{clp(FD)}$
alpha	4590	730	6.3
bridge	30	30	1
20×cars	150	60	2.5
20×crypta	480	110	4.7
donald	1170	230	5.1
20×eq10	170	130	1.3
20×eq20	300	240	1.3
lauriere	1960	630	3.1

Table 2. clp(FD, S) vs clp(FD) (using PAC).

The first thing to notice is that clp(FD, S) is always slower. The reason for this is that it is generic with respect to the semiring: it can handle both classical and soft constraints. However, the loss of efficiency is acceptable: the mean value of $\frac{clp(FD,S)}{clp(FD)}$ is 3.2. This is also due to the fact that we have used PAC, otherwise the loss would be much higher. Thus, from these initial experiments, we can see that even for problems which can be handled by clp(FD), the use of the clp(FD, S) system can be acceptable if PAC is applied.

7 Future Work

We plan to go further in the experiments with PAC. In particular, we plan to study the performances of AC and PAC on fuzzy and other soft constraint problems (we only give results for boolean problems in this paper), in order to choose the approximation with the best trade-off between precision and efficiency.

References

1. A. Aggoun and N. Beldiceanu. Overview of the CHIP Compiler System. *Constraint Logic Programming: Selected Research*, A. Colmerauer and F. Benhamou (Eds.). MIT Press, 1993.
2. Krysztof R. Apt. The essence of Constraint Propagation. CWI Quarterly vol.11 (2 & 3), pp. 215-248, 1998.
3. C. Bessière. Arc-consistency and Arc-consistency again. *Artificial Intelligence*, 65(1), 1994.
4. S. Bistarelli, U. Montanari and F. Rossi. Constraint Solving over Semirings. *Proceedings of IJCAI'95*, Morgan Kaufman, 1995.
5. S. Bistarelli, U. Montanari and F. Rossi. Semiring-based Constraint Solving and Optimization. *Journal of ACM*, vol. 44, no. 2, March 1997.
6. S. Bistarelli, U. Montanari and F. Rossi. Semiring-based Constraint Logic Programming. *Proceedings of IJCAI'97*, Morgan Kaufman, 1997.
7. P. Codognet and D. Diaz. Compiling Constraints in clp(FD). *Journal of Logic Programming*, vol. 27, no. 3, 1996.
8. P. Cousot. Asynchronous Iterative Methods for Solving a Fixed Point System of Monotone Equations in a Complete Lattice. Université Scientifique et Médicale et Institut National Polytechnique de Grenoble, RR 88, Septembre 1977.
9. D. Dubois, H. Fargier and H. Prade. The calculus of fuzzy restrictions as a basis for flexible constraint satisfaction. Proc. IEEE International Conference on Fuzzy Systems, IEEE, pp. 1131–1136, 1993.
10. Y. Georget. Extensions de la Programmation par Contraintes. Ph.D. thesis, Ecole Polytecnique, Paris, to be defended in September 1999.
11. Y. Georget and P. Codognet. Compiling Semiring-based Constraints with clp(FD,S). *Proceedings of CP'98*, Springer, 1998.
12. Y. Georget and P. Codognet. Encoding Global Constraints in Semiring-based Constraint Solving. *Proceedings of ICTAI'98*, IEEE, 1998.
13. A. K. Mackworth. Consistency in Networks of Relations. *Artificial Intelligence 8 (1977)*, pp 99-118.
14. J-F. Puget. A C++ implementation of CLP. *Proceedings of SPICIS 94*, November 1994.
15. P. Van Hentenryck. *Constraint Satisfaction in Logic Programming*. MIT Press, 1989.
16. P. Van Hentenryck, Y. Deville and C-M. Teng. A generic arc-consistency algorithm and its specializations. *Artificial Intelligence 57 (1992)*, pp 291-321.

Transformation-by-Example for XML*

Shriram Krishnamurthi, Kathryn E. Gray, and Paul T. Graunke

Department of Computer Science
Rice University
Houston, TX 77005-1892, USA

Abstract. XML is a language for describing markup languages for structured data. A growing number of applications that process XML documents are *transformers*, i.e., programs that convert documents between XML languages. Unfortunately, the current proposals for transformers are complex general-purpose languages, which will be unappealing as the XML user base broadens and thus decreases in technical sophistication. We have designed and implemented XT3D, a highly declarative XML specification language. It demands little more from users than a knowledge of the expected input and desired output. We illustrate the power of XT3D with several examples, including one reminiscent of polytypic programming that greatly simplifies the import of XML values into general-purpose languages.

1 XML and Transformations

XML [3] is a simplified version of the markup description language SGML. Because of XML's syntactic simplicity, it is easy to implement rudimentary XML processors and embed them in a variety of devices. As a result, a wide variety of applications are adopting XML as a data representation standard. Declarative programming languages must therefore provide support for XML. They can do better; as this paper demonstrates, ideas from declarative programming can strongly enhance the toolkit that supports XML.

Syntactically, XML has a structure similar to other SGML-style markup languages such as HTML. The difference between XML and a language like HTML is that XML really represents a *family* of languages. Concretely, XML provides two levels of specification:

- An XML *element* defines a tree-structured representation of terms. This representation is rich enough to express a wide variety of data. A sample element, which might represent information about music albums, is

    < *album title*="everybody else is doing it, so why can't we?">
       < *catalog*>< *num*> *A043*</ *num*>< *fmt*> *CD*</ *fmt*></ *catalog*>
       < *catalog*>< *num*> *BD34*</ *num*>< *fmt*> *LP*</ *fmt*></ *catalog*>
    </ *album*>

---

* This work is partially supported by NSF grants CCR-9619756, CDA-9713032 and CCR-9708957, and a Texas ATP grant.

E. Pontelli, V. Santos Costa (Eds.): PADL 2000, LNCS 1753, pp. 249–262, 2000.

- An XML *language* is essentially a BNF grammar that lists the valid elements and states how they may nest within each other. A language thus circumscribes a subset of the universe of all possible elements. The language of music albums may, for instance, allow an *album* element to mention only the name and catalog entries of an album.

An input whose elements meet the basic syntactic requirements of XML (such as matching and properly nested element tags) is said to be *well-formed*. A well-formed element that meets the requirements of a language, or *document type definition*, is called *valid* (with respect to that definition).

This two-level syntax makes XML documents easy to process in two phases. The first phase converts an input character stream into a stream of elements, checking only for well-formedness. The second phase, which can proceed in a top-down fashion, checks each element in the stream for conformance with a language definition. In short, XML is relatively easy to parse.

XML is commonly associated with the Web. New XML languages can be used to provide more structure to information than Web markup languages like HTML offer. These benefits can also be harnessed in several other contexts, so XML is expected to see widespread use for defining syntaxes for communication standards, database entries, programming languages, and so forth. Already, user communities are defining XML languages for business data, mathematics, chemistry, etc. XML thus promises to be an important and ubiquitous vehicle for data storage and transmission.

By itself, an XML document does nothing. It represents uninterpreted data. Its value lies in processors that understand the document and use it to perform some action. The set of processors for a language is potentially unlimited, e.g.,

XML Language	Processor	Action
HTML	Web browser	renders document on screen
music albums	inventory lister	generates HTML listing
a programming language	pretty-printer	generates HTML listing
a programming language	interpreter	runs program

A surprising number of these actions involve transforming one XML language into another. Even rendering documents on screen involves transformations. The XSL standard [6] defines an XML language for "formatting objects" that provide low-level formatting control of a document's content. As the number of domains that use XML to represent their information increases, more of these actions will be XML transformations.

Recognizing the importance of transformations, the XML standards committee is defining XSLT, a language for describing transformations between XML languages. Unfortunately, XSLT is an ad hoc language with no complete, formal semantics. Worse, XSLT appears to be a fairly complex language, and seemingly simple transformations require the user to essentially write a traditional procedural program. As XML's audience grows to encompass users of decreasing technical sophistication, XSLT's complexity imposes prohibitive demands on users, and increases the likelihood of errors.

To address this problem, we have designed and implemented XT3D, a transformation system for XML. XT3D is itself an XML language, so users do not need to learn a new surface syntax. The principal advantage of XT3D over XSLT is that it provides an extremely simple, declarative language for describing transformations over XML elements. Specifically, an XT3D specification contains little more than outlines of the expected input and the desired output of the transformation. Thus we anticipate that even users with minimal technical skills can use XT3D.

We hope the ideas of this paper will broaden the discussion on XML transformation languages. In particular, this paper includes several examples of transformations that can be implemented conveniently in XT3D, including some reminiscent of polytypic programming. We believe these examples can serve as part of a benchmark suite for evaluating transformation languages.

The rest of this paper is organized as follows. Section 2 briefly describes XML's syntax and language descriptions. Section 3 explains XT3D through a series of examples, and section 4 describes an extension and some pragmatic considerations. Section 5 describes how XT3D can automate the embedding of XML data in a general-purpose language. Section 6 describes some details about our implementation and its current status. The last two sections discuss related work and offer concluding remarks.

2 Background

XML documents consist of *elements*. The outermost element in the sample presented in section 1 describes an album. An album has one *attribute*, a title. Its *content* is a sequence of catalog entries. Each catalog entry contains a number and a format element. All elements must be properly nested, with elements represented by matching opening and closing tags, e.g., *<album>* and *</album>*. *Empty* elements, which are elements with no contents (but possibly with attributes), use only one tag, which is closed with */>*, e.g., *<empty/>*.

XML users define *languages* via an XML SCHEMA [1], which is essentially a BNF description. A schema that validates the sample XML element of section 1 is shown in figure 1. The elements in a document can specify attributes in any order, whereas content must follow the order described by the schema. The *minOccur* attribute specifies the minimum length required of a sequence of the referred element.

As the example suggests, XML SCHEMA is itself an XML language. Schemas are being proposed as an alternative to traditional markup specifications, inherited from SGML, called DTDs. Unlike schemas, DTDs are not XML languages. Section 5 exploits the fact that schemas are XML documents.

3 Transformation by Example (by Example)

We call the style of transformations employed by XT3D "transformation by example" by analogy to the work of Kohlbecker and Wand [13]. An XT3D trans-

```
<schema>                                <elementType name="catalog">
  <elementType name="album">              <sequence>
    <sequence minOccur="0">                 <elementTypeRef name="num"/>
      <elementTypeRef name="catalog"/>      <elementTypeRef name="fmt"/>
    </sequence>                           </sequence>
    <attrDecl name="title"/>            </elementType>
  </elementType>

                                        <elementType name="fmt">
  <elementType name="num">                <datatypeRef name="string"/>
    <datatypeRef name="string"/>        </elementType>
  </elementType>                       </schema>
```

Fig. 1. Sample Schema

formation consists of pairs of patterns representing the expected source and the desired output. These patterns, which are parameterized over pattern variables, are in the source and destination XML languages, respectively.

The pattern-matcher works by comparing each element in the input tree against the collection of defined patterns. An element matches a pattern if the element has the same structure as the pattern, with pattern variables in the pattern matching an arbitrary element in the actual input. The pattern matcher binds pattern variables to the corresponding parts of the inputs. It then generates an output element, substituting pattern variables with the sub-terms bound in the input. This new element is then expanded. This process continues until the input cannot be transformed further.

Figure 2 presents a sample XT3D transformation that processes elements that conform to the schema of section 2. The element *xt3d-transformation* introduces a new set of transformations. The *xt3d-macro* element represents a single transformation in this set. The *xt3d-clause* element delimits the two boxed terms, which constitute an input- and an output-pattern pair. Pattern variables are introduced as *xt3d-bind* elements in the input pattern, and *xt3d-use* elements in the output. An element's attributes (as opposed to its content) are matched by the *xt3d-attr* elements of the *xt3d-attributes* element.[1] If an attribute is specified literally in the input pattern, the pattern matcher checks that the element contains that attribute, with the value bound in the pattern.

The empty element <*xt3d-···*/> denotes an ellipsis, which affects pattern-matching. It follows a ("head") pattern in a sequence and matches a source

---

[1] This is the one point where XT3D departs from a pure "by example" syntax. We are forced to invent notation because XML attribute values can only be strings. Given a string value for an attribute, XT3D cannot determine whether the user means it to be a pattern variable (to be bound for use in the output) or a literal (to be checked for presence in the input). We rejected both embedding a special-purpose language in attribute value strings, and deviating from XML syntax.

```
<xt3d-transformation>
 <xt3d-macro>
  <xt3d-clause>
```

```
<xt3d-input>
 <album>
  <xt3d-attributes>
   <xt3d-attr name="title">
    <xt3d-bind name="name"/>
   </xt3d-attr>
  </xt3d-attributes>
  <catalog>
   <num><xt3d-bind name="num"/>
   </num>
   <fmt><xt3d-bind name="fmt"/>
   </fmt>
  </catalog><xt3d-.../>
 </album>
</xt3d-input>
```

```
<xt3d-output>
 <ul>
  <li><xt3d-use name="name"/>
  </li>
  <li>
   <b><xt3d-use name="num"/>
   </b>
   <i><xt3d-use name="fmt"/>
   </i>
  </li><xt3d-.../>
 </ul>
</xt3d-output>
```

```
  </xt3d-clause>
 </xt3d-macro>
</xt3d-transformation>
```

Fig. 2. Sample XT3D Transformation

sequence of zero or more instances of the head pattern. It binds each pattern variable in the head pattern to a sequence. This sequence consists of the sub-terms, in order, of the terms in the source sequence that correspond to the pattern variable's position in the head pattern. Ellipses can be nested to arbitrary depth. Each nesting level introduces a nested sequence in the binding of a pattern variable.[2]

This transformation converts the album element of section 2 into

```
<ul>
 <li>everybody else is doing it, so why can't we?</li>
 <li><b>A043</b><i>CD</i></li>
 <li><b>BD34</b><i>LP</i></li>
</ul>
```

The following sub-pattern of the transformation's expected source uses ellipses:

```
<catalog>
 <num><xt3d-bind name="num"/></num>
 <fmt><xt3d-bind name="fmt"/></fmt>
</catalog><xt3d-.../>
```

---

[2] Hence the name XT3D, which stands for "XML Transformations with Three Dots".

In the sample album entry, this pattern matches against

$$<catalog><num>A043</num><fmt>CD</fmt></catalog>$$
$$<catalog><num>BD34</num><fmt>LP</fmt></catalog>$$

binding *form* to the sequence "CD" followed by "LP", and *number* to "A043" followed by "BD34". The output pattern pairs numbers with formats:

```
<li>
 <b><xt3d-use name="num"/>, </b>
 <i><xt3d-use name="fmt"/></i>
</li><xt3d-.../>
```

As a second example, consider a variant on the first that lists the numbers and formats separately. We only need change the output rule:

```
<xt3d-output>
 <ul>
  <li><xt3d-use name="name"/></li>
  <li><b><xt3d-use name="num"/></b> <xt3d-.../></li>
  <li><i><xt3d-use name="fmt"/></i> <xt3d-.../></li>
 </ul>
</xt3d-output>
```

In short, this transformation is a simple version of a table transposition. (By using nested ellipses, we can handle arbitrary numbers of rows and columns.)

These examples distill the essence of similar ones presented in the XSLT document [4] and the paper by Wallace and Runciman [18]. The XT3D specifications do not involve list processing combinators or conventional procedural programming. We therefore believe XT3D will be especially helpful for users who have little or no formal programming experience.

The third example illustrates a transformation that may be useful in software that generates rudimentary English phrases from databases. Given a database of purchase records, it uses the transformations of figure 3 to generate a purchase summary such that multiple purchases are separated by commas, except for the last two, which are separated by the word "and". Two examples of the input and generated terms are

```
<purchase>
 <p>4 tinkers</p>        ⟹        <text>4 tinkers</text>
</purchase>
```

and

```
<purchase>                              <text>4 tinkers,
 <p>4 tinkers</p>                         <text>5 tailors,
 <p>5 tailors</p>                          <text>2 soldiers and
 <p>2 soldiers</p>        ⟹                 <text>1 spy</text>
 <p>1 spy</p>                              </text>
</purchase>                              </text>
                                        </text>
```

```
<xt3d-macro>                              <xt3d-clause>
 <xt3d-clause>                             <xt3d-input>
  <xt3d-input>                              <purchase>
   <purchase>                                <p><xt3d-bind name="i"/>
    <p><xt3d-bind name="i"/></p>            </p>
   </purchase>                               <xt3d-bind name="rst"/>
  </xt3d-input>                              <xt3d-···/>
  <xt3d-output>                             </purchase>
   <text><xt3d-use name="i"/>              </xt3d-input>
   </text>                                 <xt3d-output>
  </xt3d-output>                            <text><xt3d-use name="i"/>,
 </xt3d-clause>                              <purchase>
                                             <xt3d-use name="rst"/>
 <xt3d-clause>                               <xt3d-···/>
  <xt3d-input>                              </purchase></text>
   <purchase>                              </xt3d-output>
    <p><xt3d-bind name="i"/></p>          </xt3d-clause>
    <p><xt3d-bind name="i2"/></p>        </xt3d-macro>
   </purchase>
  </xt3d-input>
  <xt3d-output>
   <text><xt3d-use name="i"/> and
     <purchase>
      <p><xt3d-use name="i2"/>
      </p>
     </purchase></text>
  </xt3d-output>
 </xt3d-clause>
```

Fig. 3. Phrases from Databases in XT3D

Figure 4 presents what we believe is the equivalent transformation in XSLT. Though an XML language, XSLT encodes a special-purpose programming language in attribute strings. This language performs numerous actions such as boolean tests, mathematical operations, selections of attributes and content, and so on.[3] We believe this kind of encoding violates the spirit of XML, since it uses a flat representation for structured data (in this case, the special-purpose programs).

4 Beyond Macros

The alert reader will have noticed that our transformation language is essentially identical to the pattern-matching notation used for specifying Scheme

---

[3] Technically, the example is in XSLT's "abbreviated syntax", but the full syntax has the same flavor.

```
<xsl:template match="purchase">            <xsl:template name="lrgr">
  <xsl:choose>                              <xsl:param name="len"/>
    <xsl:when test="last()=1">              <xsl:param name="curr"/>
      <xsl:text>                            <xsl:choose>
        <xsl:apply-templates/>                <xsl:when
      </xsl:text>                               test="curr &lt; (len -2)">
    </xsl:when>                                 <xsl:text>
    <xsl:when test="last()=2">                    <xsl:apply-template
      <xsl:text>                                    select="p(curr)"/>,
        <xsl:apply-template select="p(1)"/>       <xsl:call-template name="lrgr">
        and                                         <xsl:with-param
        <xsl:apply-template select="p(2)"/>           name="len" select="len"/>
      </xsl:text>                                   <xsl:with-param
    </xsl:when>                                       name="curr"
    <xsl:otherwise>                                   select="curr+1"/>
      <xsl:call-template name="lrgr">           </xsl:call-template>
        <xsl:with-param name="len"            </xsl:text>
                       select="last()"/>    </xsl:when>
        <xsl:with-param name="curr"           <xsl:otherwise>
                       select="1"/>            <xsl:text>
      </xsl:call-template>                        <xsl:apply-template
    </xsl:otherwise>                                 select="p(curr)"/>
  </xsl:choose>                                   and
</xsl:template>                                   <xsl:apply-template
                                                    select="p(last)"/>
<xsl:template select="p">                     </xsl:text>
  <xsl:apply-templates/>                      </xsl:otherwise>
</xsl:template>                            </xsl:choose>
                                          </xsl:template>
```

Fig. 4. Phrases from Databases in XSLT

macros [11]. The last example above, for instance, is a straightforward extension to the traditional **and** macro used in Scheme implementations.

Macros work by repeated expansion. The macro processor scans the source term for the outermost use of a macro. It expands this term and recurs on the generated source. Expansion stops when there are no macro uses left. While this is convenient for simple specifications, it denies the user control of what to expand. It also presumes that the generated terms will be in the same language as the source, preventing transformations from one language to another.

Our implementation of XT3D is built atop McMicMac [15], a sophisticated macro system for Scheme. The McMicMac macro expander provides a complement to macros called *micros*. In a micro, all terms in the output pattern are left unexpanded unless the micro's author explicitly chooses to expand them. Thus programmers can construct terms in a destination language that is distinct from the source language, while recursively processing source sub-terms within the

```
<xt3d-micro>                         <xt3d-output>
 <xt3d-clause>                        <fo:basic-page-sequence>
  <xt3d-input>                         <fo:simple-page-master/>
   <doc>                                <fo:queue>
    <chapter>
     <p><xt3d-bind name="text"/>        ┌──────────────────────────────────┐
     </p><xt3d-.../>                    │ <xt3d-expand><xt3d-pattern>      │
    </chapter>                          │  <chapter>                       │
   </doc>                               │   <p><xt3d-use name="text"/>     │
  </xt3d-input>                         │   </p><xt3d-.../>                │
                                        │  </chapter>                      │
                                        │ </xt3d-pattern></xt3d-expand>    │
                                        └──────────────────────────────────┘

                                         </fo:queue>
                                        </fo:basic-page-sequence>
                                       </xt3d-output>
                                      </xt3d-clause>
                                     </xt3d-micro>
```

Fig. 5. Sample XT3D Micro

partially constructed output. In XT3D, the primitive *xt3d-expand* triggers recursive expansion, while *xt3d-pattern* expands its contained pattern in the pattern environment generated from the input pattern. Everything outside these terms in the output is assumed to be in the target language, and is therefore neither macro- nor pattern-expanded.

Figure 5 presents an XT3D micro. It converts a document language into XSL formatting objects. The salient portion is the boxed term in the output pattern. Everything outside the box is treated literally, and is thus immune to the expansion rules of the source language. (In principle, therefore, the macros in the preceding section should really have been micros. They work by accident, relying on the lack of overlap between the source and target languages.) In the boxed term, *xt3d-expand* further expands the body, which is still in the source language. The body can be an arbitrarily complex pattern that includes *xt3d-⋯*.

For example, an input and its expansion after one step are

```
                         <fo:basic-page-sequence>
                          <fo:simple-page-master/>
<doc>                     <fo:queue>
 <chapter>
  <p>Veni.</p>            ┌────────────────────────────────────────────────┐
  <p>Vidi.</p>     ⟹     │ <chapter>                                      │
  <p>Vici.</p>            │  <p>Veni.</p> <p>Vidi.</p> <p>Vici.</p>        │
 </chapter>               │ </chapter>                                     │
</doc>                    └────────────────────────────────────────────────┘
                          </fo:queue>
                         </fo:basic-page-sequence>
```

The boxed term in the expansion represents the element that is about to be expanded again. The surrounding elements are in the target language, so they are not subject to the rules of expansion for the document description language.

5 Processing XML Data in General-Purpose Languages

In this section, we outline how we can import XML data into a general-purpose language (in our case, Scheme) for processing. We accomplish this using several hundred lines of XT3D transformations. As a case study, this illustrates:

1. how to automate typeful embeddings of XML SCHEMAS into programming languages,
2. how XT3D facilitates this embedding, and,
3. the XML support we have built for Scheme.

This library therefore accomplishes similar ends as Wallace and Runciman's system [18], but does so as a consequence of our primitives rather than as an end in itself.

The library consists of three families of XT3D transformers, each of which converts (restricted) XML SCHEMAS into Scheme programs:

1. The first phase converts XML SCHEMAS into corresponding Scheme structure definitions (which introduce new types) using MzScheme's **define-struct** facility [8].
2. The second phase generates a family of *builders*, one per element type. A builder is a Scheme procedure that consumes an XML element of an expected type, validates it, and produces an instance of the structure corresponding to that type (defined in the first phase).
3. The third phase generates *walker* generators. Walkers are procedures that consume instances of the structures defined in the first phase. The walker traverses each field of the structure using the walker for the type of that field. It then combines the results from these traversals using a procedure that the programmer supplies to the walker generator. This relieves the programmer of having to know the names of the fields or access them explicitly.

These transformations therefore automate the creation of validators, and enable a programmer to process XML data in a type-driven manner.

The preceding text discusses XT3D generating Scheme code, but Scheme is not an XML language, and XT3D can only generate XML terms. We have therefore defined an XML language, XScheme, to represent Scheme programs. Our XML library enriches our Scheme implementation with a reader that accepts XScheme programs in addition to those written in traditional Scheme syntax.

As an example of putting these transformations to work, consider this schema of geometric shapes (which we restrict to two element types for brevity):

```
<elementType name="rectangle">              <elementType name="point">
 <sequence>                                   <sequence/>
  <elementTypeRef name="point"/>             <attrDecl name="x"
 </sequence>                                           required="true"/>
 <attrDecl name="wd"                         <attrDecl name="y"
          required="true"/>                           required="true"/>
 <attrDecl name="ht"                        </elementType>
          required="true"/>
</elementType>
```

A programmer can render data in this format to the screen using the following
Scheme code:

```
;; walk-rectangle : Rectangle ⟶ void      ;; walk-point : Point ⟶ (cons Nat Nat)
(define walk-rectangle                     (define walk-point
  (gen-walk-rectangle                        (gen-walk-point
    (lambda (attrs center-walker)              (lambda (attrs)
      (let* ((center (center-walker))            (cons (attr→num 'x attrs)
             (center-x (car center))                   (attr→num 'y attrs)))))))
             (center-y (cdr center))
             (wd (attr→num 'wd attrs))
             (ht (attr→num 'ht attrs)))
        (lambda (canvas)
          (draw-rectangle canvas
            (- center-x (/ wd 2))
            (- center-y (/ ht 2))
            wd ht))))))
```

The procedure *gen-walk-rectangle* creates a thunk that, when invoked, applies
walk-point to the point in the rectangle type. It provides this thunk as the value
for the parameter named *center-walker*. The XT3D transformations generate the
procedure *gen-walk-rectangle* and other supporting routines. The programmer
needs to write only a few lines of scaffolding to read in the data and validate
them using the generated builders. Due to paucity of space, we cannot present
more details here.

This example is reminiscent of *polytypic* programming [2, 10, 16]. Polytypic
programs, at least in the style of PolyP [10], typically consume a type constructor
and return functions that manipulate values of that type. They can, for instance,
generate maps, folds and other traversals that operate over a wide variety of
types. Similarly, our third phase consumes a schema, which is essentially a type
declaration for the values that are generated by the builders, and produces simple
traversals over this class of values.

The preceding operations could have been performed on any (restricted)
schema. We have also applied them to the schema for the XScheme language itself. This generates Scheme code which programmers can employ to manipulate

XScheme documents (i.e., programs) as Scheme values. Examples of such applications include interpreters, compilers and analysis engines. Languages that lack Scheme's syntactic simplicity can use such a library to simplify the transmission and processing of programs.

6   Implementation Details and Status

XT3D is part of the evolving XML library for the MzScheme [8] implementation of Scheme. We have tested all the examples in this paper using our library. The library exploits the similarity between XML elements and Scheme s-expressions. XML elements differ from s-expressions primarily in that they consist of two distinguished parts: attributes and content. We embed XML elements into s-expressions by requiring all target s-expressions to have the form

$$(tag \ ((attribute \ value) \ldots) \ element \ldots)$$

where *tag* is the name of the element. In our implementation, the attributes are sorted alphabetically to yield a canonical representation. We refer to such s-expressions as *x-expressions*.

Our library contains a reader that transforms XML source into x-expressions. It also includes two x-expression transformers: one that converts x-expressions representing XScheme into conventional Scheme syntax, and another that transforms x-expressions representing XT3D macro and micro definitions into McMic-Mac declarations.

The reader that generates x-expressions also maintains source location information for each term. It uses the source locations to generate special-purpose structures rather than conventional Scheme lists. McMicMac processes these enriched structures and uses them to perform source-correlation and source-tracking [14]. These are especially useful for determining the loci of errors.

Unlike some other toolkits, our library does not provide intrinsic support for any document type definition languages. Instead, we employ transformations, such as those described in section 5, to generate validators. This is a serendipitous consequence of the tools that comprise our library. Since MzScheme offers a rich target language for embedding, we expect to handle other document type definition standards such as SOX [5] in a similar manner.

Our library will continue to grow. For instance, the transformations that generate code from schemas (section 5) place some restrictions on the content of the schema. This is partially because our implementation is still in the prototype phase, but is also allied to our proposal (under preparation) for more extensible schemas. For the same reasons, transformations do not interact properly with XML namespaces. Also, our specifications become unwieldy for elements with several optional attributes.

7   Related Work

XT3D draws on a rich pedigree of Lisp and Scheme macro systems. The most influential of these is Kohlbecker and Wand's *macro-by-example* [13]. It also exploits the source correlation feature first described by Dybvig, et al. [7] and the micros of MCMICMAC [15]. Kohlbecker and Wand also provided a semantics for their transformation system, which can be used to formalize XT3D's transformers.

Several functional and declarative languages provide a pattern matching notation over values. By converting XML documents into structured values in these languages, programmers can exploit the built-in pattern matchers and constructor syntax to define transformers. This would, however, force the average user to learn the base language and contend with its peculiarities. In particular, small mistakes could trigger unexpected interactions with the base language. (One way to address this shortcoming is to use language levels [15].) In a declarative vein, we have recently come across a tool named PatML [9] which generates XML documents via pattern-matching, but have not been able to evaluate it.

The leading proposal for XML transformations is currently XSLT. It is difficult to compare XSLT and XT3D since XSLT is under constant revision, and is only partially formalized [17]. There are several subtle differences in the way XSLT and XT3D match and transform elements, with each having some strengths over the other. In the final analysis, we believe both styles serve useful ends. We would ideally like to see a synthesis of these styles so that simple tasks remain easy, while complex ones require more effort. We do find it unfortunate that XSLT uses strings to represent so much of its transformation language, since this inhibits the effective use of XML transformers to construct and process XSLT specifications themselves.

8 Summary and Future Work

We have designed and implemented XT3D, a transformation system for XML. The heart of XT3D is a simple declarative language for describing transformations that saves users from the burden of needing conventional programming experience. In particular, users need to know little more than the structure of the expected inputs and desired outputs. It should therefore be especially useful as XML is used by audiences with decreasing technical sophistication. Meanwhile, experts can exploit XT3D's advanced features to write sophisticated tools such as compilers and polytypic programs. This paper presents several such examples, which we believe belong in a benchmark for XML transformation tools.

XT3D must reflect the features and norms of XML. Since XML is constantly evolving, XT3D is very much a work in progress. Future work on XT3D can take several directions. First, it must support features like namespaces. Second, it can benefit greatly from primitives such as those provided by XSLT. XT3D also suggests shortcomings in and improvements to XML, such as information to create *hygienic* [12] transformers. We expect such work will expose ideas from functional and declarative languages to much broader audiences.

Acknowledgements

The authors thank Matthias Felleisen for suggestions, support, and critiques of drafts. We also thank the anonymous referees for their comments. The first author thanks Phil Wadler for useful exchanges.

References

[1] Beech, D., S. Lawrence, M. Maloney, N. Mendelsohn and H. S. Thompson. XML Schema part 1: Structures. Technical report, World Wide Web Consortium, September 1999.

[2] Bellé, G., C. B. Jay and E. Moggi. Functorial ML. In *International Symposium on Programming Languages: Implementations, Logics, and Programs*, pages 32–46, 1996.

[3] Bray, T., J. Paoli and C. Sperberg-McQueen. Exensible markup language XML. Technical report, World Wide Web Consortium, Feburary 1998. Version 1.0.

[4] Clark, J. XSL transformations. Technical report, World Wide Web Consortium, October 1999. Version 1.0.

[5] Davidson, A., M. Fuchs, M. Hedin, M. Jain, J. Koistinen, C. Lloyd, M. Maloney and K. Schwarzhof. Schema for object-oriented XML. Technical report, World Wide Web Consortium, July 1999. Version 2.0.

[6] Deach, S. Extensible Stylesheet Language XSL specification. Technical report, World Wide Web Consortium, April 1999.

[7] Dybvig, R. K., R. Hieb and C. Bruggeman. Syntactic abstraction in Scheme. *Lisp and Symbolic Computation*, 5(4):295–326, December 1993.

[8] Flatt, M. PLT MzScheme: Language manual. Technical Report TR97-280, Rice University, 1997.

[9] International Business Machines. PatML. Web document: http://www.alphaWorks.ibm.com/formula/patml/.

[10] Jansson, P. and J. Jeuring. PolyP — a polytypic programming language extension. In *Symposium on Principles of Programming Languages*, pages 470–482, 1997.

[11] Kelsey, R., W. Clinger and J. Rees. Revised[5] report on the algorithmic language Scheme. *ACM SIGPLAN Notices*, 33(9), October 1998.

[12] Kohlbecker, E. E., D. P. Friedman, M. Felleisen and B. F. Duba. Hygienic macro expansion. In *ACM Symposium on Lisp and Functional Programming*, pages 151–161, 1986.

[13] Kohlbecker, E. E. and M. Wand. Macros-by-example: Deriving syntactic transformations from their specifications. In *Symposium on Principles of Programming Languages*, pages 77–84, 1987.

[14] Krishnamurthi, S., Y.-D. Erlich and M. Felleisen. Expressing structural properties as language constructs. In *European Symposium on Programming*, March 1999.

[15] Krishnamurthi, S., M. Felleisen and B. F. Duba. From macros to reusable generative programming. In *Generative and Component-Based Software Engineering*, September 1999.

[16] Meertens, L. Calculate polytypically! In *International Symposium on Programming Languages: Implementations, Logics, and Programs*, 1996.

[17] Wadler, P. A formal semantics of patterns in XSLT. In *Markup Technologies*, December 1999.

[18] Wallace, M. and C. Runciman. Haskell and XML: Generic document processing combinators vs. type-based translation. In *International Conference on Functional Programming*, September 1999.

Modeling HTML in Haskell

Peter Thiemann

Universität Freiburg, Germany
`thiemann@informatik.uni-freiburg.de`

Abstract. We define HTML as an embedded domain specific language in Haskell. To this end, we have designed and implemented a combinator library which provides the means to create and modify HTML elements. Haskell's type classes are employed to enforce well-formed HTML to a large degree. Haskell can then be used as a meta language to map structured documents to HTML, to define conditional content, to extract information from the documents, or to define entire web sites. We introduce container-passing style as a programming convention for the library. We also pinpoint some shortcomings of Haskell's type system that make the task of this library's implementor tedious.

Key words: embedded domain specific language, HTML, functional programming, type classes

1 Introduction

Programming one web page in isolation is not hard. Programming an entire web site can be a nightmare. While simple HTML editors help with the first task [23,9], full blown web authoring systems are required for the other task. Meanwhile there is a plethora of systems available for this task [22]. These systems come in two basic flavors. Either they have a WYSIWYG front end [20], or they are purely textual [25,4,5]. The pure WYSIWYG tools never let you program a single line in HTML, you don't even have to know it. A disadvantage is that the HTML code produced by these tools is usually inscrutable and cannot easily be modified without the tool. The textual tools require some knowledge of HTML and add concepts on top of that. Usually, they come with some sort of previewing feature in a separate window. Of course, there are also tools which live in the middle ground between the extremes [19].

But you are always limited in the means to structure documents and to build your own abstractions by the tool at hand. However, programming languages are very good at structuring problems and at building abstractions. This is especially true for a functional programming language with an expressive type system like Haskell [6]. In such a language not only can you structure your problem and build your own abstractions, but on top of that the type system can provide additional structure and guarantees.

We have used Haskell to model a recent version of HTML and we are able to reap all the benefits alluded to above. Our domain specific HTML modeling

E. Pontelli, V. Santos Costa (Eds.): PADL 2000, LNCS 1753, pp. 263–277, 2000.

language is based on a combinator library in Haskell. The basic idea is to build a data structure that can be rendered to HTML text. Due to our use of type classes, the Haskell type checker guarantees the well-formedness of the generated HTML to a large degree. This exploitation of the type system is in our view the main contribution of the paper. Using a Haskell interpreter [12] it is possible to interactively create and manipulate web pages as well as entire web sites. Since we can use Haskell in all stages the creation of customized styles, site maps, or multi-language pages is just a matter of writing some Haskell code.

Overview In Section 2, we work through three simple examples to get a glimpse of the programmer's view of the library. Section 3 explains how Haskell can represent HTML elements, how they are filled with contents, and how they are supplied with attributes. Section 4 shows how type classes are used to enforce HTML's restrictions on how elements can be assembled. Next, in Section 5, we discuss some problems and features of the library, some of them originating from limitations in the Haskell type system. The section concludes with a brief assessment. Finally, we discuss related work in Section 6 and conclude.

In the paper, we assume some familiarity with Haskell and HTML.

2   Examples

To illustrate the working of the library, we work through some simple examples. The first example is a simple Hello World document. The second example shows a simple parameterized document. The last example reports a prototype implementation of a simplified version of Texinfo.

Although we are giving type signatures for clarity and documentation below, we should emphasize that no type signature is actually required. The Haskell interpreter, Hugs98, is able to infer all of them.

2.1   Hello World

The HTML definition demands that every document consists of a head and a body. Therefore, to start a new document, we must provide a head and a body.

```
doc :: HTML
doc = make_html 'add' doc_head 'add' doc_body
```

Here, `make_html` creates a new HTML element and the function `add` adds contents to this element. Each content item is itself a HTML element. In the head of the document, we provide the title of the document.

```
doc_head :: HEAD
doc_head =
  make_head
  'add' (make_title 'add' "Hello World")
```

Again, `make_head` creates a `<head>` element which contains a single `<title>` element, which in turn contains the string `Hello World`.

Not every combination of tag and contents is legal HTML. For example, putting some text into a document head is illegal. If we try this with our library, we get a type error.

```
Example> make_head 'add' "some string"
ERROR: Unresolved overloading
*** Type       : AddTo HEAD [Char] => HEAD
*** Expression : add make_head "some string"
```

The type class `AddTo` governs which element can contain which other element. Whenever there is an instance `AddTo s t` then elements of type `t` can be put into an element of type `s`. The type error tells us that there is no instance `AddTo HEAD [Char]`, so strings cannot be put into a `<head>` in HTML.

For the body, we supply a minimal content.

```
doc_body :: BODY
doc_body =
  make_body
  'add' (make_heading 1 'add' title)
  'add' ("This is the traditional \"" ++ title ++ "\" page.")
  'add' make_hr
  'add' (make_address
          'add' (make_a
                  'add' "Peter Thiemann"
                  'attr' A_HREF "mailto:thiemann@acm.org"))
  where title = "Hello World!"
```

Here, `make_body` creates a `<body>` element which contains a heading, some text, a horizontal rule, and an address. The address element contains a hyperlink, where the URL of the link is supplied as an attribute of the `<A>` (anchor) tag. Just like `add` adds content items to an element, `attr` adds attributes to it. Also, just like before, not every combination of tag and attribute is legal HTML. This is governed by the class `AddAttr` with the single method `attr`.

For example, trying to add a `src` attribute to an `<a>` tag yields a type error:

```
Example> make_a 'attr' A_SRC "xxx"
ERROR: Unresolved overloading
*** Type       : AddAttr A A_SRC => A
*** Expression : attr make_a (A_SRC "xxx")
```

Finally, the `show_html` function yields a rendition of the document in HTML.

```
Example> putStr (show_html doc)
<html><head><title>Hello World</title>
</head>
<body><h1>Hello World!</h1>
This is the traditional &#34;Hello World!&#34; page.<hr>
<address><a HREF="mailto:thiemann@acm.org">Peter Thiemann</a>
</address>
</body>
</html>
```

2.2   Parameterized Documents

So far, we have shown plain HTML programming with some legality checking. But it is just as simple to program parameterized documents. Suppose, you want all your documents to look similar in structure to the Hello World document of the preceding section. Abstracting the title and the contents yields

```
html_doc :: (AddTo HTML a, AddTo HEADING b, AddTo TITLE b) =>
              Int -> b -> (BODY -> a) -> HTML
html_doc level title add_contents =
  make_html
  'add' (make_head
          'add' (make_title 'add' title))
  'add' (make_body
          'add' (make_heading level 'add' title)
          $$ add_contents)
```

where $$ is reverse function application defined by

```
x $$ f = f x
```

The parameter `add_contents` is a "BODY transformer" that maps a `<BODY>` to some element of type `a` that can be added to an `<HTML>` element. Only BODY makes sense for `a`, so we could restrict the type somewhat further.

We call this functional style of parameterization *container-passing style*. It makes it possible to add multiple elements into a single element and it simplifies dealing with conditionals. Had we just said

```
html_body :: AddTo BODY a => a -> BODY
html_body contents =
  make_body 'add' contents
```

then we could only add one item to the `<BODY>`. This is because the library does not support grouping of elements. If it did we would lose static typechecking of HTML code, which relies on every element having a special type[1].

As an aside, there are alternative entry points for the library which provide all elements in container-passing style. For example, instead of `make_body` we would use `add_body` of type `AddTo a b => (BODY -> b) -> a -> a`. This function takes a BODY transformer, which is intended to add contents or attributes to the BODY, and inserts it in an element of type `a`. As an example of a BODY transformer and a use of the library in container-passing style, we write a function that adds a signature.

```
add_signature :: (AddTo a ADDRESS, AddTo A b, AddTo a HR) =>
                 b -> String -> a -> a
add_signature name url =
  add_hr
  # add_address (add_a (add' name # attr' (A_HREF url)))
```

---

[1] This problem could be addressed if the Haskell type system supported overlapping instances.

```
data Node =
  Node   String              -- name of node
         [Node_Content]       -- contents of the node
         [Node]               -- subnodes
  -- administrative fields:
         String Int           -- name stub & number of node
         [Int]                -- section counter

type Node_Content = String
```

Fig. 1. The type Node

Here add' = flip add, attr' = flip attr, and (f # g) x = g (f x) (re-versed function composition). The add_hr function does not have a transformer argument because this element has neither contents nor attributes. Although some definitions look more appealing in container-passing style, we stick to the "direct" style for the rest of this paper.

Finally, we can pick up these blocks and produce a template for the Hello World example considered above.

```
my_doc :: (AddTo HEADING a, AddTo BODY b, AddTo TITLE a) =>
          a -> b -> HTML
my_doc title contents =
  html_doc 1 title
    (add' contents
     # add_signature "Peter Thiemann" "mailto:thiemann@acm.org")
```

The type of my_doc specifies that the first argument must be suitable for adding it to a heading as well as to a title and the second argument is put into a body.

With this definition in place, the document from the first example is just

```
my_doc "Hello World" "This is the traditional \"Hello World!\" page."
```

2.3 Linked Nodes

The idea of Texinfo [26] is to structure a text as a set of nodes which are interconnected by hyperlinks. Each node has a unique name, by which it can be referred to, and three links. The links point to the next, previous, and up nodes, that is, the next or previous one on the same hierarchical level of nodes, whereas the up link points to a node higher up in the hierarchy. Each of these nodes is rendered to HTML in essentially the same way. This pattern is captured in a function node2html. But first, we need to discuss the basic datatype.

The datatype for a node has six fields (see Figure 1). It contains the name of the node, the contents of the node, the subnodes, and some administrative fields which are filled in automatically (name stub for the generated files, a unique number for the generated file, and a section counter).

```
node2html :: Node -> Maybe Node -> Maybe Node -> Maybe Node -> HTML
node2html (Node name contents subnodes _ _ sec_count)
          m_next m_previous m_up =
  html_doc level title
  ( makelink "Next" m_next
  # makelink "Previous" m_previous
  # makelink "Up" m_up
  # add_hr
  # makepars contents
  # makemenu node_ref subnodes)
  where
    title = show_sec_count sec_count ++ name
    level = length sec_count
```

Fig. 2. Translation of Node to HTML

```
makemenu make_ref [] =
  id
makemenu make_ref subnodes =
  add_list "menu" (foldr add_node id subnodes)
  where
    add_node node add_items = add_li (add' (make_ref node)) # add_items
```

Fig. 3. Creating the menu of subnodes

The author of such a structure only has to specify the contents of each node and to list the subnodes. The function node2html in Figure 2 translates one node into the corresponding HTML data structure. Following the standard title and heading defined above, there are three hyperlinks Next, Previous, and Up created by makelink. Then there is a horizontal rule, followed by the text structured in paragraphs (makepars) and finally a menu of the immediate subnodes (makemenu). Of these, makemenu (see Figure 3) is probably the most interesting. If the list of subnodes is non-empty, it creates a function that adds a <MENU> and then adds to it one list item for each subnode.

The complete implementation only requires some simple auxiliary functions and a main function tree2html :: Node -> Maybe Node -> String -> IO () which takes a Node data structure, possibly a reference to an enclosing document, and a filename stub. Executing this main function results in automatically assigning a filename to each node, translating every node to HTML, and writing the resulting text to the respective files.

3   Modeling HTML Elements

In this section, we explain the underlying data structures. The main tools are type classes and heterogeneous lists (lists with partially abstract elements).

```
class ELEMENT a where
  contents :: a -> ELEMENT_List
  set_contents :: a -> ELEMENT_List -> a
  attributes :: a -> ATTRIBUTE_List
  set_attributes :: a -> ATTRIBUTE_List -> a
  tag :: a -> String
  show_html :: a -> String
-- default implementations
  contents a = ELEMENT_Nil
  set_contents a x = a
  attributes a = ATTRIBUTE_Nil
  set_attributes a x = a
  tag a = ""
  show_html = show_element_standard
```

Fig. 4. Type class ELEMENT

Each basic HTML element (or tag) is modeled by its own datatype. For example, the datatype for the <hr> tag (*horizontal rule*) is

```
data HR = HR
```

In addition, every element type is a member of the type class ELEMENT defined in Figure 4. There are two methods to manipulate contents (if any) of the element. The method contents retrieves the contents and the method set_contents sets new contents. The set_contents method is purely functional, no destructive updating takes place.

Contents are values of type ELEMENT_List. This is a heterogeneous list of values of type class ELEMENT:

```
data ELEMENT_List =
  forall e . ELEMENT e => ELEMENT_Cons e ELEMENT_List | ELEMENT_Nil
```

The actual type of each element of the list is abstract, since the all-quantification of e in the type of the constructor amounts to the element having an existential type. It is only known that each element has a type belonging to ELEMENT, so the methods of this class are applicable [15,16]. This is an extension to Haskell, which is available in many implementations (e.g., Hugs98 [12]).

Attributes are dealt with in the same way as elements. Each attribute has its own datatype. Since HTML has different name spaces for tag names and attribute names whereas Haskell uses datatypes for both, the library renames all attributes consistently by prepending A_ to attribute types and constructors. For example, the type for the attribute HREF is

```
data A_HREF = A_HREF String
instance ATTRIBUTE A_HREF where
  attr_name (A_HREF url) = "HREF"
  attr_value (A_HREF url) = Just url
```

```
class ATTRIBUTE a where
  attr_name :: a -> String
  attr_value :: a -> Maybe String
  show_attr :: a -> String
-- default implementations
  attr_value a = Nothing
  show_attr = show_attr_standard
```

Fig. 5. A type class for attributes

Analogously to elements, each attribute is an instance of the type class ATTRIBUTE which is defined in Figure 5. Each attribute has a name (attr_name) and it can be converted to a string (show_attr). In addition, some attributes carry a value (attr_value).

Returning to elements, there are two methods to access (attributes) and to set attributes (set_attributes) of an element. They deal with a type ATTRIB-UTE_List, which is a heterogeneous list of instances of ATTRIBUTE in analogy to ELEMENT_List.

```
data ATTRIBUTE_List =
forall a . ATTRIBUTE a => ATTRIBUTE_Cons a ATTRIBUTE_List | ATTRIBUTE_Nil
```

The remaining two methods deal with the identification of the element (tag) and with creating a string representation (show_element).

As an example, we show the full datatype definition for the <A> element (HTML *anchors*).

```
data A = A ATTRIBUTE_List ELEMENT_List
instance ELEMENT A where
  contents (A aaa ccc) = ccc
  set_contents (A aaa _) ccc = A aaa ccc
  attributes (A aaa ccc) = aaa
  set_attributes (A _ ccc) aaa = A aaa ccc
  tag (A aaa ccc) = "a"
```

Anchors have attributes and also contents, so the data constructor takes two parameters. The get and set methods are obvious and the tag method returns the string "a". The library provides a shortcut make_a for constructing an anchor and an anchor-adding function in container-passing style:

```
make_a = A ATTRIBUTE_Nil ELEMENT_Nil
add_a f el = el 'add' f make_a
```

There are shortcuts defined for each element. The idea is now to use the add and attr methods to add contents and attributes to this empty anchor.

4   Assembling HTML

The datatypes from the previous section just provide a uniform means of accessing, modifying, and printing instances of ELEMENT and ATTRIBUTE. But they

```
class (ELEMENT s, ELEMENT t) => AddTo s t where
  add :: s -> t -> s
  add element subelement =
    set_contents element (ELEMENT_Cons subelement (contents element))

class (ELEMENT e, ATTRIBUTE a) => AddAttr e a where
  attr :: e -> a -> e
  attr e a =
    set_attributes e (ATTRIBUTE_Cons a (attributes e))
```

Fig. 6. Type classes for adding elements and attributes

do not provide any checks that the constructed data represents valid HTML. To implement the validity checks, the library provides two additional type classes AddTo and AddAttr shown in Figure 6. Both type classes have two parameters. In AddTo s t the s is the type of the container and t is the type of the content. In AddAttr e a, e is the type of the element and a is the type of the attribute. Both have default methods which rely on the provided methods for accessing and modifying contents and attributes. They are never overridden in the current version of the library.

To specify that an element is a legal content of another element, all we need to do is declare an instance of AddTo. For example,

```
instance AddTo DL DT
instance AddTo DL DD
```

states that the only allowed contents of a definition list (<DL>) are <DT> (term in definition list) and <DD> (definition of a term). It corresponds directly to the HTML DTD (document type definition) which defines the <DL> tag like this:

```
<!ELEMENT DL    - -  (DT | DD)+>
```

Actually, this phrase says a little more than our instance declarations because it insists that each <DL> contains *at least one* <DT> or <DD>. We'll return to that point later in Section 5.

Similarly, to specify that an attribute is legal for some element, we need to provide an instance of AddAttr. For example, the only possible attribute for a definition list is COMPACT, indicating that the list is to be rendered in a compact style. The declaration

```
instance AddAttr DL A_COMPACT
```

states this exactly.

5   Discussion

In this section, we consider some of the unpleasant facts of life pertaining to the library that we constructed. Some are just inconveniences for the implementor of the library, some can be fixed using a more elaborate type structure, and some may only be fixed using dynamic tests at run time.

5.1 HTML Entities

Besides the elements considered above, HTML defines *parameter entities* which can be used to name groups of elements. For example,

```
<!ENTITY % font " TT | B | I ">
<!ENTITY % phrase "EM | STRONG | CODE | SAMP | KBD | VAR | CITE ">
```

defines that %font stands for one of the elements <TT>, <B>, or <I>, and similarly for %phrase. It would be nice to model this relation directly using subclasses FONT and PHRASE of ELEMENT, but unfortunately we cannot.

To see why, consider the definition of another entity %text which relies on %font and %phrase:

```
<!ENTITY % text "#PCDATA | A | IMG | BR | %phrase | %font">
```

Hence, %text can be a character string, one of the <A>, <IMG>, or <BR> tags, or it can be a %phrase or a %font. However, the corresponding definitions

```
class ELEMENT a => FONT a
instance FONT TT
instance FONT B
instance FONT I

class ELEMENT a => PHRASE a
instance PHRASE EM
...

class ELEMENT a => TEXT a
instance TEXT A
instance TEXT IMG
instance TEXT BR
instance PHRASE a => TEXT a
instance FONT a => TEXT a
```

are rejected due to overlapping instances in the last two lines (by Hugs98). This declaration is already syntactically illegal in Haskell98 which restricts instance declarations to C (T u1 ... uk) where C is the type class and T is a type constructor.

In the present case, this is overly restrictive because the elements of PHRASE and FONT are disjoint. And even if they were not, since the instance declaration does not provide any definition, there can be no semantic ambiguities regardless of which instance path is used.

Another viable approach would be to define not type classes, but datatypes for FONT, PHRASE, TEXT, and so on. Here is an example definition.

```
data FONT = forall a . ELEMENT a => FONT a
instance ELEMENT FONT where
  contents (FONT a) = contents a
  set_contents (FONT a) x = FONT (set_contents a x)
  attributes (FONT a) = attributes a
```

```
set_attributes (FONT a) x = FONT (set_attributes a x)
tag (FONT a) = tag a
show_element (FONT a) = show_element a
```

This approach can be made to work, but it places a heavy burden on the user of the library. The user should not be concerned whether some use of `make_tt args` should really be `TEXT (FONT (make_tt args))`. So we would like to have the type checker insert these type coercions for us. (A related technique has been employed to locate a type in an extensible union type [13].) The declarations

```
class (ELEMENT source, ELEMENT target) => COERCE source target where
  coerce :: source -> target

class (ELEMENT source, ELEMENT target) => COERCE1 source target where
  coerce1 :: source -> target

instance ELEMENT x => COERCE x x where coerce x = x

instance (COERCE1 a b, COERCE b c) => COERCE a c where
  coerce a = coerce (coerce1 a)
instance COERCE1 TT   FONT where coerce1 = FONT
instance COERCE1 FONT TEXT where coerce1 = TEXT
-- and so on
```

specify the required relation `COERCE` between element types. Unfortunately, the declaration

```
instance (COERCE1 a b, COERCE b c) => COERCE a c where
  coerce a = coerce (coerce1 a)
```

is rejected because `b` does not occur in the type of `coerce :: a -> c` (this could cause a semantics ambiguity, in general). In the present case, the relation `COERCE1` is a partial function, hence it cannot give rise to semantic problems. (This kind of declaration was possible in Gofer [11], which was used to program the extensible type mentioned above [13].)

The current implementation of the library is flat. All uses of `%text`, `%font`, and so on in the DTD are tediously expanded by hand. A tool to perform this task automatically is currently in the works. Besides, the use of parameter entities is not restricted to grouping element names, but rather it is a general macro mechanism, which is best supported by such a tool.

5.2   Regular Expressions

Another feature of HTML that the library does not model is the use of regular expressions to specify the contents of an element. For example,

```
<!ELEMENT HTML O O  "HEAD, BODY">
```

specifies that the contents of `<HTML>` should be exactly one `<HEAD>` followed by exactly one `<BODY>`. The present library only approximates this by allowing an arbitrary number of heads and bodies in arbitrary sequence.

Likewise, other regular operators are only approximated. For example, the contents of <DL> should be (DT | DD)+ (see above), but this is not checked either.

This problem could be addressed in two ways, one static and one dynamic. In the dynamic approach, the ELEMENT class would have additional methods to model a deterministic finite automaton [7] and each addition of a content element would step the automaton. The add method of the AddTo class would have to check dynamically that the automaton of the added element is in a final state, otherwise it would raise an exception.

The static approach would encode the states of this finite automaton into the datatypes. In the case of the HTML element, this would mean

```
data HTML_0 = HTML_0
data HTML_1 = HTML_1 HEAD
data HTML_2 = HTML_2 HEAD BODY
instance HTML HTML_2              -- final state
instance HEAD h => AddTo' HTML_0 h HTML_1 where
  add HTML_0 h = HTML_1 h
instance BODY b => AddTo' HTML_1 b HTML_2 where
  add (HTML_1 h) b = HTML_2 h b
```

and there would be a type class for each element capturing the types corresponding to final states of the automaton (cf. HTML_2). Despite the imminent flood of types and classes, we expect that the usability of the library is not affected by this gain of precision. Hence, we are currently pursuing this approach by automatically generating all type and class definitions using a parser for DTDs.

Using the same approach, multiple occurrences of attributes could be rejected and the presence of required attributes could be guaranteed.

5.3   Exceptions

An exception declaration in an element declaration of a DTD indicates that, within the scope of the declared element, certain elements are admissible regardless of the content indicator of the nested elements. Dually, there are negative exceptions, which abolish the use of some elements, regardless of the content indicator of the nested elements. For example,

```
<!ELEMENT SELECT - - (OPTION+) -(INPUT|SELECT|TEXTAREA)>
```

indicates that a <SELECT> element is composed of a non-empty sequence of <OPTION> elements *and these elements must not contain the elements <INPUT>, <SELECT>, or <TEXTAREA>*.

While type classes can encode "permissions" which allow values to be used in certain ways, they cannot encode "denials", which would be required in the present case. However, this kind of negative information is required in type systems for records, which need to express the absence of a particular label [24,30]. Similar information can also be expressed using qualified types [10].

Progressing from HTML to XML [2] would also solve the problem because XML does not support exceptions, anymore.

5.4 Assessment

We found the library surprisingly easy and intuitive to use. Especially, programming HTML in container-passing style results in a fairly natural syntax. The possibility to abstract commonly used patterns pays off enormously, its benefits are already visible in the examples shown in Section 2. We also found the type checking capabilities of the current version sufficient because it captures common errors (using an element in the wrong place). We need some more experience to see if the more elaborate scheme outlined in Section 5.2 is worth the effort.

On the negative side, type errors are a bit hard on users who are not deeply into Haskell. It would be nice if type errors could be filtered and translated so that they are more informative to casual users of the library. These users would also appreciate a syntax which is closer to HTML.

Another idea that would widen the scope of the library is to put the show_element method into a monad, i.e., give it the type Monad m => a -> m String. In this way, the show methods could print directly to a file and we would gain some more flexibility in modeling configurable web sites (e.g., parameterized over a language).

6 Related Work

TkGofer [28,27] is a toolkit for building graphical user interfaces using Gofer [11] and Tcl/Tk [21]. It employs multi-parameter constructor classes to govern parameters passed to instances of widgets. This use of type classes statically avoids errors that would otherwise only be detected dynamically at execution time. Our approach is simpler because there are fewer type classes to learn and there is no parameterization over constructors. In addition, we can type check the way in which HTML elements (widgets) are put together.

There are libraries for CGI (a standard for generating dynamic documents) programming by Hughes [8] and Meijer [18], both are monad-based (or a generalization thereof) and concentrate on modeling the interaction between client and server and on encoding issues. They provide only little support for checking the validity of generated HTML. We believe that the present work is complementary to these works.

Type classes are also used as a structuring tool in the various functional hardware modeling frameworks [17,1]. However, they employ type classes in a more conventional way, namely to structure the operations that may be applied to certain values. In contrast, we use the class and instance declarations as a logic program (just a finite automaton) to rule out invalid programs (see our complaints in Section 5.1).

Wallace and Runciman [29] propose two alternative ways of using Haskell represent XML documents. They have one generic encoding, which represents documents in a similar way than we propose. But their generic encoding is a general tree structure which does not impose any validity constraints on generated or processed documents. In particular, the use of the type system for guaranteeing validity to a large degree is novel to our work. In addition, Wallace and

Runciman do have a type-based encoding, which guarantees valid documents by modeling them directly with Haskell datatypes. However, this approach is less flexible when it comes to parameterized documents. Finally, they have developed a combinator library for processing the generic XML representation. This library could be ported to our representation, thus reaping the benefits of their combinators while enjoying strongly typed XML at the same time.

In the logic programming world, there are several toolkits for generating HTML pages. The PiLLoW toolkit [3] allows for easy creation of documents including CGI functionality. It is widely used to connect logic programs to the WWW. LogicWeb [14] offers an even tighter integration which includes client-side scripting.

7 Conclusion

We have designed and implemented a convenient embedded domain specific language for meta programming of web pages and web sites in Haskell. Haskell's type classes and facilities to program with partially abstract types were instrumental in the construction. We have introduced container-passing style as a means to concisely construct abstractions and fragments of web pages.

References

1. Per Bjesse, Koen Claessen, Mary Sheeran, and Satnam Singh. Lava: Hardware design in Haskell. In Paul Hudak, editor, *Proc. International Conference on Functional Programming 1998*, pages 174–184, Baltimore, USA, September 1998. ACM Press, New York.
2. Tim Bray, Jean Paoli, and C.M. Sperberg-MacQueen. Extensible markup language (xml) 1.0 (w3c recommendation). http://www.w3.org/TR/REC-xml, feb 1998.
3. Daniel Cabeza and Manuel Hermenegildo. Www programming using computational logic systems (and the PiLLoW/CIAO library). http://www.clip.dia.fi.upm.es/Software/pillow/pillow_www6/pillow_www6.h%tml, March 1997.
4. Allaire Corp. HomeSite. http://www.allaire.com/.
5. Ralf S. Engelschall. Website meta language (wml). http://www.engelschall.com/sw/wml/.
6. Haskell98, a non-strict, purely functional language. http://www.haskell.org, December 1998.
7. John E. Hopcroft and Jeffrey D. Ullman. *Introduction to automata theory, languages and computation*. Addison-Wesley, 1979.
8. John Hughes. Generalising monads to arrows. *Science of Computer Programming*, 1999. To appear.
9. SoftQuad Software Inc. HoTMetaL. http://www.softquad.com/.
10. Mark P. Jones. A theory of qualified types. In Bernd Krieg-Brückner, editor, *Proc. 4th European Symposium on Programming '92*, volume 582 of *Lecture Notes in Computer Science*, pages 287–306, Rennes, France, February 1992. Springer-Verlag.
11. Mark P. Jones. *Gofer, Functional Programming Environment*, June 1994. Version 2.30.

12. Mark P. Jones. Hugs Online — embracing functional programming. http://www.haskell.org/hugs/, June 1999.
13. Sheng Liang, Paul Hudak, and Mark Jones. Monad transformers and modular interpreters. In *Proc. 22nd Annual ACM Symposium on Principles of Programming Languages*, pages 333–343, San Francisco, CA, January 1995. ACM Press.
14. Seng Wai Loke and Andrew Davison. Logic programming with the World-Wide Web. pages 235–245, Washington DC, USA, mar 1996.
15. Konstantin Läufer. Type classes with existential types. *Journal of Functional Programming*, 6(3):485–517, May 1996.
16. Konstantin Läufer and Martin Odersky. An extension of ML with first-class abstract types. In *Proc. ACM SIGPLAN Workshop on ML and its Applications*, pages 78–91, San Francisco, CA, June 1992.
17. John Matthews, John Launchbury, and Byron Cook. Microprocessor specification in Hawk. In *IEEE International Conference on Computer Languages, ICCL 1998*, Chicago, USA, May 1998. IEEE Computer Society Press.
18. Erik Meijer. Server-side web scripting with Haskell. *Journal of Functional Programming*, 1999. To appear.
19. Microsoft. Microsoft Frontpage98. http://www.microsoft.com/frontpage.
20. NetObjects Fusion. http://www.netobjects.com.
21. J. K. OusterHout. *Tcl and the Tk Toolkit*. Addison-Wesley, 1994.
22. PC Magazine. Web authoring tools. http://www.zdnet.com/pcmag/features/htmlauthor/_open.htm, January 20 1998.
23. John Punin and Mukkai Krishnamoorthy. ASHE (a simple HTML editor) - xhtml. http://www.cs.rpi.edu/~puninj/ASHE/, November 1996.
24. Didier Rémy. Typing record concatenation for free. In *Proc. 19th Annual ACM Symposium on Principles of Programming Languages*, pages 166–176, Albuquerque, New Mexico, January 1992. ACM Press.
25. Internet Software Technologies. HTMLed Pro32. http://www.ist.ca.
26. Texinfo. http://texinfo.org.
27. Ton Vullinghs, Wolfram Schulte, and Thilo Schwinn. The design of a functional GUI library using constructor classes. In *PSI-96: Andrei Ershov Second International Memorial Conference, Perspectives of System Informatics*, volume 1181 of *Lecture Notes in Computer Science*, pages 398–408, Novosibirsk, Russia, June 1996. Springer-Verlag.
28. Ton Vullinghs, Daniel Tuijnman, and Wolfram Schulte. Lightweight GUIs for functional programming. In Doaitse Swierstra and Manuel Hermenegildo, editors, *International Symposium on Programming Languages, Implementations, Logics and Programs (PLILP '95)*, volume 982 of *Lecture Notes in Computer Science*, pages 341–356, Utrecht, The Netherlands, September 1995. Springer-Verlag.
29. Malcolm Wallace and Colin Runciman. Haskell and XML: Generic combinators or type-based translation? pages 148–259.
30. Mitchell Wand. Type inference for record concatenation and multiple inheritance. In *Proc. of the 4th Annual Symposium on Logic in Computer Science*, pages 92–97, Pacific Grove, CA, June 1989. IEEE Computer Society Press. To appear in *Information and Computation*.

A Logic Programming Approach to Supporting the Entries of XML Documents in an Object Database*

Ching-Long Yeh

Department of Computer Science and Engineering
Tatung University
40 Chungshan North Road, Section 3
Taipei, 104, Taiwan
chingyeh@cse.ttu.edu.tw

Abstract. In this paper we employ the parsing and generation capabilities of DCG in Prolog to convert XML documents into object definitions to be stored in an object database. The system mainly consists of a DTD parser, a schema generator and a DI parser generator. The DTD parser is used to analyze the structure of DTD. The two generators take the parsing results of the DTD parser, and then produce database schema definitions and the DI parser. The database schema for a DTD is built by executing the generated schema definitions. The DI parser analyzes the document instance and produces the corresponding object definitions. The elements in the document are then stored in the object database by executing the object definition.

1 Introduction

XML [15, 9] improves upon HTML in capturing the meaning of a document and extending the tag set. At the same time, it also reduces the complexity of SGML [8]. It is believed that XML will soon be the standard of data exchanges on the Web. XML documents can be stored in file systems. However, due to lack of indices in files, we are not able to make full use of the meaning (or metadata) in XML documents. Since an XML document can be easily viewed according to the object-oriented model [16], a promising solution is to employ object database technology to manage the access of XML documents [3, 12, 1].

The arrangement of elements in an XML document is governed by the element and attribute list declarations in document type definition (DTD) [15]. The creation of DTD in a sense is closely related to defining new data types and hierarchical relationship in an object database. Thus, to enter an XML document into an object database, at first a new schema corresponding to a DTD is generated in the object database, and then the document conforming to that

---

* This research was partially supported by the Taiwan National Science Council under Contract No. 88-2213-E-036-004.

E. Pontelli, V. Santos Costa (Eds.): PADL 2000, LNCS 1753, pp. 278–292, 2000.

DTD is fragmented into objects and entered into the database. The XML documents can then be queried and managed by using the facilities provided by the object database.

Both the tasks of creating a schema in object database for a DTD and fragmenting XML documents into objects can be divided into two parts: analysis and generation. For the former task, an input DTD is analyzed according to the formation rules specified in the XML recommendation[15], and the schema definitions are produced for the structures found in the analysis of DTD. The other task is to analyze XML document instances and produce object definitions for the elements found in them.

In this paper, we employ the definite clause grammar (DCG) in Prolog [4] as a tool to implement the analysis and generation tasks mentioned above. The basic idea is to encode the analysis task in the context-free rule part and the generation task in the action part of the DCG rules.

In Sec. 2, we give a brief description about the document type definition in XML. In Sec. 3, we describe the system architecture. In Sec. 4, we describe the DTD parser. In Secs. 5 and 6, we describe the database schema generator and the DI parser generator. In Sec. 7, we show the implementation result. Finally some conclusions are drawn.

2 DTD in XML

The composition of an XML document is governed by the rules specified in the Document Type Definition (DTD) of XML [15]. A DTD in XML consists of a sequence of element type declarations as follow:

```
<!ELEMENT list    (item+)>
<!ELEMENT item    #PCDATA>
```

An element type declaration has a name, such as list and item above, which identifies the element in the structure of a document instance. Following the name of an element type declaration is the content model, such as (item+) and #PCDATA, which specifies what contents can appear within the element in a document instance. For example, the content model of the first declaration specifies that one or more items can appear as the children of a list element, and the second specifies that nothing but character data can appear in an item element. Note that an occurrence indicator following a name or list indicates that the element or content particle can occur one or more (+), zero or more (*), or zero or one times (?). Using the above element declarations, we may create an XML document as follows:

```
<list><item>apple</item>
      <item>banana</item>
      <item>cherry</item>
      <item>water melon</item>
</list>
```

A further example that a section contains a title, followed by an optional abstract, followed by one or more paragraphs can be declared shown in the following element.

```
<!ELEMENT section (title, abstract, paragraph+)>
```

The commas in the content model specify that the sub-elements must appear in that order. In addition to the sequential list, a choice list can appear in the content model. For example, the following element declaration specifies that a list of zero or more elements, which may be p or list or notes, can be inserted between the head and div2 list within a div1 element.

```
<!ELEMENT div1 (head,(p|list|notes)*,div2*)>
```

An element declaration can have an attribute list declaration to give the attributes, or metadata, of the element. For example, the following attribute list declaration specifies that a section has two attributes, id and status, whose values are given as of ID type, and the default value, final.

```
<!ATTLIST section
          id ID #IMPLIED
          status (draft|final) "final">
```

The above introduction about XML is sufficient for the purpose of this paper. More detailed descriptions about XML can be found in [15, 9].

3   System Architecture

The system architecture is shown in Fig. 1. In the system, the DTD parser takes a DTD as the input and produces the parse tree of the DTD. The knowledge source of the DTD parser comes from the rules of document type declaration defined in the XML specification [15]. Following the DTD parser are two sets of generation rules: the schema generation rules and the DI parser generation rules, which are consulted by the generators to produce the schema definitions of a DTD in the object database and the parser for parsing document instances, respectively. After executing the schema definitions represented in the object definition language of the object database, the schema corresponding to the DTD is then built in the object database.

The generated DI parser is used to analyze the structure of the document instance conforming to the DTD. It works along with the object generation rules to produce the object definitions program of the input document instance. Similarly, after executing the object definitions program, the input document instance (DI) is then entered into the object database. The user can then access the XML documents by using the query facilities provided by the object database. We will not investigate the development of the user interface because it falls outside the scope of this paper.

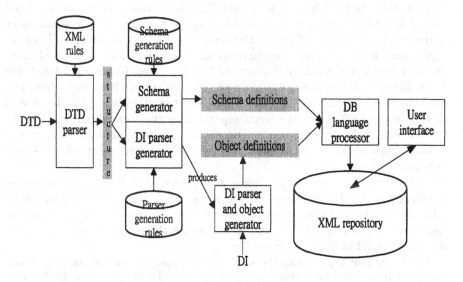

Fig. 1. System architecture

4   DTD Parser

The rules of document type declaration defined in the XML specification are represented in the Extended BNF (EBNF) [15]. The definite clause grammar (DCG) aims at implementing context-free grammars such as the EBNF. A grammar stated in DCG is executed directly by the Prolog inference engine as a syntax analyzer. Semantic interpretation routines can be interleaved within the DCG rules. Thus it is straightforward to build the parser for a DTD by taking advantage of the parsing and generation capabilities of the DCG in Prolog.

Due to the declarative feature of the DCG syntax parser, the essential step towards building a DTD parser based on the DCG is to convert the document type declaration rules in EBNF into the DCG rules. The first two EBNF rules of the element type declaration in the XML specification can be converted into DCG rules as follows.

```
elementdecl::=                 elementdecl(contentModel(N,C))-->
    '<!ELEMENT' S Name S           elementPrefix,
    contentspec S? '>'             name(N),
                                   contentSpec(C),
                                   rightAngle.


contentspec::=                 contentSpec(C)-->
    'EMPTY' | 'ANY' |              empty,{C='EMPTY'};
    Mixed | children              any,{C='ANY'};
                                   mixed(C);
                                   children(C).
```

The terms in the right-hand side of the DCG rules correspond to the right-hand side of the EBNF rules, except the white space markers, S. The white space characters in the input DTDs are filtered out by the lexical analyzer. Thus the white space marker will not be placed in the right-hand side of the DCG rules. Without being separated by the vertical bar, the terms in the right-hand side of an EBNF rule are a sequential order. We use conjunctive connectors, i.e., commas, to represent the sequential order. On the other hand, for the case of choices in the EBNF, i.e., the terms separated by the vertical bar, such as the contentspec rule shown above, we use disjunctive connectors, i.e., semicolons, as the separators in the DCG rules. Enclosed in the brackets are the semantic interpretation routines.

In the first DCG rule, the parameter contentModel(N,C) is used to represent the structure, C, of the element, N. The structure C itself can be a terminal or a list of sequence or choice terms, depending upon the content model of the element. The parse tree of the input DTD can be obtained by starting from the tt contentModel of the root element in the DTD.

In the contentspec rule, the nonterminal types of content models, Mixed and children, need be further specified by other DCG rules. The EBNF rule for the Mixed type, as shown below, indicates that a content model of type Mixed contains a character string #PCDATA optionally interspersed with child elements. The DCG rules for the Mixed type element are shown as below.

```
Mixed ::=                           mixed(mixed([pcdata|Ns]))-->
    '(' S? '#PCDATA' (S? '|'            leftParen,
    S? Name)* S? ')*'                   pcdata,
    |'(' S? '#PCDATA' S? ')'            altNames(Ns),
                                        rightParen,star.
                                    mixed(mixed([pcdata])) -->
                                        leftParen, pcdata,rightParen.
                                    altNames([N|Ns]) -->
                                        verticalBar,name(N),altNames(Ns).
                                    altNames([]) --> [].
```

We use a new rule, altNames, to account for the optional part of the Mixed rule. The resulting structure of the Mixed type element is represented by the structured term, mixed, with a list of child elements in it.

The other nonterminal type of the contentspec rule, children, specifies the sequence and choice structures as shown below.

```
children ::= (choice|seq)('?'|'*'|'+')?
   choice ::= '(' S? cp ( S? '|' S? cp )* S? ')'
      seq ::= '(' S? cp ( S? ',' S? cp )* S? ')'
       cp ::= (Name|choice|seq)('?'|'*'|'+')?
```

The children rule consists of either a choice or a seq followed by one of the repetition indicator. Both the choice and seq rules contain repetitive patterns, as shown in the underlined parts. Similarly we create the following DCG rules to deal with them.

```
children(R/X) -->                      altCp([Cp|Cps]) -->
   (seq(SeqList),{R=SeqList}             verticalBar,
   ;                                     cp(Cp),
    choice(CpList),{R=CpList}),          altCp(Cps).
   (question, {X=question};            altCp([]) -->[].
    star,{X=star};                     seqCp([Cp|Cps]) -->
    plus,{X=plus};                       comma,
    [],{X=null}).                        cp(Cp),
choice(Output) -->                       seqCp(Cps).
   leftParen,                          seqCp([]) -->[].
   cp(Cp),                             cp(R/X) -->
   altCp(Cps),                           (name(N),{R=N}
   rightParen,                           ;
      {Output=alt([Cp|Cps])}.             choice(CpList),{R=CpList}
seq(Output) -->                           ;
   leftParen,                             seq(SeqList),{R=SeqList}),
   cp(Cp),                              (question, {X=question};
   seqCp(Cps),                           star,{X=star};
   rightParen,                           plus,{X=plus};
      {Output=seq([Cp|Cps])}.            [], {X=null}).
```

In the above DCG rules, the sequence and choice structures are represented by the terms, seq and alt, respectively. The repetitive indicators are appended with the seq and alt terms. There are trivial DCG rules for terminals or tokens in the EBNF rules not shown in this paper. Their purposes are for recognizing separator markers, punctuation marks, repetitive markers, names and reserved words, and so on.

Before the input DTD can be analyzed by the DTD parser, it must be tokenized into a string of tokens. We have implemented a DTD tokenizer based on a finite state machine [2]. Fig. 2 shows a DTD and its parsing result represented in a Prolog list.

5   Database Schema Generation

Before an XML document can be entered into the object database, it is necessary to create the object database schema of the DTD that the XML document is conformed to. In this section, we describe the generation of database schema for a DTD.

The task described in this section corresponds to the schema generator module in Fig. 1. The input of the schema generator module is the structure of the DTD produced by the DTD parser and the output is the object database schema definitions of the DTD. The knowledge source of the schema generator is a set of generation rules that are consulted to produce the schema definitions of the elements in a DTD.

An element type declaration in a DTD defines the composition relationship with its subelement(s). Starting from the root element thus forms a composition hierarchy. A simple way is to define a class for each element type in the object

```
<!ELEMENT top (p,spec,div1)>
<!ELEMENT p (#PCDATA|a|ul|b|i|em)*>
<!ELEMENT spec (front,body, back?)*>
<!ELEMENT div1 (head,(p|list1|note)*, div2*)>
<!ELEMENT name (#PCDATA)>    <!ELEMENT a (#PCDATA)>
<!ELEMENT ul (#PCDATA)>      <!ELEMENT b (#PCDATA)>
<!ELEMENT i (#PCDATA)>       <!ELEMENT em (#PCDATA)>
<!ELEMENT front (#PCDATA)>   <!ELEMENT body (#PCDATA)>
<!ELEMENT back (#PCDATA)>    <!ELEMENT head (#PCDATA)>
<!ELEMENT list1 (#PCDATA)>   <!ELEMENT note (#PCDATA)>
<!ELEMENT div2 (#PCDATA)>
```

```
[contentModel(top,seq([p/null,spec /null,div1/null])/null),
 contentModel(p,mixed([pcdata,a,ul,b,i,em])),
 contentModel(spec,seq([front/null,body/null,back/question])/star),
 contentModel(div1,seq([head/null,alt([p/null,list1/null,note/null])
             /star,div2/star])/null),
 contentModel(name,pcdata), contentModel(a,pcdata),
 contentModel(ul,pcdata), contentModel(b,pcdata),
 contentModel(i,pcdata), contentModel(em,pcdata),
 contentModel(front,pcdata), contentModel(body,pcdata),
 contentModel(back,pcdata), contentModel(head,pcdata),
 contentModel(list1,pcdata), contentModel(note,pcdata),
 contentModel(div2,pcdata)]
```

Fig. 2. Example of a DTD parsing result

database schema, thus forming a flat list of element type classes. The flat list approach is easy to implement and maintain. However, it bears the disadvantage that it is unable to make use of inheritance to reduce code redundancy and express common behavior [7]. Another approach is to group element types having similar features into a class, which forms a hierarchical structure of element types. A problem of making a hierarchy of element types is that it is difficult to obtain a generic hierarchy that is able to classify the features of all types of elements [7].

The approach used in HyperStorM [3] is to divide the element types into two groups: flat and non-flat. The elements of non-flat type are represented by individual database objects, while the flat ones are not. Non-flat element types are in the higher level in the element type hierarchy; in other words, they are more informational. Flat element types are in the lower level or are leaves in the hierarchy. A group of flat elements is represented by a database object, with complete markup in the object. The decision of flatness of an element type is subject to the configuration of the particular document type.

The approach used in HyperStorM needs to consider the information units in the document types, which largely relies on the domain knowledge of the document type. In this paper, we divide the element types into two classes: structured and unstructured. The elements of the latter class are the ones containing only character data, i.e., PCDATA. The other class is further divided into mixed, single sequential, multiple sequential, single alternative, and multiple alternative, as shown in Fig. 3, among which the single and multiple classes are further generalized as the Single and Multiple classes, respectively. The sequence and alternative classes correspond to the content models containing sequence and choice subelements. An element of the Single class has its content model without repetition, while an element of the Multiple class has a repetitive content model. For illustration, we show in Fig. 4 the schema definition of the elements in the DTD of Fig. 2.

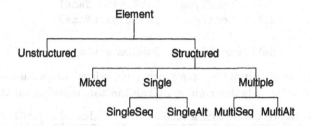

Fig. 3. The hierarchy of element types

```
defineClass Top super: SingleSeq{        defineClass P super: Mixed{
    instance:                                 instance:
        P   p;                                    List<Mixedp> mixedp;}};
        Spec  spec;                       defineClass Spec super: MultiSeq{
        Div1  div1;};                         instance:
defineClass Mixedp super: SingleAlt{              List<Seqspec>  seqspec;};
    instance:                             defineClass Seqspec super: SingleSeq{
        String pcdata;                        instance:
        A   a;                                    Front  front;
        Ul  ul;                                   Body   body;
        B   b;                                    Back   back;};
        I   i;                            defineClass Div1 super: SingleSeq{
        Em em;};                              instance:
defineClass Alt1 super: SingleAlt{                Head   head;
    instance:                                     List<Div2>  div2;};
        P   p;                            defineClass Name super: Unstructured{
        List1  list1;                         instance:
        Note   note;};                            String pcdata;};
```

Fig. 4. Schema definition of elements in Fig. 2

The schema definitions shown in Fig. 4 are written using the object definition language of the Jasmine object database, ODQL [6], which is close to the standard object database language defined by the ODMG [5]. The classes in Fig. 3 can be defined similarly as the ones in Fig. 4. The schema generator proceeds as follows, where the contentModel term is the output of the DTD parser as described in Sec. 4.

```
for each contentModel(ElementName,ContentStructure) do
    output the following definition
        defineClass ElementName super: SuperClass {
            class:
                String Repetition;
            instance:
                SubElementType1   SubElementName1;
                SubElementType2   SubElementName2;
                ...
                SubElementTypen   SubElementNamen;};
```

In the above definition, we omit other class-level properties and methods. The field SuperClass is determined by rules in the following table.

value of ContentStructure	value of SuperClass
pcdata	Structured
seq(...)/null or seq(...)/question	SingleSeq
alt(...)/null or alt(...)/question	SingleAlt
seq(...)/star or seq(...)/plus	MultiSeq
alt(...)/star or alt(...)/plus	MultiAlt

The instance-level properties in the above definition are filled in according to the subelements listed in ContentStructure. For a subelement of a single name without repetition, for example spec, the name of the subelement is taken as the type and the name of the property, for example, Spec spec. Note that a class name is capitalized in our naming convention. We use a list type to represent a subelement of single name with repetition. For example, for the subelement, div2*, the property definition is List<Div2> div2. For a nested subelement with repetition, we create a new class to deal with it. For example, for the nested choice subelement, (p|list1|note)*, the property definition is List<Alt1> alt1, where the name alt1 is created by the schema generator. We use seq$i$ for a sequential nested subelement. Alt1 as shown below is the auxiliary class for the nested element.

```
defineClass Alt1 super: SingleAlt{
    instance:
        P    p;
        List1  list1;
        Note   note;};
```

For an element of the Mixed type, we create an auxiliary class similar to the above to deal with the repetition occurring within the element. The class definitions of the p and spec elements in Fig. 2 are shown in Fig. 4 to illustrate the cases of nested and mixed elements.

6   DI Parser Generation

In this section, we describe the generation of the DI parser for a given DTD. First we describe the construction of the DI parser for a given DTD and the generation of object representation for elements in the input XML document. Then we describe the automatic generation of the DI parser given a new DTD.

6.1   Construction of a DI Parser

The structure of elements in an XML document is governed by the DTD of the document. An XML document can be segmented into a hierarchy of elements. To enter an XML document into the object database, it is necessary to convert each element in the hierarchy as an instance of the respective class in the database schema. A DI parser along with the object generator is used for this purpose.

Again, we use the parsing capability of DCG to develop a DI parser. The essential step is to convert the rules in the DTD into DCG rules. For example, for the DTD in Fig. 2, the DCG rules for the DI parser is shown in Fig. 5.

```
top(V) -->
   stg(top),p(P),spec(Spec),div1(Div1),etg(top).
p(V) -->
   stg(p),mixedp(Mixedp),etg(p).
mixedp(V) -->
   (pcdata(Pcdata);a(A);ul(Ul);b(B);I(I);em(Em);
   {false}),mixedp(_);[].
spec(V) -->
   stg(spec),spec1(Spec),etg(spec).
spec1(V) -->
   front(Front),body(Body),(back(Back);[ ]),spec1(_);[].
div1(V) -->
   stg(div1),head(Head),alt1(Alt1),div21(Div21),etg(div1).
alt1(V) -->
   (p(P);list1(List1);note(Note);{false}),alt1(_);[].
div21(V) -->
   div2(Div2),div21(_);[].
name(V) -->
   stg(name),pcdata(Pcdata),etg(name).
```

Fig. 5. A sample DI parser

The right-hand side of a DCG rule is formulated according to the content model of the corresponding element definition. For example, consider the top element which consists of three sequential subelements, p, spec and div1. In a document of the above DTD, a top element is enclosed by the start and end tags of top, and inside the tags are the three tag-enclosed elements. The DCG rule for top is thus formed according to the above structure. For the case of alternative structure, we use disjunctive connector, semicolon, instead of the conjunctive connector, comma, in the sequential case.

For a content model having repetition, we use an auxiliary rule to deal with the repetition. First, consider the content model having a outside repetition marker, for example, the spec element in Fig. 2. The left-hand side of an auxiliary rule retains the name of its original rule with a numeric suffix, for example, spec1. The right-hand side of the auxiliary rule manages the repetition of subelements within the start and end tags of the original element. See, for example, the spec and spec1 rules in Fig. 5.

Then we consider the content model having repetition marker occurring within it, for example, the div1 element in Fig. 2. In this case, we use an auxiliary rule to handle the inner repetition. The left-hand side of this kind of rule is a system-generated name, and the right-hand side of the rule manages the repetition of the subelements. See, for example, the div1, alt1 and div21 rules in Fig. 5.

6.2   Generation of Element Objects

The DI parser described in the preceding subsection is used to analyze the structures in an XML document. We then add semantic action routines in the right-hand side of the DCG rules to generate the object definitions of the document. In general, the semantic action routines are attached to the right end of the right-hand side of the rule, which means that after successfully recognizing the elements mentioned, do the semantic actions. For the terminal element, the semantic action routine is to generate the object definition of the unstructured element. For example, the object definition for the name element in Fig. 2 is as follows.

```
Name name0;
name0=Name.create(pcdata:=Pcdata);
```

The variable, name0 of the Name type is a system-generated name. The next line is to create a new object and store the character string obtained. The resulting object is bound to the variable name0, which is then passed up one level to be the subcomponent of element object in the next higher level.

We attach a procedure, genUnstructuredCode(ElementName,Pcdata,Result), to the DCG rules of name below, for example, to achieve the above task.

```
name(V) -->
    stg(name),
    pcdata(Pcdata),
    etg(name),{genUnstructuredCode(name,Pcdata,V)}.
```

The body of the `genUnstructuredCode` procedure is an output template of the above object definition, where the first parameter `ElementName` is used to decide the class of the object variable, for example, `Name`, and generate the name for the object variable, for example, `name0`. The second parameter is used to assign the value of `pcdata`, and `Result` is instantiated to the object variable as the resulting object, here `V`.

For the structured element types, we design a procedure to handle each of the following structures: mixed, single sequence, single alternative, multiple sequence and multiple alternative. To save space, we only describe the part of single sequence type. An element of this type consists of a sequence of subelements. To create an object for an element of the single sequence type, we first declare a variable of the class and then assign the object of each subelement to the corresponding slot. For example, the code for creating an object of a `top` element is shown as follows.

```
Top top0;
top=Top.new(p:=P,spec:=Spec,div1:=Div1);
```

The DCG rule for the `top` element is as follows. The procedure, `genSingleSeq-Code`, is similar to the code for unstructured element, except that the second parameter is a list of subelements and their resulting variables.

```
top(V) -->
    stg(top),p(P),spec(Spec),div1(Div1),etg(top),
    {genSingleSeqCode(top,[p/P,spec/Spec,div1/Div1],V)}.
```

6.3   Semantic Actions for Generating DI Parser

In Sec. 6.1 and 6.2, we describe the construction of a DI parser using the DCG and the associated semantic action routines attached to the DCG rules to generate object definitions of a document instance. In the following, we describe the generation of the above codes for a new DTD. The task described here corresponds to the DI Parser Generator in Fig. 1. Basically, the task of generating a DI parser is similar to the schema generation in that they both interpret the structures obtained after executing the DTD parser.

As mentioned in Sec. 6.2, a DI parser consists of a number of parsing rules expressed as the following general pattern.

```
Rule_Head -->
    Start_Tag, Rule_Body, End_Tag, {Semantic Actions}.
```

The task of the DI parser generator is to consult the generation rules to produce the parsing rule for each content model obtained from the DTD parser, which is outlined as follows:

```
for each contentModel(ElementName,ContentStructure) do
    generate the rule head for ElementName;
    generate the start tag for ElementName;
```

```
generate the rule body for ContentStructure;
generate the end tag for ElementName;
generate the semantic action;
```

As outlined above, the generation of the rule head and both tags are trivial, which are accomplished simply by giving the element name, as shown in the examples in Sec. 6.2.

The generation of rule body is determined by consulting the generation rules. The generation rule for the unstructured type is trivial. For an element of structured type, we need to distinguish the arrangement of subelements in it, i.e., either sequential or alternative, and the case of repetition. For the content model without repetition, we use conjunctive connectors (,) to connect the subcomponents of the rule body for the sequential case, while disjunctive connectors (;) for the alternative case. If the content model is appended with an optional indicator (?), then the rule body must add a subcomponent to deal with the optional case. We use examples of the generation results as shown below to illustrate the generation for the above cases.

Element	The parsing rule
`<!ELEMENT x (a,b,c)>`	`x(V)-->stg(x),a(A),b(B),c(C),etg(x).`
`<!ELEMENT x (a|b|c)>`	`x(V)-->stg(x),(a(A);b(B);c(C)),etg(x).`
`<!ELEMENT x (a,b,c)?>`	`x(V)-->stg(x),(a(A),b(B),c(C);[]),etg(x).`
`<!ELEMENT x (a|b|c)?>`	`x(V)-->stg(x),(a(A);b(B);c(C);false;[]),etg(x).`

For a content model with repetition, we create an auxiliary parsing rule to deal with the repetition. Then the rule body of the parsing rule for the element becomes a call for the auxiliary rule. The following examples illustrate the idea.

Element	The parsing rule
`<!ELEMENT x (a,b,c)*>`	`x(V)-->stg(x),x1(V),etg(x).`
	`x1(V)-->a(A),b(B),c(C),x1(_);[].`
`<!ELEMENT x (a,b,c)+>`	`x(V)-->stg(x),a(A),b(B),c(C),x1(V),etg(x).`
	`x1(V)-->a(A),b(B),c(C),x1(_);[].`

Furthermore, since a subelement may be a structure with or without repetition, when generating the code for each subelement, we need to consider the cases of structured subelements as well. When the generator detects an occurrence of nested subelements, it creates auxiliary parsing rules to handle the nested subelements.

7   Implementation

We have built a prototype of the system using LPA Win-Prolog V3.5 [10] on personal computer. It consists of a DTD parser, Schema generator and DI parser generator as described in Secs. 4, 5 and 6. After creating the physical store and class family for XML documents, we can proceed to build the database schema for DTD by executing the ODQL codes generated by the DTD schema generator.

A DI parser, as shown in Fig. 1, is generated by the DI parser generator. It is used to analyze an input document instance and produce the object definitions of the document in ODQL. After executing the object definitions, the document are then entered into the object database.

User can use the Jasmine Studio environment to view the XML element classes and objects stored in the database, and develop applications that access the XML documents stored in the database. Java and the programming environments having access to ActiveX controls, such as Visual Basic and Visual C++, can be used to develop XML applications as well.

Currently, we focus on the data modeling of elements definitions in XML documents. We will include the processing of other components, such as attribute list declaration, in the document type declaration. In addition to data modeling, one of our future work is to carry out the behavior modeling of the classes of XML elements in the object database. That is the generation of the procedure codes, such as `getElementContent()` and `getIThElement()`, for the element classes in database.

To make effective use of the XML database, we are developing a template-based query interface to help user easily access the XML documents stored in the object database without knowing the structure of the document [17].

8   Conclusions

In this paper, we employ the DCG in Prolog to translate XML documents into the schema and object definitions of an object database. The features of back-tracking in Prolog and the CFG formalism in the DCG are useful that we can construct the parsers easily by expressing the rules in the XML specification in DCG. We need not worry about providing information to choose which production rule to use as the recursive-descent parser does [2]. Similarly, because of the features we can easily generate the DCG rules for the DI parser as the result of the parsing process. Our experience encourages us to use the DCG to build XML translators for other types of applications, such as the transformation of XML documents to conform various DTDs [11].

Acknowledgment

We gratefully acknowledge the support of the object database software, Jasmine, from Computer Associates Taiwan Ltd. The anonymous reviewers provided helpful comments to improve the paper.

References

[1] Abiteboul, S., Cluet, S., Christophides, V., Milo, T., Moerkotte, G., Simeon, J.: Querying documents in object databases. International Journal on Digital Libraries. (1997) 5-19.

[2] Appel, A. W.: Modern Compiler Implementation in Java: Basic Techniques. Cambridge university Press. (1997)

[3] Bohm, K., Aberer, K., Neuhold E. J., Yang, X.: Structured document storage and refined declarative and navigational access mechanisms in HyperStorM. VLDB Journal (1997).

[4] Bratko, I.: Prolog Programming for Artificial intelligence, 2nd ed. Addison-Wesley. (1990)

[5] Catell, R. G. G. (ed.): The Object Database Standard: ODMG-93. (1996) Morgan Kaufmann

[6] Computer Associates: http://www.cai.com/products/jasmine.htm

[7] El-Medani, S.: Support for Document Entry in a Multimedia Database. (1996) Technical Report TR 96-23, Department of Computing Science, University of Alberta.

[8] Goldfarb, C.: The SGML Handbook. Oxford University Press. (1990)

[9] Goldfarb, C., Prescod, P.: The XML Handbook. Prentice Hall. (1998)

[10] Logic Programming Associates: http://www.lpa.co.uk/

[11] Maler, E., Andaloussi, J. E.: Developing SGML DTDs: From Text to Model to Markup. Prentice Hall. (1996)

[12] Ozsu, M.T., Szafron, D., El-Medani, G., Vittal, C.: An object-oriented multimedia database system for a news-on-demand application. Multimedia Systems. Vol. 3. (1995) 182-203

[13] POET Software: XML: the foundation for the future. Available at http://www.poet.com. (1997)

[14] Vittal, C.: An Object-Oriented Multimedia Database System for News-on-Demand Application. Technical Report TR 95-06. Department of Computer Science, University of Alberta. Canada. (1995)

[15] W3C. Extensible Markup Language (XML) 1.0. W3C Recommendation 10-February-1998. Available at http://www.w3.org/TR/REC-xml. (1998)

[16] W3C. Document Object Model (DOM) Level 1 Specification Version 1.0. W3C Recommendation 1 October, 1998. Available at http://www.w3.org/TR/REC-DOM-Level-1/. (1998)

[17] Yeh, C. L., Chen, H.C.: An extensible template-based query interface to accessing XML object databases. Accepted for presentation in 1999 International Symposium on Multimedia Information Processing, Taipei, Taiwan.

A Hybrid Approach for Solving
Large Scale Crew Scheduling Problems

Tallys H. Yunes*, Arnaldo V. Moura, and Cid C. de Souza**

Institute of Computing, University of Campinas,
Campinas, SP, Brazil
tallys@acm.org, arnaldo@dcc.unicamp.br, cid@dcc.unicamp.br,
Group on Applied Optimization,
http://goa.pos.dcc.unicamp.br/otimo

Abstract. We consider several strategies for computing optimal solutions to large scale crew scheduling problems. Provably optimal solutions for very large real instances of such problems were computed using a hybrid approach that integrates mathematical and constraint programming techniques. The declarative nature of the latter proved instrumental when modeling complex problem restrictions and, particularly, in efficiently searching the very large space of feasible solutions. The code was tested on real problem instances, containing an excess of 1.8×10^9 entries, which were solved to optimality in an acceptable running time when executing on a typical desktop PC.

1 Introduction

Urban transit crew scheduling problems have been receiving a great deal of attention for the past decades. In this article, we report on a hybrid strategy that is capable of efficiently obtaining provably optimal solutions for some large instances of specific crew scheduling problems. The hybrid approach we developed meshes some classical Integer Programming (IP) techniques and some Constraint Programming (CP) techniques. This is done in such a way as to extract the power of these two approaches where they contribute their best towards solving the large scheduling problem instances considered. The resulting code compiles under the Linux operating system, kernel 2.0. Running on a 350 MHz desktop PC with 320 MB of main memory, it computed optimal solutions for problem instances with an excess of 1.8×10^9 entries, in a reasonable amount of time.

The problem instances we used stem from the operational environment of a typical Brazilian transit company that serves a major urban area. In this scenario, employee wages may well rise to 50 percent or more of the company's total expenditures. Hence, in these situations, even small percentage savings can be quite significant.

* Supported by FAPESP grant 98/05999-4, and CAPES.
** Supported by FINEP (ProNEx 107/97), and CNPq (300883/94-3).

E. Pontelli, V. Santos Costa (Eds.): PADL 2000, LNCS 1753, pp. 293–307, 2000.
© Springer-Verlag Berlin Heidelberg 2000

We now offer some general comments on the specific methods and techniques that were used. We started on a pure IP track applying a classical branch-and-bound technique to solve a set partitioning problem formulation. Since this method requires that all feasible duties are previously inserted into the problem formulation, all memory resources were rapidly consumed when we reached half a million feasible duties. To circumvent this difficulty, we implemented a column generation technique. As suggested in [5], the subproblem of generating feasible duties with negative reduced cost was transformed into a constrained shortest path problem over a directed acyclic graph and then solved using Dynamic Programming techniques. However, due to the size and idiosyncrasies of our problem instances, this technique did not make progress towards solving large instances.

In parallel, we also implemented a heuristic algorithm that produced very good results on large set covering problems [2]. With this implementation, problems with up to two million feasible duties could be solved to optimality. But this particular heuristic also requires that all feasible duties be present in memory during execution. Although some progress with respect to time efficiency was achieved, memory usage was still a formidable obstacle.

The difficulties we faced when using the previous approaches almost disappeared when we turned to a language that supports constraint specification over finite domain variables. We were able to implement our models in little time, producing code that was both concise and clear. When executed, it came as no surprise that the model showed two distinct behaviors, mainly due to the huge size of the search space involved. It was very fast when asked to compute new feasible duties, but lagged behind the IP methods when asked to obtain a provably optimal schedule. The search spaces of our problem instances are enormous and there are no strong local constraints available to help the resolution process. Also a good heuristic to improve the search strategy does not come easily [4].

To harness the capabilities of both the IP and CP techniques, we resorted to a hybrid approach to solve the larger, more realistic, problem instances. The main idea is to use the linear relaxation of a smaller core problem in order to efficiently compute good lower bounds on the optimal solution value. Using the values of dual variables in the solution of the linear relaxation, we can enter the generation phase that computes new feasible duties. This phase is modeled as a constraint satisfaction problem that searches for new feasible duties with a negative reduced cost. This problem is submitted to the constraint solver, which returns new feasible duties to be inserted in the IP problem formulation, and the initial phase can be taken again, restarting the cycle. The absence of new feasible duties with a negative reduced cost proves the optimality of the current formulation. This approach secures the strengths of both the pure IP and the pure CP formulations: only a small subset of all the feasible duties is efficiently dealt with at a time, and new feasible duties are quickly computed only when they will make a difference. The resulting code was tested on some large instances, based on real data. As of this writing, we can solve, in a reasonable time and with proven optimality, instances with an excess of 150 trips and 12 million feasible duties.

This article is organized as follows. Section 2 describes the crew scheduling problem. In Sect. 3, we discuss the IP approach and report on the implementation of two alternative techniques: standard column generation and heuristics. In Sect. 4, we investigate the pure CP approach. In Sect. 5, we present the hybrid approach. Implementation details and computational results on real data are reported in sections 3, 4 and 5. Finally, in Sect. 6, we conclude and discuss further issues.

In the sequel, execution times inferior to one minute are reported as *ss.cc*, where *ss* denotes seconds and *cc* denotes hundredths of seconds. For execution times that exceed 60 seconds, we use the alternative notation *hh:mm:ss*, where *hh*, *mm* and *ss* represent hours, minutes and seconds, respectively.

2   The Crew Scheduling Problem

In a typical crew scheduling problem, a set of trips has to be assigned to some available crews. The goal is to assign a subset of the trips to each crew in such a way that no trip is left unassigned. As usual, not every possible assignment is allowed since a number of constraints must be observed. Additionally, a cost function has to be minimized.

2.1   Terminology

Among the following terms, some are of general use, while others reflect specifics of the transportation service for the urban area where the input data came from. A *depot* is a location where crews may change buses and rest. The act of driving a bus from one depot to another depot, passing by no intermediate depot, is named a *trip*. Associated with a trip we have its *start time*, its *duration*, its *departure depot*, and its *arrival depot*. The duration of a trip is statistically calculated from field collected data, and depends on many factors, such as the day of the week and the start time of the trip along the day. A *duty* is a sequence of trips that are assigned to the same crew. The *idle time* is the time interval between two consecutive trips in a duty. Whenever this idle time exceeds *Idle_Limit* minutes, it is called a *long rest*. A duty that contains a long rest is called a *two-shift duty*. The *rest time* of a duty is the sum of its idle times, not counting long rests. The parameter *Min_Rest* gives the minimum amount of rest time, in minutes, that each crew is entitled to. The sum of the durations of the trips in a duty is called its *working time*. The sum of the *working time* and the *rest time* gives the *total working time* of a duty. The parameter *Workday* is specified by union regulations and limits the daily total working time.

2.2   Input Data

The input data comes in the form of a two dimensional table where each row represents one trip. For each trip, the table lists: *start time*, measured in minutes after midnight, *duration*, measured in minutes, *initial depot* and *final depot*.

We have used data that reflect the operational environment of two bus lines, Line 2222 and Line 3803, that serve the metropolitan area around the city of Belo Horizonte, in central Brazil. Line 2222 has 125 trips and one depot and Line 3803 has 246 trips and two depots. The input data tables for these lines are called OS 2222 and OS 3803, respectively. By considering initial segments taken from these two tables, we derived several other smaller problem instances. For example, taking the first 30 trips of OS 2222 gave us a new 30-trip problem instance. A measure of the number of active trips along a typical day, for both Line 2222 and Line 3803, is shown in Fig. 1. This figure was constructed as follows. For each (x, y) entry, we consider a time window $T = [x, x + Workday]$. The ordinate y indicates how many trips there are with start time s and duration d such that $s \in T$ or $s + d \in T$, i.e., how many trips are active in T.

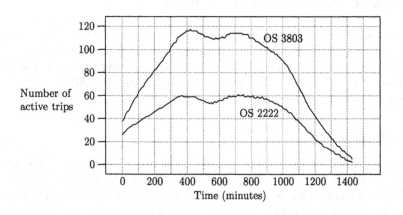

Fig. 1. Distribution of trips along the day

2.3   Constraints

For a duty to be feasible, it has to satisfy constraints imposed by labor contracts and union regulations, among others. For each duty we must observe

$$total\ working\ time \leq Workday$$
$$rest\ time \geq Min\_Rest.$$

In each duty and for each pair (i, j) of consecutive trips, $i < j$, we must have

$$(start\ time)_i + (duration)_i \leq (start\ time)_j$$
$$(final\ depot)_i = (initial\ depot)_j.$$

Also, at most one long rest interval is allowed, in each duty.

Restrictions from the operational environment impose *Idle_Limit* = 120, *Workday* = 440, and *Min_Rest* = 30, measured in minutes. A *feasible duty* is a duty that satisfies all problem constraints. A *schedule* is a set of feasible duties and an *acceptable schedule* is any schedule that partitions the set of all trips. Since the problem specification treats all duties as indistinguishable, every duty is assigned a unit cost. The cost of a schedule is the sum of the costs of all its duties. Hence, minimizing the cost of a schedule is the same as minimizing the number of crews involved in the solution or, equivalently, the number of duties it contains. A *minimal schedule* is any acceptable schedule whose cost is minimal.

3   Mathematical Programming Approaches

Let m be the number of trips and n be the total number of feasible duties. The pure IP formulation of the problem is:

$$\min \sum_{j=1}^{n} x_j \tag{1}$$

$$\text{subject to} \quad \sum_{j=1}^{n} a_{ij} x_j = 1, \quad i = 1, 2, \ldots, m \tag{2}$$

$$x_j \in \{0, 1\}, \quad j = 1, 2, \ldots, n. \tag{3}$$

The x_j's are 0-1 decision variables that indicate which duties belong to the solution. The coefficient a_{ij} equals 1 if duty j contains trip i, otherwise, a_{ij} is 0. This is a classical set partitioning problem where the rows represent all trips and the columns represent all feasible duties.

We developed a constraint program to count all feasible duties both in OS 2222 and in OS 3803. Table 1 summarizes the results for increasing initial sections (column "# Trips") of the input data. The time (column "Time") needed to count the number of feasible duties (column "# FD") is also presented. For OS 2222, we get in excess of one million feasible duties, and for all trips in OS 3803 we get more than 122 million feasible duties.

3.1   Pure IP Approach

In the pure IP approach, we used the constraint program to generate an output file containing all feasible duties. A program was developed in C to make this file conform to the CPLEX[1] input format. The resulting file was fed into a CPLEX 3.0 LP solver. The node selection strategy used was *best-first* and branching was done upon the most fractional variable. Every other setting of the branch-and-bound algorithm used the standard default CPLEX configuration.

The main problem with the IP approach is clear: the number of feasible duties is enormous. Computational results for OS 2222 appear in Table 2, columns

---

[1] CPLEX is a registered trademark of ILOG, Inc.

Table 1. Number of feasible duties for OS 2222 and OS 3803

OS 2222 (1 depot)			OS 3803 (2 depots)		
# Trips	# FD	Time	# Trips	# FD	Time
10	63	0.07	20	978	1.40
20	306	0.33	40	6,705	5.98
30	1,032	0.99	60	45,236	33.19
40	5,191	5.38	80	256,910	00:03:19
50	18,721	21.84	100	1,180,856	00:18:34
60	42,965	00:01:09	120	3,225,072	00:57:53
70	104,771	00:03:10	140	8,082,482	02:59:17
80	212,442	00:05:40	160	18,632,680	08:12:28
90	335,265	00:07:48	180	33,966,710	14:39:21
100	496,970	00:10:49	200	54,365,975	17:55:26
110	706,519	00:14:54	220	83,753,429	42:14:35
125	1,067,406	01:00:27	246	122,775,538	95:49:54

under "Pure IP". Columns "Opt" and "Sol" indicate, respectively, the optimal and computed values for the corresponding run. It soon became apparent that the pure IP approach using the CPLEX solver would not be capable of obtaining the optimal solution for the smaller OS 2222 problem instance. Besides, memory usage was also increasing at an alarming pace, and execution time was lagging behind when compared to other approaches that were being developed in parallel. As an alternative, we decided to implement a column generation approach.

3.2 Column Generation with Dynamic Programming

Column generation is a technique that is widely used to handle linear programs which have a very large number of columns in the coefficient matrix. The method works by repeatedly executing two phases. In a first phase, instead of solving a linear relaxation of the whole problem, in which all columns are required to be loaded in memory, we quickly solve a smaller problem, called the *master* problem, that deals only with a subset of the original columns. That smaller problem solved, we start phase two, looking for columns with a negative reduced cost. If there are no such columns, we have proved that the solution at hand indeed minimizes the objective function. Otherwise, we augment the master problem by bringing in a number of columns with negative reduced cost, and start over on phase one. The problem of computing columns with negative reduced costs is called the *slave* subproblem. When the original variables have integer values, this algorithm must be embedded in a branch-and-bound strategy. The resulting algorithm is also known as *branch-and-price*.

Generating Columns. In general, the slave subproblem can also be formulated as another IP problem. In our case, constraints like the one on two-shift

Table 2. Computational results for OS 2222 (1 depot)

# Trips	# FD	Opt	Pure IP		CG+DP		Heuristic	
			Sol	Time	Sol	Time	Sol	Time
10	63	7	7	0.02	7	0.01	7	0.05
20	306	11	11	0.03	11	0.07	11	0.30
30	1,032	14	14	0.06	14	0.52	14	10.37
40	5,191	14	14	3.04	14	9.10	14	13.02
50	18,721	14	14	14.29	14	00:01:29	14	00:30:00
60	42,965	14	14	00:01:37	14	00:07:54	14	00:30:22
70	104,771	14	14	00:04:12	14	00:44:19	14	00:03:28
80	212,442	16	16	00:33:52	16	03:53:58	16	00:16:24
90	335,265	18	18	00:50:28	18	08:18:53	18	00:22:42
100	496,970	20	20	02:06:32	20	15:08:55	20	00:50:01
110	706,519	22	-	-	-	-	22	01:06:17
125	1,067,406	25	-	-	-	-	25	01:55:12

duties substantially complicate the formulation of a pure IP model. As another approach, Desrochers and Soumis [5] suggest reducing the slave subproblem to a constrained shortest path problem, formulated over a related directed acyclic graph. When this process terminates, it is easy to extract not only the shortest feasible path, but also a number of additional feasible paths, all with negative reduced costs. We used these ideas, complemented by other observations from Beasley and Christofides [1] and our own experience.

Implementation and Results. To implement the branch-and-price strategy, the use of the ABACUS[2] branch-and-price framework (version 2.2) saved a lot of programming time. One of the important issues was the choice of the branching rule. When applying a branch-and-bound algorithm to set partitioning problems, a simple branching rule is to choose a binary variable and set it to 1 on one branch and set it to 0 on the other branch, although there are situations where this might not be the best choice [13]. This simple branching rule produced a very small number of nodes in the implicit enumeration tree (41 in the worst case). Hence, we judged that any possible marginal gains did not justify the extra programming effort required to implement a more elaborated branching rule (c.f. [12]). In Table 2, columns under "CG+DP", show the computational results for OS 2222. This approach did not reach a satisfactory time performance, mainly because the constrained shortest path subproblem is relatively loose. As a pseudo-polynomial algorithm, the state space at each node has the potential of growing exponentially with the input size. The number of feasible paths the algorithm has to maintain became so large that the time spent looking for columns with negative reduced cost is responsible for more than 97% of the total execution time, on the average, over all instances.

---

[2] http://www.informatik.uni-koeln.de/ls_juenger/projects/abacus.html.

Table 3. Heuristic over OS 3803 (2 depots)

# Trips	# FD	Opt	Sol	Time
20	978	6	6	0.35
40	6,705	13	13	3.60
60	45,236	15	15	52.01
80	256,910	15	15	00:08:11
100	1,180,856	15	15	00:13:51
110	2,015,334	15	15	00:23:24

3.3 A Heuristic Approach

Heuristics offer another approach to solve scheduling problems and there are many possible variations. Initially, we set aside those heuristics that were unable to reach an optimal solution. As a promising alternative, we decided to implement the set covering heuristic developed by Caprara et al. [2]. This heuristic won the FASTER competition jointly organized by the Italian Railway Company and AIRO, solving, in reasonable time, large set covering problems arising from crew scheduling. Using our own experience and additional ideas from the chapter on Lagrangian Relaxation in [11], an implementation was written in C and went through a long period of testing and benchmarking. Tests executed on set covering instances coming from the OR-Library showed that our implementation is competitive with the original implementation in terms of solution quality. When this algorithm terminates, it also produces a lower bound for the optimal covering solution, which could be used as a bound for the partition problem, as well. We verified, however, that on the larger instances, the solution produced by the heuristic turned out to be a partition already.

Computational results for OS 2222 appear in Table 2, columns under "Heuristic". Comparing all three implementations, it is clear that the heuristic gave the best results. However, applying this heuristic to the larger OS 3803 data set was problematic. Since storage space has to be allocated to accommodate all feasible columns, memory usage becomes prohibitive. It was possible to solve instances with up to 2 million feasible duties, as indicated in Table 3. Beyond that limit, 320 MB of main memory were not enough for the program to terminate.

4 Constraint Programming Approach

Modeling with finite domain constraints is rapidly gaining acceptance as a promising programming environment to solve large combinatorial problems. This led us to also model the crew scheduling problem using pure constraint programming (CP) techniques. All models described in this section were formulated using the ECL^{i}PS^e [3] syntax, version 4.0. Due to its large size, the ECL^{i}PS^e formulation for each run was obtained using a program generator that we developed in C.

---

[3] http://www.icparc.ic.ac.uk/eclipse.

A simple pure CP formulation was developed first. It used a list of items, each item being itself a list describing an actual duty. A number of recursive predicates guarantee that each item satisfies all labor and regulation constraints (see Sect. 2.3), and also enforce restrictions of time and depot compatibility between consecutive trips. These feasibility predicates iterate over all list items. The database contains one fact for each line of input data, as explained in Sect. 2.2. The resulting model is very simple to program in a declarative environment. The formulation, however, did not reach satisfactory results when submitted to the ECL^iPS^e solver, as shown in Table 4, columns under "First Model". A number of different labeling techniques, different clause orderings and several variants on constraint representation were explored, to no avail. When proving optimality, the situation was even worse. It was not possible to prove optimality for instances with only 10 trips in less than an hour of execution time. The main reason for this poor performance may reside on the recursiveness of the list representation, and on the absence of reasonable lower and upper bounds on the value of the optimal solution which could aid the solver discard unpromising labelings.

4.1 Improved Model

The new model is based on a two dimensional matrix X of integers. The number of columns (rows) in X, $UBdutyLen$ ($UBnumDut$), is an upper bound on the size of any feasible duty (the total number of duties). Each X_{ij} element represents a single trip and is a finite domain variable with domain $[1..NT]$, where $NT = UBdutyLen \times UBnumDut$. Real trips are numbered from 1 to N, where $N \leq NT$. Trips numbered $N+1$ to NT are *dummy trips*. To simplify the writing of some constraints, the last trip in each line of X is always a dummy trip. A proper choice of the start time, duration and depots of the dummy trips avoids time and depots incompatibilities among them and, besides, prevents the occurrence of dummy trips between real trips. Moreover, the choice of start times for all dummy trips guarantees that they occupy consecutive cells at the end of every line in X. Using this representation, the set partitioning condition can be easily met with an `alldifferent` constraint applied to a list that contains X_{ij} elements.

Five other matrices were used: *Start*, *End*, *Dur*, *DepDepot* and *ArrDepot*. Cell (i, j) of these matrices represents, respectively, the start time, the end time, the duration, and the departure and arrival depots of trip X_{ij}. Next, we state constraints in the form `element`$(X_{ij}, S, Start_{ij})$, where S is a list containing the start times of the first NT trips. The semantics of this constraint assures that $Start_{ij}$ is the k-th element of list S where k is the value in X_{ij}. This maintains the desired relationship between matrices X and *Start*. Whenever X_{ij} is updated, $Start_{ij}$ is also modified, and vice-versa. Similar constraints are stated between X and each one of the four other matrices. Now, we can write:

$$End_{ij} \leq Start_{i(j+1)} \qquad (4)$$

$$ArrDepot_{ij} + DepDepot_{i(j+1)} \neq 3 \qquad (5)$$

$$Idle_{ij} = BD_{ij} \times \left(Start_{i(j+1)} - End_{ij}\right) \qquad (6)$$

Table 4. Pure CP models, OS 2222 data set

			First Model		Improved Model			
			Feasible		*Feasible*		*Optimal*	
# Trips	# FD	Opt	Sol	Time	Sol	Time	Sol	Time
10	63	7	7	0.35	7	0.19	7	0.63
20	306	11	11	12.21	11	0.47	11	9.22
30	1,032	14	15	00:02:32	15	0.87	14	00:29:17
40	5,191	14	15	00:14:27	15	0.88	-	> 40:00:00
50	18,721	14	15	00:53:59	15	0.97	-	-
60	42,965	14	-	-	15	2.92	-	-
70	104,771	14	-	-	16	3.77	-	-
80	212,442	16	-	-	19	8.66	-	-
90	335,265	18	-	-	24	17.97	-	-
100	496,970	20	-	-	27	29.94	-	-
110	706,519	22	-	-	27	39.80	-	-
125	1,067,406	25	-	-	32	00:01:21	-	-

for all $i \in \{1, \ldots, UBnumDut\}$ and all $j \in \{1, \ldots, UBdutyLen-1\}$. Equation (4) guarantees that trips overlapping in time are not in the same duty. Since the maximum number of depots is two, an incompatibility of two consecutive trips is prevented by (5). In (6), the binary variables BD_{ij} are such that $BD_{ij} = 1$ if and only if $X_{i(j+1)}$ contains a real trip. Hence, the constraint on total working time, for each duty i, is given by

$$\sum_{j=1}^{UBdutyLen-1} (Dur_{ij} + BI_{ij} \times Idle_{ij}) \leq Workday, \tag{7}$$

where BI_{ij} is a binary variable such that $BI_{ij} = 1$ if and only if $Idle_{ij} \leq Idle\_Limit$. The constraint on total rest time is

$$Workday + \sum_{j=1}^{UBdutyLen-1} (Idle_{ij} - Dur_{ij} - BI_{ij} \times Idle_{ij}) \geq Min\_Rest \tag{8}$$

for each duty i. For two-shift duties, we impose further that at most one of the $Idle_{ij}$ variables can assume a value greater than $Idle\_Limit$.

4.2   Refinements and Results

The execution time of this model was further improved by:

Elimination of Symmetries – Solutions that are permutations of lines of X are equivalent. To bar such equivalences, the first column of the X matrix was kept sorted. Since exchanging the position of dummy trips gives equivalent solutions, new constraints were used to prevent dummy trips from being swapped when backtracking.

Domain Reduction – For instance, the first real trip can only appear in $X_{1,1}$.

Use of Another Viewpoint – Different viewpoints [3] were also used. New Y_k variables were introduced representing "the cell that stores trip k", as opposed to the X_{ij} variables that mean "the trip that is put in cell ij". The Y_k variables were connected to the X_{ij} variables through *channeling constraints*. The result is a redundant model with improved propagation properties.

Different Labeling Strategies – Various labeling strategies have been tried, including the one developed by Jourdan [9]. The strategy of choosing the next variable to label as the one with the smallest domain (*first-fail*) was the most effective one. After choosing a variable, it is necessary to select a value from its domain following a specific order, when backtracking occurs. We tested different labeling orders, like increasing, decreasing, and also middle-out and its reverse. Experimentation showed that labeling by increasing order achieved the best results. On the other hand, when using viewpoints, the heuristic developed by Jourdan rendered the model roughly 15 % faster.

The improved purely declarative model produced feasible schedules in a very good time, as indicated in Table 4, under columns "Improved Model". Obtaining provably optimal solutions, however, was still out of reach for this model. Others have also reported difficulties when trying to solve crew scheduling problems with a pure CP approach [4, 8]. Finding the optimal schedule reduces to choosing, from an extremely large set of elements, a minimal subset that satisfies all the problem constraints. The huge search spaces involved can only be dealt with satisfactorily when pruning is enforced by strong local constraints. Besides, a simple search strategy, lacking good problem specific heuristics, is very unlikely to succeed. When solving scheduling problems of this nature and size to optimality, none of the these requirements can be met easily, rendering it intrinsically difficult for pure CP techniques to produce satisfactory results in these cases.

5 A Hybrid Approach

Recent research [6] has shown that, in some cases, neither the pure IP nor the pure CP approaches are capable of solving certain kinds of combinatorial problems satisfactorily. But a hybrid strategy might outperform them.

When contemplating a hybrid strategy, it is necessary to decide which part of the problem will be handled by a constraint solver, and which part will be dealt with in a classical way. Given the huge number of columns at hand, a column generation approach seemed to be almost mandatory. As reported in Sect. 3.2, we already knew that the dynamic programming column generator used in the pure IP approach did not perform well. On the other hand, a declarative language is particularly suited to express not only the constraints imposed by the original problem, but also the additional constraints that must be satisfied when looking for feasible duties with a negative reduced cost. Given that, it was a natural decision to implement a column generation approach where new columns were generated on demand by a constraint program. Additionally, the discussion in Sect. 4.2 indicated that the CP strategy implemented was very efficient when

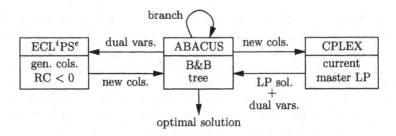

Fig. 2. Simplified scheme of the hybrid column generation method

identifying feasible duties. It lagged behind only when computing a provably optimal solution to the original scheduling problem, due to the minimization constraint. Since it is not necessary to find a column with *the* most negative reduced cost, the behavior of the CP solver was deemed adequate. It remained to program the CP solver to find a set of new feasible duties with the extra requirement that their reduced cost should be negative.

5.1 Implementation Issues

The basis of this new algorithm is the same as the one developed for the column generation approach, described in Sect. 3.2. The dynamic programming routine is substituted for an ECL^{i}PS^e process that solves the slave subproblem and uses sockets to communicate the solution back to the ABACUS process. When the ABACUS process has solved the current master problem to optimality, it sends the values of the dual variables to the CP process. If there remain some columns with negative reduced costs, some of them are captured by the CP solver and are sent back to the ABACUS process, and the cycle starts over. If there are no such columns, the LP solver has found an optimal solution. Having found the optimal solution for this node of the enumeration tree, its dual bound has also been determined. The normal branch-and-bound algorithm can then proceed until it is time to solve another LP. This interaction is depicted in Fig. 2.

The code for the CP column generator is almost identical to the code for the improved CP model, presented in Sect. 4.1. There are three major differences. Firstly, the matrix X now has only one row, since we are interested in finding *one* feasible duty and not a complete solution. Secondly, there is an additional constraint stating that the sum of the values of the dual variables associated with the trips in the duty being constructed should represent a negative reduced cost. Finally, the minimization predicate was exchanged for a predicate that keeps on looking for new feasible duties until the desired number of feasible duties with negative reduced costs have been computed, or until there are no more feasible assignments. By experimenting with the data sets at hand, we determined that the number of columns with negative reduced cost to request at each iteration of the CP solver was best set to 53. The redundant modeling, as well as the heuristic

Table 5. Hybrid algorithm, OS 2222 data set (1 depot)

# Trips	# FD	Opt	DBR	# CA	# LP	# Nodes	PrT	LPT	TT
10	63	7	7	53	2	1	0.08	0.02	0.12
20	306	11	11	159	4	1	0.30	0.04	0.42
30	1,032	14	14	504	11	1	1.48	0.11	2.07
40	5,191	14	14	1,000	26	13	8.03	0.98	9.37
50	18,721	14	14	1,773	52	31	40.97	3.54	45.28
60	42,965	14	14	4,356	107	41	00:04:24	14.45	00:04:40
70	104,771	14	14	2,615	58	7	00:01:36	4.96	00:01:42
80	212,442	16	16	4,081	92	13	00:01:53	18.84	00:02:13
90	335,265	18	18	6,455	141	11	00:02:47	31.88	00:03:22
100	496,970	20	20	8,104	177	13	00:06:38	51.16	00:07:34
110	706,519	22	22	11,864	262	21	00:16:53	00:02:28	00:19:31
125	1,067,406	25	25	11,264	250	17	00:19:09	00:01:41	00:21:00

suggested by Jourdan, both used to improve the performance of the original CP formulation, now represented unnecessary overhead, and were removed.

5.2 Computational Results

The hybrid approach was able to construct an optimal solution to substantially larger instances of the problem, in a reasonable time. Computational results for OS 2222 and OS 3803 appear on Tables 5 and 6, respectively. Column headings # Trips, # FD, Opt, DBR, # CA, # LP and # Nodes stand for, respectively, number of trips, number of feasible duties, optimal solution value, dual bound at the root node, number of columns added, number of linear programming relaxations solved, and number nodes visited. The execution times are divided in three columns: PrT, LPT and TT, meaning, respectively, time spent generating columns, time spent solving linear programming relaxations, and total execution time. In every instance, the dual bound at the root node was equal to the value of the optimal integer solution. Hence, the LP relaxation of the problem already provided the best possible lower bound on the optimal solution value. Also note that the number of nodes visited by the algorithm was kept small. The same behavior can be observed with respect to the number of columns added.

The sizable gain in performance is shown in the last three columns of each table. Note that the time to solve all linear relaxations of the problem was a small fraction of the total running time, for both data sets.

It is also clear, from Table 5, that the hybrid approach was capable of constructing a provably optimal solution for the smaller data set using 21 minutes of running time on a 350 MHz desktop PC. That problem involved in excess of one million feasible columns and was solved considerably faster when compared with the best performer (see Sect. 3.3) among all the previous approaches.

The structural difference between both data sets can be observed by looking at the 100 trip row, in Table 6. The number of feasible duties on this line is,

Table 6. Hybrid algorithm, OS 3803 data set (2 depots)

# Trips	# FD	Opt	DBR	# CA	# LP	# Nodes	PrT	LPT	TT
20	978	6	6	278	7	1	2.11	0.08	2.24
30	2,890	10	10	852	19	1	9.04	0.20	9.38
40	6,705	13	13	2,190	48	1	28.60	1.03	30.14
50	17,334	14	14	4,220	94	3	00:01:22	3.95	00:01:27
60	45,236	15	15	8,027	175	1	00:03:48	14.81	00:04:06
70	107,337	15	15	11,622	258	1	00:07:42	40.59	00:08:37
80	256,910	15	15	8,553	225	1	00:10:07	47.12	00:10:58
90	591,536	15	15	9,827	269	1	00:14:34	00:02:04	00:16:43
100	1,180,856	15	15	13,330	375	1	00:39:03	00:04:37	00:43:49
110	2,015,334	15	15	13,717	387	1	01:19:55	00:03:12	01:23:19
120	3,225,072	16	16	18,095	543	13	04:02:18	00:09:09	04:11:50
130	5,021,936	17	17	28,345	874	23	06:59:53	00:30:16	07:30:56
140	8,082,482	18	18	27,492	886	25	13:29:51	00:28:56	13:59:40
150	12,697,909	19	19	37,764	1,203	25	21:04:28	00:49:13	21:55:25

approximately, the same number of one million feasible duties that are present in the totality of 125 trips of the first data set, OS 2222. Yet, the algorithm used roughly twice as much time to construct the optimal solution for the first 100 trips of the larger data set, as it did when taking the 125 trips of the smaller data set. Also, the algorithm lagged behind the heuristic for OS 3803, although the latter was unable to go beyond 110 trips, due to excessive memory usage.

Finally, when we fixed a maximum running time of 24 hours, the algorithm was capable of constructing a solution, and prove its optimality, for as many as 150 trips taken from the larger data set. This corresponds to an excess of 12 million feasible duties. It is noteworthy that less than 60 MB of main memory were needed for this run. A problem instance with as many as $150 \times (12.5 \times 10^6)$ entries would require over 1.8 GB when loaded into main memory. By efficiently dealing with a small subset of the feasible duties, our algorithm managed to surpass the memory bottleneck and solve instances that were very large. This observation supports our view that a CP formulation of column generation was the right approach to solve very large crew scheduling problems.

6   Conclusions and Future Work

Real world crew scheduling problems often give rise to large set covering or set partitioning formulations. We have shown a way to integrate pure Integer Programming and declarative Constraint Satisfaction Programming techniques in a hybrid column generation algorithm that solves, to optimality, huge instances of some real world crew scheduling problems. These problems appeared intractable for both approaches when taken in isolation. Our methodology combines the strengths of both sides, while getting over their main weaknesses.

Another crucial advantage of our hybrid approach over a number of previous attempts is that it considers *all* feasible duties. Therefore, the need does not arise to use specific rules to select, at the start, a subset of "good" feasible duties. This kind of preprocessing could prevent the optimal solution from being found. Instead, our algorithm implicitly looks at the set of all feasible duties, when activating the column generation method. When declarative constraint satisfaction formulations are applied to generate new feasible duties on demand, they have shown to be a very efficient strategy, in contrast to Dynamic Programming.

We believe that our CP formulation can be further improved. In particular, the search strategy deserves more attention. Earlier identification of unpromising branches in the search tree can reduce the number of backtracks and lead to substantial savings in computational time. Techniques such as dynamic backtracking [7] and the use of *nogoods* [10] can be applied to traverse the search tree more efficiently, thereby avoiding useless work.

References

[1] J. E. Beasley and N. Christofides. An algorithm for the resource constrained shortest path problem. *Networks*, 19:379–394, 1989.

[2] A. Caprara, M. Fischetti, and P. Toth. A heuristic method for the set covering problem. Technical Report OR-95-8, DEIS, Università di Bologna, 1995.

[3] B. M. W. Cheng, K. M. F. Choi, J. H. M. Lee, and J. C. K. Wu. Increasing constraint propagation by redundant modeling: an experience report. *Constraints*, 1998. Accepted for publication.

[4] K. Darby-Dowman and J. Little. Properties of some combinatorial optimization problems and their effect on the performance of integer programming and constraint logic programming. *INFORMS Journal on Computing*, 10(3), 1998.

[5] M. Desrochers and F. Soumis. A column generation approach to the urban transit crew scheduling problem. *Transportation Science*, 23(1), 1989.

[6] C. Gervet. Large Combinatorial Optimization Problems: a Methodology for Hybrid Models and Solutions. In *JFPLC*, 1998.

[7] M. L. Ginsberg. Dynamic backtracking. *Journal of Artificial Intelligence Research*, (1):25–46, 1993.

[8] N. Guerinik and M. Van Caneghem. Solving crew scheduling problems by constraint programming. In *Lecture Notes in Computer Science*, pages 481–498, 1995. Proceedings of the First International Conference on the Principles and Practice of Constraint Programming, CP'95.

[9] J. Jourdan. *Concurrent Constraint Multiple Models in CLP and CC Languages: Toward a Programming Methodology by Modeling*. PhD thesis, Université Denis Diderot, Paris VII, February 1995.

[10] J. Lever, M. Wallace, and B. Richards. Constraint logic programming for scheduling and planning. *BT Technical Journal*, (13):73–81, 1995.

[11] C. R. Reeves, editor. *Modern Heuristic Techniques for Combinatorial Problems*. Wiley, 1993.

[12] D. M. Ryan and B. A. Foster. An integer programming approach to scheduling. In A. Wren, editor, *Computer Scheduling of Public Transport*. North-Holland Publishing Company, 1981.

[13] F. Vanderbeck. *Decomposition and Column Generation for Integer Programming*. PhD thesis, Université Catholique de Louvain, CORE, September 1994.

Knowledgesheet: A Graphical Spreadsheet Interface for Interactively Developing a Class of Constraint Programs*

Gopal Gupta and Shameem F. Akhter**

Laboratory for Logic, Databases, and Advanced Programming
Department of Computer Science
New Mexico State University
Las Cruces, NM, USA

Abstract. We introduce a generalization of the spreadsheet paradigm, called Knowledgesheet, for solving a *class of* constraint satisfaction problems. The traditional spreadsheet paradigm is based on attaching arithmetic expressions to individual cells and then evaluating them; our Knowledgesheet interface instead allows *finite domain constraints* to be attached to individual cells that are then solved to obtain a solution. This extension provides an easy-to-use interface for solving a large class of constraint satisfaction problems—those whose specification and solution conforms to a 2-dimensional structure, e.g., scheduling problems, time-tabling problems, etc. A prototype for the Knowledgesheet has been developed and applied to solve many different types of problems.

1 Introduction

Many problems that arise in daily life are NP-hard in nature. For instance, course scheduling at Universities, resource allocation, task scheduling, and examination timetabling. Most NP-hard problems can be elegantly expressed as constraints. A solution to these problems can then be found by constraint solving. However, formulating the problem as a set of constraints is not an easy task. Very often a lot of experimentation is involved and different constraints need to be tried. In this paper, we present a spreadsheet based interface, called Knowledgesheet, for finite-domain constraint programming. We show that this interface facilitates the interactive development of constraint-based solutions to a large class of practical NP-hard problems. A prototype implementation of Knowledgesheet, implemented in Java, is operational [9,5].

The Knowledgesheet interface is based on the observation that most combinatorial problems are naturally modeled as a set of variables and a set of constraints on these variables. While the facilities provided by constraint languages (such as logic programming languages and constraint programming languages) precisely

* The authors have been partially supported by NSF grants CDA 97-29848, CDA 98-02251, CCR 99-00320, CCR 99-04063.
** Currently at Technology CAD Group, Intel Corporation, Portland, Oregon, USA.

E. Pontelli, V. Santos Costa (Eds.): PADL 2000, LNCS 1753, pp. 308–323, 2000.
© Springer-Verlag Berlin Heidelberg 2000

match the requirements for modeling combinatorial problems, the way in which the solution has to be programmed requires deep knowledge of the language. The Knowledgesheet programming interface that we present in this paper bridges this gap, at least for a class of such problems. The Knowledgesheet interface allows novice users to program a large class of constraint satisfaction problems (CSPs), just in the same manner as an ordinary spreadsheet allows a novice user to program a large class of problems involving arithmetic computations.

In traditional spreadsheets only atomic values (numbers and constants) and arithmetic expressions can be attached to individual cells. In a Knowledgesheet, finite domain constraints can also be attached to individual cells. This generalization of a spreadsheet, or Knowledgesheet, is inspired by the idea that the solution to many constraint problems, such as course scheduling, examination timetabling, resource scheduling, etc., can be expressed via finite domain (FD) constraints entered in a 2-dimensional table. These constraint satisfaction problems thus can be programmed using the spreadsheet paradigm if FD constraints are also allowed to be attached to individual cells of the spreadsheet.

Consider the problem of course scheduling at an academic department in a University. The course schedule consists of a table with a number of rows (one row per course) and a number of columns. For each course, the table specifies the instructor who is going to teach the course, the room in which the class is going to be taught, etc., under appropriate columns. The person who designs this course schedule essentially uses a *pencil-and-paper* approach. He/she starts out with a blank table on a piece of paper that has one empty row per course. He/she then gradually schedules the instructors and the classrooms for each course following certain constraints. These constraints are imposed by certain facts, such as: which instructors have the expertise to teach which courses, which room is big enough to hold the maximum number of students allowed in that course, etc. The designer will make some guesses, and then use trial and error to manually come up with a correct schedule. Experience shows that this process of trial and error is quite hard, and mistakes are invariably made. A tool such as Knowledgesheet can automate this process for the designer. The idea behind the Knowledgesheet approach is to let the designer just state the constraints regarding instructors' expertise, room capacities, etc., in the various empty cells of the table. The possible ways in which the boxes in the table can be filled is also stated (domain or set of values that a particular slot or box can take). This domain information as well as the constraints are collected in a program, which is then executed to compute the results. The computed results are then displayed in the table. So given the Knowledgesheet tool, a designer's task boils down to stating the constraints and domains. An automatic constraint solver does the task of computing exact values that constitute a schedule of courses. If the designer doesn't like the solution, he/she can interactively change the constraints to obtain more acceptable solutions.

The Knowledgesheet tool consists of three parts: (i) a spreadsheet like interface for entering the constraint and domain information, (ii) an off-the-shelf back-end CLP(FD) engine that solves constraints, and, (iii) a protocol for communicating between the interface and the back-end engine. We use the ECLiPSe CLP(FD) System [1] as the back-end engine for solving the constraints. The Knowledgesheet interface provides facilities to enter constraints interactively. It also provides facilities for copying constraints entered in one box to another box with appropriate transformations (much in the fashion of a traditional spreadsheet). Thus, repetitive computations are not programmed as loops (or using recursion), rather an instance of the computation is entered in a Knowledgesheet cell, and then this computation is copied on remaining cells.

The major advantage of the Knowledgesheet interface is that it facilitates problem modeling and interactive problem solving. Essentially, it forces the programmer (or problem solver) to think in an intuitive and structured (tabular) way. The problem solver still has to come up with all the constraints, and a model of the solution based on constraints—the interactive nature of the Knowledgesheet and its enforcement of the spreadsheet discipline make the task of the programmer, we believe, considerably easier. It also allows novice users to be able to interactively solve CSPs. The disadvantage is that it can be used for solving only a class of constraint satisfaction problems.

It should be emphasized that the Knowledgesheet Interface is an interactive tool and involves the programmer in finding a solution that is acceptable. Essentially, the programmer has to keep experimenting until a satisfactory solution is found. All the Knowledgesheet does is that it makes the process of interactive development of the solution easier. The responsibility of modeling the solution still rests with the programmer.

2   Constraint Logic Programming

Traditional logic programming languages, such as Prolog [7], are inefficient for solving complex search problems. These programming languages use the *generate and test* paradigm. In the generate and test paradigm, constraints (or tests) are applied *a posteriori* to detect failures after values have been chosen for the unknown variables in the problem model. Constraint languages remove this pitfall of LP by using consistency techniques. The idea is to actively use constraints to prune the search space *a priori* by removing combinations of values that cannot appear together in a solution. Consistency techniques divide the task of searching for a solution into two steps: (1) propagate the constraints as much as possible, and (2) choose values for some of the variables. Step (1) and (2) are applied until the problem is solved. Essentially, instead of using the generate and test paradigm, as done in traditional logic programming, constraint languages use *test and generate*. Constraints considered *a priori* that cannot be solved are suspended until enough values are generated that they can be solved.

CLP is a result of integration of consistency techniques into logic programming. The integration is done in such a way that the semantic properties of Logic Programming are preserved. CLP is a result of merging of two declarative paradigms: logic programming and constraint solving. The combination helps make CLP programs both more expressive and flexible. CLP can be viewed as a general and very efficient tool for solving NP-hard problems. More details on CLP can be found in many of the books and articles available [1,2,3]. We do assume for this paper that the reader has some familiarity with CLP(FD). An important class of CLP languages is finite domain based constraint languages, referred to by the generic name CLP(FD), e.g., CHIP [1] and ECLiPSe [8]. In CLP(FD) languages the possible values that a variable can take are restricted to a finite set. Finite domain constraint are useful for solving many real life problems such as scheduling, time tabling, etc.

3   The Knowledgesheet System

3.1   The Knowledgesheet Paradigm

The Knowledgesheet paradigm for building application programs is inspired by the spreadsheet paradigm. The spreadsheet paradigm can be thought of as a pencil-and-paper solution technique. In the spreadsheet paradigm a user enters data and functions (arithmetic expressions) in a 2-dimensional grid of cells. The functions may take other cell values as inputs. Once the data and functions have been entered, they are evaluated and the resulting values displayed on the grid. For particular types of applications, especially those that involve 2-dimensional structures (e.g., financial accounts), the spreadsheet paradigm is perhaps the most convenient tool available. The spreadsheet paradigm, however, is limited because only data or arithmetic expressions can be entered in the cells (though most modern spreadsheet packages permit the user to write Macros, which are programs written in powerful Turing-machine equivalent programming languages).

For many applications that have a 2-d structure, the spreadsheet paradigm is not enough, because of its limitations to functions only. For example, a schedule of classes at a University is a 2-dimensional structure, where data in the various cells is related in complex ways. However, this relationship is not functional in nature, therefore, the spreadsheet paradigm is not adequate for developing schedules. However, the development of such applications on a spreadsheet becomes possible if we generalize functions to predicates or constraints. This generalization of spreadsheets to include constraints is termed Knowledgesheet by us. We chose the name Knowledgesheet because certain applications that fall in the realm of AI can now be programmed using the spreadsheet paradigm.

There are a large number of applications that can be structured as a 2-d grid of cells, where the values of different cells are related via complex constraints. Class scheduling at Universities, resource allocation, task scheduling, examination timetabling, work assignment, intelligent cost-accounting, and many types of puzzles fall in this category. The solution of each one of these problems involves building a 2-d table. The different data-items that constitute the solution table must satisfy certain constraints.

In the Knowledgesheet paradigm, constraints on a particular data item will be attached to the cell where that data-item is to appear. A cell corresponds to a variable (thus, an empty cell corresponds to an unbound variable). Once all the constraints are laid out (analogous to attaching expressions to cells in the spreadsheet paradigm), the constraints are collected and solved (using a finite domain constraint logic programming engine). The values calculated as a result of this constraint solving are then displayed. One can choose any type of constraints (for example, constraints over reals, finite domain constraints, etc.), and once the type of constraints allowed is decided, the appropriate constraint solver has to be selected by the engine. Indeed, spreadsheet interface that allows constraints over reals [16], as well as spreadsheet interfaces for specific problems [12], have been designed in the past. For our project, we consider constraints over finite domains, as developing tools for interactively solving scheduling problems was one of our primary goals.

3.2   The Knowledgesheet Interface

Based on the Knowledgesheet paradigm, we have developed a spreadsheet based interface for solving a class of constraint satisfaction problems. The tool is just a prototype, however, it has enough functionality to solve many interesting CSP problems. The prototype interface has all the major windows, dialog boxes and the required set of functions. The visual layout gives the user a good idea regarding how to use the system. In order to use the system, the user first develops a mental model of the problem in terms of 2-dimensional tables. The user needs to have some idea of the basic concepts of constraint programming, such as domain, constant, and constraints (just as in the traditional spreadsheet, the user must be familiar with arithmetic expression, data values, etc.). However, no detailed knowledge of any constraint programming language is needed.

The interface has two major parts: (i) a data area and, (ii) the scrolling view window. The data area is used for inserting data into the cell objects and the scrolling view window displays a part of the whole worksheet. The actual appearance of the interface is shown in Figure 1 and is similar to an ordinary spreadsheet. The Knowledgesheet interface is implemented in Java and supports multiple tables. Using the interface the user specifies relations (or facts) and queries in a tabular form. The constraints involved in the query are next entered in the cells of the query table (the user chooses which table is the query table). Once the tables are filled, the system will assemble the CLP(FD) program and communicate it to the back-end CLP(FD) engine, which will compute values for the empty cells in the query table. The system will then display these results in the query table. This process is akin to an ordinary spreadsheet, where arithmetic expressions are attached to cells of various tables, and the values of these expressions are displayed once they have been computed. Note that if there are multiple solutions to a given problem, then these solutions can be displayed one after the other when the user selects next solution menu option.

In the Knowledgesheet interface the columns are labeled A, B, C, D, E, etc., and the rows are labeled 1, 2, 3, ... (Figure 1). Thus, the cells are referred to in a manner identical to ordinary spreadsheets. There is also a data area on top where the value of the current active cell (most recently clicked cell) is displayed, just as in an ordinary spreadsheet. This area is also used for entering data (constraints and domain values) in the current active cell (additionally, data can be entered through pop-up windows; see below). One can scroll around the Knowledgesheet window using the mouse. The Knowledgesheet window can be increased or decreased in size just like any ordinary window. The various other operations such as selecting a cell or a range of cells, entering data, text, a constant, a domain, a constraint or resetting a cell are performed by selecting the appropriate command from a floating pop-up menu that appears when the left mouse button is clicked. Menus are also available for loading data (constraints, domain values, etc.) from a file, saving data, etc.

The syntax used for entering the constraints and domain values for a particular cell is the same as for CLP(FD), except that the constraints are enclosed within special <C> markers, the domain values between special <D> markers, and the constants between special <k> markers. These markers are displayed when the contents of a particular cell are examined. Also, these markers need not be typed in when input is given using the mouse and pop-up windows as they are automatically inserted.

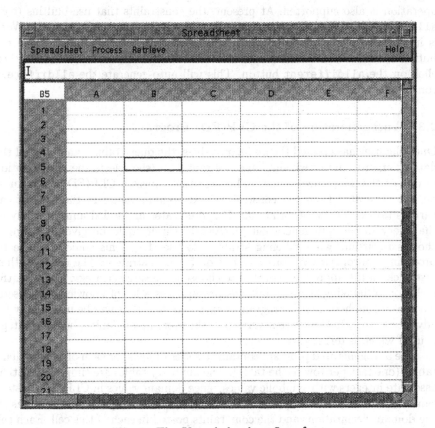

Fig. 1. The Knowledgesheet Interface

The primary operation that the user will be performing using the Knowledgesheet Interface are the following: (i) entering auxiliary tables, (ii) entering the query table, (iii) entering constants, domain values, and constraints in cells of the query table. The user may further copy the constraints and domains in a cell to other cells. These are copied with appropriate transformation applied just as in an ordinary spreadsheet. For example, the constraint A1 + B1 #= 2 in cell C1 when copied to cell C2 will become A2 + B2 #= 2. (Note that #= is the *forward checkable* CLP(FD) operator [1,2] for checking equality over domain variables.) Both absolute reference as well as relative reference can be made to a cell, just as in an ordinary spreadsheet. The copying feature gives the user the power to copy the active-cell to another cell or to an array of cells selected with the mouse. The references between cells may be either absolute or relative in either their horizontal (A, B, C, ...) or vertical index (1, 2, 3, ..). All copies of an absolute reference will refer to the same row, column or cell whereas a relative reference refers to a cell with a given offset from the current cell. Most of the operations use mouse for input and event control, keyboard is used to type data (constants, domains, constraint). Most of the events associated with the Knowledgesheet need to be performed with the help of the mouse. The range selection operation is also supported. At present, the constraints that use builtins (e.g., alldifferent, element, cumulative, etc.) have to be manually entered. Work is in progress to to provide these in the interface as buttons. Thus, given the button for the alldifferent constraint, the user will select a range of cells, then click on the alldifferent button. This will auto-generate the alldifferent constraint for variables corresponding to the selected cells.

3.3   Autogeneration of the CLP(FD) Program

Once the user has created the auxiliary tables, the query tables, and entered the data, domains, and constraints in these tables, he/she selects the solve option in one of the drop-down menus. This selection causes a CLP(FD) program to be autogenerated from the constraints and domain values in the cells of the various tables. The appropriate labeling predicates are added automatically to the query in the autogeneration process. The user could be given a range of choices regarding what labeling strategy to use [1,2]. This could be done by providing appropriate buttons, one button for each strategy. The user will then just click on the appropriate button to choose the desired strategy. However, the inclusion of labeling strategy buttons presupposes a lot of knowledge on users' part regarding how a CLP program is executed, and thus will be useful only for advanced users. In the current version of the system, a default labeling strategy is used which is deleteffc [1].

The autogenerated program contains a series of facts for each of the auxiliary tables (one fact per row of the table). The auxiliary tables are simple maps that associate integers with symbolic values, since domain values in CLP(FD) system can only be integral. The query table is translated into a query, and contains all the domain declarations and the constraints posted in each of this cell. Each cell in the query table is treated as an unbound variable whose value is sought. The query along with the facts is passed to a CLP(FD) engine, that solves the query. The engine writes the value of the unknown variables in a file, from where the front-end interface reads the values and displays them in the table.

3.4 Structure of the Generated Program

The structure of the constraint logic program generated by the Knowledgesheet interface is based on the constraint (or test) and generate methodology of CLP. The Knowledgesheet interface will always produce a non-recursive program for the constraint part, because of the non-recursive nature of the spreadsheet paradigm. The information contained in each cell of the spreadsheet is mapped into a constraint. The generate (labeling) section of the synthesized program (which is automatically added) is recursive, since it mainly consists of labeling predicates, which are recursive.

There is only one main rule involved in the program, which is generated from the query-table (the table in which the user is trying to represent a solution). The autogenerated program file thus contains a section containing CLP(FD) facts corresponding to the auxiliary tables, and a main rule corresponding to the query table. The main rule contains a domain declaration part (all domain declarations from the query table are placed here), a constraint declaration part (all constraints entered in the cells of the query table are placed here), and the labeling section which is automatically added (default labeling strategy is `deleteffc`). The final part of the main rule is autogenerated CLP(FD) code that deals with extraction of the result so that it can be passed to the front-end interface for display. Example auto-generated programs (e.g., for the class-scheduling problem) can be found in [9].

4 Examples

4.1 Scheduling Resources

Resource scheduling is frequently needed in various situations. Consider a large retail store that is open 14 hours a day (e.g., Walmart); such stores typically hire a number of managers. The schedule of these managers has to be drawn in such a way that, for example, at least one manager is present at any given time. Also, the schedule has to be fair to all the managers. Thus, some of the constraints under which the schedule has to be drawn are: every manager should get 2 days off during the week; every manager should be assigned the same number of morning, afternoon, and evening shifts over the long run; a manager who is present during the evening shift to supervise the closing of the store should not be assigned to a morning shift the following day to supervise the opening of the store; etc. In most of these store, this assignment is done manually, primarily because the constraints can vary in time (e.g., store hours may change, a manager may call sick), frequently resulting in unfair and/or wrong schedules.

Let's try to solve this scheduling problem using the Knowledgesheet approach. Assume that the retail store opens from 8AM to 11PM, 7 days a week.

Assume that there are 5 managers (Bill, Mary, John, Gary, and Linda) in the store each of whom is supposed to work 40 hours per week. There must be one manager present at any given time when the store is in operation. Each manager is supposed to get 2 days off every week (obviously, these 2 off days cannot always be Saturday and Sunday for every manager, since the store is open on Saturday and Sunday too). Each manager works no more than 8.5 hours a day (which includes half hour for lunch), either in the morning shift (8:00 PM to 4:30 PM), or the midday shift (10:00 AM to 6:30 PM), or the evening shift (2:30PM to 11PM). The schedule should obey the following constraint: a manager doing an evening shift should not be scheduled for a morning shift for the immediately following day. The schedule should also take manager preferences into account to the extent possible (e.g., a manager may want specific days off during a particular week). The schedule should be fair to all the managers: in the long run everybody should have an equal number of days of morning mid-day and night shifts. Most managers prefer the two off-days to fall on Saturday and Sunday. The scheduler should be fair in assigning Saturdays and Sundays as off-days to all the managers. In the long run, everybody should get the same number of Saturdays and Sundays off.

Suppose we want to draw a schedule for 1 week (we choose one week to keep the example simple). To solve this problem, the user will invoke the tool, which will display a table just like most spreadsheets do when they are invoked. The user will then label the columns and rows appropriately with the names of the managers and days of the week (See Figure 2). Because we are drawing a schedule for only one week, the constraint for ensuring fairness of allocating Saturdays and Sunday as the two days off cannot be enforced, so we'll ignore it. We'll enforce all the other constraints. At this point the user would have defined an empty table with 5 rows (one per manager) and 7 columns (one per day).

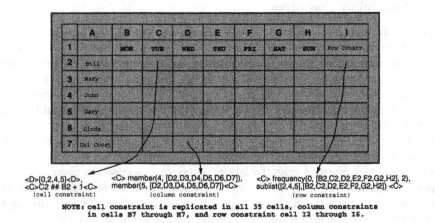

<D>[0,2,4,5]<D>,   <C> member(4, [D2,D3,D4,D5,D6,D7]),   <C> frequency(0, [B2,C2,D2,E2,F2,G2,H2], 2),
<C>C2 ## B2 + 1<C>   member(5, [D2,D3,D4,D5,D6,D7])<C>   sublist([2,4,5],[B2,C2,D2,E2,F2,G2,H2]) <C>
(cell constraint)   (column constraint)   (row constraint)

NOTE: cell constraint is replicated in all 35 cells, column constraints
in cells B7 through H7, and row constraint cell I2 through I6.

Fig. 2. Table after Adding Further Constraints

We will assume that there are three shifts: morning, midday and evening. These will be denoted by numbers 5, 2, and 4 respectively (see later for justification for this peculiar choice). 0 will be used to indicate a manager's day off. The cells in the table will finally display either the shift that a manager is suppose to be present for during that day, or 0, which means (s)he has the day off. Note that each cell in the table can only take values from the domain $\{0, 2, 4, 5\}$. The user will indicate this finite domain by entering this set in each cell (of course, the user has to enter this domain in one cell and then copy it in the remaining cells just as in a regular spreadsheet). This is shown in Figure 2. For example, in the cell C2, the user will enter, <D>[0,2,4,5]<D> to indicate the domain of cell C2. This will be copied in all other cells. However, to keep figure uncluttered, the domain values of all the cells are not shown in Figure 2. The use of finite domains is very important in constraint solving, because otherwise the search space may be very large. In fact, the search space is quite large even now (with 35 total cells each of which can be assigned any one of the 4 values from the set $\{0, 2, 4, 5\}$ there are 4^{35} possible candidates to check for an acceptable solution), but when we enter further constraints, these constraints will be used to *actively prune* this massive search space and produce a solution.

Once the domain value has been entered, the user will indicate the other constraints that each cell must obey. Some of these constraints are local (i.e., apply to each cell), while some have to be applied to an entire row or entire column. The first constraint that we need to attach to each cell (except those in the first column) is that a person cannot be assigned to the morning shift if (s)he has worked on an evening shift the previous day. This constraint can be entered by adding, for example, in cell C2 the constraint: C2 $\neq$ B2 + 1. The constraint is shown in figure 2, and is labeled *cell constraint*, since it is associated with each cell. This constraint can then be copied everywhere in the table except in column B (while copying, appropriate transformations are automatically applied just as in a regular spreadsheet, e.g., when copied in cell D2, this cell constraint will be transformed to D2 in [0,2,4,5], D2 $\neq$ C2 + 1). One can now see why we chose the values 2, 4, and 5 to denote midday, evening, and morning shifts respectively, and 0 to indicate the day off. We wanted to make sure that only the value assigned to morning shift is 1 more than that for the evening shift, so that this constraint can be expressed numerically.

Now we have to ensure the global constraints, namely: (i) at least one manager is present at any time during the day, (ii) no manager works more than 5 days a week, and (iii) every manager has more or less the same proportion of morning, midday and evening shifts. These are global constraints because they involve more than one cells, and are to be enforced over each column or row in the table. We'll add an extra column to the right of the table, and an extra row at the bottom of the table where such constraints will be placed.

Let's consider constraint (i) first. The person defining the constraints can use his/her knowledge (domain-specific knowledge) of the fact that if there is at least one person present in the morning shift and at least one person present in the evening shift, then we are assured that there is at least one manager present at any given time when the store is in operation. Thus, the column constraint that we need, for example for column D is member(4, [D2, D3, D4, D5, D6]) and member(5, [D2, D3, D4, D5, D6]). This constraint is placed in row 7 in column D. Note that [D2, D3, D4, D5, D6] refers to a list of values consisting of those computed for cells D2, D3, D4, D5, and D6. This constraint will then be copied across the extra row at the bottom (row 7). The member constraint is a builtin constraint provided as a button.

Let's now consider row constraints (ii), namely, every manager has exactly 2 days off, and constraint (iii), namely, no manager works more than 5 days a week and that the shifts are fair. To check for (ii) we have to ensure that in each row there are exactly two 0s (2 days off). Constraint (iii) can be more or less achieved by ensuring that every manager is working at least one morning, one midday, and one evening shift during the week. Constraint (ii) can be checked by defining an auxiliary table that maps days-off to 1, and morning, midday, and evening shifts to 0, and then checking that there are exactly two 1s in each row resulting from the mapping. To each of the cells in the extra column to the right (Column I), we'll add the appropriate constraint. For example, in the top most cell in the column I (cell I2), we'll add the constraint: frequency(0, [B2, C2, D2, E2, F2, G2, H2], 2). The constraint frequency is provided as a builtin; frequency(N, L, K) checks that the value N appears in the list L exactly K times. It can be implemented using the element constraint provided in most clp(FD) systems [1]. Constraint (iii) can then be checked by using the sublist builtin predicate. For the first row, this constraint will be: sublist([2,4,5], [B2, C2, D2, E2, F2, G2, H2]), where the sublist(S, R) builtin checks that the list S is a completely contained in the list R.

	A	B	C	D	E	F	G	H	I
1		MON	TUE	WED	THU	FRI	SAT	SUN	Row Constr.
2	Bill	5	5	5	2	0	4	0	
3	Mary	4	3	0	5	4	5	0	
4	John	0	5	2	4	2	0	2	
5	Gary	0	2	4	0	4	2	5	
6	Linda	0	4	2	2	0	2	4	
7	Col Const								

Fig. 3. Displaying a Solution

The final table decorated with all the different types of constraints is shown in Figure 2 (all the constraints in each cell are not shown to avoid clutter). Once the constraints have been defined, the user selects SOLVE menu-option, and the system calculates the values for all of the 35 variables using a CLP(FD) engine, which are then displayed. Figure 3 shows one solution.

4.2   The 3x3 Grid Puzzle

Consider the well-known 9-squares puzzle, where all the squares of a 3x3 grid have to be filled with integer values from 1 to 9 with no two squares having the same value. The sum of the values in the squares across all rows, columns and major diagonals must be 15.

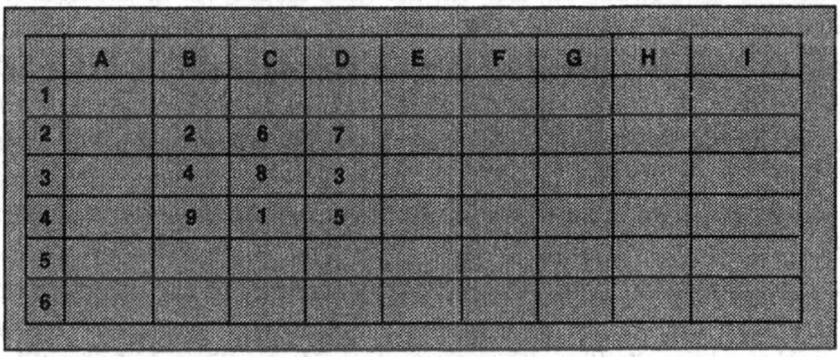

	A	B	C	D	E	F	G	H	I
1									
2		2	6	7					
3		4	8	3					
4		9	1	5					
5									
6									

Fig. 4. The 3x3 Puzzle

To solve this problem using the Knowledgesheet paradigm, we will define a 3x3 query table in which we will attach appropriate constraints (Figure 4). Suppose the table is defined in columns B, C, and D, and rows 3, 4, and 5. Then in the cell B3 we should add the constraint B3+C3+D3 #= 15. This constraint should then be copied in the cells B4 and B5. The constrains C3+C4+C5 #= 15 should be next attached to the cell C3, and copied to the cell D3. The cell B3 should be augmented with the constraint B3+B4+B5 #= 15. The diagonal constraints should be next specified, and, finally, the domain of each cell should be set to 1..9. The constraints in each cell of the grid are shown below.

```
Cell    Constraints
B3:     B3+C3+D3 #= 15, B3+B4+B5 #= 15
C3:     C3+C4+C5 #= 15
D3:     D3+D4+D5 #= 15
B4:     B4+C4+D4 #= 15
B5:     B5+C5+D5 #= 15, B5+C4+D3 #= 15
D5:     B3+C4+D5 #= 15, alldifferent([B3,B4,B5,C3,C4,C5,D3,D4,D5])
```

In the above table, all the cells do not contain constraints. The cells without any constraints cells can have constraints, but that may introduce duplicate or redundant constraints. Introduction of redundant or duplicate constraints does not seriously compromise performance, however, the user should be careful while using them. To model the problem and to display the solution we need a mapping table (auxiliary table, not shown), which maps symbolic names attached to the cells in the query table to actual integer values. Once the mapped table and query tables have been specified, the back-end CLP(FD) engine is invoked. The solutions are computed by the engine and displayed on the Knowledgesheet interface as shown below.

The Knowledgesheet interface can also be used to graphically solve cryptarithmetic puzzles, such as SEND + MORE = MONEY (Figure 5). The constraints are specified for just the rightmost column, and then copied to other columns. The constraints can then be solved, and the solution displayed. In the figure, we have a auxiliary table that associates the letters s, e, n, d, m, o, r and y with empty cells (the constant letters are shown in column G and the empty cells in the column H). The query table consists of the rectangle with diagonal corners B2, E2, B5, and E5 plus the cell A5. The user enters the constraint for computing the sum in cell E5, and the carry in cell D2. The expression in E5 is copied to cells B5, C5, and D5, the expression for carry in cell D2 is copied into cells C2 and B2. In the figure, we have shown variable names on the cells, in reality they will be blank. To make the association between multiple occurrence of the same letter (e.g., O that occurs in C4 and D5), we set equality constraints between each letter and its position in the column H. Thus, the constraints C4 #= H7 and D5 #= H7 will have to be explicitly generated (this is done by clicking with the mouse on the two cells to be equated and then clicking on the button corresponding to the equality operator. Finally, the alldifferent([H2,H3,H4,H5,H6,H7,H8,H9]) constraint is generated and placed in one of the cells of the query table. Now the specification is complete and these constraints can be solved to display a solution.

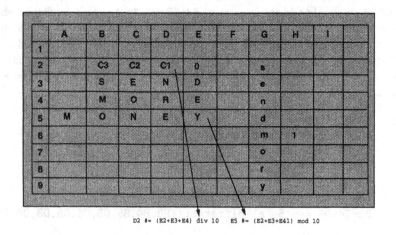

D2 #= (E2+E3+E4) div 10   E5 #= (E2+E3+E41) mod 10

Fig. 5. Cryptarithmetic Puzzle

5   Discussion

5.1   Interactive Problem Solving with Knowledgesheet

The Knowledgesheet tool can also be useful for solving large, intractable CSPs (e.g., course scheduling for 50 courses). For most scheduling problems, the person designing the schedule can manually come up with a partial solution (e.g., coming up with a schedule for, say, 40 of the 50 courses), for the rest of the schedule, the Knowledgesheet system can be used. Essentially, the user will fill out all the constraints and the domains in the various cells of the query table, then he/she will enter constants for those values that he/she can determine manually. For computing the rest of the values the back-end constraint solver of the Knowledgesheet system will be called. Given the user's initial choice, there may not be any solution feasible, however, the user can experiment by incrementally finding the solution row by row, or by slightly changing the manually determined solution, or both. Thus, the interactive nature of Knowledgesheet can be very helpful in solving large problems. Essentially, the Knowledgesheet system permits cooperative problem solving—the user and the CLP(FD) system cooperate via the Knowledgesheet interface to solve a problem. The same situation applies to an over-constrained system when the system cannot produce a solution. In this case as well, the user can incrementally remove constraints and finally find a solution.

5.2   Previous Work

The concept of a spreadsheet interface for general purpose programming has been proposed by, among others, Yoder and Cohen [14]. They show how spreadsheets can be utilized as a programming tool via their spreadsheet-based tool called Mini-SP. However, the application of Mini-SP system is limited. It can be used for solving some well-known problems, such as sorting, and temperature gradient simulation. Most of the spreadsheet based programming tools are for specific tasks. Lai, Malone and Yu developed *Object Lens* system [13], a spreadsheet for cooperative work. Hofe has developed the ConPlan [15] interface that takes tabular input and is specifically designed for scheduling nurses. The SD-spreadsheet, a constraint-spreadsheet based application specifically for solving financial planning problems has been developed by Shvetsov, Kornienko, and Preis [16]. The system is based on a variant of interval constraint programming rather than on CLP(FD). Recently, Configuration Spreadsheet has been developed by Renschler [12] for configuring the mobile phone network transceivers. The configuration spreadsheet uses CLP(FD), however, it is a problem specific tool and not a general purpose tool for developing solutions to CSPs.

6   Conclusions and Future Work

In this paper we presented the design and implementation of the Knowledgesheet Interface. The Knowledgesheet interface is a generalization of the traditional spreadsheets that enables interactive solving of a class of constraint satisfaction problems. A large class of CSPs can be modeled as consisting of values arranged in a 2-d table, where the values are related to each other via constraints. In the Knowledgesheet interface, the user states only these constraints, which are then solved to obtain a solution. The Knowledgesheet interface enables non-experts to solve CSP problems.

We believe that the Knowledgesheet interface has many potential applications and that it can be used by novice users for solving many practical problems, such as course scheduling, resource allocation, task scheduling, examination time-tabling, work assignment, intelligent cost-accounting, etc. A patent for the interface is pending [5]. The Knowledgesheet tool also has pedagogical value, as we believe that it is a good aid for teaching solving of CSPs and puzzles to non-expert users, since its graphical interactive nature allows for experimentation.

A Knowledgesheet-like approach can also be applied for building interfaces for solving engineering and other types of decision support problems. Engineering design problems can also be modeled in terms of a set of variables related via constraints. One can envisage a graphical tool in which the various design constraints are attached to the drawing of the part being designed; the constraints are next solved to obtain concrete values for the various design parameters. Likewise, decision trees can be graphically programmed: the nodes of the decision tree that contain constraints are mapped to the various cells of the Knowledgesheet. Thus, a class of expert systems can be quickly designed and implemented by non-expert users. These extensions are planned in the future.

We plan to extend the Knowledgesheet system further in the future, to make it more sophisticated: e.g., supporting multiple sheets, buttons for more powerful builtin constraints, buttons for choosing more sophisticated labeling strategies, etc. We also plan to provide readymade builtin templates for solving standard problems (e.g., for scheduling managers at a store, class scheduling in an academic department) that are encountered most commonly. This will be useful because one could argue that even though the Knowledgesheet tool makes the task of designing a schedule easier, it is still beyond the capabilities of most retail store managers or other similar users. This is in the spirit of the builtin readymade templates provided in many of the general purpose software tools available in the market today (e.g., Microsoft Office Software Suite). We also plan to support hierarchical constraints, as this is crucial for solving certain type of practical problems. Many features that are available in commercial spreadsheets can be included in the Knowledgesheet to make it more easy to use (e.g., ability to change sizes of rows/columns, use of keyboard for operations that are currently only possible via the mouse, etc.). Incorporation of these extensions is in progress.

References

1. Van Hentenryck, P., Constraint Satisfaction in Logic Programming, The MIT Press, Cambridge, MA, England, 1989.

2. Marriott, K., and Stuckey, P. J., Programming with Constraints: An Introduction, The MIT Press, Cambridge, MA, England, 1998.
3. Cohen, J., Logic Programming and Constraint Logic Programming, The Computer Science and Engg. Handbook, pp. 2066-2093, CRC Press, Inc., Florida, US, 1996.
4. H.-J. Goltz and D. Matzke. University Timetabling Using Constraint Logic Programming, Proc. PADL'99, Springer LNCS 1551, 1999.
5. G. Gupta and S. F. Akhter. Knowledgesheet: A Spreadsheet-based Interface for Interactively Solving Scheduling Problems. Patent pending. Feb. 1999.
6. Boizumault, P., Delon, Y., and Peridy, L., Constraint Logic Programming for Examination Timetabling, The Journal of Logic Programming, pp. 217-233, 1995.
7. Sterling, L., and Shapiro, E., The Art of Prolog, The MIT Press, 1994.
8. Meier, M., ECLiPSe User's Manual, IC-PARC Tech. Rep., 1997.
9. S. F. Akhter. Knowledgesheet: A User-Interface for Solving Constraint Satisfaction Problems. Master's thesis. New Mexico State University, July '98.
10. Henz, M., and Würtz, J., Using Oz for College Timetabling, In proceedings of the 1995 Int'l Conf. on Automated Timetabling, Edinburgh, Scotland.
11. Colorni, A., Dorigo, M., and Maniezzo, V., Metaheuristics for High-School Timetabling, Computational Optimization and Applications, 9(3): 277-298, 1998.
12. Renschler, M., Configuration Spreadsheet for Interactive Constraint Problem Solving, Conference Proceeding, Proc. Practical Applications of Constraint Tech., 1998.
13. Lai, K., Malone, T., W., and Yu, K., Object-Lens: A "Spreadsheet" for Cooperative Work, ACM Transactions on Office Information Systems, 6(4): 332-353, 1998.
14. Yoder, A., G., and Cohn, D., L., Real Spreadsheets for Real Programmers Proc. International Conference on Computer Languages, IEEE, pp. 20-30, 1994.
15. Hofe, H., M., ConPlan/SIEDAplan: Personnel Assignment as a Problem of Hierarchical Constraint Satisfaction, Conference Proceeding, PACT 97, pp. 257-271.
16. Shvetsov, I., Kornienko, V., and Preis, S., Interval Spreadsheet for problems of financial planning, Conference Proceeding, PACT 97, pp. 373-385.

Current Trends in Logic Programming: Prospects and Promises

(Abstract)

I.V. Ramakrishnan

Department of Computer Science
SUNY Stony Brook
Stony Brook, NY
ram@cs.sunysb.edu

Over the last decade significant theoretical and practical advances have been made in several key logic programming technologies, notably abstract interpretation, program transformations, constraint processing, tabling and semantics of negation. These advances have contributed to the development of a new generation of powerful and efficient logic programming systems that are beginning to be deployed as the implementation platform in state-of-the-art tools in different application domains.

This talk will describe the current status and future plans of two such systems, XMC and WebRover, implemented using the XSB tabled logic programming system that embodies many of these advances.

XMC is a tool used for the specification and verification of concurrent systems. Specifically, it is an efficient and flexible model checker for finite-state systems that uses XSB as a programmable fixed point engine. XMC is written in under 200 lines of tabled Prolog code, which constitute a declarative specification of CCS and the modal mu-calculus at the level of semantic equations. Despite the high-level nature of XMC's implementation, its performance is comparable to that of highly optimized model checkers such as Bell Lab's Spin and Stanford University's Murphi on examples selected from the benchmark suite contained in the standard Spin distribution.

WebRover is a web-based information system designed for querying dynamic web content, i.e., data that can only be extracted by filling out multiple forms. Systems such as WebRover are popularly referred to as "shopbots" since they allow end users to shop around for products and services on the web without having to tediously fill out forms manually. WebRover, built using XSB as the implementation platform, is operational and is being used to mine parts data from various web catalogs for the Department of Defense.

E. Pontelli, V. Santos Costa (Eds.): PADL 2000, LNCS 1753, pp. 324–324, 2000.
© Springer-Verlag Berlin Heidelberg 2000

Production-Quality Proof-Carrying Code
(Abstract)

Peter Lee

Computer Science Department
Carnegie Mellon University
Pittsburgh, PA
petel@cs.cmu.edu

For the past year I have been involved in a "technology transfer" experiment to take ideas based on theoretical principles, namely proof-carrying code (PCC) and certifying compilers, directly out of the laboratory and into commercial use. In a PCC system, code objects include an easy-to-verify encoding of a proof that the code is safe to execute, for a definition of safety provided by the host system. A certifying compiler takes source programs and compiles them automatically into PCC target programs.

In this lecture, I will describe this project, which has involved the development of an optimizing certifying compiler for the Java programming language. I will focus mainly on the technical lessons that we learned while attempting to scale up a laboratory prototype into a production-quality system. These lessons include specific technical problems that we encountered—some solved and others not yet solved—as well as advice for future writers of certifying compilers. In addition, I will also give some assessment of the practical viability of PCC, both in technical and in business terms. Ultimately, I will argue that there are tremendous advantages in arranging for the compiler to produce easy-to-verify code, and hence that future compilers will all be certifying.

E. Pontelli, V. Santos Costa (Eds.): PADL 2000, LNCS 1753, pp. 325–325, 2000.
© Springer-Verlag Berlin Heidelberg 2000

Author Index

Lecture Notes in Computer Science

For information about Vols. 1–1681
please contact your bookseller or Springer-Verlag

Vol. 1716: K.Y. Lam, E. Okamoto, C. Xing (Eds.), Advances in Cryptology – ASIACRYPT'99. Proceedings, 1999. XI, 414 pages. 1999.

Vol. 1717: Ç. K. Koç, C. Paar (Eds.), Cryptographic Hardware and Embedded Systems. Proceedings, 1999. XI, 353 pages. 1999.

Vol. 1718: M. Diaz, P. Owezarski, P. Sénac (Eds.), Interactive Distributed Multimedia Systems and Telecommunication Services. Proceedings, 1999. XI, 386 pages. 1999.

Vol. 1719: M. Fossorier, H. Imai, S. Lin, A. Poli (Eds.), Applied Algebra, Algebraic Algorithms and Error-Correcting Codes. Proceedings, 1999. XIII, 510 pages. 1999.

Vol. 1720: O. Watanabe, T. Yokomori (Eds.), Algorithmic Learning Theory. Proceedings, 1999. XI, 365 pages. 1999. (Subseries LNAI).

Vol. 1721: S. Arikawa, K. Furukawa (Eds.), Discovery Science. Proceedings, 1999. XI, 374 pages. 1999. (Subseries LNAI).

Vol. 1722: A. Middeldorp, T. Sato (Eds.), Functional and Logic Programming. Proceedings, 1999. X, 369 pages. 1999.

Vol. 1723: R. France, B. Rumpe (Eds.), UML'99 – The Unified Modeling Language. XVII, 724 pages. 1999.

Vol. 1724: H. I. Christensen, H. Bunke, H. Noltemeier (Eds.), Sensor Based Intelligent Robots. Proceedings, 1998. VIII, 327 pages. 1999 (Subseries LNAI).

Vol. 1725: J. Pavelka, G. Tel, M. Bartošek (Eds.), SOFSEM'99: Theory and Practice of Informatics. Proceedings, 1999. XIII, 498 pages. 1999.

Vol. 1726: V. Varadharajan, Y. Mu (Eds.), Information and Communication Security. Proceedings, 1999. XI, 325 pages. 1999.

Vol. 1727: P.P. Chen, D.W. Embley, J. Kouloumdjian, S.W. Liddle, J.F. Roddick (Eds.), Advances in Conceptual Modeling. Proceedings, 1999. XI, 389 pages. 1999.

Vol. 1728: J. Akoka, M. Bouzeghoub, I. Comyn-Wattiau, E. Métais (Eds.), Conceptual Modeling – ER '99. Proceedings, 1999. XIV, 540 pages. 1999.

Vol. 1729: M. Mambo, Y. Zheng (Eds.), Information Security. Proceedings, 1999. IX, 277 pages. 1999.

Vol. 1730: M. Gelfond, N. Leone, G. Pfeifer (Eds.), Logic Programming and Nonmonotonic Reasoning. Proceedings, 1999. XI, 391 pages. 1999. (Subseries LNAI).

Vol. 1731: J. Kratochvíl (Ed.), Graph Drawing. Proceedings, 1999. XIII, 422 pages. 1999.

Vol. 1732: S. Matsuoka, R.R. Oldehoeft, M. Tholburn (Eds.), Computing in Object-Oriented Parallel Environments. Proceedings, 1999. VIII, 205 pages. 1999.

Vol. 1733: H. Nakashima, C. Zhang (Eds.), Approaches to Intelligent Agents. Proceedings, 1999. XII, 241 pages. 1999. (Subseries LNAI).

Vol. 1734: H. Hellwagner, A. Reinefeld (Eds.), SCI: Scalable Coherent Interface. XXI, 490 pages. 1999.

Vol. 1564: M. Vazirgiannis, Interactive Multimedia Documents. XIII, 161 pages. 1999.

Vol. 1591: D.J. Duke, I. Herman, M.S. Marshall, PREMO: A Framework for Multimedia Middleware. XII, 254 pages. 1999.

Vol. 1624: J. A. Padget (Ed.), Collaboration between Human and Artificial Societies. XIV, 301 pages. 1999. (Subseries LNAI).

Vol. 1635: X. Tu, Artificial Animals for Computer Animation. XIV, 172 pages. 1999.

Vol. 1646: B. Westfechtel, Models and Tools for Managing Development Processes. XIV, 418 pages. 1999.

Vol. 1735: J.W. Amtrup, Incremental Speech Translation. XV, 200 pages. 1999. (Subseries LNAI).

Vol. 1736: L. Rizzo, S. Fdida (Eds.): Networked Group Communication. Proceedings, 1999. XIII, 339 pages. 1999.

Vol. 1737: P. Agouris, A. Stefanidis (Eds.), Integrated Spatial Databases. Proceedings, 1999. X, 317 pages. 1999.

Vol. 1738: C. Pandu Rangan, V. Raman, R. Ramanujam (Eds.), Foundations of Software Technology and Theoretical Computer Science. Proceedings, 1999. XII, 452 pages. 1999.

Vol. 1739: A. Braffort, R. Gherbi, S. Gibet, J. Richardson, D. Teil (Eds.), Gesture-Based Communication in Human-Computer Interaction. Proceedings, 1999. XI, 333 pages. 1999. (Subseries LNAI).

Vol. 1740: R. Baumgart (Ed.): Secure Networking – CQRE [Secure] '99. Proceedings, 1999. IX, 261 pages. 1999.

Vol. 1741: A. Aggarwal, C. Pandu Rangan (Eds.), Algorithms and Computation. Proceedings, 1999. XIII, 448 pages. 1999.

Vol. 1742: P.S. Thiagarajan, R. Yap (Eds.), Advances in Computing Science – ASIAN'99. Proceedings, 1999. XI, 397 pages. 1999.

Vol. 1743: A. Moreira, S. Demeyer (Eds.), Object-Oriented Technology. Proceedings, 1999. XVII, 389 pages. 1999.

Vol. 1744: S. Staab, Extracting Degree Information from Texts. X; 187 pages. 1999. (Subseries LNAI).

Vol. 1745: P. Banerjee, V.K. Prasanna, B.P. Sinha (Eds.), High Performance Computing – HiPC'99. Proceedings, 1999. XXII, 412 pages. 1999.

Vol. 1746: M. Walker (Ed.), Cryptography and Coding. Proceedings, 1999. IX, 313 pages. 1999.

Vol. 1747: N. Foo (Ed.), Adavanced Topics in Artificial Intelligence. Proceedings, 1999. XV, 500 pages. 1999. (Subseries LNAI).

Vol. 1748: H.V. Leong, W.-C. Lee, B. Li, L. Yin (Eds.), Mobile Data Access. Proceedings, 1999. X, 245 pages. 1999.

Vol. 1749: L. C.-K. Hui, D.L. Lee (Eds.), Internet Applications. Proceedings, 1999. XX, 518 pages. 1999.

Vol. 1750: D.E. Knuth, MMIXware. VIII, 550 pages. 1999.

Vol. 1751: H. Imai, Y. Zheng (Eds.), Public Key Cryptography. Proceedings, 2000. XI, 485 pages. 2000.

Vol. 1753: E. Pontelli, V. Santos Costa (Eds.), Practical Aspects of Declarative Languages. Proceedings, 2000. X, 327 pages. 2000.

Vol. 1754: J. Väänänen (Ed.), Generalized Quantifiers and Computation. Proceedings, 1997. VII, 139 pages. 1999.